I0837356

Am. Photo-Relief Printing Co., Philadelphia.

THE AMERICAN SYSTEM.

SPEECHES

ON

THE TARIFF QUESTION,

AND ON

INTERNAL IMPROVEMENTS,

PRINCIPALLY DELIVERED IN

THE HOUSE OF REPRESENTATIVES OF THE UNITED STATES.

BY

ANDREW STEWART,

LATE M. C. FROM PENNSYLVANIA.

WITH A PORTRAIT

PHILADELPHIA:

HENRY CAREY BAIRD,

INDUSTRIAL PUBLISHER,

406 WALNUT STREET.

1872.

A BIOGRAPHICAL SKETCH.

ANDREW STEWART, now in his eighty-second year, was born in Fayette county, Pa., and never lived out of it. His father, Abraham Stewart, was born in York, Pa., and his mother, Mary Oliphant, in Chester county, Pa. They emigrated while young to Fayette county, where they were married in 1789. They raised a family of children, of whom the eldest was Andrew, the subject of this notice, who was born June 11th, 1791, near Uniontown, where he now lives. At an early age he became self-dependent; till eighteen he worked on a farm and taught a country school; afterwards, to pay his way while going to school and reading law, he acted as a scrivener and as clerk at a furnace. At the age of twenty-three he was admitted to the bar, and in the same year was elected to the Legislature; was re-elected for three years, and when a candidate for the Senate, without opposition, President Monroe tendered him the appointment of District Attorney for the United States, which, preferring to a seat in the Senate, he accepted, but resigned it after his election to Congress, in 1820, where he served eighteen years, out of a period of thirty, going in and going out with the Hon. Thos. H. Benton; and he is now the only surviving member of the seventeenth Congress, as stated by President Buchanan, in a speech in Philadelphia, shortly before his death, that he and "Mr. Stewart, of Fayette, were the only survivors of the seventeenth Congress," to which they were elected in 1820.

In 1848, when Mr. Stewart was a candidate for the Vice-Presidency, he declined a nomination for Congress, and in the Convention in Philadelphia, after the nomination of President Taylor, it was left to the Pennsylvania delegation to nominate a candidate for Vice-President, who, after having retired to agree upon a nominee, upon the first ballot Mr. Stewart had fourteen out of twenty-six, the remaining twelve voting for Mr. McKennan and several others, when, without taking a second ballot, to make it *unanimous*, the chairman of the delegation hurried back into the Convention and reported that they had failed to agree, whereupon Mr. Fillmore was nominated and confirmed, as was stated and published at the time without contradiction.

On the accession of General Taylor to the Presidency, the Pennsylvania delegation in Congress recommended Mr. Stewart for Secretary of the Treasury; but, being at the time confined to a sick bed, he declined the appointment; and it may be stated, as a remarkable fact, true of no other man, living or dead, that Mr. Stewart served in Congress with every President before General Grant, except the first five and Taylor, who was never in Congress. This fact will appear by reference to the Congressional Biographical Dictionaries.

While in Congress, it will be seen that Mr. Stewart served on several of the most important committees, among them as Chairman of the Committee on the *Tariff*, and the Committee of *Internal Improvements*, constituting together, what was well called by Mr. Clay, "*The American System*"—in the advocacy of which, Mr. Stewart commenced and ended his political life. This system, he always contended, lay at the foundation of the national prosperity—the one protecting the *national industry*, and the other developing the *national resources*. He called it the "political *thermometer*," which always had and always would indicate the rise and fall of the national prosperity. In concluding one of his speeches, he put this whole matter in a nutshell when he said:

The true American policy is this:

1st. *Protect* and *cherish* your *national industry* by a wise system of finance, selecting in the first place those articles which you can and ought to supply to the extent of your own wants—*food*, *clothing*, *habitation*, and *defence*—and to these give ample and adequate protection, so as to secure at all times an abundant supply at home. Next select the LUXURIES consumed by the *rich*, and impose on them such duties as the wants of the Government may require for revenue; and then take the necessaries of life consumed by the poor, and articles which we cannot supply, used in our manufactories, and make them *free*, or subject to the lowest rates of duty.

2d. Adopt a system of *national* improvements, embracing the great rivers, lakes, and main arteries of communication, leaving those of a LOCAL character to the care of the States; and on these expend the *surplus revenue* only; thus uniting and binding together the distant parts of our common country, and at the same time securing the most efficient system of defence in war, and the cheapest and best system of commercial and social intercourse in peace.

3d. Introduce enlightened economy in every branch of the public expenditures. Lighten the burdens, diversify the employments, and secure and increase the rewards of labor in all its departments. And,

4th. In your foreign relations follow the advice of the father of his country—"observe good faith and justice towards all nations—cultivate peace and harmony with all." Thereby illustrating the beauty and perfection of our Republican institutions, holding up a great example of "liberty and independence," for the nations of the earth to admire and imitate. This was the great and true *American system* which he hoped yet to see adopted and carried out. We owe a great example to the world—let it be given; this was the duty, as he trusted it would be the destiny of this, our great and glorious Republic.

Mr. Stewart belonged to the Democratic party up to 1828, when the party, at the dictation of the South, under the lead of Van Buren, Buchanan, and others, gave up the tariff and internal improvements for office, exchanging measures for men, principles for pelf; here Mr. Stewart took an independent stand. He said he would stand by his measures, going with those who went for, and against those who went against them. He came home in the midst of the excited contest between Jackson and Adams for the Presidency, in 1828, when his constituents were known to be more than two to one for Jackson; and in a public speech declared his intention "to vote for Adams, whose friends supported his measures, whilst the Democratic party, as such, opposed them. If for this they chose to turn him out, so be it; he would never surrender his principles for office. If he did, he would be a political hypocrite, unworthy the support of any honest man; he would rather go out endeavoring to support what, in his conscience, he believed to be the true interests of his constituents and his country, than to go in by meanly betraying them."

The Democrats took up Mr. Hawkins, of Greene county, then Speaker of the Senate, and used every means, fair and foul, to exasperate the Jackson men against Mr. Stewart; yet, with all their efforts, although Jackson had a majority of 2800—more than two votes to one—in his district, Mr. Stewart was elected over the Jackson candidate by a majority of 235, a result unprecedented; showing a degree of personal popularity on the one side, and of magnanimity and forbearance on the other, without a parallel in the history of elections. Mr. Stewart was afterward re-elected for four terms, when he peremptorily declined a re-nomination.

At the age of thirty-four Mr. Stewart married the daughter of David Shriver, of Cumberland, Md., and raised a family of six children, who are all living except Lieutenant-Commander Wm. F. Stewart, U. S. N., who was lost on the U. S. S. Oneida, on the 24th of January, 1870; being at the time executive officer of the ship, and one of the most promising officers of his age in the service—so pronounced, in letters of condolence after his death, by all of the officers under whom he had served. His last heroic words, on being urged to take the boat as the ship was going down, were, "*No;* let others take the boat, my duty is on board my ship," and he went down with her.

Mr. Stewart has frequently been urged by friends, clubs, and committees, to collect and prepare for publication a selection from his speeches, especially on the tariff question, addressed to the "farmers, mechanics, and workingmen;" but, owing to the multiplicity of his business engagements, he has been unable so to do until, by reason of a recent confinement to his house by sickness for some months, he has been enabled, with the assistance of one of his sons, to collect such of those on the subjects of the Tariff and Internal Improvements as remained after the burning of his office in 1844, selections from which will be found in this volume.

Mr. Stewart has carried into private life the same devotion to these measures that distinguished him while in the public service; and in his eighty-second year he is found among the foremost in advocating railroad improvements, which, when completed, will make his native county one of the richest and most prosperous in the State. To show his constant zeal and restless activity in the cause of domestic industry, and home manufactures, it may be stated that he has erected a blast furnace (now in operation), rebuilt a glass works, has built eleven saw mills, four flouring mills, planing mills, etc., besides more than 200 tenant and other houses; has bought and sold over 80,000 acres of land, and has between 30,000 and 40,000 acres still left, much of it in the West, and yet twenty-one years of the prime of his life were devoted to the services of his country in her State and National Legislatures.

Among his many patriotic and benevolent acts, the following is one of the most recent, the account of which is copied from the *American Standard*, of May 23, 1872:

UNIONTOWN SOLDIERS' ORPHAN SCHOOL.—It will be remembered that some time ago a correspondence appeared in the papers between Hon. Andrew Stewart, Prof. Wickersham, and the Principal of the Uniontown Soldiers' Orphan School, relative to an endowment which Mr. Stewart generously proposed to make for the benefit of the children in the Uniontown school. As nothing has since been published, it may be thought that the proposition has never been carried into effect. To correct such an impression, I desire to say that Mr. Stewart has put into execution his design by appropriating the interest of $10,000 annually, to be distributed among the children who leave the school at the age of sixteen years, according to merit, based upon scholarship, industry, and good conduct. Several have already received the benefit of this fund, and during the present year about thirty will become recipients in proportion to their merits as above indicated.

Though but recently introduced, the plan gives great promise of accomplishing much good. It is certainly one happily conceived, most generously executed, and as one of the last acts of a long and useful life, will be a prouder and more enduring monument to its projector, when he rests from his labors, than the most imposing granite obelisk.

It is to be hoped that it will be the beginning of a system of education and training for a large class of poor and neglected children, for whom no one cares, and many of whom will find their way to houses of correction, and finally be added to the list of criminals. That this plan may eventually lead to the establishment of such a school here, and others throughout the State, is, I believe, Mr. Stewart's earnest wish.

A. H. WATERS,
Principal of Uniontown S. O. School.

Such is a brief outline of the life and services of a self-made man, who commenced life with nothing. Should not such examples encourage and stimulate the efforts of every young man of this great and free country, where all start in the great race of life with the same prospects of future wealth, fame, and position?

CONTENTS.

SPEECHES.

FIRST DIVISION—THE TARIFF.

SPEECH I.

SPEECH II.

SPEECH III.

SPEECH IV.

SPEECH IX.

SECOND DIVISION—INTERNAL IMPROVEMENTS.

SPEECH I.

SPEECH II.

[*Extract.*]

SPEECH III.

SPEECH IV.

SPEECH V.

SPEECH VI.

SPEECHES ON THE AMERICAN SYSTEM.

IN DEFENCE OF THE PROTECTIVE POLICY.

DELIVERED IN THE HOUSE OF REPRESENTATIVES, U. S., ON THE 14th DAY OF MARCH, 1846.

MR. STEWART said he regretted that this great question of national protection, the most important that could possibly occupy the attention of American statesmen, was constantly resolved by gentlemen on the other side into a mere question of *party*. Separated from the pernicious influences of *party*, he was sure there could be but one opinion upon the subject. The contest was for the *American market*. *Foreigners*, and especially the *British*, were the parties on the one side, and the *Americans* on the other; and the only question was, which side should we take? By adopting "*free trade*," we give our markets and our money to *foreigners;* by adhering to *protection*, we secure both to our own people. Disguise it as you will, this is the true and only question to be decided, and the fate of the country depends on the result. He trusted gentlemen would decide in favor of their own country—in favor of their own farmers, mechanics, and laboring men—that they would protect their own people employed in the fields and in the workshops, in the conversion of our own agricultural produce into articles for use, instead of importing them from abroad; for it was demonstrable that more than one-half of the hundred millions of dollars annually sent abroad to purchase foreign goods, went to pay for foreign agricultural produce worked up in these goods by labor employed and fed in foreign countries, instead of our own.

Mr. S. begged gentlemen upon this great American question, to separate themselves from party prejudice, and come up to its consideration in a true American spirit. It was a question that soared far above and beyond the reach of mere party interests and party considerations. Why, then, these *party* appeals? Was it because gentlemen were afraid to meet the question on its own intrinsic and independent merits—was this the motive of these appeals to the poor, pitiful and paltry purposes of party politics? Was this a time or an occasion for such appeals? No. Let this great question of protecting American industry be discussed on great—broad American principles, and it would be so discussed by every one who had a true American heart in his bosom.

Mr. S. said he would now proceed to answer the arguments that had been urged against *protection*, and in favor of *free trade*, and then give his own views as to the true American policy to be adopted and maintained by this country; and in doing so he would study clearness and simplicity, for "truth needs not the foreign aid of ornament;" he would state facts—facts which he was prepared to establish by official, or other conclusive evidence, with the inferences fairly deducible from them—and he would submit them with confidence to the candor and good sense of this House and of the American people.

In the first place, then, he would notice some of the arguments urged upon all occasions against protection, and just now repeated by the gentleman from Alabama [Mr. Payne], who had spoken last.

EFFECT OF PROTECTIVE DUTIES ON PRICES.

The first argument of the gentleman had been the position, that the effect of a protective tariff was oppressive, especially on the poor, and on the interests of agriculture and labor. How was it oppressive upon these? No other interest in the country was half so much benefited by the tariff as the farmers, and mechanics, and workingmen. The gentleman said that it injured them by increasing the price of manufactured commodities; for the gentleman's assertion was, that protection did invariably increase the price of the articles protected. Now, in reply, Mr. S. would distinctly put forth this assertion, to which he challenged contradiction, viz: that there never was a protective duty levied in this country, on any article which we could and did manufacture extensively, which had not resulted in bringing down the price of that article; and he challenged gentlemen to point him to a single instance in reference to which this was not true. The prices of commodities, instead of being raised by protection, had been reduced to one-third, one-fourth, and even to one-tenth and one-twelfth part of what had been paid for them when imported from abroad. The gentleman, if he had walked up to the Fair, might there have seen American cotton, such as had cost, when the enormous minimums were first imposed for its protection by Mr. Lowndes and Mr. Calhoun, eighty-five cents a yard, now ready to be delivered in any quantity, and of better quality, at seven cents; and woollen jeans, sold in 1840 at sixty-five cents, now selling, of superior quality, for thirty-five; and these articles were subject to the very highest duties in the whole catalogue—proving, beyond all contestation, the truth of the proposition denounced as an absurdity by the gentleman, that the highest duties often produce the lowest prices, when levied on articles which we can supply to the extent of our own wants. Here was the result of American industry, skill, and improvement, when left free to act out their own energies, and occupy, fully and freely, their own appropriate markets, without the disturbing and destructive competition of the pauper labor of Europe. Mr. S. had mentioned the article of cotton, because it afforded a striking illustration of the general doctrine, showing that the minimums, the highest protective duties, had produced the greatest reduction of prices. But the same thing was true, to a greater or less extent, with respect to every protected article in the entire list. Mr. S. stated incontrovertible matters of fact. He challenged contradiction—he courted investigation—he defied gentlemen to disprove an atom of what he had asserted. And, to put this truth in the strongest light, he repeated that the highest and most obnoxious duties, those abhorred minimums, against which gentlemen had wasted such furious denunciations, presented precisely the very cases where the reduction of price had been the greatest. Those duties, it is said, now amounted to two and three hundred per cent. *ad valorem.* And why? Because they were fixed specific duties. They remained stationary, however prices might change; and, of course, as the price went down, the duty bore a larger and still larger proportion to it. At first, the duty was, say, half the price of the article; as the price declined, the duty became equal to the price; then it became greater than the price; then double the price; and, at length, treble; and then gentlemen exclaimed in horror, "What an abominable duty! It is three hundred per cent. on the total value of the article! What horrible profits! How the duty must raise the price!" when, all the while, the duty remained the same, and its effect had been, not to increase, but to bring down the price to one-third of what it was—from thirty cents down to ten cents per yard; and this was robbery and plunder! And still the gentleman said it was an absurdity, which no man could swallow, to say that the higher the protective duty the lower the price. Now, Mr. S. would venture to say, that if the duty on iron and its manufactures were increased to-morrow five hundred per cent., the rapid rush of capital into that business, and the vast increase of supply would be such, and the consequent reduction of price so great, that the United States would soon supply the world with iron, its capacity for its production being unlimited. He had stated facts, showing that high duties had produced low prices. Can the gentleman deny them? There they stand on impregnable foundations, firm as the hills! Let the gentleman and his friends disprove them as they can. That such is the practical operation of the system is fully established by the fact, that whilst manufactures of various kinds had declined to one-fourth of their former price, *agricultural* produce and the *wages* of labor had undergone little or no reduction, owing to the constantly increasing home demand for both, resulting from the protective policy. He submitted it as a matter of fact, known to every man, woman and child in the country, where manufactures existed, that they *paid less* for manufactured goods, and *received more* for their *labor* and their *produce*, owing to an increased demand. Yet, in the face of these universally admitted facts, we are told every day on this floor, that the tariff increases prices, and robs and plunders the farmers!!

But Mr. S. wished to be understood correctly. He did not say that the effect of all duties was to diminish prices; on the contrary, he did not deny that it was the effect of some duties to increase prices. But what he said was this: that duties levied on articles we could make, to the extent of our own wants, and with a view to protect and increase our own manufactures, did in all cases operate, in the end, to lower prices, by increasing capital, competition, and supply. Duties imposed on foreign articles which we could not make for ourselves, would generally increase the prices, because they did not increase the supply by increasing home competition. His position was this: *duties levied for revenue on articles we cannot produce, generally increased prices; whilst protective duties, levied on articles we can and do produce, always, in the end, diminished prices.* The truth of both these propositions was proved by undeniable facts, and by all experience. And the reason was just as obvious as the fact. When the supply of an article was not equal to the demand, he admitted the immediate effect of a high duty might for the moment increase the price and profits of its manufacture, but this very increase induced capital to rush into it, and the competition and increased supply resulting, soon brought down the price and profits to the lowest rates, proving the truth of the proposition, that the "higher the duty, the lower the price." The imposition of a duty on an article produced here, gave an impulse to American enterprise; the machinery employed in its production was studied and improved; an increased supply was the natural consequence; and increased supply, while the demand remained the same, must always diminish prices. Would the gentleman undertake to deny that the proportion between demand and supply regulated price? Mr. S. hardly thought that he would go so far as that. But, as the gentleman had asserted that duties raised prices, he was bound to prove the truth of his position by quoting facts. The man who asserted a thing to be a fact was bound to prove it, in court or out of court. As a lawyer the gentleman knew this to be so. Now, Mr. S. challenged the gentleman to put his finger on one solitary case where his assertion was true. What one *protected* article, the product of American skill and industry, had been permanently increased in price, after the duties, however high, had been first imposed for its protection? Mr. S. had challenged gentlemen, one and all, to point out a single article, a pin or a needle, the price of which had been increased after the imposition of a protective duty. They had failed to do it. He had called on them at the commencement of the session to hunt up some article. Nearly six months had elapsed, yet they had failed to find one; and he now called on gentlemen to point out one if they could. He heard no answer. No article could be found. And yet, gentlemen stood up in the face of the country and the world, and advanced the position that protective duties always increased prices. Mr. S. made his appeal to facts. Let the gentlemen meet him with facts. They could not; they dealt altogether in assertions against facts. Now if, as Mr. S. had proved, protective duties had not *increased* but *reduced* prices, what became of all this clamor about high prices, robbery, oppression, and plunder? It vanished into thin air; it had no foundation to stand on; and gentlemen were bound by their own principles to go for the protective policy, which reduced the price of manufactured goods by increasing the supply; whilst, on the other hand, it increased the price by increasing the demand for agricultural produce, and enhanced the wages of labor by increasing its employments.

THE EFFECT OF THE TARIFF ON LABOR AND INVESTED CAPITAL.

But gentlemen said, that while the tariff was oppressive on the interests of agriculture and of labor, it was highly beneficial to invested capital, to the rich monopolists, the lords of the loom. Now, Mr. S. said that just the reverse of this was true. While protection greatly benefited both agriculture and labor, it was but a small advantage, if any, to *vested capital.* The gentleman and his friends, without knowing it, were in fact doing more for the benefit of *vested capital,* by keeping up this agitation and opposition to the tariff, and thereby establishing a monopoly by checking competition, than all the tariff men in that House put together. In the case of vested capital the tariff had done its work; it had built the manufactories up; it had introduced improved machinery and increased skill; it had done all that fixed capital required. Vested capital was now on its feet—it could get along without help. They had exported during the last year between four and five million dollars worth of cotton cloth; they had beaten the British out of their own markets. The great manufacturers of these goods feared no foreign competition; they had overcome that, and Great Britain was compelled to impose discriminating duties in her East India colonies on American cottons—first 8, then 10, and finally 15 and 20 per cent., to enable her manufacturers to keep the possession of her own colonial markets. Our manufacturers had thus beaten down British competition in the Chinese and other foreign markets. What invested capital now feared, was American competition at home. But gentlemen exultingly say, if you can beat the foreigner, what do you want with protection?

I answer, the invested capital in these branches don't want it. But I want it, not to favor them, but to encourage further investments, and build up competition elsewhere. The protective tariff raised against them that very competition. While advocating, therefore, the continuance of our existing tariff, and resisting its reduction, Mr. S. was working in the most direct and efficient manner for the interests of American labor—he was resisting foreign; he was going for the interests of the American farmers and the American laborers, and not for the interests of large vested capital; he went to destroy existing monopoly, by increasing investments and competition—the only thing that could destroy it. It was the gentlemen, and those who acted with them, by keeping up this tariff agitation—who were aiding vested capital. This agitation operated to check new investments, and of course to promote and secure monopoly. Those who were contemplating the investment of new capital would defer it. One would say to another, "Don't build a new mill or furnace now, the tariff is going to be reduced." Mr. S. knew this to be true. He had heard of twelve large companies who had intended to build furnaces in Pennsylvania this spring, but had suspended their purpose till they should see what Congress would do with the tariff at the present session. Did this hurt those who already owned manufacturing establishments? Certainly not; it was the very thing to aid them. This gave New England a monopoly; it secured in her hands that which the people of Pennsylvania and the people of the South most wanted. They wanted protection—New England could do without it. Virginia wanted it, North Carolina wanted it, so did South Carolina, and Georgia, and all the West. They wanted protection to build them up; in New England the tariff had done its work—it had fulfilled its office. New England might now say to this Government, "Father, I am now of age; I am on my own feet; I can make my way through the world: I have met John Bull and beat him; I thank you very much for what you have done for me, and I will be a burden on you no longer; now take care of the younger branches of the family."

The rest of the country was comparatively young in manufactures. They still needed the helping hand of Government; they wanted protection in their infancy. New England was magnanimous and patriotic; she wished to see other portions of the country prosper by following her example; when the South and West supplied, as they could, the coarser goods, she would go to work on the finer fabrics. Did not gentlemen see that by reducing the tariff they were checking investments in their own country and in mine, in the South and West, and thereby securing a monopoly and high profits to vested capital, wherever it existed, which could only be reduced by enlarged competition at home? Was not this true? Was it not common sense? He put it to every man's understanding. It was not only common sense, but, what was more, it was proved by universal experience.

To show the practical operation of the protective policy, he would take, by way of illustration, the neighboring iron-works at Mount Savage, near Cumberland. That establishment has been built up within a few years. Sometime before it was commenced, land could be bought there for two and three dollars an acre, which could not now be purchased under twenty or thirty dollars; and mineral lands had lately been sold at hundreds of dollars per acre, which, a few years before these improvements were made, were comparatively worthless. Such were the effects of the protective policy. Was this system hurtful to agriculture? Then let gentlemen look at the Laurel Factory, not far from this city. The proprietor of that factory lately bought the ground on which it stood for five dollars an acre; and the same proprietor was now trying to purchase land in the neighborhood at fifty, and could not get it. This was the effect of giving the farmers a market. Manufacturing establishments multiplied the value of farms in their vicinity often ten, twenty, and sometimes, mineral lands, an hundred fold. And what was its effect upon labor? Did it not increase the price of labor? What raised prices, but an increased demand? What depressed prices, but the destruction of employment? The protective policy, by increasing the number of manufacturing establishments, of course increased the number of persons employed in them, thereby creating a greater demand and higher wages for labor. Laborers of all descriptions flock to the furnaces—coal-diggers, choppers, teamsters, and a thousand others. Now, suppose the gentleman should quit his agitation, make no more appeals to party, and no more anti-tariff speeches, what would be the effect? Would not others go to building up new establishments? And would not that furnish new markets for farmers, and employment for labor of all sorts? The Mount Savage works employed in various ways, on the ground and in the neighborhood, four or five thousand men. Let three or four more such establishments go up in that vicinity, and you would have at once a demand for three or four times as many hands, and for all sorts of agricultural produce in the same proportion. How, then, could gentlemen assert that the protective policy favored invested *capital*, and was oppressive to *labor* and *agriculture?*

[Mr. Holmes, of S. C., put a question to Mr. Stewart, whether all this was not done by taxing the South for the benefit of New England?]

The gentleman asked whether all this benefit did not grow out of a tax upon the South? Mr. S. would answer the gentleman; if these factories were built by Government, then this might, to some extent, be true. But they were built, not by Government, but by individual enterprise; and what sort of a tax was it upon the South, to give them better goods for one-fourth the price they formerly paid? Mr. S. said he was very sorry that his excellent friend from South Carolina should feel such deep regret at the prosperity of New England. If he thought New England was getting rich by manufactures, he would advise him to go home and do likewise—to follow their example, and grow rich also. The gentleman said that the planters of the South were working the whole year for a profit of four or five per cent., while the manufacturers of New England were getting forty or fifty. This was a great error—but, if true, was it not a free country? Who gave New England exclusive privileges? Why did not the South engage in the same forty or fifty per cent. business, instead of working on at four or five? Why did not they commence with coarse fabrics, made from their own cotton, just as New England had done before them? But New England was now passing from that stage, and going into the higher and finer branches. The South, he was glad to learn, were now commencing. True, they were yet in the A B C of the business; they were in their infancy; they wanted the fostering care and protection of Government. The tariff on the coarse fabrics was now for their benefit. New England wanted it no longer on the coarse, but only on the higher and finer fabrics, in which they were now struggling with foreigners, who were endeavoring to break them down by flooding our markets with these articles at an under-value, hoping to indemnify themselves for temporary losses by future exorbitant prices, extorted from us when American competition is put down and destroyed.

Mr. S. said he had been greatly amused by listening to the ingenious but sophistical reasoning of gentlemen who had gone into extended calculations to prove that cotton manufacturers were now realizing 100 per cent., clear profits, annually—yes, exactly 100 per cent. Yet the fact was notorious—seen in all the eastern papers—that the stocks of those very manufacturing establishments were selling every day, on change, often below par. Would men realizing 100 per cent. sell their stock under par? or would other capitalists suffer it to be thus sold? Besides, if these calculations of gentlemen be correct, do they not see, at a glance, that all the capital of the country, (for capital is quick and clear-sighted,) would rush at once into this 100 per cent. business—capital from England, and all Europe, would soon be into it, and what then? The business would soon be overdone—and then what? It would become the very worst business in the world. Gentlemen must be very credulous themselves, or think others so, to indulge in such absurdities. Business was like a pendulum—if you give it a strong impulse in one direction, the reaction was sure to carry it as far in the opposite direction. If any branch of business, by protection or otherwise, become highly profitable, the rush of capital into it would soon bring it down to the very lowest rates of profit.

POLICY OF THE SOUTH.

How was it that Southern gentlemen could shut their eyes to the result of their own unwise policy? Let them look how they stood, and then look at the North. The North applied their shoulder to the wheel; they went to work to better their condition; they husbanded their own resources; they employed and diversified their labor; they lived upon their own means; kept their money at home to reward their own industry, instead of foolishly sending it abroad to purchase what they could so well and so profitably supply at home. But South Carolina and her Southern sisters would touch neither hammer nor shuttle. They sent away their money to New England or to old England. And what was the consequence of these two opposite systems? South Carolina was poor and dependent, while New England was independent and prosperous. South Carolina, when the Federal Constitution was adopted, had five representatives, North Carolina five, and Virginia ten representatives on this floor. They all cherished a deadly hostility to everything connected with the manufactures, internal improvements, and progress of every kind. They denied to this Government the power of self-protection and self-improvement; they went for the stand-still, lie-down, go-to-sleep, let-us-alone, do-nothing policy; they had tried to live on whip syllabub, political metaphysics, and constitutional abstractions, until it had nearly starved them to death, while the Northern States had wisely pursued the opposite policy; and what had been the effect on their relative prosperity? New York began with six representatives in that hall; now she had thirty-four. Pennsylvania began with eight, and now she had twenty-four. Virginia, with North and South Carolina, had commenced with twenty representatives, and now they have, altogether, but thirty, and New York alone has thirty-four. Such are the fruits of the opposite systems of policy adopted by the North and South. Judge the tree by its fruits. Will men never learn wisdom from experience? He would rejoice to see the South as prosperous and as happy as the North. They had all the elements of wealth and prosperity in profusion around them—the raw materials and bread stuffs, minerals, and water-power in abundance, running to waste. If they would allow him to offer them advice, it would be to abandon an exploded and ruinous policy; follow the example of the North, and share in their prosperity. Instead of coming here repining and complaining that the North was rich and prosperous, making forty or fifty per cent. profit on their capital, whilst the South realized but four or five, just turn round, quit your four or five per cent. profits, and go to work, at what you allege yields forty or fifty. If the tariff was confined to the North, you might complain; but it was free to all alike—North and South, East and West. Go to the hammer and the loom, the furnace and the forge, and become prosperous in your turn. All these blessing are within your reach, if you will but put forth your hands to grasp them; they are offered freely to your acceptance. You enjoy great advantages. You have not only all the advantages enjoyed by the North for manufacturing, but you have others superadded; you supply the raw material, and above all, you have *labor without wages,* perfectly available for such purposes; the hands of the young and old, now useless for the field, might, in factories, become highly profitable and productive operatives. Take hold, then, of the same industry which had made New England great, and especially on those branches of it which New England now could and would spare. Then South Carolina would be, thus far, independent both of New England and of all the world. She could no longer hope to compete with Texas and the rich lands of the Southwest in the production of cotton. Her wornout fields must sink in the contest with the virgin soil of the new States. Then let her address herself to manufactures. The gentleman from South Carolina seemed to observe, with grief and envy, that New England was enjoying profits of from forty to fifty per cent. That was not true; but what if it was? If she gave that to South Carolina for six cents per yard, which Carolina once could not get from abroad under thirty-six, the question for Carolina to look at was, not what profits New England *made*, but what prices she *charged* her.

That gentleman wanted his State to go to old England for all she required. We were all to depend on Europe for our manufactured articles. Foreign countries were to enjoy exclusively the profitable business yielding forty and fifty per cent., while we were all to turn farmers, and join the gentleman in working, as he said, for a profit of four and five per cent. (and when all became farmers it would be ten times worse), competition having ceased, old England would again make the gentleman pay twenty-five cents a yard for what New England now offered them for six. Was not this patriotic? Was it not a noble, an enlarged American policy? England was to be allowed to monopolize all the profitable business, the result of labor-saving machinery, while we were to content ourselves with the plough and the hoe, and profits at the rate of two or three per cent. Was that the policy for America to pursue? They might be Americans who recommended it, but they were certainly playing into the hands of our trans-Atlantic competitors. If manufacturing was such profitable business as these gentlemen represented it to be, why not let Americans have it rather than foreigners? Why not keep our money and our profits to ourselves, instead of giving both to the labor of Great Britain? The profits of manufacturing were chiefly owing to an enlarged market, and to the use and constant improvement of labor-saving machinery. The saving of labor and the increase of human power produced in this manner was almost incalculable. By its aid one feeble woman or child was enabled to accomplish more in a day than would pay for the productions of forty able-bodied, hard-handed men without it. Did gentlemen desire, and was it their policy, to let England enjoy all this benefit, and keep it to herself as a monopoly? It was this labor-saving machinery, and this alone, that kept the British Government from bankruptcy. This prolific source of wealth and power enabled the British people to stand up under a debt of four thousand millions of dollars, and to pay taxes to the Government amounting to more than two hundred and fifty millions every year. This was the result of her immense labor-saving machinery, estimated to be equal to the labor of eight millions of men. Was it the policy of gentlemen to let England have this profitable business of manufacturing all to herself? That seemed to be the policy of the Secretary of the Treasury. Indeed, he had avowed it in his report to be his settled policy to break down the manufacturers of our own country, and derive his revenue from British and other foreign goods. His policy was in his own words, to prevent "*the substitution of domestic rival products for imported articles.*" This policy of *substituting American for foreign goods*, he says, is injurious to the revenue, and must be arrested by reducing the duties so as to let in the productions of foreign labor, and thus break down American mechanics and manufacturers, and put an end to this growing evil of "*substituting American rival products for foreign goods.*" This sentiment the Secretary has repeated several times in his report. See pages 3 and 6. His policy was to increase the revenue by increasing importations; and, as he would reduce the average of duties one-third, of course, to get the same amount of revenue, we must add ½ to our imports. This was manifest and undeniable. Our present imports amounted to one hundred millions; to carry out the Secretary's plan we must raise them to one hundred and fifty millions. Our exports were about one hundred millions, and of course fifty millions in specie would be required annually to pay the balance. The whole specie of the country had never been estimated at more than eighty millions. How, then, was his policy to work? How was he to make up this deficit? Not from the banks, for they would be broken up within the very first year of such a system; and then what was Mr. Secretary going to do for his revenue? The duty on foreign iron, he tells us, is 75 per cent. He was for reducing it to 30 per cent.—less than one-half. We must, of course, import more than double the amount of foreign iron to get the present amount of revenue, and to that extent break up American supply. Now, it was impossible to make our people double their consumption, and so the result must necessarily be to get them to take foreign goods where they now took domestic, thus supplying the demand from abroad, and of course destroying the domestic article to that extent. Was not all this plain? Could any man in his senses deny it? And then, besides, where was the Secretary going to get the money to pay for all these foreign goods? There was the rub. The gentleman from Virginia [Mr. Bayly] talked about exporting potatoes to Ireland. Export potatoes to Ireland! He would tell that gentleman that last year we imported 211,327 bushels, paying a duty of ten cents per bushel—15,045 from Ireland, while Ireland took of all our grain only 790 bushels of corn, not a barrel of flour, corn-meal, or a bushel of grain, or its productions in any other form. The whole of our mighty export of breadstuffs to England, Scotland, and Ireland, amounted to less than $224,000, less than one-fourth of a million—less than could be furnished by a single Western county. Potatoes were cheaper in Ireland than in the United States, yet the people are starving, because they had no protection against England, no money, no *employment.* This was the effect of "free-trade" with England, and it was precisely the condition into which "free-trade" with England would soon bring this country, if it were adopted. "Free-trade" with England reminded him of an anecdote of an Irishman, who, when complaining of starvation in Ireland, was asked whether potatoes were not very cheap? he answered, "Chape! the Lord love ye, they're but saxpence a bushel." "How is it, then, you are starving?" "Just because we have no work, and can't get the saxpence." [A laugh.] Such were the fruits of exchanging agricultural products for manufactured goods—the products of manual labor for the products of machinery—working the hoe against the loom. Such had been, and always would be, the result of this miserable system of policy, whenever and wherever adopted.

TAXATION.

Next, the gentleman complained of taxation. If protective duties, as he had proved, *reduced* prices, where was the taxation? But suppose it to be admitted that the duties on foreign goods are added to the price. Then I ask what tax did farmers and laborers now pay the United States? Nothing. Many of them used nothing but domestics. They bought no *foreign* goods except tea and coffee, and they were free. Thousands and hundreds of thousands of our people don't pay a dollar a year into the National Treasury, and thousands not a cent. How would it be under a system of direct taxation? The burdens of the Federal Government would fall on farmers and laborers more heavily than the heaviest State taxation. Under a system of direct tax the proportion of Pennsylvania would be *three millions* a year—more than double her present heavy State taxation. But all these burdens put together are nothing compared to the taxes imposed on us by the *British.* To form an idea of its extent, let every gentleman ascertain the number of stores selling *British goods* in his district. These merchants are all tax-gatherers for England, taking millions and tens of millions of specie from our farmers for British agricultural produce, wool, and everything else converted into goods, and sent here and sold to our farmers, who have those very materials on their hands rotting for want of a market; and this is the ruinous system recommended to our farmers by these "free-trade" advocates. The farmers understand it, and they will let gentlemen know it at the polls. They will let gentlemen know what they think of this "*buy everything and sell nothing policy.*" They know that the farmer who sells more than he buys gets rich, and he who buys more than he sells gets poor; and they know that the same theory is true with regard to nations; they know that, to sell more and buy less, is the way to wealth, and that the opposite course is the road to bankruptcy and ruin. A striking illustration of the truth of this may be found in the fact that during the reduction of duties under the compromise act our imports exceeded our exports upwards of three hundred millions, and the consequence was that our specie was all exported, our banks broken, the treasury empty, people impoverished, and two hundred millions of State six per cent. bonds sent to Europe to pay this unfavorable balance of trade, where they still remain, drawing away our specie to pay the interest—a dead weight upon the energies of the people. Such are the blessings and benefits of low duties, and should this destructive bill pass, they will soon return in all their bitterness.

The idea that a balance of trade against us is not an unfavorable indication, was a plausible absurdity into which sensible men were sometimes seduced. The error consisted in the assumption that our imports consisted of cash or were converted into cash: whereas they were imported for consumption, and were *consumed.* Now, was it not manifest that if a nation sold one hundred millions, and bought and *consumed* one hundred and fifty millions of foreign goods, the nation would be fifty millions in debt? Suppose an individual sells one hundred dollars worth of produce, and buys and consumes one hundred and fifty dollars worth of goods, is he not fifty dollars in debt? And if true of an individual, is it not equally true of a nation?

The true American policy was PROTECTION and INDEPENDENCE. It was to make America independent of all the world. That was sound American policy; and he trusted no man would suffer himself to be so carried away by mere party politics as to advocate "*free-trade*" and *starvation,* twin sisters, "one and inseparable." *Protection* was the policy which would spread comfort and happiness over the face of a smiling land. Its effect would penetrate our forests, and reach to the remotest hamlet in the West. This would keep our money at home, instead of sending it across the ocean to enrich British farmers and manufacturers to the ruin of our own.

EFFECT OF THE PROPOSED BILL ON THE REVENUE.

What was the theory of our learned Secretary? We must reduce duties to increase our revenue. Now, Mr. S. said, and he defied contradiction, that as truly as the thermometer indicated the increase or diminution of heat in the atmosphere, just so truly did the increase or diminution of the tariff mark the increase or the diminution of revenue. He appealed to the record, and defied his opponents to the test.

This Mr. S. pronounced a most extraordinary scheme—the greatest absurdity that ever entered into the imagination of man. The Secretary's plan was to *increase the revenue.* And how was it to be accomplished? By *reversing* the rule adopted in this and every other country from the beginning of time. His plan was, not to *increase,* but *reduce,* duties, the source of revenue. Now, he wished to state a few plain facts, derived from this very report of Secretary Walker's itself, utterly subversive of his whole theory. In the first place, his voluminous tables showed, at pages 956 and 957, that for the last 25 years the tariff and the revenue had invariably gone up and down together. 2d. That, in 1842, under a 20 per cent. tariff, the net revenue was only $12,780,173, while under the present tariff, averaging, he says, near 40 per cent., the last year (1845) the net revenue was $27,528,112, as given at page 23, more than double that of 1842, and corresponding exactly with the increase of the duties. Yet, in the face of these facts, he proposes to reduce the duties to increase the revenue! But this is not all; this report further shows this fact, that the present tariff is now yielding more revenue than has ever been received, with the exception of a single year (1836), since the foundation of the Government. But what is most astonishing, the Secretary, at page 47 of his report, gives the amount of revenue his favorite standard, 20 per cent., would yield on the whole imports of the last year, free, dutiable, and all, and

He makes it..............................	$22,636, 864
From which deduct amount on tea and coffee, made free..........................	2,400,000
Leaves	$20,236,864
And from this deduct the expenses of collection	3,500,000
And he has left only.............	$16,736,864
And this was subject to a still further reduction on $15,346,830 of goods re-exported	3,069,000
	$13,667,864

Thirteen millions less than the present tariff. And this is a war measure, leaving only $13,767,864 assessed on the imports of 1845, which were 25 millions more than the average imports of the last 9 years; and at an average duty of 25 per cent., according to the same calculation, the revenue would be only $17,097,330. This was the Secretary's own calculation. See page 47 of his report. But if the Secretary will take 67 millions, the average of dutiable imports (page 9), his 20 per cent. will give him less than ten millions net revenue.

Yet the Secretary recommended a reduction of duties to an average rate of 20 per cent., and in support of this recommendation he had accompanied his report with a table, at page 956, showing the revenue under different tariffs for the last twenty-five years, viz., four years immediately before the tariff of 1824, four years under the tariff of 1824, four years under the tariff of 1828, ten years under the compromise bill, and three years under the tariff of 1842. And what was the result?

For the four years preceding the tariff of 1824 the average gross revenue was $22,753,000. Under the tariff of 1824, which its opponents at the time predicted would ruin the revenue and compel a resort to direct taxation, the average for the four years of its duration was $28,929,000. Next came the "bill of abominations," the "black tariff of 1828," which it was said would bankrupt the treasury beyond all question; and what was the result? The average revenue during the four years of its operation increased to $30,541,000. Then came the compromise bill of 1833, which brought the tariff down by biennial reductions to a horizontal duty of 20 per cent.; and what was its effect upon the revenue? The revenue declined *pari passu* with the tariff, yielding for ten years an average of $21,496,000, and the last year of its operation under the 20 per cent. duty only $16,686,000 gross revenue, netting $12,780,000, while our expenditures were more than double that amount. Then came the present tariff, which yielded more than $32,000,000 gross—$27,500,000 net revenue. Now, what does our profound Secretary of the treasury propose to do to improve the revenue? Mark it! He proposes to reduce the tariff to an average of about 20 per cent., which "experience proves," he says, will give the *highest revenue,* and yet this very report shows the fact that a 20 per cent. tariff in 1842 yielded only $12,780,000, while the present tariff last year yielded $27,526,000. Thus, according to the Secretary, *twelve is more than twenty-seven!* A new discovery in arithmetic. The new "free-trade" system of finance says—"reduce the duties to increase the revenue," a doctrine not only urged upon Congress by the Secretary and *The Union,* his organ, but by all the advocates of this new tariff on this floor. "Reduce the duties to increase the revenue!" Can anything be more absurd? Are not duties the source of revenue; and would it not be just as sensible to say "reduce the revenue to increase the revenue?" Duties and revenue being convertible terms. Suppose you want twenty-five millions from the tariff—that sum must be raised, no matter how you impose the duties; and why not so arrange them as to protect and sustain your own national industry—thus making taxation itself prolific of benefits and blessings to the people? Making it the means of protecting national industry, enlarging the markets for agriculture, increasing the employments and wages of labor, developing your own national resources, and securing your national prosperity and independence; thus making taxation itself a blessing, instead of a curse, to your country?

On the subject of the revenue, he would venture to predict, that if the system of measures recommended by the Secretary—the reduction of the tariff, the change from specific to ad valorem duties, the Subtreasury, and the warehousing system were adopted—the revenue next year would *not be half* the amount it will be this year. Mark the prediction, *not half.*

Who could deny the fact that with the raising of the tariff the revenue increased, and with its diminution the revenue fell off, till at last under 20 per cent., which the Secretary considered the very *beau ideal*—the very perfection of a revenue system—the nett revenue sank down to less than thirteen millions? There was the Secretary's theory—and there, alongside of it, stood his proof; and his proof utterly subverted his theory. Did it prove that reducing duties to 20 per cent. raised the revenue to its highest point! Just the reverse. It reduced it to the very lowest point of depression. While his theory said that 20 per cent. would give the "*highest,*" his proof showed that it gave the very "*lowest.*"

FOLLY AND EXTRAVAGANCE OF THIS ADMINISTRATION.

And was not this a pretty time to select for the reduction of duties? Now, when we had just entered into a war, whose duration no man could predict or calculate. When we went to war in 1812 we doubled the duties: now it was proposed to cut them down one-half! What a consummate proof of political wisdom and financial ability was here exhibited? Why, then, destroy the present admirable tariff, that had worked so well, and adopt such a miserable and rickety system as this? Why destroy a tariff that had paid, since 1842, inclusive, no less than $34,307,224 of the principal and interest of your public debt, and leaving in your treasury, on the first of July, 1845, a balance of $7,658,306, which added to the above, gives a surplus revenue, over and above the ordinary expenditures, of $41,965,520, derived from the tariff of 1842, including the payments of that year? This he stated from official annual Treasury reports of 1843, page 31, of 1844, page 19, and of 1845, page 25. Yet this tariff, which had yielded this large surplus, is to be destroyed in the midst of war, to carry out an absurd resolution adopted some years ago by an irresponsible political cabal assembled at Baltimore; and this was their leading and almost only argument in its favor. Mr. S. called the attention of the chairman of the Committee of Ways and Means to the fact, and he should like to hear his explanation of it. The estimates made by the Secretary of the Treasury, before there was a word said about war or the prospect of war—estimates rendered in a time of profound peace to meet the ordinary expenses of the Government—had been more by six millions and a half than the expenditures of the preceding year. If gentlemen doubted it, he would refer them to the Secretary's report. He wished the chairman to explain how it was that the peace estimates for this year exceeded by more than six millions the peace expenditures of the last year; and, besides this, we had had a bill appropriating a million and a half to make good deficient appropriations. Add this million and a half to the six millions and a half he had just mentioned, and it would make eight millions, by which amount our peace expenditure for the present year surpassed those of the last. There stood the fact in the Secretary's own report, and Mr. S. challenged the chairman of the Committee of Ways and Means, or any friend of the Secretary or of the Administration, to deny it. Was this war brought about to conceal these enormous and unprecedented expenditures in time of peace, exceeding by six or seven millions the expenditures of preceding years? The war would smother up all this extravagance, and conceal it from the public view. All wasteful expenditures would now be attributed to the war. The war would be a blanket wide enough to cover all. And here he would add another fact—it was one the people ought to know—it was this: That the appropriations reported passed, and to be passed, amounted already this session to the enormous sum of $57,237,075; and would, perhaps, reach sixty millions before the adjournment—nearly three times our ordinary appropriations. And, in the face of all this, we are to pass this miserable party bill reducing the revenue fully one-half.

There was another thing of which the tariff was an index, and that was the public *prosperity*. When the people are poor they could not afford to consume luxuries; imports fell off, and down went the revenue. But when duties were high and domestic competition was excited, agriculture having abundant markets, and labor full and profitable employment, the people became prosperous; they lived in comfort; they could afford to pay for fine goods and luxuries—and up went the revenue. Reduce the tariff, break up American industry, and you clothed the people in rags, and your treasury became bankrupt. The national *revenue* and the national *prosperity* went up and down together, and were always coincident with national *protection*. This he asserted as an undeniable fact, proved by every page of our financial history, from the days of the revolution up to the present hour.

A CHAPTER FOR WORKING MEN TO READ.

Mr. S.'s system was this: Select the articles you can manufacture to the full extent of our own wants, then, in the language of Thomas Jefferson, "impose on them duties lighter at first, and afterwards heavier and heavier as the channels of supply were opened." This was Jefferson's plan; the reverse of modern democratic "free-trade." Next Mr. S. went for levying the highest rates of duty on the luxuries of the rich, and not on the necessaries of the poor. Encourage American manufactures, and while on the one hand the poor man found plenty of employment, on the other he got his goods cheap. He could clothe himself decently for a mere trifle. He wanted no foreign commodities but his tea and his coffee, and they were free, and should remain free. The poor man could now buy cloth for a full suit from head to foot for less than *one dollar* of substantial American manufacture. He had himself worn in this hall a garment of this same goods, at ten cents per yard, and it was so much admired that more than a dozen members had applied for similar garments, and they had been supplied to Senators and others; yet we are told the tariff taxes and oppresses the poor. Put high revenue duties on wines, on brandies, on silks, on laces, on jewelry, on all that which the rich man alone consumed and which the poor man did not want. Take off the duties from the poor man's necessaries, and give him high wages for his work. That was the way to diffuse happiness and prosperity among the great body of the people. That was good sound democratic policy. He was for lifting up the poor. He was for "levelling upward;" for increasing the domestic comfort of our own laboring population—the true *democracy* of the country. The rich could pay, and ought to be made to pay, and they should pay; the poor man could not, and should not, with his consent. Mr. S. went for the system which elevated the poor man in the scale of society; that promoted equality, that essential element in all free Governments, not by pulling down the higher, but by lifting up the lower classes to their level. The gentleman from Alabama and his friends advocated a policy which would have precisely the opposite effect. Their system would truly make the "rich richer and the poor poorer." The gentleman advocated a system whose direct and undeniable tendency was to destroy competition, and thereby give a monopoly to the heavy capitalists. He would benefit those very "millionaires" of whose presence here he complained so loudly. Free-trade would inevitably degrade the wages of labor in every department of industry, whether employed in the fields or in the workshops, to the level of wages in Europe; this was as certain as the ebbing and flowing of the tides. What could be plainer? Take two coterminous States—Kentucky and Ohio. Suppose in Kentucky, as in Europe, wages was 12½ cents per day, and in Ohio, as in the U. S., 75 cents per day. Now was it not perfectly clear that, unless Ohio protected her prosperous labor, the productions of the low price labor of Kentucky, boots, shoes, hoes, everything would come in, and compel the mechanics and laborers of Ohio to come down to 12½ cents a day, or give up their markets, quit work, buy everything, sell nothing, and *get rich!* And he submitted, would not this be the effect of "free-trade" with Europe? The only difference was the cost of transportation across the Ohio and across the Atlantic; and with the modern facilities of steam, a ton of iron could be brought from Europe to this country for less than $4; less than it would cost to cart it 20 miles on common roads. Such would be the manifest and ruinous effects of "free-trade," on the wages of labor in every department of the national industry; and any reduction of protection would be a reduction to the same extent of the wages of labor.

It would degrade the free labor of this country to the

miserable condition of the serf labor of foreign lands, where men were slaves—without the means of educating their children—working from the cradle to the grave, and never aspiring to anything beyond a scanty and miserable subsistence; and such was the condition to which "free-trade" must inevitably bring the now protected and prosperous labor of this great country. Pull down the walls built up by the tariff of '42 to protect and defend American labor—let the cheap productions of the low-priced labor of Europe flow *freely* into your markets, and you must sooner or later come down to their degraded *condition—moral* and *political.* He, therefore, earnestly appealed to the laboring people of this country—the sovereigns of the land—who "made all and paid all," to come quickly to the rescue, to save themselves from the degrading and disastrous effects of "free-trade." The *power* was in their own hands—they could protect themselves at the *ballot-box*, and, if they did not, they would deserve the degradation to which they would be doomed. To every candidate for office propound this question: "*are you in favor of protecting American against foreign labor by a* PROTECTIVE TARIFF?" And let his answer be conclusive. This is the remedy—the only remedy. Let it be adopted, and all will be well. He stood there the firm friend and humble advocate of the *laboring man.* He had been a laboring man himself; he knows their privations and had participated in their toils; and to deserve and receive the approbation of the *laboring poor*, of the *mechanics*, and *log-cabin* men of this country, would be more grateful to his heart than all the praises of all the presses of the land. It would be the crowning and cherished reward of all his efforts—the only reward to which he aspired.

Labor, productive labor, was the great source of national wealth. Its importance was incalculable. Compared with this all other interests dwindled into perfect insignificance. What is all other capital combined compared to the capital of labor—hard-handed, honest labor—the toiling millions—the great fountain of our national prosperity—look at it. Suppose we have but two millions of working men in the United States, whose wages average $180 per year—this is equal to the interest of $3000 at six per cent. Each laborer's capital, then, is equal to $3000 at interest. Multiply this by two millions, the number of laborers, and it gives you a capital amounting to the enormous sum of *six thousand millions of dollars*, producing, at six per cent., *three hundred and sixty millions* of dollars a year. This was the "*labor capital*" he wished to sustain and uphold. This was the great *national industry* he wished to protect and defend against the ruinous and degrading effects of a free and unrestricted competition with the pauper labor of foreign lands. He went to secure the American market for American labor. In the great struggle for the American market he took the American side. On the other hand, the gentleman from Alabama and his friends went for the British; for foreigners; for "free-trade;" for opening our ports to the manufacturers of all the world; for bringing in freely the pauper productions of Great Britain, to overwhelm the rising prosperity of our own poor but industrious citizens. They went for crushing American enterprise; grinding down American labor, and putting their countrymen on a footing with the very sweepings of the poor houses of Europe; and would, in the end, bring them down to their *political*, as well as their pecuniary and moral condition. Mr. S. was for cherishing American labor; for giving it high wages; for surrounding it with all the substantial comforts of life. Which was the true friend of the PEOPLE? And yet these "free-trade" advocates, from the Secretary down, professed to be the exclusive friends of the "poor man," and we are denounced as the friends of "millionaires and monopolists." We now imported fifty millions worth of British goods annually, and therein we imported twenty-five millions worth of British agricultural products—of English wool, English grain, English beef and mutton, English flax, English agricultural productions of every kind. And yet gentlemen would rise here and talk of a British market for our breadstuffs. Why, how much of this did England take? Not a quarter of a million, in all its forms!

Here was a beautiful reciprocity. Here were the beauties of free trade. Here was our equality of benefits. We took fifty millions in British goods, one-half of it agricultural produce, while she took one-quarter of a million of our breadstuffs. This was our boasted British market. What was this British market to us? The American market consumed annually nearly a thousand millions of American grain; the British market one-quarter of one million. Great Britain took of our flour not a twentieth part as much as Massachusetts, not a tenth part of the amount taken by the East and West Indies; not a third part as much as Brazil; not as much as the little Island of Cuba; and not much more than half as much as Hayti. Poor, miserable, negro Hayti, took last year 53,144 barrels of our flour, while England, Scotland, and Ireland together, took but 35,355 barrels of flour, and *one* barrel of corn-meal. Yet we are told, in the face of these official facts, by the Secretary of the Treasury, that we must take more British goods, otherwise she will have to pay us "*cash for our breadstuffs, and, not having it to spare,* she will not buy as much of our cotton." What an insult to American farmers is this. As an honorable man, must he not blush for his reputation when he looks upon these facts? But what better could we expect from this American Secretary, who, over and over, in his report, denounces the *substitution of American manufactures for foreign goods,* and declares that *direct taxation* is more equitable and just than *duties on foreign goods,* especially in its operations on the poor! Better levy taxes on our own productions than on those of foreigners! Such are the doctrines openly avowed by this Secretary to favor his miserable system of "free-trade." Away with such British doctrines as these! They could never find favor with the American people, while a spark of patriotism animates their hearts, or a drop of Revolutionary blood runs in their veins.

The gentleman from Alabama will no doubt discover another terrible absurdity when Mr. S. stated that Great Britain exported and sold more agricultural produce than any other country in the world. Yet it is strictly and undeniably true. Exported, not in its original form, but worked up and converted into goods, iron, cloths, etc., consisting of raw materials and breadstuffs. Great Britain exported, on an average, more than two hundred and fifty millions of dollars' worth of manufactures, one-half of the whole value of which consisted of the produce of the soil. The United States took about one-fifth part of all the exports of Great Britain—being more than all Europe put together. In a report of a committee in the British Parliament, made some years ago, it appeared that the British goods consumed by the people of the different countries of Europe,—France, Russia, Prussia, Austria, Spain, Belgium, etc., amounted to *fourteen cents'* worth per head, while the people of the United States at the same time consumed *three hundred and fifty-four cents'* worth per head! This showed the immense importance of the American market to

Great Britain, and accounted for her great solicitude to retain it. It also showed the superior wisdom of the European Governments in excluding British goods by high and prohibitory tariffs; thus developing and relying upon their own resources, encouraging and sustaining their own national industry, promoting their own prosperity, and thus establishing (as we should do) their own national independence on the most solid and lasting foundations.

Mr. S. invited scrutiny into the facts he had stated; he challenged contradiction. He put them before gentlemen, and begged them to examine and disprove them if they could. He invited them to reflect upon them in a spirit of candor. To dismiss from their minds all party bias; to rise for once superior to the low grovelling prejudices of party; to wake up to the great interest, and feel for the real strength and true glory and independence of their native land.

BENEFITS OF THE TARIFF TO FARMERS.

Gentlemen dwelt entirely on the benefits of foreign trade. They went altogether in favor of importing foreign goods, and creating a market for the benefit of foreigners. Would our own agriculture be benefited by a process like this? Nothing could more effectually divert the benefit from our own people and pour it in a constant stream upon foreign labor. No American interest was so much benefited by a protective system as that of *agriculture*. The foreign market was nothing, the home market was everything to them; it was as one hundred to one. The tariff gave us the great home market, while the gentleman's scheme was to secure us, at best, but the chance of a market abroad, while it effectually destroyed our secure and invaluable market at home. Gentlemen were very anxious to compete with the pauper labor of Europe. I will tell them one fact: With all the protection we now enjoy, Great Britain sends into this country eight dollars' worth of her agricultural productions to one dollar's worth of all our agricultural productions (save cotton and tobacco) that she takes from us.

This I will prove by the returns furnished by Mr. Walker himself in support of the bill which he has laid before the Committee of Ways and Means. Now, I assert, and can prove, that more than half the value of all the British merchandise imported into this country consists of agricultural products, changed in *form*, converted and manufactured into goods. And I invite a thorough analysis of the facts. I challenge gentlemen to the scrutiny. Take down all the articles in a store, one after another—estimate the value of the raw material, the bread and meat, and other agricultural products, which have entered into their fabrication, and it will be found that one-half and more of their value consists of the productions of the soil—agricultural produce in its strictest sense.

Now, by reference to Mr. Walker's report, it will be seen that, for twelve years back, we have imported from Great Britain and her dependencies annually fifty-two and a half millions of dollars' worth of goods, but call it fifty millions, while she took of all our agricultural products, save cotton and tobacco, less than two and a half millions of dollars' worth. Thus, then, assuming one-half the value of her goods to be agricultural, it gives us twenty-five millions of her agricultural produce to two and a half millions of ours taken by her, which is just ten to one; to avoid cavil, I put it at eight to one. To test the truth of his position, he was prepared, if time permitted, to refer to numerous facts. But for the information of gentlemen who are such great friends to the poor and oppressed farmers, I will tell them that we have imported yearly, for twenty-six years, (so says Mr. Walker's report,) more than ten millions of dollars' worth of *woollen goods*. Last year we imported $10,666,176 worth. Now, one-half and more of the value of this cloth was made up of wool, the subsistence of labor and other agricultural productions. The general estimate is, that the wool alone is half. The universal custom among farmers, when they had their wool manufactured on the shares, was to give the manufacturer half the cloth. Thus we import, and our farmers have to pay, for *five* millions of dollars' worth of foreign wool every year in the form of cloth, mostly the production of sheep feeding on the grass and grain of Great Britain, while our own wool is worthless for want of a market; and this is the policy gentlemen recommend to American farmers. Yes, sir; and not satisfied with *five* millions, they wish to increase it to *ten* millions a year for foreign wool. Will gentlemen deny this? They dare not. They supported Mr. Walker's bill, reducing the duties on woollens nearly one-half, with a view to *increase* the revenue; of course, the imports must be doubled, making the import of cloth twenty millions instead of ten, and of wool ten instead of five millions of dollars per annum.

This was the plan to favor the farmers, *British* farmers, by giving them the *American* market. Their plan was to buy everything, sell nothing, and get rich. (A laugh.) What was true as to cloth was equally true as to everything else. Take a hat, a pair of shoes, a yard of silk or lace, analyze it, resolve it into its constituent elements, and you will find that the raw material, and the substance of labor, and other agricultural products, constituted more than one-half its entire value. The pauper labor of Europe employed in manufacturing silk and lace got what it eat, no more; and this is what you pay for when you purchase their goods. Break up your home manufactures and home markets, import everything you eat and drink and wear, for the *benefit of the farmers.* Oh, what friends these gentlemen are to the farmers and mechanics and laborers of this country—no, sir, I am wrong, of *Great Britain.*

As a still stronger illustration of his argument, Mr. S. referred to the article of iron. Last year, according to Mr. Walker's report, we imported $9,043,396 worth of foreign iron, and its manufactures, mostly from Great Britain, four-fifths of the value of which, as every practical man knew, consisted of agricultural produce—nothing else. Iron is made of ore and coal; and what are the ore and coal buried in your mountains worth? Nothing—nothing at all, unused. What gives them value? The labor of horses, oxen, mules and men. And what sustained this labor but corn and oats, hay and straw for the one, and bread and meat and vegetables of every kind for the other. These agricultural products were purchased and consumed, and this made up nearly the whole price of the iron which the manufacturer received and paid over to the farmers again and again, as often as the process was repeated. Well, is not iron made in England of the same materials that it is made of here? Certainly; then is not four-fifths of the value of British iron made up of British agricultural produce? And if we purchase nine millions of dollars' worth of British iron a year, do we not pay six or seven millions of this sum for the produce of British farmers—grain, hay, grass, bread, meat, and other provisions for man and beast—sent here for sale in the form of iron? He put it to the gentleman from Virginia (Mr. Bayly) to say if this was not true to the letter. He challenged him to deny it, or disprove it if he could. The gentleman's plan was to break down these great and growing markets for our own farmers, and give them to the British; and yet he *professed* to be a friend to American farmers!! "From such friends, good Lord, deliver *them!*" One remark more on this topic. Secretary Walker informs us that the present duty on iron is 75 per cent., which he proposes to reduce to 30 per cent., to *increase the revenue.* To do this, must he not then double the imports of iron? Clearly he must. Then we must add ten or twelve millions per year to our present imports of iron, and of course destroy that amount of our domestic supply to make room for it. Thus, at a blow, in the single article of iron, this bill is intended to destroy the American markets for at least eight millions of dollars worth of domestic agricultural produce to be supplied from abroad; and this is the American—no! the *British*—system of policy which is now attempted to be imposed upon this country by this *British-hating Administration!* Let them do it, and in less than two years there will not be a specie-paying bank in the country. The people and the Treasury will be again bankrupt, and the scenes and sufferings of 1840 will return; and with it, as a necessary consequence, the political revolutions of that period.

REPEAL OF THE CORN LAW—ITS EFFECTS.

But the gentleman congratulates the West on the prospect of an early repeal of the corn laws. But, in his opinion, if the corn laws were repealed, the people of the West would scarcely get a bushel of their grain into England on any terms.

[*Mr. Bayly.* Do you mean what you say, that not one bushel will go there?]

Mr. Stewart. I will answer the gentleman by giving him Lord Ashburton's speech in the House of Lords a few days ago. He states that nine-tenths of the grain now imported in Great Britain is supplied from the north of Europe, although they pay a tax of fifteen shillings the quarter; while that from Canada, and the United States passing through Canada, pays but four shillings. Repeal the duty of fifteen shillings, and will they not supply the whole? Most clearly they will. The fact is notorious, that most of our grain and flour now goes to England through her colonial ports, and at colonial duties, thus evading the operation of the corn laws, while the grain and flour from the north of Europe must always pay the highest duties imposed by the corn laws. Hence Lord Ashburton very justly argues, that we must be overwhelmed if the corn laws are repealed, and this great advantage, now enjoyed by Canada and the United States, of importing flour and grain at about one-fourth of the duty paid by the importers from the Baltic and Black sea. Repeal the corn laws—put them on an equal footing with us, and is not the question settled, and the market lost to our grain and flour in all time to come? Nothing can be clearer. And yet gentlemen exult in the prospect of the repeal of the corn laws, and are ready to sacrifice the whole of our manufactures and home markets to bring it about. Such will be the operation of the repeal of the corn laws on American agriculture, and such is the statement of Lord Ashburton, who perhaps knows as much about the matter as even the learned gentleman from Virginia. But this is not all. This opinion of Lord Ashburton is sustained by the most intelligent merchants in Great Britain. Such is the uniform tenor of the testimony recently taken before a select committee of the House of Commons on this subject. *Henry Cleaver Chapman*, one of the witnesses, and one of the most intelligent men in the kingdom, says: "Repeal the corn laws, and the growing trade with Canada and the *Western States of America* will be crushed by the cheaper productions of the Baltic and the Black sea; consequently," he adds, "*America*, Canada, and British shipping would receive a severe and decisive blow by the repeal of the corn laws." But still the gentleman from Virginia exults in the prospect of the repeal of the corn laws, and boasts of the market it will open to our Western farmers, to whom, however, he will not give one dollar for their rivers and improvements—not a cent—but is anxious to seduce them into this British free-trade *trap;* but he would say to the West, "timeo Danaos," trust your friends, and beware of your enemies. Look at the boasted foreign market, what is it? Comparatively nothing. Look at facts. The agricultural productions of the United States, exclusive of cotton and tobacco, are estimated at one thousand millions per year. Our exports to all the world amounted last year to $11,195,515. Of this, Great Britain took about two and a half. All the rest was consumed at home. So the foreign markets of the world amounted to 11 millions, and the home market to 989 millions. Yet the gentleman had just pronounced the foreign markets everything to the farmers, and the home markets comparatively nothing. We are told by the gentleman, as well as by the Secretary of the Treasury, that if we will reduce our tariff, England will repeal her corn laws, and open her ports to our bread stuffs to enrich our farmers. Now, sir, I beg farmers to look at official facts sent to us by this Secretary a few days since. Look at the report on commerce and navigation, and you will be astonished to see that England, Scotland, and Ireland last year took from the United States 2010 *bushels!* of wheat, and 35,355 barrels of flour, equal in all to 178,785 bushels of wheat—not equal to the production of a single county in Pennsylvania or Ohio. England imports about eighteen millions of bushels of wheat yearly. For six years, prior to 1843, she imported annually more than twenty millions, and of this only 178,785 from the United States—not a hundredth part of her foreign supply. What an immense market for our bread-stuff! And will the repeal of the corn laws help you? Clearly not. It will favor other countries just as much as it will favor you; if the duty is taken off of your grain, it is taken off of theirs. So it leaves you just where you are; nay, worse. For we now get a large amount of grain to England through the Canadian ports at 4 shillings duty, while the grain of Europe now pays 18. Repeal the corn laws, and this advantage is lost forever, and our trade through the colonial ports is at an end. Clearly, then, the repeal of the corn laws will be an injury, and a great injury, to our farmers on the Canadian frontier, without in the least favoring anybody else.

Last year Great Britain and Ireland took of all the grain and bread-stuffs of the United States, wheat, rye, oats, corn, flour, and meal of all kinds, 223,251 dollars' worth, not a quarter of a million; and we took from her 49,684,059 dollars' worth of her goods—nearly fifty millions of dollars. These are official facts, yet the Secretary of the Treasury, who communicates them, says, if we don't reduce our tariff, and take more British goods, England will have to pay us specie for our *bread-stuffs*. What an absurdity. She takes one-fourth of a million of our bread-stuffs, and we take fifty millions of her goods; yet she must pay specie for our bread-stuffs!! But Great Britain took in the same year $35,675,859 worth of cotton, yet this *cotton-growing* Secretary is not satisfied. We of the West must break up our markets, send our *specie* to England to purchase wool and other agricultural produce, converted into goods, and support labor, fed by British bread and meat, so that England may have plenty of specie to pay high prices for Mr. Walker's cotton. Farmers of the West, what say you to this? Will you submit? If you do, you are slaves, and you deserve it. But another fact. Our exports of manufactures last year, including those of wood, amounted to $13,429,166. Assuming, as in the case of British manufactures, that one half their value is made up of American agricultural produce, then we export nearly *seven* millions of dollars' worth of agricultural produce in the form of manufactures, which does not glut or injure the foreign markets for our flour and grain in its original form. To use a familiar illustration: Western farmers send their corn, hay, and oats, thousands of dollars' worth, every year to the Eastern market, not in its rude and original form, but in the form of hogs and horses; they give their hay-stacks life and legs, and make them trot to market with the farmer on their back. [A laugh.] So the British converted their produce, not into hogs or horses, but into cloth and iron, and send it here for sale. And, viewing the subject in this light, he could demonstrate that there was not a State in the Union that did not now consume *five* dollars' worth of British agricultural produce to *one* dollar's worth she consumes of theirs. Time would not permit him to go into details; but he would furnish the elements from which any one could make the calculation. Assuming that *consumption* and *exportation* are in proportion to population, then we import 50 millions of British goods, and 25 millions—one-half—is agricultural produce. We export to England agricultural produce [excluding cotton and tobacco] 2½ millions. Divide these sums, 25 and 2½ millions, by 223, the number of Representatives, and it gives $112,108 as the amount of British agricultural produce consumed in the form of goods in each Congressional district; and $11,210 as their export to Great Britain of agricultural produce. This gives the proportion of ten to one. Yet gentlemen are not satisfied, and wish still further to increase the import of British goods, and still further prostrate and destroy the American farmer, and mechanic, and laboring man, to favor foreigners.

EFFECT UPON CURRENCY.

To show the effect upon currency, as well as agriculture, suppose the gentleman from Virginia [Mr. Bayly] wants a new coat; he goes to a British importer and pays him twenty dollars, hard money, and hard to get. England takes none of your rag money. [A laugh.] Away it goes, in quick time. We see no more of it; as far as circulation is concerned, the gentleman might as well have thrown it into the fire. I want a coat. I go to the American manufacturer and buy $20 worth of American broadcloth. He wore no other, and he would compare coats with gentlemen on the spot. [A laugh.] Well, the manufacturer, the next day, gave it to the farmer for wool; he gave it to the shoemaker, the hatter, and blacksmith; they gave it back to the farmer for meat and bread; and here it went from one to another. You might perhaps see his busy and bustling $20 note five or six times in the course of a day. This made money plenty. But where was the gentleman's hard money? Vanished; gone to reward and enrich the wool-growers and farmers, shoemakers, hatters, and blacksmiths of England. Now, I go for supporting the American farmers and mechanics, and the gentleman goes for the British—that's the difference. Can the gentleman deny it? There are but two sides in this matter, the *British* and the *American* side; and the simple question is, which side shall we take? The great struggle is between the *British* and *American* farmers and mechanics for the American market, and we must decide which shall have it.

BRITISH INFLUENCE AND SIR ROBERT PEEL'S POLICY EXPOSED.

Mr. S. would here take occasion to state a *fact* that would startle the American people.

The *British manufacturers* have, at this moment, possession of this Capitol. Yes, sir, I tell you and the country—one of the principal committee rooms in this house is now, and has been for weeks past, occupied by a gentleman formerly residing in Manchester, England, who has a vast number, perhaps hundreds, of specimens of goods sent from Manchester (priced to suit the occasion) to be exhibited to members of Congress to enlighten their judgments, and, in the language of his letter of instruction from Manchester of the 3d January, '46, accompanying these specimens, to enable members of Congress "to arrive at just conclusions in regard to the proposed alterations in the present tariff." Yes, sir, agents, specimens, and letters from Great Britain, instructing us how to make a tariff to suit the British.

Speaking of the President's message, this Manchester letter-writer calls Mr. Polk "a second Daniel come to judgment, a second Richard Cobden;" and so delighted were they in England with Mr. Walker's celebrated free-trade report, that it was ordered to be printed by the House of Lords. After all this, having our President and Secretary on their side, they ought to have been content, without sending their letters of instructions here to direct us what kind of a tariff they wish us to pass. But if their chancellor had sent us a revenue bill, he could not have furnished one to suit Great Britain better than the one furnished by the Secretary of the Treasury. Parliament would pass it by acclamation. Sir Robert Peel understands his business; he proposes to take the duties off bread-stuffs and raw materials of all kinds used by their manufacturers, and remove every burden, so as to enable them to meet us and beat us in our own markets, and in the markets of the world, where Yankee competition is beginning to give them great uneasiness. Last year we exported hundreds of thousands of dollars' worth of cotton goods into the British East Indies, and beat the British in their own markets, after paying discriminating duties imposed to keep us out, first 8, then 10, and finally 15 per cent. In this great struggle, Sir Robert Peel comes to the rescue; he repeals the duty on cotton and wool, and bread and meat, and everything used by British manufacturers, to enable them to go ahead in this struggle with the Americans. He understands the great interests of his country, and, like a great and true statesman, he takes care of them. He sees a new crisis, and he meets it like a man. He sees that the manufacturers of Great Britain, the great pillars of her national prosperity, are tottering to their fall; he sees that powerful rivals are springing up in the United States and in Europe, who are not only supplying themselves, but threatening to drive Great Britain out of the markets of the world. To meet this new and fearful crisis, what does he do? He addresses the lords and landholders of England, with whom he had been always politically identified, thus: "Gentlemen, stern necessity now demands that you surrender some temporary advantages to save your country and yourselves. Our manufactures are threatened with destruction; they are your great and only markets; they consume, carry abroad, and sell *one hundred and twenty-five* millions of your agricultural produce annually—thus making England the greatest agricultural exporting country in the world. But if you suffer your manufactures to be destroyed by foreign competition, what becomes of you? Where are your markets? Can you carry your bread and meat, your wool and other products abroad in a raw and unmanufactured form? Our manufacturers are giving way; last year the United States sold in the foreign markets more than THIRTEEN MILLIONS of manufactured goods, and the question is now presented, will you sustain your manufacturers in this struggle by cheapening their living, or will you hold on and break them down, and with them your country and yourselves?" This noble and patriotic appeal had its effect; the corn laws were repealed. And what does Mr. Walker do? Just the reverse. He proposes to take off all protective duties, and impose heavy burdens on the raw materials, dye-stuffs, etc., used by our manufacturers, so as effectually to prostrate and break them down. Sir Robert Peel takes burdens off his steed, while Sir Robert Walker piles bags of sand on his—then crack their whips—clear the road—a fair race! [A laugh.] Such is the difference between British and American policy. Sir Robert Peel's present system furnishes powerful arguments for adhering to our protective system—his object is, not to favor, but to beat us; and our course is, not to defeat, but to favor his purpose. This will not only be the effect of the tariff proposed by our Secretary, but it is its open and avowed purpose and design. Is it not the proclaimed purpose of the message and report to increase the importation of British goods, and of course, to that extent, destroy American supply? Does not the Secretary propose to reduce the protective duties on most articles more than one-half for the purpose of *increasing* revenue; and if the revenue is *increased* by *reducing* duties one-half, must not the imports be more than doubled? This is self-evident; and if you double your imports of foreign goods, must you not destroy to that extent American supply? Most certainly, unless the Secretary can, in his wisdom, devise a plan to make people eat, drink, and wear double as much as they now do. But where will we find money to pay for them? But, startling and extraordinary as it may appear, our Secretary, for the first time in the history of the world, has boldly and openly avowed it as the object of the Government to break down and destroy its own manufactures, for the purpose of making way for those of foreigners. In the very first paragraph of his argumentative report, he sets out with stating that the revenue of the first quarter of this year is two millions less than the first quarter of the last, and that this has been occasioned by the *substitution of highly protected American manufactures for foreign imports;* and this evil, this terrible evil, this *American* Secretary proposes to remedy by reducing the protective duties, and thus breaking up this abominable business of "*substituting domestic products,*" made by *American* labor out of *American* produce, for *British* goods, made by *British* labor out of *British* produce. Oh, but he hates the *British.* Now, sir, this is not only the doctrine of his *text,* but it runs through his whole sermon of 957 pages. No wonder it was printed by the House of Lords; and let our Secretary carry through this bill, and Queen Victoria would gladly transfer the seals from Sir Robert Peel to Sir Robert Walker, for the latter will have rendered her a greater service than any other man, dead or living.

But this is not only the doctrine of the Treasury report, but of the message itself. The revenue standard laid down in the message aims a death blow at all American industry. It suggests a kind of "*sliding scale*" so that whenever any branch of American industry begins to beat the foreigner, and supply the market, and thereby diminish imports and revenue, this is evidence that the duty is too high, and ought to be reduced, so as to let in the foreign rival productions; but let the President speak for himself—here is his revenue standard in his own words:

"The precise point in the ascending scale of duties at which it is ascertained from experience that the revenue is greatest, is the maximum rate of duty which can be laid for the bona fide purpose of collecting money for the support of Government. To raise the duties higher than that point, and thereby diminish the amount collected, is to levy them for protection merely, and not for revenue. As long, then, as Congress may gradually increase the rate of duty on a given article, and the revenue is increased by such increase of duty, they are within the revenue standard. When they go beyond that point, and as they increase the duties the revenue is diminished or destroyed, the act ceases to have for its object the raising of money to support Government, but is for protection merely."

What is this but a rule to favor foreigners and break down Americans? The moment the American by his superior industry and skill begins to succeed, and by supplying the market imports and revenue diminish, then the duty must come down so as to increase foreign imports and the revenue. This is the plain and inevitable operation of the rule, and who would go into manufacturing under such an anti-American rule as this, making the penalty—death by the law—certain and inevitable? And yet we are told that this system is to be *permanent*—a system based upon fluctuations and continual change, is to be permanent! Under this executive rule, what duty could be permanent? It was "a sliding scale," *working by legislation.* The President says, continue to increase the duty so long as it increases revenue, but reduce it when it is so high as to reduce revenue. What would be the practical result? The President runs up his revenue duty on articles we do not now produce; these duties at length induce the investment of capital; machinery and labor go to work and supply the market; imports and revenue consequently fall off; then down with the duties till you destroy *American* competition and supply. This done, and again the President puts up his revenue duties till he again starts competition; then down with the duties again; and so on forever. Such must be the practical working of the system. Yet it is recommended as a *permanent* system, to put at rest the agitations of the tariff! So far from it, Congress would have to remain in session permanently to watch and adjust this Executive "sliding scale," to suppress and keep down American labor, and secure to foreigners the undisputed possession of the American market. In the language of the Secretary, to prevent the "*substitution of American rival fabrics for foreign goods;*" and this system was certainly admirably calculated to accomplish this, its avowed, object.

EFFECT OF AD VALOREM DUTIES.

Ad valorem duties had been universally rejected throughout the world, and whenever *specific* duties could be adopted, they were substituted for ad valorems. And why? Because all experience had proved that they led to all kinds of frauds and evasions, and were utterly inadequate to the purposes of either *revenue* or *protection.* They favored the foreign manufacturer and foreign importer at the expense of the honest American. The foreign *manufacturer* sold his goods to his *own agent,* who was the importer. They made out and swore to their invoice at any price they pleased, thus cheating the revenue, whilst they broke down our honest shippers, mechanics, and manufacturers. For these destructive effects there was no remedy. On the other hand, specific duties, levied on the *thing,* and not its *price,* must be fairly and honestly paid.

Another pernicious effect of ad valorem duties was this—they gave *protection* when it was *not* wanted, and took it away when it *was*—thus when goods went down in price abroad, and consequently ran into our markets, the duties went down with the prices, but when the prices rose so high abroad that they could not be imported, then the duties were high in proportion; for instance, when iron was $60 per ton abroad, and could not be imported, then 30 per cent. ad valorem would be $18 per ton; but if iron fell to what it was a few years ago, $25 per ton, when it could and would be imported to the ruin of our manufacturers, then the duty, 30 per cent., would fall down from $18 to $7.50 per ton; thus making dear goods dearer and cheap goods cheaper—giving *high* protection when none was wanted, and no protection at all when it was. These were a few of the many objections to this miserable and ruinous system of ad valorems, adopted here when cast off and rejected everywhere else; but this was in perfect harmony with the Secretary's whole scheme, which was avowedly to prevent the "*substitution of American manufactures for British goods.*" Its purpose was to favor the British and break down the Americans, and it would answer its purpose. It was playing into the hands of Sir Robert Peel, and carrying out the policy of this British-hating Administration. Giving up Oregon was nothing, but giving up our national independence, and reducing us again to the condition of colonies, was too bad. The remedy is with the People, and they must apply it. If gentlemen desired an appropriate title for their bill, he would furnish one, and move it as an amendment if the bill passed, viz:

"A bill to reduce the duties on luxuries of the rich, and to increase them on the necessaries of the poor; to bankrupt the Treasury, strike down American farmers, mechanics, and working men; to make way for the products of foreign agriculture and foreign labor; to destroy American competition, thereby establishing a foreign monopoly in the American market; and, by adopting the principles of free-trade, to reduce the now prosperous labor of this country to the degraded level of the pauper labor of Europe, and finally destroy the prosperity and independence of these United States, and again reduce them to the condition of colonies and dependencies of Great Britain."

A CHAPTER FOR MECHANICS AND FARMERS.

The operation of this bill upon the national industry will be seen from the following examples, assuming that the reduction of wages will always be in proportion to the reduction of *protection*, and that as home consumption cannot be increased, home production must be diminished to the extent of the increased importations:

Employments, etc.	Importations under the present duties.	Estimated increase of importations under the proposed duties.	Proposed duties, as per Mr. Walker's report—table C.	Proposed duties, as per Mr. McKay's bill.
Shoemakers	$42,250	$45,000	45 per ct.	30 per ct.
Tailors	1,173,028	200,000	50 "	30 "
Blacksmiths	....	200,000	61 "	30 "
Hatters	16,646	110,000	49 "	30 "
Tanners	128,277	100,000	40 "	20 "
Iron makers	4,489,553	1,185,000	75 "	30 "
Miners of coal	223,919	125,000	67 "	30 "
Glass makers	106,905	100,000	90 "	25 "
Paper makers	51,724	150,000	75 "	30 "
Hemp, cordage, etc.	355,875	275,000	65 "	25 "
Lead	....	....	92 "	20 "
Pins	45,078	50,000	70 "	20 "
Nails and spikes	....	....	66 "	20 "
Manufactures of wool.	10,057,875	2,000,000	40 "	30 "
" " cotton	13,863,383	5,150,000	90 "	25 "
" " silk	10,650,000	700,000	42 "	25 "
Salt	898,663	1,000,000	76 "	20 "
Sugar	4,780,555	630,000	75 "	30 "
Brandy and sp'ts dist'd from grain, etc.	1,045,363	365,650	180 "	100 "
Wool	1,689,794	200,000	40 "	30 "
Blankets	1,000,000	20,000	30 "	20 "
Potatoes	58,949	150,000	36	20 "

The question, then, is distinctly presented to all these mechanics, manufacturers, and farmers, whether they are prepared to submit to these reductions in their prices and wages, or give up the market to foreigners? One or the other they must do—and why? Mr. Walker says, to increase the revenue; but this is manifestly not true; for when you take all the increase of imports Mr. Walker himself estimates, and assess on these the proposed reduced duties there will be, on his own showing, a loss instead of a gain of revenue. Then why the proposed reduction? To substitute *foreign* for *American* fabrics, as declared in Mr.

Walker's report. To favor *foreigners*, by breaking down *American mechanics, manufacturers, and farmers;* and this *anti-American* measure is to be passed under the party lash of this Administration, and to be approved by the people. We shall see!

But gentlemen were in love with the scheme, and the party had ordained that it should be tried. Let its advocates go home and tell the shoemakers, and carpenters, and blacksmiths, and tanners, and hatters, that they had voted to take twenty per cent. off those articles which were the products of their labor. Tell the shoemakers that the Secretary of the Treasury proposed to double the import of shoes for the purpose of increasing the revenue, but that the real effect would be to reduce the revenue; and when these honest and hard-working men asked their representatives why they voted for such a scheme, their only answer must be, to break up your labor. Let them go into their districts and tell the hatters that the Secretary intended to bring in one hundred and ten thousand dollars more of foreign hats. Tell the blacksmiths that Mr. Walker intended to bring in two hundred thousand dollars worth of iron manufactures. Go and tell the tailors that he intended, in like manner, to bring in two hundred thousand dollars' worth more of ready-made clothing, reducing the protection on that article from fifty down to thirty per cent., and let them understand that the fruit of this reform would be to reduce the revenue and reduce the price of their work twenty per cent., to throw multitudes of them out of employment, and to supply the place of their labor in the market by the labor of English and French shoemakers, English hatters, English blacksmiths, and English tailors; and how was it probable these men would be pleased; and, what was of more consequence to certain gentlemen, how was it likely they would vote? [A good deal of restlessness was here manifested.] Mr. S. said he knew it was a very unpleasant topic in certain quarters, but what he said was true, and gentlemen would find it to be true. He warned them to remember his words, that, just so sure as they passed this new tariff bill, so certainly would they destroy the revenue, destroy the country, and destroy their party; and, if the last was the only consequence, he would not regret it—it would be a godsend to the country. He told them beforehand they would not have money to pay the ordinary expenses of the Government, let alone the expenses of the war.

GENERAL OPERATIONS OF THE BILL.

Mr. S. said he had been considering the subject somewhat in detail; he now wished for a moment, in conclusion, to present the subject in a more general and comprehensive point of view. He wished gentlemen to turn to the 47th page of the Secretary's report, and they would there see these statements: that the dutiable imports last year were $95,-106,724, which exceeds by twenty-five millions the average of dutiable imports for the last nine years. (See page 71.) The Secretary further states, that the average amount of the duties imposed by the present tariff is 32.40 per cent.; which at first he proposed to reduce 19½ per cent., but since the war has raised to 22. But to simplify the calculation, let us put the dutiable imports at one hundred millions, the present duties at 33 and the proposed duties 22 per cent.—just one-third off. If you reduce the duties one-third, you must, to get the same revenue, increase your imports one-third—that is, instead of one hundred, you must have one hundred and fifty millions of dutiable imports. Then, is it not clear that the only effect of the measure is to increase the foreign imports fifty millions of dollars! Without increasing the revenue one cent, or lightening the burdens of the people one farthing, you get exactly the same revenue. The people pay precisely the same amount to Government, but they pay fifty millions more to foreigners, lose that much specie, destroy fifty millions of our productions, and with it the hundreds of millions of capital and thousands of honest and industrious people thrown out of employment!

Now we pay one hundred millions to foreigners, and twenty-seven to Government—making one hundred and twenty-seven millions of dollars. By this bill we will pay one hundred and fifty millions to foreigners, and twenty-seven millions to Government, making one hundred and seventy-seven millions—just fifty more than the people now pay. And why? To favor foreigners and destroy American labor. That was the effect, and the only effect, of this measure. It was to increase the burdens of the people just fifty millions of dollars a year. You may increase your imports, but you cannot increase your exports; you cannot force them upon other countries. They will take what they want, and no more. And what follows? First, you must send fifty millions in specie abroad, to pay for one year's excess of imports. Next year, having no specie, you will send your State and National bonds, at 6 per cent., as you did under your 20 per cent. duties and excessive imports a few years since; and then again follows repudiation and bankruptcy, State, National, and individual. But this is not all; there is another and a worse consequence. You may add one-third to your supply of foreign goods, but you can't compel the people to eat, drink, or wear one-third more; and if you could, it would ruin them. Then, if you can't increase *consumption*, it follows that you must destroy fifty millions of American production, to make room for this additional fifty millions of foreign goods.

But can you, by reducing duties, increase your imports fifty millions? The attempt will be a failure, and the effect will be to reduce your revenue one-half, and to reduce the wages of labor here; just as you reduce the duties, your laborers must continue to work on at these reduced rates or starve. They will work on, and your imports and your revenue will be reduced together. The people, ground down and impoverished by this levelling and degrading system, can purchase and consume nothing from abroad. If you want to replenish your Treasury, protect your national industry, and keep it prosperous; and then, having the ability, they will purchase foreign goods and enrich your Treasury. A poor people make a poor Treasury, and a rich people a rich one. This resulted from the fact, that in this country the revenue was a *voluntary* and not *compulsory* contribution by the people to the Government. When did they contribute by the purchase and consumption of foreign goods? When they had the ability—when they were prosperous; and hence it always happened that when the people were protected and prosperous, under high tariffs, we had a full Treasury; and when the people were impoverished by "free trade," the Treasury and the country always had and always would become bankrupt together. Such was our uniform experience—such the unbroken evidence of our financial history, and no man could deny it.

CONSEQUENCES OF THIS POLICY FORETOLD.

Let gentlemen go on and pass this bill; let them carry out their system; let them involve the country in war—double the expenditures of Government, as they had done—create a large national debt—reduce the revenue by reducing the duties to one-half of what they now are—destroy the national industry—bankrupt the Treasury and the people with your ad valorem and warehousing system, your *hard money* Subtreasury, and your *paper money* Treasury note bills;—go on, gentlemen, and see where you will come out. You will do one good thing, at least—you will relieve the country from the curse of this whole anti-American and British free-trade system, and restore the true American policy in 1848. Carry out your measures; prostrate all the walls that now surround and protect the national industry; break down your manufacturing establishments throughout the length and breadth of the land; compel them, as the only means of saving what they have, to close their doors, and turn out 850,000 operatives into the streets, without work, to beg or starve; let them go to the farmer for employment, and he will tell them his markets are gone, and that his condition is no better than theirs. It will then be seen who the tariff benefits. What will these people do? Go back, and tell the manufacturers to go on, and they will work for half price; and the farmer offering his produce at the same rate, then the manufacturer can resume, when loss of protection is made up by reduction of prices. Reduce the tariff and you reduce wages in precisely the same ratio—proving clearly that the operation and object of protective duties are to enable the manufacturers to pay high prices to laborers and to agriculture. Carry out your measures, and you will soon find where the "*shoe pinches*"—you will find out who the tariff protects; or, if you do not, the farmers and laborers will tell at the polls.

Gentlemen could not escape it. The tariff, after all, would be the great absorbing question. It was in its effects national and diffusive—felt not merely in the thronged cities, but reaching in its consequences the remotest hamlet in the far West. Texas, Oregon, and other exciting questions of the day, were ephemeral, and would soon pass away; but the *tariff* and *protection* lay at the very foundation of the national prosperity, and could never cease to interest deeply the American people.

Sir, pass this "free trade" bill, submitted to and approved, as he understood, by the *cabinet;* bring back the scenes of 1840; and in eighteen months you will scarcely have a specie-paying bank, or a specie dollar left in the country; and again will be heard throughout the land the cry of "*change! change! any change must be for the better.*" Political revolutions are the fruits of popular suffering and discontent; in prosperity the cry is "*let well enough alone.*"

[*A voice.* Then as a Whig you ought to go for the new tariff.]

Yes, said Mr. S., if I was like some gentlemen on this floor—If I loved my *party* more than my *country*, I would; but as I love my country more than my party, I will not. If it were not for the lash and drill of party discipline, this "*British bill*" would find few advocates on this floor. It was the bantling of party—the illegitimate offspring of the Baltimore Convention—that Pandora's box, whence originated most of the troubles that now afflict this country. But he again warned gentlemen—pass this bill, and, in the strong language of a Democratic Senator on a late occasion, it will sink "*the party* so low that the arm of resurrection could never reach it."

But this measure, we are told, is to be a measure of permanency; it is to give peace and repose to the country. If so, it would be the peace and repose of *death*. No, sir, you may strike down the country, but the blow would but rouse and excite the people to return it with such vigor and energy as to prostrate the aggressors. This bill a measure of peace! No; it is a measure of war—war upon the people—worse, far worse, than a war with England—a war upon the national industry in all its departments; and the people will make war upon it—war, unceasing and interminable war—war on the hustings, and war at the ballot-box. Pass this destructive bill, and Mr. S. said he would call on the people—the honest hard-handed farmers, mechanics, and laboring men of the land, to fling their banners to the breeze, with this inscription: "*The British free-trade tariff of* 1846—*Repeal!* REPEAL!! REPEAL!!!" and never lower it till it triumphed—as triumph it would most gloriously—in the renewal of the tariff of 1842, and with it the restoration of our national *prosperity* and *independence*.

THE TRUE AMERICAN POLICY

The true American policy is just the reverse of that recommended by this administration. It is this:

1st. *Protect* and *cherish* your *natural industry* by a wise system of finance, selecting in the first place those articles which you can and ought to supply to the extent of your own wants—*food, clothing, habitation* and *defence*—and to these give ample and adequate protection, so as to secure at all times an abundant supply at home. Next select the

LUXURIES consumed by the *rich*, and impose on them such duties as the wants of the Government may require for revenue; and then take the necessaries of life consumed by the poor, and articles which we cannot supply used in our manufactories, and make them *free*, or subject to the lowest rates of duty.

2d. Adopt a system of *national* improvements, embracing the great rivers, lakes, and main arteries of communication, leaving those of a LOCAL character to the care of the States; and on these expend the *surplus revenue* only; thus uniting and binding together the distant parts of our common country, and at the same time securing the most efficient system of defence in war, and the cheapest and best system of commercial and social intercourse in peace.

3d. Introduce enlightened economy in every branch of the public expenditures. Lighten the burdens, diversify the employments, and secure and increase the rewards of labor in all its departments. And:—

4th. In your foreign relations follow the advice of the father of his country—"Observe good faith and justice towards all nations—cultivate peace and harmony with all." Thereby illustrating the beauty and perfection of our Republican institutions, holding up a great example of "liberty and independence," for the nations of the earth to admire and imitate. This was the great and true *American system* which he hoped yet to see adopted and carried out. We owe a great example to the world—let it be given. This was the duty, as he trusted it would be the destiny, of this, our great and glorious republic.

COMMENTS AND OPINIONS OF THE PRESS.

To show the fact that the "*American system*"—Tariff and Internal Improvements—has been supported by the *Republican* and opposed by the *Democratic party* for nearly half a century, we copy a number of notices and opinions of the press, running back to 1824, and of which those immediately following are a part, from papers published in every State *then* in the Union, taken from a scrap-book kept by Charles Stewart. These notices also show a very remarkable coincidence of opinion, expressed by these papers simultaneously throughout the United States, not only in reference to the merits of these speeches, but also as to the policy and measures they advocate. It appeared that there was 155,000 copies of this speech printed in pamphlet form in Mr. Gideon's office alone, in Washington, to supply the orders of members of Congress and others; besides hundreds of thousands, in German as well as English, printed elsewhere, and distributed throughout the country. Besides, these notices, by the ablest editors in the country, contain important facts and arguments worthy of preservation.

"We finish this masterly effort of Mr. Stewart, this week. Those who have read the two first portions as published in the *Watchman*, are doubtless waiting impatiently for this paper. This speech contains more common sense and plain truth on the subject of the tariff than any we have seen for some time. It exposes as with a sunbeam the darkness and hidden folly of those who would make the American people 'hewers of wood and drawers of water' for England. It exposes that suicidal policy which would crush our own, and build up the manufactories of Europe. And it also shows how false is the pretended policy of *free-trade* which England proposes, in a spirit of boasted liberality, to adopt; and how mischievous it would prove to us, to be deceived thereby. A paper of such value has rarely been published."—*Watchman, N. C.*

"It must be a source of as much pride and pleasure to the Whigs of Pennsylvania, as it is gratifying to Mr. Stewart, to have such a compliment paid to his talent, as the following, by a Bostonian. As a man of talent, Mr. Stewart ranks among the first in Congress, and what is most consoling to the people, is the fact that all his talent and time are devoted to their welfare. Conscious of the rectitude of his principles, he is bold and fearless in the discharge of his duty, and while he strips the verbiage and sophistry from the false arguments of his free-trade opponents, and exposes their selfishness to the entire world, he is also decorous and respectful, and never says aught to wound the private character or feelings of any one. As great, powerful, and convincing as he is in debate, just in proportion is he spoken of in his private relations. Pennsylvania may well be proud of him, and their pride is increased from the fact that Mr. Stewart is selected as a man worthy of respect for his services to the Industrial world, by such a man as Hon. Abbott Lawrence, of Boston. Who is not proud of him?

"The speech referred to was published in the *Advocate* on the 22d ult., consequently our readers know that the speech is entitled to the confidence of such a liberal patriot as Mr. Lawrence; several patrons have asked its republication, but we have not determined to do so yet, as it is fresh to the recollections of all.

"THE HON. ABBOTT LAWRENCE.—This gentleman, with his characteristic liberality and patriotism, has authorized the printing, at Washington, of twenty thousand copies of Mr. Stewart's Speech in defence of the protective policy for distribution, directing the printer to draw on him for all expenses. The diffusion of such documents, at this time, in the South and West, cannot fail to produce salutary effects. The author of this speech may well be proud of such a compliment from such a source."—*Boston Advocate.*

"Read it, and after you have read it, hand it to your neighbor and ask him to read it; no matter what party he belongs to, every body, every man, woman and child ought to read thoroughly Mr. Stewart's remarks upon the tariff. It is an excellent speech, upon a most important subject. The question is whether we shall do our own manufacturing at home, by our own citizens, and with our own capital, where our farmers raise the provisions to feed the operatives, or let it be done abroad for the benefit of foreigners, Is it cheaper, is it better for the public interest, for the people of the United States, to patronize foreign work-shops, than to sustain those which they have at home? That is the question, and we desire every *freeman* in Vermont to ask himself that question, and to make up his mind upon this important subject. We say again, read it attentively."—*Vermont Gazette.*

"A considerable portion of our paper to-day is occupied with the admirable speech of the Hon. Andrew Stewart on the tariff, to which we invite the attention of our readers. It is one of the many most triumphant replies of this great defender of the protective policy, to the free-traders in Congress, which completely annihilates their absurd theory of free-trade. The arguments of Mr. Stewart are unanswerable, and cannot fail to convince every man who reads them, we care not how prejudiced he may be against protection, that the tariff policy is the only true policy for the nation. He shows clearly in this speech, that all experience has proved, that whenever the protective doctrine has been abandoned the country has labored under embarrassments and the people have suffered—the poorer classes especially; while on the contrary, when the tariff has been high the country has flourished, and the people, rich and poor, have prospered. The speech abounds in facts which prove this beyond contradiction, and if every locofoco in the country could be furnished with a copy of it and read it, he could not fail to be convinced at least of its truth, and, if he had a true American heart in his bosom, would cease his senseless opposition to this great measure of his country's prosperity. We recommend to our Whig readers, after they have read this speech themselves, to hand it to their locofoco neighbors, and induce them to read it also. They may do some good in this way.

"Mr. Stewart is the great champion of the tariff in the present Congress, and is an honor to the State he represents. Pennsylvania has not now, and never had a more able and faithful guardian of her interests in that body. His manly, vigorous and able defence of the tariff of 1842, the life blood of Pennsylvania prosperity, cannot fail to endear him to his constituents, and make them feel proud of him. We trust he will be kept in the position he is, until this question is finally put at rest, by being settled upon some permanent basis. To such men as Mr. S. we owe our prosperity, and to such men we must look for its continuance."—*New York Chronicle.*

"Mr. Stewart of Pa. made a speech an hour long, every line of which is worth a golden eagle, if it could only reach every working-man in the country.

"He then turned to Mr. Bayly, and said he would notice some of his assertions. Mr. Stewart then made one of the most successful attempts ever witnessed in Congress to annihilate the arguments of a political opponent."—*New York Tribune*

"We have published in this week's paper another of Mr. Stewart's admirable speeches on the tariff. It exhibits facts and arguments that are unanswerable; and shows Mr. Secretary Walker's free-trade policy to be not only false and unfounded, but that exactly the reverse of his theories is true. Mr. Stewart, in referring to the scenes of 1840, said: 'Pass this Treasury bill, approved, as he understood, by the cabinet,—restore your 20 per cent. tariff—bankrupt your treasury—paralyse your national industry—break down your farmers, manufacturers and mechanics, by *importing goods and exporting money*—pass this bill, and in eighteen months you will scarcely have a specie-paying bank, or a specie dollar in the country. Pass this bill, and you will not only bring back the scenes, but you will bring back with them the political revolutions of 1840.' [A voice:] 'Then as a Whig you ought to go for the new tariff.' To this Mr. Stewart answered—and his answer is worthy of all praise. Brief as it is, it contains more genuine patriotism than could be sifted out of the thousand and one braggadocio speeches that have been delivered on the Oregon question.

"'Yes,' said Mr. Stewart, 'if I was like some gentlemen on this floor, if I loved my party better than my country, I would; but, as I love my country more than my party, I will not.'

"Let unprincipled slaves of party read Mr. Stewart's answer, and reflect whether it is nobler to serve their country faithfully or to act as traitors, with the venal desires and hopes of participating in the plunder of a despoiled and conquered republic!

"Mr. Stewart's speech should be extensively circulated and read, in order that the country may be fully apprised of its true situation on this vital question."—*Delaware Journal.*

"The important fact that the inevitable tendency of a protective tariff is to reduce the price of the protected goods, is fully and clearly established, and the Hon. gentleman shows with great power, the exceeding love which is felt by the Secretary of the Treasury, for the 'poor man.' He shows that under the operation of a protective tariff, the 'poor man' is able to buy his cotton at six cents a yard, instead of paying thirty-six cents a yard for an inferior article, under the system of free-trade the Secretary desires; that the young carpenter who is about to erect a house for his wife and children, pays but four cents a pound for nails, under a protective tariff, while in 1816, under a system of free-trade, his father paid sixteen cents a pound for the same article.

"The British manufacturers whom Mr. Secretary Walker seems so much disposed to favor, instead of the manufacturers of the North and East, the British agriculturists whom Mr. Secretary Walker is so desirous of assisting to the injury of the farmers of the Western and Middle States, are under deep obligations to our *American* Secretary, and most faithfully does Mr. Stewart present him to the American people. Massachusetts alone consumes annually thirty-three millions of the agricultural produce of the other States of the Union. Great Britain consumes but two and a half millions of the products of our grain-growing States, while we import from her about fifty millions annually of manufactured goods, and yet all the energies of the Secretary of the Treasury are bent to the accomplishment of his purpose of benefiting the British manufacturer, while our own labor is to be unrewarded and our workshops to be abandoned."—*Transcript, R. I.*

"We invite the special attention of our readers to the very searching and pointed remarks of the Hon. Andrew Stewart of Pa., which we publish in to-day's paper. The speech is somewhat lengthy, and occupies a considerable share of our small sheet. We looked over it intending to abridge—give our readers the *strong* points, leaving out the balance, But on examination we could find no part that should be left out. The *strong* points embraced the whole speech. The speech is characteristic of Mr. Stewart—plain, practical, demonstrative in its character. He places Mr. Walker's celebrated report in the most unenviable position. How Mr. Walker, or his friends for him, will get out of those egregious blunders, not to say falsehoods, which are now, for the first time, dragged into the light, and presented for the consideration of the American people, we cannot see. On the subjects of the tariff and commerce, Mr. Stewart has no superior in Congress. He has the statistics at hand that he has been treasuring up for years, and the member that takes hold of him must come into the conflict doubly equipped, or he will be badly used up. Figures will not lie, and on these Mr. Stewart plants himself, and shakes defiance in the teeth of Mr. Walker and his friends.

"We are informed that the members have ordered some forty or fifty thousand copies of the speech to be printed on their own private account, to be circulated throughout the country."—*Record, Md.*

"Mr. Andrew Stewart of Pennsylvania has stood up manfully for the cause of protection to American industry, in the House of Representatives. The opponents of the tariff, in Congress, aided by the agents of British manufacturers out of doors, are making great efforts to bring us again under the system of low duties and large importations. The country, it is true, had a fair trial of this system during the Van Buren administration; and we would think that the results of the experiment then were not such as to make the people anxious to try it again. Yet the very same policy which proved insupportable in 1840, which had brought the country into extreme distress and broke down a powerful party—the very same policy, Sub-Treasury and all, is now to be again forced upon us. Treasury notes, defalcations and bankruptcy, will ensue afterwards —in due order as before.

"The influences which determine the issues of popular elections —what are they? It would require a minute analysis to detect and discriminate them. A party making war upon American industry, yet calling itself democratic, after it has prostrated every great interest of domestic labor, disordered the currency and spread an irredeemable circulation over the land, impoverished the Treasury, and created a public debt—is finally driven from power by an overwhelming popular majority. What then? Why after a brief interval, the Whigs having possession of power only long enough to pass one great measure of protection to home industry, and to repeal one hurtful measure, the Sub-Treasury—the return of prosperity, produced by these measures, caused former sufferings and the occasions of them to be forgotten; and now we see the same party, whose destructive policy had become insupportable, restored again to power to recommence the same identical policy which every man of sense must know will produce the same inevitable results.

"But let us hear Mr. Stewart; he is speaking of the war which the Administration is now waging upon American industry—the destruction of which is to be preliminary to the general system of national prostration likely to follow from the adoption of the government policy." (Speech follows.)—***Reville, Kentucky.***

"A few days since, the Hon. A. Stewart, one of the ablest and most distinguished members of Congress from this State, reviewed the free trade doctrines contained in the annual report of the Secretary of the Treasury. The speech excited much attention at the time, because of the many important facts and arguments which it embodied. Its author has since revised it, and in this corrected form, it will be found at length in our first page. We bespeak for it a candid and careful consideration. It is especially worthy the attention of every Pennsylvanian, of all who are in favor of adequate protection to home industry. Perhaps there is no man in the country better acquainted with this subject than the fearless and talented representative of the Eighteenth District."—*Inquirer, Phila.*

"Upon the tariff question, the greatest that can claim the attention of any legislative body, there have been no less than 78 speeches made during the present session—25 in the Senate, and 53 in the House of Representatives. In the Senate, Evans, Choate, and Wright of the North, Berrien and McDuffie of the South, and Benton and Crittenden of the West—all master spirits of the land; yet none of the speeches of these great men has received any considerable notice or circulation. Look, too, in the other branch of Congress, and you will find the same state of things. The same state, do I say? No, not exactly; there is *one* bright exception, but *only one.* Although the wisdom and genius of that great body of statesmen and orators have been concentrated upon this one question—although this was the *focus* at which every ray of intellect centred, yet every other speech fell still born from the press, while that of Andrew Stewart has passed through several editions in pamphlet form, amounting to some 100,000 copies, translated into German, and republished in almost every Whig newspaper of the day."—*Examiner, Md.*

"Side by side with Mr. Clay, has Mr. Stewart, through years of Congressional labor, through success and defeat, advocated and sustained the same principles. While the one, from his elevated position, saw and indicated the way, the other has more effectually and powerfully aided to make it plain. We venture to say that no man in America has, with so much power and practical common sense, simplified, and brought home to the understandings of the people, the true sources of national greatness and of the happiness of the common people. He is, as our readers and the whole country know, an eminently practical man. No stronger evidence could be given of the truth of these suggestions than the immense editions which have been published at various times, and in different sections of the Union, of his numerous speeches on the tariff. These have amounted to several hundreds of thousands of copies."—*Free Press, Va.*

"We publish upon our first page an extract from the recent speech of Mr. A. Stewart in review of Secretary Walker's Report, and shall continue the publication in subsequent numbers. This speech is well worth a careful study. It would be impossible to conceive a more thorough explosion than it makes of the doctrines of Secretary Walker and the free-traders."—*Sentinel, Flor.*

"We have transferred to our columns to-day the admirable speech of the Hon. Andrew Stewart, of Pennsylvania, in the House of Representatives in Congress, on the subject of the tariff. It is an able exposition of the fallacies and false arguments of the President and Secretary of the Treasury in the Message and Secretary's Report, and deserves a careful perusal."—*Independent, Mass.*

"We invite attention to some extracts from a late speech of Andrew Stewart, and regret that our columns forbid publishing the speech entire. It is a caustic and withering reply to Mr. R. J. Walker's labored report, and exposes with truth and severity the mis-statements and fallacies of the secretary."—*Miscellany, Ga.*

"The speech of Mr. Stewart in reply to the sophistries of Sir Robert J. Walker, the President's bold advocate of British interests, to the destruction of our own, will be read with satisfaction by every friend of his country. It is able, interesting, and conclusive, and justly commands the attention of all men of intelligence throughout our country.

"We have been obliged to delay the publication of the speech for some time, on account of the press of legislative proceedings."—*Whig, Flor.*

"We commend to perusal the eloquent speech of Mr. Stewart of Pennsylvania. The fine-spun free-trade Utopian schemes of the visionary Secretary of the Treasury are brushed away by this speech, as easily as the sun doth dispel the early dew.

"The speech was not made merely to take up the time of the House; but to expose the falsity of the Treasury Report, and we have not met with a more searching and investigating speech in a long time."—*Telegraph, Mich.*

"We would particularly call the attention of the members of all parties to Mr. Stewart's speech. It is certainly conclusive, as the returns there used are derived from official sources. Editors throughout the country should publish it as a matter of general information to their readers, and besides, it should be preserved for political reference hereafter."—*Democrat, Mo.*

"We call the special attention of our readers to the speech of the Hon. Andrew Stewart of Pennsylvania contained in this number of the *Palladium*. It is too long for most articles published in a country newspaper; but long as it is, owing to its particular merits, it is worth the time of a hundred careful readings. Let no man who takes or can get the *Palladium*, lay it aside for good, till he thoroughly reads the speech. Again we say, read, read. Please lay it up for future reference."—*Palladium, Ohio.*

"This able and distinguished friend of domestic industry, Mr. Andrew Stewart of Pa., whose recent speech in the House of Representatives we have already noticed, having seen his remarks on the tariff, commented on in the *Union*, has addressed a letter, through the *National Intelligencer*, to Mr. Secretary Walker, explaining and vindicating his views; and dealing powerful blows at the fallacies in the Secretary's Report. Mr. Stewart and the friends of the tariff, need not, however, discuss over and over again the tariff subject. Argument has been exhausted—facts have become burdensome, reasons are piled mountain high—Pelion upon Ossa. The great matter is now in the hands of *the party*—to be settled as a *party* question. Particularly is it in the hands of the Representatives from Mr. Stewart's own State. If Pennsylvania is willing to see the tariff prostrated, and protection to home manufactures abandoned—what other State ought to resist the mandate of *the party*—or why should the Whigs waste their energies in vain attempts to stop the determined action of the dominant power? We cannot see the use, in this case, of contending unnecessarily, against what will be done —because, if the experiment is to be tried, we want the whole responsibility thrown upon those who effect the mischief."—*Gazette, D. C.*

"We give our readers in to-day's paper, to the exclusion of almost every thing else, the speech of the Hon. A. Stewart, of Pennsylvania, delivered in Congress on the subject of the tariff—and request our friends, particularly our democratic friends, to peruse it attentively and impartially. The tariff is no *party* question, it is an AMERICAN question. Gen. Washington, Mr. Jefferson, Mr. Madison, Mr. Monroe, and Gen. Jackson, were all advocates of both the constitutionality and expediency of protecting *home* industry by the General Government."—*Mail, Camden, N. J.*

"We most sincerely wish that every man in the State could read this able speech; we are clearly of the opinion that every one would acknowledge the truth and force of Mr. S.'s arguments and facts, and feel a consciousness of pride thrill his entire frame, to know, that Pennsylvania has one Whig in Congress, able and willing to take care of her interests. We feel proud of Mr. Stewart, and the people of York county may also feel proud, for, although he is not a York county man, still he reveres this county, (not for her locofocoism, however,) but because the remains of his ancestors are deposited in her soil, and because he has warm friends and admirers, who appreciate his worth, residing within her confines."—*The Advocate, Pa.*

"We commence in this day's paper the publication of Hon. A. Stewart's late Speech in Congress, on the Protective Policy. Mr. Stewart is a Pennsylvania member, and one of the ablest men in the present Congress. His speech abounds in sound, logical argument, and cannot fail of pleasing all who will take the pains to read it. We hope all our readers will give it an attentive perusal. We shall give the conclusion next week."—*Whig, Ill.*

"Andrew Stewart has obtained for himself a name as the defender of that policy (the tariff,) which is the common source of prosperity to the agriculturalist, the mechanic and the laborer, and no eulogy of ours can stimulate him to renewed ardor and zeal, in the defence of the rights of the poor, or endear him to his constituents and to the nation any more, we know, but we feel it due to ourself and to the country to advise them of his manly efforts in their and our behalf.

"Time and again, when the protective system has been threatened by demagogues on the one hand, and the ignorant and skeptical on the other, has he stept forward, and by his almost unbounded knowledge and overwhelming illustrations driven off and kept at bay these disturbers of American industry. And as a proof of his continued devotedness and fond attachment to a policy, which has caused the country to rise from her folorn condition, and to put on her wonted mantle of cheerfulness, no sooner had Congress assembled at its present session, than he made a powerful speech, in which he stripped the flimsy arguments of his excellency James K. Polk, of their sophistry, and exposed the naked skeleton to an indignant public." —*Telegraph, N. H.*

"We are indebted to the *National Intelligencer* for a copy of the speech of Mr. Stewart, which we publish on the first and second pages of to-day's paper. The facts and arguments presented in this speech are such, we think, as cannot be refuted—and whatever fate may await the present tariff, Mr. Stewart deserves, and will receive, the thanks, not only of his immediate constituents, but of the friends of domestic industry throughout the Union, for his efforts to save it."—*Herald, Maine.*

"We ask the careful perusal, on the part of our readers, of the excellent speech of the Hon. A. Stewart, of Fayette, on the tariff, which we publish to-day. It is a master production, exposing in a clear and forcible manner the numerous fallacies and unfounded arguments contained in the Free-Trade Report of Secretary Walker. There is no man in Congress better prepared to meet the opposition in its onslaught upon the tariff of 1842 than Mr. Stewart. Upon every matter relating to the protective policy he is perfectly at home, and he has thus far proven more than a match for those who are bent upon prostrating the industrial energies of the nation. Would that *every member of Congress* from Pennsylvania, without distinction of party, would stand up thus nobly in defence of our dearest interests."—*Berks Journal, Pa.*

"The excellent speech of this *first rate* representative in the Congress of the United States occupies a very large space in to-day's paper, but, as it is a very interesting document, both as regards the questions discussed and the able manner in which they are handled, we doubt not that our readers will be pleased with its publication. We ask for it, on the part of all intelligent and honest men, an impartial perusal.

"Since ever Mr. Stewart has occupied a place in the councils of the nation, he has evinced a degree of devotion to the interests of the country unsurpassed, and exhibited such a profound knowledge of its institutions and the policy that should govern it, that he has gained for himself, from one end of the Union to the other, a reputation of which any man might be proud."—*Free Press, Cin.*

"We have just finished the perusal of the speech of the Hon. A. Stewart, of Pennsylvania, delivered in the House on the 11th ult., on the subject of Mr. Walker's report, and the operation and effects of his tariff. Gross and numerous as we knew were the errors of Mr. Walker, both in theory and in figures, our examination of his estimates and statements had not been sufficiently searching to give us a correct idea of the magnitude of these errors, false theories, and premises, until the perusal of this speech from Mr. Stewart. We shall endeavor, shortly, to find room for the whole of it, as it ought to be perused by every citizen. In the meantime, we will take up some of the points alluded to."—*State Journal, N. O., La.*

"We commend to the attention of our readers Mr. Stewart's admirable speech on the tariff, which will be found in our columns to-day; do not fail to read it carefully—it will abundantly repay you for the time you may devote to it—read it and pass it round to your Democratic friends."—*Herald, Ala.*

"Mr. Andrew Stewart, member of Congress from Pennsylvania, has in a recent speech demonstrated the insufficiency of the tariff of 1846, and thoroughly exposed the chicanery of the Secretary of the Treasury's report. Read the following extracts. We have seen nothing on the subject so conclusive."—*Courier, S. C.*

"Mr. Stewart's speech in the House yesterday was a masterly *exposé* of the British partialities and predilections of our free-trade advocates, and defence of the true American interests and rights of the American mechanic and farmer and American labor. Mr. Stewart is a strong man, and his speech is unanswerable. He made the true issue—American labor *versus* British pauper labor—and called upon those who were for placing British pauper labor above the labor of the mechanic and farmer of America, to array themselves against the present admirable tariff, while those who were for sustaining American labor against the pauper labor of Europe would of course stand by the American tariff."—*Baltimore Patriot, Md.*

"Hon. Andrew Stewart, of Fayette county, is deservedly esteemed as one of the most useful and efficient Representatives in Congress from this State. He has indeed acquired a high reputation throughout the country as an able champion of protection to American industry, so that our whole State has cause to be proud of him as a bold and fearless advocate of her interests, involved as they are in the present tariff. He has made another excellent speech in defence of that measure, for a copy of which we are indebted to the politeness of Hon. John Strohm, Representative in Congress from Lancaster, and which we lay before our readers this week, commencing on our first page. It will be seen that he has in a brief and comprehensive manner reviewed and exposed the fallacious humbugs raised against the tariff by the anti-protectionists of the South, and their panders at the North."—*Montrose Register, Pa.*

The foregoing notices and comments are taken from hundreds of others of the same tenor, and expressing the same opinions, both as to the speech and the policy advocated.

LETTERS.

Copy of a letter from Baron Charles Dupin, member of the House of Peers, and the ablest advocate of the protective policy in France, dated

PARIS, 16*th May*, 1846.

"HONORABLE SIR:—Be so kind as to accept a copy of my speech [60 pages in French] upon the commercial interests of nations, contrasted with those of Great Britain. If I had known of your most able speech of the 14th of March, it would have been highly useful to me for the light it spreads upon that matter.

"I am, Sir, with the highest esteem, your most obedient servant,

"BARON CHARLES DUPIN.

"To MR. A. STEWART, of Pennsylvania."

Extract from a letter from Henry Clay, dated

ASHLAND, 26*th June*, 1846

"MY DEAR SIR:—I have read your excellent speech on the protective policy with great satisfaction. It is a most triumphant vindication of that policy, and I concur with you heartily in most of what you have so well said. I differ with you on the first part of your position—'*That duties levied for revenue on articles we cannot produce increased prices, whilst protective duties levied on articles we can and do produce diminished prices;*' or rather I should say, that it should be received with some qualification. Duties levied for revenue on articles we do not produce do not always enhance the price. . . . . If, however, I am right in this view, it does not affect the main and strong current of your able speech.

"What will be the fate of the pending measure? I wish you would give my respects to some of our Democratic friends in the Pennsylvania delegation, and ask them whether they *now* think the President (Polk) is a better tariff man than I am.

"I am your friend and obedient servant,

"H. CLAY."

Extract from a letter from J. & G. Gideon, dated

WASHINGTON, *October* 27*th*, 1846.

"DEAR SIR:—The number of your speech printed by us during the last session is as follows:

Number furnished individuals (members)...	60,000	copies.
" " by order of Mr. A. Lawrence, Boston.......	20,000	"
" " Committees	60,000	"
	140,000	"
After adjournment to Committees.......	25,000	"
To others, etc., number not known.		

"Yours truly,

"J. & G. GIDEON.

"HON. A. STEWART."

ON THE PORTION OF THE PRESIDENT'S MESSAGE AND TREASURY REPORT RELATING TO THE TARIFF.

DELIVERED IN THE HOUSE OF REPRESENTATIVES, U. S., ON TUESDAY, 9th DECEMBER, 1845.

THE House having under consideration the resolution to refer that portion of the President's message in relation to the tariff to the committee of ways and means—

Mr. Stewart moved to amend the resolution by inserting thereafter instructions to the committee to report "as the sense of this house that the tariff of 1842 ought not to be disturbed." In supporting this motion, Mr. S. said, that he thought the house ought to meet this question at once, and give an expression of its views and purposes. The people had heard with alarm the language of the executive message on the subject of the tariff. Mr. S. was in possession of letters just received from individuals who had commenced manufacturing establishments, and who wished to know whether it would be safe for them to proceed. Their inquiry of him was, what was going to be done? Whether the entire system of protective policy was to be overturned, as had been recommended by the executive? That inquiry was coming up from all parts of the country; he could not answer them; and he thought it the duty of this house to reply to these inquiries, and to let the people know at once whether the policy of protecting American industry was to be subverted or established. Surely it was their obvious duty to come up to the question fairly and openly, and at once, and give a distinct expression of their views.

It had been intimated by a gentleman from Alabama, over the way, [Mr. Payne,] that the report from the Secretary of the Treasury was a most extraordinary document. Extraordinary it certainly was, and many new and very extraordinary doctrines did it contain. Mr. S. concurred very heartily with the gentleman in thus much of what he had said.—The report was a document setting forth doctrines in political economy such as never before had been promulgated by any authorized officer of government, and the positions there assumed were such as had startled the country. It was therefore manifestly proper and highly obligatory on this body that it should give as prompt an expression as possible of its views and intentions in the premises. Mr. S. proposed to draw forth to view, and to public examination, in as brief a manner as he could, some of these opinions and doctrines.

The first doctrine which he should notice, and which was most distinctly avowed in the secretary's report, was that the protective policy was *unconstitutional*, and if so, there must be an end of it. The secretary said expressly that the tariff of 1842 was "too unequal and unjust, too exorbitant and oppressive, and too clearly in conflict with the fundamental principles of the constitution."

These were his express words; that the tariff of 1842 was clearly in conflict with the fundamental principles of the constitution; and he had made an argument to prove this. He quoted the Constitution, and then argued, by way of inference, that the power to lay a duty for protection was not in this government. His report says:

"A *partial* and a *total prohibition* are *alike in violation of the true object of the taxing power*. They only differ in degree, and not in principle. If the revenue limit may be exceeded *one per cent.*, it may be exceeded one hundred. If it may be exceeded upon any one article, it may be exceeded on all; and there is no escape from this conclusion but in contending that congress may lay duties on all articles so high as to collect no revenue, and operate as a total prohibition.

"The constitution declares that 'all bills for raising revenue shall originate in the house of representatives.' A tariff bill, it is conceded, can only originate in the house, because it is a bill for *raising revenue*. That is the only proper object of such a bill. *A tariff is a bill* to 'lay and collect taxes.' It is a bill 'for raising revenue;' and whenever it departs from that object, in *whole* or in *part*, either by *total* or *partial* prohibition, *it violates the purpose of the granted power*."

Mr. S. here referred to the messages of Washington, Jefferson, Madison, and Monroe, all of whom over and over again, in the strongest and most emphatic language, urged upon congress the propriety of protecting domestic manufactures. He then came to the message of Gen. Jackson—a name which, he should suppose, would still have some small measure of authority, at least, with those who once professed themselves pre-eminently his friends. Mr. S. would place in distinct and open contradiction the opinions held by the present executive and his Secretary of the Treasury, as contained in the message of the one and the report of the other, and the opinions of Andrew Jackson as contained in his executive messages to congress. He had already presented the doctrines of the existing administration as they were embodied in the report of the secretary of the treasury.

He would now proceed to read a paragraph from the message of President Jackson, by way of refreshing gentlemen's recollection as to what had been the opinions on this subject avowed by that distinguished man. Mr. S. considered the passage he was about to quote as containing one of the clearest and strongest vindications of the constitutional power to lay duties, for the purpose of protection, that had ever been put forth to the world. Here it is:

"The power to impose duties upon imports originally belonged to the several states. The right to adjust these duties, with a view to the encouragement of domestic industry, is so completely identical with that power, that it is difficult to suppose the existence of the one without the other. The states have delegated their whole authority over imports to the general government, without limitation or restriction, saving the very inconsiderable reservation relating to the inspection laws. This authority having thus entirely passed from the states, the right to exercise it for the purpose of protection does not exist in them; and, consequently, if it be not possessed by the general government, it must be extinct. Our political system would thus present the anomaly of a people stripped of the right to foster their own industry, and to counteract the most selfish and destructive policy which might be adopted by foreign nations. This surely cannot be the case; this indispensable power, thus surrendered by the states, must be within the scope of authority on the subject expressly delegated to congress. In this conclusion I am confirmed, as well by the opinions of Presidents Washington, Jefferson, Madison, and Monroe, who have each repeatedly recommended this right under the constitution, as by the uniform practice of congress, the continued acquiescence of the states, and the general understanding of the people."—*Jackson's Second Annual Message.*

Yet now congress was to learn, for the first time, by executive instruction, that they possessed no *constitutional power* to protect our own home industry—no power to countervail the injurious regulations of other countries—no power to protect the labor of our own citizens from the destruction which must be brought upon it by an unrestricted competition with the pauper labor of Europe; but our own hardy sons of toil must be impoverished and ground down so long as the wretched beggars under a foreign government were compelled by their necessities, to labor at lower rates than freeborn Americans—were the doctrines distinctly promulgated by the President in his message, and especially by his Secretary of the Treasury. Well might they be called extraordinary, for such they certainly were. Were the American people prepared to sustain opinions like these? Would they subscribe to the dogma that their own government had no power to protect them? That was the doctrine—there was no evading it, and Mr. S. desired to know whether this house was prepared to give it the impress of its sanction?

This, however, was but one of the extraordinary doctrines in this most extraordinary production. It contained others equally strange, equally new, equally pernicious in tendency, equally destructive in practical operation. Would the people believe it? This document from the secretary recommended the imposition of an *excise* on American manufactures—to take the duties off British goods, and put them on the American.

[*Mr. Johnson*, of Tennessee, here interposed, and desired to ask him a question. When the government protected these manufactures, who paid the duties?]

Mr. Stewart disliked these interruptions; but since the question was put, he would answer it. The gentleman asked him who paid. The gentleman and his friends held the doctrine that the consumer always paid the duty, and the secretary told the nation that the poor man was taxed eighty-two per cent. on cotton goods over the rich man. Yes, this poor man seemed a special favorite of the honorable secretary. He had introduced him ten times in the course of two paragraphs of the report. His sympathy was greatly excited that this unhappy "poor man" was taxed one hundred and fifty per cent. on his cotton shirt, because there was a specific duty on imported cotton goods of nine cents a yard. Now, if this specific duty of nine cents amounted to a hundred and fifty per cent. *ad valorem*, that fixed the price of the cotton to the "poor man" at but six cents a yard, for nine cents was just one hundred and fifty per cent. on six cents. So the practical effect of this horrid tax was, that this "poor man" got a good shirt at sixpence a yard. And Mr. S. would tell the gentleman another thing. When those most abominable minimums, which so excited the wrath of the secretary had first been introduced, in 1816, by William Lowndes—one of the purest patriots and most enlightened statesmen that had ever graced these legislative halls, and sustained, too, by John C. Calhoun, scarcely less distinguished—India cotton goods, of the very coarsest quality, known to every lady at the time by the name of hum-hums, cost thirty-three cents a yard; so that the "poor man" would then have had to pay four dollars for twelve yards of it, and the effect of the infamous minimums had been that every poor man in the country could now get a better article for six and a quarter cents. That was the way the people were taxed and oppressed by the protective system; and this was the manner in which the "poor man" was ground down to the dust to benefit the rich monopolist! The secretary persuaded this poor man that he was taxed eighty-two per cent. more than the rich man, and this was quite insufferable, and yet he paid only six cents for what formerly cost him thirty-six cents, and of an inferior quality at that. On that thirty-six cents, the tariff of 1816 laid a duty of nine cents, which was then but twenty-five per cent. *ad valorem;* it is now one hundred and fifty per cent., and why? Because the price is reduced from thirty-six to six cents per yard.

These dreadful minimums had, in their practical consequences, given the farmers a market, given their children employment, made their land profitable, filled the country with the hum of contented industry, and had brought down the price of the poor man's clothing from thirty-six cents a yard, down—down—down, as the system proceeded, till, at last, it gave it to him at six cents a yard. Now the secretary cried out that the duty on these cottons was a hundred and fifty per cent. *ad valorem!* Enormous! Horrid! And why? The duty had not changed, but the price had. As the price went down the duty went up. At thirty-six cents per yard, nine cents duty would be twenty-five per cent.; at six cents a yard, the duty would be one hundred and fifty per cent; and if the price descended to one cent a yard, then the duty would be nine hundred per cent.! The poor man robbed, plundered, and oppressed by a duty of nine hundred per cent., simply because he got a yard of cotton goods for one cent a yard! Let the manufacturer run up the price to thirty-six cents again, and the oppression is all over; the duty of nine cents a yard falls instantly to twenty-five per cent., a moderate revenue duty. No more complaint; these friends of the "poor man" are perfectly satisfied.

Such was the practical operation of these odious minimums which had reduced the poor man's cotton goods from twenty-five and thirty cents per yard to six and eight cents Yet this was the system which must be given up; this was the operation which was so oppressive and so *unconstitutional* that it must be suffered to exist no longer upon our statute book! The duty was to be taken off the foreign goods, and put upon American manufactures; such was the doctrine of this report and message which says—

[*Mr. Johnson*, of Tennessee, here again asked Mr. Stewart, if the tariff brought down the prices of articles, why did the manufacturer want it, and what was it that brought down the price of other goods in proportion?]

Mr. Stewart replied that such was not the fact. Other goods, not manufactured here, silks, velvets, etc., had not declined in the same ratio, nor had wages or agricultural produce; because the protective tariff had increased the supply of domestic goods by increasing competition, and had sustained wages and agricultural produce by creating an increased demand for both. If the gentleman could comprehend that demand and supply regulate price, it would be all plain to him.

Yes, sir, and could the secretary accomplish what seems to be his purpose, the destruction of our domestic cotton manufactures—which he says now amount to eighty-four millions per annum, and which, of course, adds that much annually to our national wealth, strike this out of existence, destroy this immense competition and supply—soon, very soon, the "poor man," without employment and with diminished means would have to pay the foreigner two or three times the price he now pays at home. Such are the favors this administration would confer upon "poor men." The gentleman asks, if protection reduces prices, why do manufacturers want it? It was not increased prices, but increased business they wanted—a wider market; it was the advantage of improved machinery, increased skill, and enlarged sales that reduced prices; 5 per cent. profit on a business of $5000 a year was more than 20 per cent. profit on $1000; and the sale of six pairs of shoes a day, at ten cents profit, was better than the sale of one pair at fifty cents profit. Is the gentleman satisfied?

When interrupted, he had been controverting the doctrines put forth by the secretary in his report. He had. referred to a table which had been reported by the committee of ways and means, for the purpose of showing the enormous tax which was imposed by the system of *minimums;* but when the secretary, by the assistance of the honorable chairman of the committee of ways and means, was preparing with great labor and pains this document, he seemed to forget that he was, at the same moment, furnishing mathematical proof of the exact extent to which protection had reduced prices. By converting specific into *ad valorem* duties, the duty runs up precisely as the price runs down; so by showing an increased rate of duty, the gentlemen have only shown reduced prices.

The duty is fixed, and cannot vary. The *ad valorem* duties are always the same. None were imposed by the tariff of 1842 above 50 per cent. How, then, does the President, in his message, get duties of 200 per cent.? This can only be done by converting the *specific* duties into *ad valorem* duties; and, when this is done, a high duty only shows a low price. If the duty is 200 per cent., the price must be one-half only of the duty. Thus, we are told that glass pays the enormous duty of 200 per cent., and why? Because the duty is $4 per box, and the price $2 per box; but if the glass went down to $1 per box, the duty would be 400 per cent. Thus we are told by the Secretary of the Treasury that the people paid in all a tax of eighty-four millions, of which but twenty-seven went to the government, and fifty-four to the manufacturers; and he referred to a list of sixty or seventy articles paying specific duties, which, when converted into *ad valorem*, amounted to more than a hundred per cent. Very well; and what did this prove? Why, simply that the prices of those articles had been greatly diminished, as in the case of cottons. The same duty which, when levied, had been but 25 per cent., had now become 100 per cent., simply because the price had gone down to one-fourth part of what it was. So the main result of all the labor and cyphering of the secretary and chairman of the committee of ways and means had been to furnish to the whole country official demonstration that prices had been reduced by a protective tariff to one-fourth or one-fifth of what they had been in 1816. Take a plain illustration: the tariff imposed a duty of four cents per pound on nails; the price of nails in 1816 had been 16 cents per pound; so that the duty was then 25 per cent. on the price; but the same duty, we are told in this report, is now 100 per cent.; and how so? Because the price had fallen from sixteen cents to four cents per pound.

very oppressive on the "poor man," who has thus to pay 100 per cent. on nails! The explanation of all this was perfectly plain and easy. The effect of competition, machinery, skill, and industry, had increased the supply, and by an increased supply, in this as in all other cases, had reduced the price of glass, cotton, etc., whilst it had rendered the whole country prosperous by the increased demand for all the productions of the farmers.

Mr. S. thanked the secretary for his reference to his document; it had furnished to him and to the country undeniable proof, from the highest authority, to what an extent prices had been reduced, insomuch that the duty on one article, though reasonable at first, had now risen to three hundred and eighty-nine per cent. *ad valorem,* brought about solely by the *reduction* of the price. Mr. S. defied escape from this position. Let any gentleman take the report and examine it, and the more they examine, the more would they be convinced that this was a true explanation of the whole matter. Yet this was held forth for the purpose of exciting alarm; it furnished a topic for popular declamation; it might persuade the "poor man" that he was greatly oppressed, because he paid a tax of two hundred per cent. on his window glass; and he perhaps would not understand that if glass fell to a dollar a box, he was taxed four hundred per cent., or if by any improvement in the manufacture he should be enabled to get his glass at fifty cents a box, why then he would be paying the enormous unheard of tax of *eight hundred per cent.* This same "poor man" of the secretary sometimes wanted to buy a few nails, and the secretary alarmed him by the intelligence that nails were taxed a hundred per cent. on their value. So they were; but what did they pay for them? He used to pay sixteen cents a pound, but this wicked oppressive tariff had brought them down to four cents. Now, who did not see that if a specific duty of four cents a pound on nails was converted into an *ad valorem* duty, it amounted to a hundred per cent., and should nails be brought down to a cent a pound, the duty would be four hundred per cent.! What an oppression to get nails at a penny a pound. Surely the "poor man" was likely to be utterly crushed and ruined.

Mr. S. said he had wished to point out some other of the extraordinary doctrines contained in this paper of the secretary, and there was one which would startle the country; it was covered up in cautious language, but when the veil was drawn aside, and the truth exposed, he again warned gentlemen that it would startle the country. This free-trade secretary had recommended an EXCISE on American manufactures. Yes, that was the protection he had provided for American industry; it was to take off the duty from foreign manufactures, and put it on our own. Hear him:

"In accordance with these principles, it is believed that the largest practicable portion of the aggregate revenue should be raised by maximum revenue duties upon luxuries, whether grown, produced, or manufactured *at home or abroad*."

Let mechanics and manufacturers hear that.—Every American artizan should hear it. The duty was to be on articles, etc., whether grown, produced, or manufactured at *home* or abroad. Here was an American secretary distinctly recommending to levy the highest rate of revenue duties on goods manufactured *at home*. What was this but an excise? —What else was an excise than a tax on the manufactured goods of this country? Yet this was the secretary's recommendation. How would American people like it?

Both in the message and in the report, the administration had given its own definition of what, according to its understanding, was a revenue standard of duty; and this was the language of the President's message:

"The precise point in the ascending scale of duties at which it is ascertained from experience that the revenue is greatest, is the maximum rate of duty which can be laid for the *bona fide* purpose of collecting money for the support of government.—To raise the duties higher than that point, and thereby diminish the amount collected, is to levy them for protection merely, and not for revenue. As long, then, as congress may gradually increase the rate of duty on a given article, and the revenue is increased by such increase of duty, they are within the revenue standard. When they go beyond that point, and, as they increase the duties, the revenue is diminished or destroyed, the act ceases to have for its object the raising of money to support the government, but it is for protection merely."

Here was the rule by which duties were to be laid. The moment an American manufacturer had succeeded in supplying our own market, and began to thrive in his business, that would be a proof that the duty was too high for revenue; it was no longer a revenue duty but a *protective* duty, and it must forthwith be reduced. As the American furnished *more* goods to the country, *less* foreign goods would be imported, revenue would be diminished, and the duty must come down; that was the rule. And now Mr. S. would ask, under such a rule as this, what man in his senses would invest a dollar in manufactures? What was the prospect before him? The moment when, by industry and enterprise, he should succeed in getting the better of his foreign competitor, down with the duty. If a shoemaker or a hatter, by making better or cheaper hats or shoes, had got possession of the market, the eye of this free-trade system was fastened on him like a vulture. The secretary found he was doing too well, and the duty must be reduced to let in the foreigner. Such was the plan of this administration. The mechanic, finding his protection thus diminished, and having no other resource but his business, would go on to work longer and to work harder than before, and when, by working out of hours, he had contrived to get over the opposition of his own government, and his foreign competitor, and began to get together a little profit, the same doctrine would repeat the process: the duty would evidently be too high—down with it! The "poor man" would now take his children from school and bring them into the shop. They, too, would now work, while the man himself worked harder and harder. But what would be the result? It would only bring him under the President's rule; the duty must be again lowered, and still go on to be lowered, more and more, till at last this free-born American must be ground down by the action of his own government to the degraded and wretched condition of an English pauper or a Russian serf. The moment an American laborer succeeded by his exertions in shutting out foreign competition, the foreigner must be let in and put over him. What sort of a rule was this? For whom would one suppose it to be made? For the American manufacturer or the European? Clearly it was a rule for the benefit of the foreigner. And could an independent and intelligent American consent to live under such a rule? The moment the American rises to his feet, in this struggle with foreigners for the American market, he is to be knocked down by this executive *poker*, and *walked over* by his Secretary Walker. [A laugh.] And this was their *American system*. Mr. S. insisted it was a British system. It was just such a system as Sir Robert Peel would have recommended, could he have spoken through President Polk as his trumpet; its practical, its universal operation, would be what he had just now described. And would the house endorse a system like this? This was the far-famed "*free-trade* system," now for the first time promulgated by an American fiscal officer.

Since the improvements in steam, the cost of transportation was comparatively nothing. Take off the duty, and the British workshops would be brought to our doors. Suppose these British laborers were in Alexandria, working at twenty-five cents, was any man so blind as not to see that they must soon break down the workmen of Washington, who were receiving seventy-five cents a day? The employer would soon begin to talk to them in a very intelligible language. "My competitors in Alexandria get labor for twenty-five cents a day, and you must take the same or quit." Now, where was the difference, whether the distance was a little greater or a little less? The practical operation of the system would be just the same. And this was the blessed system of free trade! The workmen of England and France could work cheaper than ours, and the free-trade doctrine held that we must buy wherever we could buy cheapest. Down went the duty, in came foreign goods, out went American money; and out and out it went till we had no more money to send, and the people and their government became bankrupt together. This was the blessing which the compassionate secretary had in store for the "poor man!" Oh, how he loved him! He brought in "the poor man" ten times in two paragraphs! But his love would be very apt to operate like the love a certain bear once had for a "poor man," when he hugged him to death. [A laugh.]

Mr. S. had seen Mr. Walker's name announced for the presidency. Now, an uncharitable observer might perhaps say that Mr. Walker was looking to be the "poor man's" candidate. If so, he proposed a wise plan, for his system would soon make all the people poor, and then he would go in by acclamation. [Much merriment.]

The secretary's system might not inaptly be termed a plan to manufacture "poor men." Such would be its practical result, and there would be no escaping it. Let the gentleman from Alabama [Mr. Payne] examine the report as long as he pleased, and see if he could make anything else out of it.—And now Mr. S. would ask the members of this house, and his countrymen generally, whether the adoption of such a plan would not be equivalent to passing a law that henceforth no further capital should be invested in manufactures? It was in the nature of a notice beforehand, and it ran in this wise: "Gentlemen, you may invest your money in such way as you deem best, but we here notify you that, as soon as you shall have supplied the

American market, and we find that in consequence of your success imports begin to diminish, the duties must be reduced, and foreign goods must be let in until we get revenue enough to pay all government officers." With such a notice before him, who would engage in manufactures? Who would invest the capital he had received by inheritance or accumulated by his own enterprise and toil with the certainty before his eyes that just as soon as he began to gather a little strength, to acquire greater skill to improve the modes of labor, and to realize its reward by getting the better of foreign competition, he must be knocked down, and the foreigner let in to ruin him? This might be called, in certain parts of the country, "legging for the British." Gentlemen from the West understood what was meant by the term "legging." [Yes, yes, and a laugh.] This rule would guaranty the American market to the foreigner forever, or until American labor was ground down and degraded to the half-starved and wretched condition of the serfs and paupers of Europe; and the American masses, thus deprived of the means of educating their children, would be obliged to work as in Europe, from the cradle to the grave, and their *moral* and *political* condition would in the end be no better than theirs.

Such most clearly must be the practical and inevitable operation of this rule, if carried out. And are these the benefits and blessings this administration has in reserve for the "poor man?"

But the Secretary of the Treasury had made other very wonderful discoveries in finance. What did he tell us? "*Experience proves* that, as a general rule, a duty of *twenty per cent. ad valorem* will yield the largest revenue." Yes; *experience* proved that an *ad valorem* duty of twenty per cent. would yield the greatest amount of revenue. Twenty per cent. yield the greatest revenue! Why, what was the great, broad, universally-known experience of the country? We had a tariff of twenty per cent. in 1841–2, and what was our revenue? Not one-half of what it now is. The whole amount of revenue from imports was then about thirteen millions, and this year it was twenty-seven millions. Was thirteen more than twenty-seven? If so, the secretary is right; if not, he was clearly wrong? And what was the effect of their twenty per cent. horizontal duty? Under its operation the country was prostrated, the government itself was bankrupt, and the people were little better. Yet this man could say, in the face of these well-known facts, and of the American people, any one of whom knew better, that an average duty of twenty per cent. yielded the greatest amount of revenue. The secretary had even gone further yet than this: in his famous circular he had assumed that *twelve and a half* per cent. *horizontal* was the true revenue standard. Some western scribbler asked him, through the press, how much revenue 12½ per cent. would give on one hundred millions of imports? (that being more than the average amount). The answer must be twelve and a half millions; then deduct three and a half millions, the expense of collection, and but nine millions of nett revenue would be left to pay twenty-six millions of expenditures. To make up the revenue, you must add more than one hundred millions to your imports, while your whole specie has never been estimated at more than eighty-five millions; then all your specie goes for your first year, and where will you get money for the next year?—These questions, being rather troublesome, were never answered.

The truth was, that the revenue resulted from the tariff, and followed it. When the tariff was low, the revenue was low; when the tariff was high, the revenue was high. That had been the uniform experience of the country, and he challenged gentlemen to show the contrary. It must be so; it could not be otherwise. And why? Because the result of protection was to make the people rich, and taking off protection was to make them poor. When the people were rich the treasury was full; as the country became poor the treasury was impoverished.—In this country the revenue was a *voluntary*, and not, as in other states, a *compulsory* contribution, made by the people to the government. The condition of the treasury was, in fact, a political thermometer, to test the prosperity of the country. According to the national prosperity, so would the revenue ever be found. When men were impoverished, could they purchase goods freely? Certainly not. When prosperous, their wives and daughters could purchase costly clothing and rich furniture, and then many goods were always imported. But when the country was impoverished, by the ruinous policy now recommended, men would wear their old coats, their wives and daughters stay at home and mend them, merchants could not get money to import goods, and the treasury would be bankrupt.

Under the compromise law the duties ran down till they

reached the point of 20 per cent.; then was the gentleman's Utopia; then according to the secretary, the revenue ought to have been abundant; but who had yet forgotten, or could ever forget, what had been then the condition of the treasury, and of this entire nation? The treasury was so perfectly bankrupt that it could not borrow one dollar. The states were everywhere repudiating their debts, and the national character lay prostrate and bleeding. That was the condition, and every body knew it, to which a twenty per cent. tariff had brought this land; and yet at this day the first fiscal officer of the government had the front to recommend a return to that state of things. In our great humiliation and distress the tariff of '42 came in like a delivering angel; it raised and restored the revenue; it replenished a famished treasury; it brought repudiation into disrepute; it made a bankrupt law useless; in a word, it struck the whole country as with the wand of an enchanter, and brought back plenty, and credit, and enterprize, and hope, and public character. Why, then, disturb it? What mischief had it done? The secretary deprecated agitation, but who agitated the country? It was the secretary himself and his friends. The friends of protection everywhere cried out, "give the country repose," "give the country prosperity and peace under the tariff as it is."

His hour, Mr. S. said, was fast drawing to a close. He must hasten on, and merely glance at many of the remaining topics of the message and report, some of which, had time permitted, he should have been glad to have noticed somewhat more at large. The report, for the first time in an *official* form, had promulgated the doctrine of "free trade," which is openly and distinctly avowed; and, to enforce the argument, reference is made to the "free-trade" existing among the states: and it is declared that "reciprocal *free-trade* among nations would best promote the interest of all;" that "the manufacturing interest opposes reciprocal *free-trade* with foreign nations;" "and if it desired reciprocal *free-trade* with other nations, it would have desired a very different tariff from that of 1842."

These are his positions, and they fully sustain the doctrine of "free-trade."

But the policy recommended by this administration, if carried out, would be ruinous to Pennsylvania, because her iron and other manufactures are carried on mostly by *manual labor*, and not, as in New England, by *labor-saving machinery*, and therefore, to induce the investment of capital and the acquisition of skill and experience, she must be protected against a too free competition with the depressed and low priced labor of Europe.

The report represents the foreign market as all important to the farmer, whilst the home market it considers of small comparative consequence; yet it appears from official documents that our annual exports of agricultural products (deducting cotton, tobacco, and rice) have not for a series of years exceeded an average of ten millions of dollars, whilst the domestic market amounts to more than fifty times that sum. Massachusetts, it is ascertained, imports and consumes annually thirty three millions of dollars worth of the agricultural products of the other states, whilst Great Britain, from whence we import about fifty millions of dollars' worth of manufactured goods annually, (one-half of the whole value of which consists of agricultural produce, raw material, and the substance of labor,) does not take, of all the agricultural productions of the United States (excluding cotton, tobacco, and rice) two and a half millions of dollars' worth a year: thus estimating one-half the value of our imports to consist of agricultural produce converted into goods, it follows that we import and consume about twenty-five millions of British agricultural produce in the form of manufactures, whilst she takes less than two and a half from us; so that we purchase and consume ten dollars' worth of British agricultural produce, converted into cloth, iron, and other goods, to one dollar's worth of the same articles she takes from us. Yet according to the report, the *foreign* market to the farmer is every thing and the *home* market nothing.

The report says that *protective* duties are levied exclusively for the benefit of the rich monopolists at the expense of the farmers and laborers. Now, he contended that just the reverse of this was the truth. That the practical effect of protection was to increase the number of manufacturing establishments, and thus destroy *monopoly* by promoting *competition;* and that by withdrawing labor from agriculture to manufactures, you not only diminish the *supply*, but at the same time increase the *demand* for agricultural produce, and of course increase its price; whilst on the other hand, by increasing manufacturing establishments you increase the supply of manufactured goods, and of course *reduce* their price, so that the farmer is thus enabled to *sell for more and buy for less.* If demand and supply regulate price, this conclusion is inevitable. Yet the report says "the tariff is a *double benefit* to the manufacturer and a *double loss* to the farmer."

The Secretary of State (Mr. Buchanan) understood this much better, when he sent a toast some time since to the manufacturers of Pittsburg to this effect: "The election of James K. Polk has saved the manufacturers from being ruined and overwhelmed by excessive competition." He was right. It certainly did favor the invested capital, the *monopolists*, by checking competition, and thereby keeping down the wages of labor and the produce of the farmer, which would, in a different result, have been enhanced in price by an increased demand. This is illustrated by the fact that at Pittsburg, shortly before the tariff of 1842, the laborers in the factories were put on half work, and of course *half pay;* and almost immediately after its passage they were restored to full work and *full pay.* It was for the sake of the laborer and farmer, therefore, that he advocated the protective policy, and not for the "rich monopolists"—the only class that will be benefited by the course of this administration in the check their policy will give to *competition* and new investments of capital, while the "poor laborer and the farmer" will be the only sufferers by it.

I submit to every man of practical common sense, whether such must not be the result. And yet we are gravely told by both the message and report that *protective* duties operate exclusively for the benefit of the rich capitalists at the expense of the "poor laborer and the farmer!"

But, finally, this whole question, so interesting to the American people, turns upon a simple question of *fact:* "Do *protective* duties ultimately *increase* or *reduce* the *prices* of the articles on which they are levied?"

Now, the message and the report *assume* (but fail to prove in a single instance) that *protective* duties have increased prices, and are therefore oppressive and burdensome; while, on the other hand, he asserted, and was ready to prove by the documents referred to, by every price current and every merchant in the country, that the prices of *protected* goods have been reduced by competition since the odious *minimums* and specific duties were first imposed for *protection* in 1816 to one-half, one-third, one-fourth, and in some instances to one-sixth part of what they were at that time, as in the case of coarse cottons, glass, iron, nails, etc.;

yet, in the face of these undeniable facts, it is asserted that the duty (nine cents a yard—150 per cent.) is added to the price of the *domestic* as well as the imported goods, and is paid by the consumer, and that the "poor man" is thus taxed on his coarse cotton goods 82 per cent. more than the rich; when the fact is admitted that the poor now get a better article made at home, and paid for in *labor* or *produce*, at one-fourth of the price he paid in 1816, when the minimum duties were first imposed; while on the other hand, the wages of labor and the produce of the farm, flour, grain, meat, etc., have undergone little or no reduction of price, owing to the increased demand produced by the increase of manufactures. Such has been the effect of *protective* duties. But *revenue* duties levied on articles not produced or manufactured at home, may and do generally increase prices, because they do not produce competition and *increased supply*. But to the facts. I call upon the President and secretary for their *proofs*. Show me the evidence that in a single instance *protective duties* have permanently increased prices. This you assert, and I deny. This is an issue of *fact*, and not of argument. Produce, then, your evidence, that *protective* duties have permanently increased prices, and then go on and denounce protection as plunder, robbery, and oppression. But first *prove* your *facts*, and then make your argument. I ask the secretary as a lawyer, would any court in Christendom tolerate for a moment the course you pursue? You bring a suit against A. who denies your claim. Are you at liberty to assume the facts without proof to be just as you want them, and then make your speech, and ask a verdict? Surely not. Yet such is the course pursued on this great question. You *assume* without proof, that *protective* duties increase prices, and then contend that the "poor man" and the farmer are oppressed and plundered by the tariff. Now, if this be found to be untrue in point of fact, and that the reverse is true, that they *reduce* prices, and of course *lessen* burdens, then what becomes of all your arguments and speeches against the oppressions of the tariff? They fall lifeless to the ground.

He denied the right of the enemies of the tariff to *assume* these facts, and called on them for the proof. The facts lie at the foundation of the whole question, and he trusted they will be furnished.

The President and secretary tell us they want a revenue tariff—a tariff that will just yield revenue enough to meet expenditures, and no more. Well, according to their own showing, the present tariff is the very thing they want. They tell us officially that the expenditures this year have been $29,968,207, and the revenue has been $29,769,133. Now is it possible to get the tariff nearer right than it is? Why, then, disturb or change it, when, according to their own theory, it is exactly right? Last session we were threatened with a large surplus, and were then told we must "reduce the tariff to *reduce* the revenue." Now we are told we must "reduce the tariff to *increase* the revenue." So, whether there was too much or too little, the remedy was always the same—"reduce the tariff—reduce the tariff." Doctor Sangrado's cure for all things—"bleeding and warm water." [A laugh.]

We are told by the secretary that the manufacturers are all making immense profits—20 or 30 per cent. But can this be possible? Is not capital free everywhere? and will it work for 4 or 5 per cent. at agriculture, as is alleged, when, by going into manufactures, it could realize 20 or 30? If this were true, the rush of capital into manufactures would soon be so great as to reduce it to the very lowest rates of profit. But if the manufacturers supply goods at one-fourth of their former cost, and still make money, why complain? And why break down or drive away this profitable business, where, by the use of labor-saving machinery, one hand will do the work of forty? Why drive this 30 per cent. business abroad, and continue to labor here at 4 or 5 per cent. profit, and exchange the productions of forty hard working men here for the labor of one woman, with the aid of labor-saving machinery abroad? Why not keep this profitable business in our own country?

The secretary, in his report, tells us that "on coal and iron the duties are far too high for revenue," and that they ought to be reduced to the "revenue standard," which he assumes to be about 20 per cent. Now, if the average duty on these articles exceeds, as the secretary alleges, 60 per cent., then according to his views, more than two-thirds of the duty must be taken off of iron and coal, which would extinguish the fires of every furnace and every forge in Pennsylvania, destroying millions of capital, and sending millions abroad to purchase the agricultural produce of foreign countries, converted into iron. Try this Anti-American system, and hear what Pennsylvania has to say to it! I need not anticipate her; she will speak for herself.

This is not what she understood by the Kane letter, and she will say so.

The secretary says: "Where the number of manufactories is not great, the power of the system to regulate the wages of labor is inconsiderable; but as the profit of capital invested in manufactures is augmented by the protective tariff, there is a corresponding increase of power, until the control of such capital over the wages of labor becomes irresistible." Was there ever a greater error entered into the imagination of man? There is not a laboring man in this country who does not know that quite the reverse of this is the fact; that where the demand for labor is small, wages go down; and where manufactories multiply, and as the demand for labor increases, wages go up. Yet the secretary has it, that when the demand for labor is small, wages are high; and when the demand is great, wages are low!

The secretary tells us, exultingly, that "England has repealed her duties on cotton, and reduced them on breadstuffs." True, but is not this the work of the protective policy? The American manufacturer is abroad throughout Europe with his goods, underselling England even in her own markets. Hence she is obliged to take every burden off her manufacturers to enable them to maintain the competition. Hence they repeal the duty on cotton and provisions, not for favor, but to beat us—not to benefit us, but to save themselves. The secretary boasts of British liberality, with the notorious fact before his eyes, that except on cotton, the average duties levied at this moment in Great Britain on all our imports exceed 300 per cent.; while our duties on her imports do not average 33. This is British liberality, so extolled and eulogized by the *American* Secretary. England, we are told, will follow our example, if we adopt "free-trade." Will she? Hear what she says on this subject through her ministry. The Duke of Wellington, very recently, in reply to Earl Grey and others, stated in the house of peers, "that when free-trade was talked of as existing in England, it was an absurdity. There was no such thing, and *there could be no such thing as free-trade in that country.* We proceed (says he) on the system of protecting our own manufactures and our own produce—the produce of our labor and our soil; of protecting them for exportation, and protecting them for home consumption; and on that universal system of protection it was absurd to talk of free-trade."

The secretary says, if we do not take British goods, they will have to pay cash for our cotton; and, "*not having it to spare*," they will buy less, and at lower prices. We must cease manufacturing, and send our money to England, so that she may have "money to spare" to buy southern cotton. This is the idea. The north and the west are to be sacrificed to make a market for southern cotton. But does not the secretary see that by impoverishing the north and west, a worse result would follow? They would soon be unable to buy anything; whereas, if protected and prosperous, having the means, they would have the will to purchase and consume foreign goods. Thus the secretary's "free-trade" plan would most effectually defeat his own purpose, *if carried out.*

But England, we are told by the secretary, will, if we relax, repeal her corn laws. She may for the moment, to avoid starvation; and not an hour longer. But, if repealed, would it inure to our benefit? Would she not obtain her supplies of wheat much cheaper from the North Sea and the Baltic, from Odessa, Warsaw, Dantzic, and Hamburgh, where, for seven years, ending 1840, the price of wheat was seventy-seven cents per bushel, while here it was $1.40 on the seaboard; and freight from there was but thirteen cents per bushel, and from here thirty-six? At this time the price there is ninety cents, and here $1.15. But the repeal of the corn laws would equally favor the wheat of the Baltic, while a great portion of our wheat finds its way to Great Britain, through Canada, at the colonial duties, thus escaping the operation of the corn laws.

But let the administration adopt its system, and let the manufacturers close their doors and turn out seven or eight hundred thousand people to beg or starve, and they will soon hear a voice that will make them tremble. Yes, and this Secretary of the Treasury himself will hasten to declare, as did the Emperor of Russia, who tried this system of free-trade for a short time, but soon renounced it in this emphatic language:

"*Agriculture left without markets, industry without protection,* LANGUISH AND DECLINE. SPECIE IS EXPORTED AND THE MOST SOLID COMMERCIAL HOUSES ARE SHAKEN. The public prosperity would soon feel the wound inflicted on private fortunes, if new regulations did not promptly change the actual state of affairs.

"*Events have proved that our* AGRICULTURE *and our* COMMERCE, *as well as our* MANUFACTURING INDUSTRY, *are not only paralyzed,* BUT BROUGHT TO THE BRINK OF RUIN."

Such would be the effects of the system now recommended for our adoption, and such would soon be the language this administration or its successors would be obliged to adopt. Sir, if I loved my *party* more than my *country*, I would rejoice to see this administration carry out its measures, for its speedy overthrow would be inevitable.

Mr. S. said he would now present the doctrines of this administration in direct opposition to Thomas Jefferson and Andrew Jackson, and let the people decide for themselves. Protection is not only denounced by this administration as *unconstitutional*, but also as oppressive to the farmer and laborer. Well, what says General Jackson on this subject? He says:

"If we omit or refuse to use the gifts which God has extended to us, we deserve not the continuation of his blessings. He has filled our mountains and our plains with minerals—with lead, iron, and copper; and given us climate and soil for the growing of hemp and wool. These being the grand materials of our national defence, they ought to have extended to them adequate and fair *protection* that our own manufactories and laborers may be placed on a fair competition with those of Europe. I will ask, what is the real situation of the agriculturist? Where has the American farmer a market for his surplus product? Except for cotton, he has neither a foreign nor home market. Does not this clearly prove, when there is no market either at home or abroad, that there is too much labor employed in agriculture, and that the channels for labor should be multiplied? *Common sense points out, at once, the remedy.* Draw from agriculture this superabundant labor; employ it in mechanism and manufactures; thereby creating a home market for your breadstuffs, and distributing labor to the most profitable account; and benefits to the country will result. Take from agriculture, in the United States, 600,000 men, women, and children, and you will, at once, give a home market for more breadstuffs than all Europe now furnishes us. In short, sir, we have been too long subject to the policy of British merchants. It is time that we should become a little more *Americanized;* and, instead of feeding the paupers and laborers of *England*, feed our *own;* or else, in a short time, by continuing our present policy, we shall all be rendered paupers ourselves."

The secretary's report says we ought not to adopt *protective* duties because other nations do so, and says, "with revenue duties only throw open our ports to all the world." But what says Thomas Jefferson; here are the words of that profound and patriotic statesman in his report to Congress on this subject:

"But should any nation, contrary to our wishes, suppose it may better find its advantage by continuing its system of prohibitions, duties, and regulations, it *behooves us to protect our citizens, their commerce and navigation, by counter prohibitions*, duties, and regulations also. Free commerce and navigation are not to be given in exchange for restrictions, and vexations, nor are they likely to produce a relaxation of them. Where a nation imposes high duties on our productions, or prohibits them altogether, it may be proper for us to do the same by theirs; first, burdening or excluding those productions which they bring here in competition with our own of the same kind; selecting next, such manufactures as we take from them in greatest quantity, and which, at the same time, we could the soonest furnish to ourselves, or obtain from other countries; imposing on them duties, lighter at first, but HEAVIER and HEAVIER afterwards, as other channels of supply open. Such duties *having the effect of indirect encouragement to domestic manufactures* of the same kind, *may induce the manufacturer to come himself into these states.*"

Now President Polk says, that duties can be imposed only for *revenue*, and not for *protection*, and that when the home supply diminishes revenue, the duties ought to be reduced so as to increase imports. But Jefferson's rule is precisely the reverse. He says, as the domestic supply increases the duties ought to be *increased*, not *reduced* as Mr. Polk has it. The duties, according to Jefferson's plan, ought to be made *heavier* and *heavier* to favor the Americans. Polk's lighter and lighter to favor foreigners.

Which is right, Jefferson or Polk? one or the other must be mistaken, as they are directly at issue.

Here they stand directly opposed—which side as Americans ought we to take? He had always been and still was attached to the old *Jeffersonian democracy*, the opposite of modern *progressive democracy*, and he believed that a majority of the old and honest democrats of Pennsylvania would still be found faithful to the tried and true Jeffersonian principles when brought to the test.

On the subject of the tariff Jefferson's plan was the only true one, "select the articles we can and ought to manufacture for ourselves, give them full and adequate protection, 'lighter at first, but heavier and heavier' as the domestic supply increases, and for revenue increasing the duties on luxuries consumed by the rich." This is the true American system as expounded by Thomas Jefferson himself; it is the standard around which all his friends should now rally—and those who desert this standard are traitors to his principles.

Mr. S. said, he wished to consider for a moment the tariff as connected with agriculture, and it might startle the secretary to tell him that Massachusetts now exported to foreign markets more agricultural produce then any other state in the Union. She exported it as the British exported it, not in its raw form, but converted into manufactures; and, what was still more important to the grain-growing states, she exported it in a form not to compete with, or at all affect, the price of produce, in its raw condition in the foreign markets. And it might startle the secretary still more to tell him that millions of dollars' worth of hay, oats, straw, grass, and corn, were transported annually over the mountains to the Atlantic markets, from Ohio, Kentucky, and the other Western States. But is it not strictly and undeniably true? Not in its original form, but like British goods, converted and changed into a condition in which it can be transported to market. Converted into hogs, horses, and fat cattle; for what are these but the corn, oats, and hay, of the Western farmer, changed into animated forms, and made to *carry itself*, to market. A fat hog carries eight or ten bushels of corn to market, and a fine Western horse carries seventy or eighty dollars' worth of hay and oats to the Eastern market, with the farmer on top of it, who sells it for cash, and returns home to repeat the process. And thus foreigners convert *their* agricultural produce, not into hogs and horses, but into cloth, iron, hats, shoes, every thing you find on the merchant's shelf, and send them here for sale and consumption. Our merchants throughout the country, so far as they sell foreign goods, are in fact but retailers of foreign agricultural produce, converted into goods and sent here for sale; and, when we look abroad at their vast numbers, is it surprising that money should be scarce? It has clearly proved that more than half the value of a yard of cloth consists of wool, and the substance of labor employed in its manufacture. That nine-tenths of the value of pig iron consists of agricultural produce, and even a yard of lace is but little else than the *subsistence* of the foreign pauper labor employed in its fabrication. Yet the farmer seems not to be aware, that when he pays twenty dollars for a suit of British cloth he sends ten dollars of the twenty in *hard* money (they take no paper) to purchase British wool, and bread, and meat, while he has no market for his own. Yet is it not true? And is not this the policy recommended by his administration? He was admonished to be brief, but he would, while on this point, state another fact susceptible of the clearest demonstration, that the constituents of every member in this house from Ohio, Indiana, Illinois, and all the grain-growing states, are, and at this moment, purchasing and consuming five dollars' worth of British agricultural produce to one dollar's worth Great Britain takes of theirs. By referring to the official reports on commerce and navigation for ten or twenty years back, it would be found that our imports of British goods amount to nearly $50,000,000 a year, while she has taken, of all the agricultural products of the grain-growing states of this Union, flour, grain, meat, etc., less than two millions and a half. Now, if only half the value (and it was much more) of these goods consisted of agricultural produce, this would give ($25,000,000) twenty-five millions of British agricultural produce taken annually by us, to two and a half millions of ours taken by them, just *ten to one*. Now, assuming that consumption is in proportion to population; then these Western gentlemen's constituents are consuming not five but *ten dollars'* worth of British agricultural produce to *one* Great Britain takes from them; and yet the secretary is not satisfied, but wishes to increase the import of foreign goods to favor the *farmers!* Reduce the duties, says the administration, to increase imports, and amen, say most of the representatives of these Western farmers. But what would these farmers say to their representatives when they come to look *practically* and not *theoretically* at this matter? He, Mr. S., intended to call their attention to it. He intended, after the example of the secretary, to address some questions to the farmers of this country, and he hoped soon to have their answers to lay before the house; he wanted the facts on both sides. He would ask, for instance, how much agricultural produce there was in a yard of domestic cloth, or a ton of iron? and whether, if brought from England, (where it was made of the same materials,) they did not purchase English wool and provisions converted into cloth, iron, etc., when they had no market for their own? He would ask the merchants and manufacturers what were the prices of cotton and woollen goods, glass, iron, nails, etc., in 1816, when the first protective tariff was adopted, and what were they now? He would ask the working men what would be the effect of "free-trade," recommended by the Secretary of the Treasury, on the wages of labor in this country? Such questions, in his judgment, would not only furnish important facts, but, what was more important, it would bring the farmers and laborers to investigate this subject in a common sense practical point of view, and to figure it out for themselves; in this way more would be done to bring the people to a right understanding of this highly interesting subject, than by all the speeches made here or elsewhere.

The message tells us that a *protective tariff* benefits the rich at the expense of the laboring poor. No, sir; it is just the reverse. The tariff is a rampart thrown around our national labor, the great element of our national wealth. The tariff furnished the only security our laborer had against the degrading and leveling effects of an unrestricted competition with the pauper labor of Europe. As you reduce this wall of protection, you reduce the wages of labor. As you reduce labor, you reduce the national wealth, which is the sum of your productive industry.

Sir, I stand here the advocate of *labor*—labor in the field and in the workshops—this struggle for national *protection* is a struggle for national prosperity. Who can estimate the value of our national labor? It amounted to hundreds of millions of dollars. A poor man's labor is his capital; if he earns only $120 per annum, this is equal to a capital of $2000, at 6 per cent.; if you have a million only of laborers, this gives you a capital of *two thousand millions of dollars;* and is this not worth your care and your protection? Must this vast American labor be prostrated and trodden down to make a market for foreign goods? to increase revenue by increasing the imports, sending millions abroad to sustain foreign labor, to obtain a few thousand dollars of revenue? The naked question presented is, shall we favor foreign industry or our own? Shall we take the *foreign* or the *American* side in this great struggle for the American market? This is the great and true question involved in this issue of *protection* or *no protection.* This administration has taken the foreign side of the question. They denounce all *protection* as *unconstitutional.* I take the American side. And I fearlessly appeal to the good sense, the enlightened patriotism of the American people, the *farmers* and *laborers,* whose interests are at stake, to decide this question. The issue is now fairly made up, and must be decided. Is protection constitutional or not? Has Congress the power to protect the national industry? Sir, let gentlemen pull down this wall of protection thrown around the national industry by the tariff of 1842, inundate the country again with foreign goods, send all our money abroad to pay for them, again bankrupt the people and the treasury as in 1841; let gentlemen do this, and go home, to meet the frowns of an indignant and ruined people.

COMMENTS AND OPINIONS OF THE PRESS.

We copy from the scrap book already referred to, the following notices from among hundreds of others of like tenor published in newspapers throughout the United States.

"The report of Robert J. Walker, Secretary of the Treasury, submitted to Congress at the opening of the present session, lauded the tariff of 1846, as the greatest measure perhaps that has been adopted since the formation of our government—it was truly a wonderful measure, and that report has called forth from his Democratic friends the most extravagantly fulsome laudations, and its author pronounced the greatest financier of the age. It was truly a Democratic document of the modern kind.

"On the 11th of January, Hon. Andrew Stewart, of Pennsylvania, made a speech in the House of Representatives, in which, among other things, he scathingly reviewed Mr. Secretary Walker's report, and pointed out some of his misstatements in very plain language, and in such a way as is not calculated to increase confidence in the accuracy or veracity of the honorable secretary. It will be seen from the extracts which we present in another column, and to which the reader's attention is directed, that Mr. Stewart openly and directly impeaches the truth and fairness of Mr. Walker's statements, and calls upon him to substantiate them. Mr. Stewart also holds himself bound to maintain his statements if they are denied." —*Knoxville Tribune, Tenn.*

"Hon. Andrew Stewart, of Pennsylvania, made sad work with Secretary Walker's annual report, proving it full of falsehoods and misstatements. He is just the man that can do it successfully and with effect. He puts his words down and clinches them so tight, that no locofoco need ever attempt to overset them. If we can get a copy of the speech, we will publish it."—*Traveller, Louisiana.*

"We invite the special attention of both the friends and foes of the doctrine of Protection, to the lucid exposition of the Hon. Andrew Stewart, in the House of Representatives. The speech speaks for itself—and we hope every one will avail himself of the privilege of giving it an attentive perusal. No man in the Union understands this subject as thoroughly as Mr. Stewart, and the Secretary of the Treasury will find in him a knight who can tilt the lance with such precision and accuracy, as to extort a cry for quarter. It is a most scathing review of the document in which Mr. Walker set forth the beauties of free-trade—a trade free for all other countries but our own—free for every other nation on which the sun shines; but restricted, when our own country attempts to trade or traffic with a neighboring nation."—*Gazette, D. C.*

"We ask every reader of the *Whig* to give the speech of Mr. Stewart, of Pennsylvania, a perusal. It will be found on the first page of this week's paper. Mr. Stewart most successfully exposes the errors and intentional misstatements of Mr. Secretary Walker, made in his annual report to Congress. And, as this report of Mr.

Walker has been extensively circulated, we hope the speech of Mr. Stewart will be also extensively circulated and read. So effectually did Mr. Stewart expose the errors of Mr. Walker, that he has since come out and confessed to an error of four millions in amount, in one of his statements."—*Leavenworth Whig, Ind.*

"We are under obligations to the Hon. George Ashmun, the accomplished and fearless member of Congress from the 6th District, for a copy of the last speech of Mr. Stewart, of Pennsylvania, upon the tariff. A part of this speech will be found in to-day's paper, and the remainder we shall lay before our readers next week. We hope it will be read and weighed by every one who has anything at stake, or a duty to discharge, in the impending attacks on the tariff. The views of Mr. Stewart upon this great question, which he has made his study, and to the consideration of which he always brings an earnestness in some measure commensurate with the importance of the subject, we have seldom read more clearly or forcibly stated or more boldly uttered than in the speech before us."—*Transcript, Mass.*

"No man in the country has risen more rapidly in the public esteem than the Hon. Andrew Stewart, of Pennsylvania. The industry and research displayed in his masterly efforts in behalf of a Protective Tariff, on the floor of Congress, have won him the highest respect among the first minds in the country, and stamped him as a true representative of the genius of his State. Mr. S. has a fine talent for elucidating difficult and complex questions, overcoming by a sort of intuition, what requires plodding industry with most men."—*Gazette, Ohio.*

"We have perused this able speech, and consider it one among the best we ever read. We intended to have published a large portion if not all of the speech, but, unfortunately, it got misplaced, and could not be found till too late to publish it. It is well worth a place in every Whig paper in the country; '*the people*' should see and read it, and we regret that we cannot give our readers more than the closing remarks."—*Weldon Herald, N. C.*

"Upon our first page will be found an extract from the lucid speech of the Hon. A. Stewart, of Pennsylvania, which will be read with interest. Mr. Stewart has won golden opinions in the House of Representatives for his manly exposition of the 'withering curses' of locofocoism, and we are happy in being able to give extracts from a speech so sound and so patriotic."—*Voice of Freedom, Vt.*

"We regret that our limits will not permit us to make extracts from this speech, which proves that the secretary's theories and facts are always at war. He cites a number of instances of the contradictory character of his report, and stamps falsehood upon his vaunting on the admirable workings of the tariff of '46, which were made by the secretary to mislead and deceive the people with regard to its practical operations. Gross and palpable misstatements are fastened upon the report, of millions of dollars."—*Lexington Advertiser, Miss.*

"Mr. Stewart's speech upon the tariff, at the commencement of the session, has been circulated throughout the Union, and everywhere with interest. It is the most sensible, plain and candid exposition of the tariff policy that has yet been published; and will do more to enlighten the public mind upon that subject, than ten thousand reports like that of the Secretary of the Treasury. Mr. S. has examined the whole subject with the greatest care, and probably possesses more information upon the practical operations of the different systems which have been imposed upon the country, than any other man in it. He is extremely desirous of obtaining well authenticated facts respecting the prices of produce, of all kinds of home manufactures, and foreign manufactures of similar articles, and of the wages of labor at different periods since 1816."—*Rhode Island Chronicle.*

"Our readers will find in this day's *Era* the speech of the Hon. Andrew Stewart, of Pennsylvania, in answer to that of Mr. McClernand, of Illinois. We read the latter with a view to see what excuses a man could find for voting against the obvious interests and welfare of his constituents. His fulsome and nauseous flattery of the President is really too great even for a time-serving politician in Congress. The way in which he is handled by Mr. Stewart will afford our readers a treat. As to Mr. McClernand's *model* President and *model* Secretary of the Treasury, they meet with no mercy. The gross blunders of the latter are ably exposed."—*New Era, St. Louis, Mo.*

"The able and distinguished friend of domestic industry, Hon. A. Stewart, of Pennsylvania, who recently made a speech in the House of Representatives, we have already noticed, having seen his remarks on the tariff commented on in the *Union*, has addressed a letter, through the *National Intelligencer*, to Mr. Secretary Walker, explaining and vindicating his views; and dealing powerful blows at the fallacies in the Secretary's Report.—*Alexandria Gazette, D. C.*

"Mr. Stewart, in his speech on the floor of Congress some weeks since, took occasion to expose the false positions which the President, in his message, and the Secretary, in his report to Congress, had assumed in regard to the operation of the present tariff. For this, it appears, Mr. Stewart is assailed through the columns of the Goverment paper, in an article which he supposes to have been written by the secretary himself, and in which his statements are denounced as 'egregious misrepresentations;' whereupon he joins issue with the secretary on questions of fact, and calls upon that dignitary to sustain his position by proof, offering at the same time to substantiate all his own statements by official documents. Mr. Stewart has taken a stand on this question from which he cannot be driven, either by the sophistry of the President and his Secretary or the Government paper—and Mr. Polk and Mr. Walker owe it to their own characters as well as to the nation, to bring forward their facts, if any they have, or, in case they have none, then come out manfully and honorably and acknowledge that they have assumed false positions and promulgated erroneous doctrines."—*The Whig, Ky.*

"Well may the people of Fayette and the 18th District be proud of their representative in Congress. He is everywhere receiving the highest plaudits for the firm, decisive, and able stand which he has taken in defence of the American policy of protecting our own labor. In Pennsylvania, such is the enthusiasm which he has excited, that the presses, in counties where there is no Whig representative, put in a claim on him to represent *their* people, as well as his own more immediate constituents."—*The Herald, Ill.*

"In Mr. Stewart the friends of the tariff have an able champion. There is no man in Congress probably who has paid more attention to this subject, who understands it more thoroughly than Mr. S., or who is more vigilant and active in its support. War having been proclaimed by the Democratic administration of James K. Polk, against this great measure, he is prompt to sound the alarm, and array himself in its defence. In this he is well fortified by facts and arguments, and will be backed by his Whig colleagues, but the power and force of party drill may prove too strong to be resisted, and the tariff must fall! The Democracy will doubtless be found rallying almost in a body to *the standard of Free-Trade*, unfurled by the President—that President, too. who was represented by his friends in Pennsylvania, as being '*a better Tariff man than Mr. Clay!*' Shame upon the recreants who thus imposed upon and cheated a confiding people."—*The Banner, N. Y.*

"We are gratified by the returns from Pennsylvania, to see that our esteemed and distinguished friend, Andrew Stewart, is returned to Congress by a majority near six times as large as heretofore. This is not less complimentary to himself than it is creditable to the State. Mr. Stewart is a noble fellow, an ornament to our National Assembly—a man of eminent ability—long devoted to the interests of his country. To the subject of the tariff he has devoted all the energies of his powerful mind for years past, and is perfectly at home in all its intricacies. He is the great champion on this subject in the House. Devoted to the Protective Policy—armed with the argument of omnipotent fact at every point, he stands forth the able expounder of Pennsylvania's interests—the eloquent and powerful advocate of the nation's policy. Well may Pennsylvania do honor to such a man; and we prophecy that the day is not far distant when he will not only be honored as the great exponent of Pennsylvania's interests, but likewise as the champion of the rights and interests of American Freemen."—*The Press, Conn.*

"The readers of the *Voice* will notice that we occupy a large share of this number with the speech of Mr. Stewart. We have done this because we think it as valuable matter as we could present to both Whigs and Democrats, and we hope no one will leave this speech unread on account of its length. Our general plan is to put the *whole* of such documents in one number of the paper, that they may the more conveniently be preserved. Let each Democrat who sees the speech but read it attentively, and we think it will make an impression on his mind favorable to seeing things in their true light, unless he is *so* far gone that the truth cannot save him."—*Voice, N. C.*

"We have been favored with a pamphlet copy of the speech of the Hon. A. Stewart, in relation to the tariff of 1842, as recently delivered in the House of Representatives. Many of the views of Mr. Stewart are particularly interesting and able, and they will be read with the more interest now that the President and his political friends have thrown off all disguise and avowed themselves foes to a measure so vital to the interests of Pennsylvania and the nation at large. Instability of legislation is indeed one of the greatest curses of this country."—*Inquirer, N. Y.*

"We this week make some valuable extracts from the speech of Andrew Stewart, Esq., member of Congress from Fayette county, Pa., on the subject of the tariff, to which we would direct the attention of all into whose hands this number of our paper may fall. That is the grand rallying point, and the one to which we desire most to see all eyes directed. If we had nothing else in view, the honor, the prosperity, and the perpetuation of the free institutions of our country should prompt us to urge the protective policy."—*Freeman, Ga.*

"The last *Volunteer* contains the greater portion of Mr. Secretary Walker's free-trade report, and as a thorough exposure and refutation of its gross fallacies, absurdities, and sophistries, we give the able speech of the Hon. Andrew Stewart, of the Fayette district of the State. We hope our readers will give it a careful perusal, and then lend the paper to their locofoco friends who may desire to have the mysteries of Mr. Walker's report unravelled."—*Chronicle, N. J.*

"We embrace this first opportunity to find room for the unanswerable argument of Hon. Andrew Stewart, a noble son of Pennsylvania, in refutation of the sophisms of Mr. Polk and Mr. Walker, on the tariff. The speech was delivered in the House of Representatives of the United States, on Tuesday, December 9. In the first part of the speech, the 'Constitutional' objections of Southern men are answered, in relation to protection, by quotations from Washington, Jefferson, Madison, Monroe, and Jackson."—*Gazette, Mich.*

"We regret our inability to give the whole of Mr. Stewart's speech on the subject of the tariff, but we have prepared as large a portion of it for this day's weekly as we could find room for. It is one of those plain, practical illustrations of well known facts that will not fail to strike the good sense of every man who reads it."—*The News, Va.*

"The remarks of the Hon. Andrew Stewart, in defence of the tariff, and in protection to our own industry, will be found in today's paper, and we hope will be universally read, as it is a masterly and irresistible argument, and holds up the President and Secretary Walker to the gaze and the scorn of every Northern man. Never did the enemies of the prosperity of any country—never did a Tory in the Revolution receive so scathing, so withering a rebuke as has been dealt to these free-trade Tories by the Representative from Fayette. We repeat the hope that it will be read by all, and extensively published over the land, as an antidote to the poison of Polk's message and Walker's report, that will be understood by all. Circulate the document."—*Register, Maine.*

"Hon. Andrew Stewart, of Pennsylvania, the ablest champion and defender of a protective tariff in the nation, has been using up the late report of the Secretary of the Treasury. Read a portion of his speech in to-day's *Courier.*"—*Courier, New Castle, Del.*

"Would that *every member of Congress* from Pennsylvania, without distinction of party, would stand up thus nobly in defence of our dearest interests. It is a scandal and a shame that prominent and influential members from this State, whose constituents look to them to stand by a measure that has done so much to advance the prosperity of our citizens, should basely 'crook the supple hinges of the knee,' and follow the *party* in the destruction contemplated. The time may come when these faithless servants will repent in sackcloth and ashes the course they are now pursuing. In the meantime, it affords us no small pleasure to know that the Whigs will stand up to a man, and contend with the opposition inch by inch, every foot of ground upon which the tariff of 1842 rests for support. They may be defeated in their gallant endeavors to uphold a measure so fraught with benefits and blessings to all classes of the community—we fear they will—but come what may, we have the assurance they will remain true to their principles—true to their plighted faith—true to their constituents, and true to the best interests of the great body of the people."—*The Herald, Pa.*

"The speech of Mr. Stewart is one of the best, in behalf of Whig principles, which has been spoken in the Halls of Congress during the present session, and therefore, young gentlemen, as you value the privilege and feel proud of the dignity of being or soon becoming 'Independent sovereigns,' we ask you to read and study it."—*Herald of Freedom, N. H.*

"If you want your understanding enlightened upon the subject of the tariff, by clear, sound, matter-of-fact argument, don't lay this paper down until you have read the speech of the Hon. Andrew Stewart, of Pennsylvania. It is the best tariff speech we have ever read. It should be posted up in every farmer's house, in every shoe-shop, hat-shop, smith-shop, and every other kind of shop and factory from Maine to Louisiana."—*Galaxy, Vt.*

"Having referred to the *men* and *measures* most prominent in the recent Presidential canvass, we will proceed to give our impressions as to the 'why and wherefore' of victory enuring to the Whigs. Briefly, then, we regard the action of the 29th Congress upon the subject of the tariff as the principal cause of Whig success.

"Pending the discussion of the tariff bill of '46, it was declared by Mr. Stewart, of Pennsylvania, in debate, that 'the passage of said bill would be the greatest Godsend the Whigs ever had, and would inevitably cause the defeat of the Democracy in '48.'

"Prophecy has become history, and hence, not the veto, not the sub-treasury, not the Mexican war, not internal improvements, not the 'Wilmot proviso,' not the eclat of General Taylor's military services, not 54° 40′, not the extraordinary and efficient services of the Whig Congressional Committee, not Whig clubs, speeches, documents, and organization; nor yet Democratic default in these—not 'France, its king and court'—nor yet the 'extra' pay, and inclination of General Cass to 'swallow all Mexico, Cuba, and Yucatan,' caused his defeat, but mainly the reduced duty upon *coal* and *iron*. Indeed, all of these combined, though each, doubtless, measurably tending to the success of the Whigs, would have been essayed in vain but for the manifest disregard of Pennsylvania interests shown by the aforesaid *Democratic* Congress."—*Sun, Baltimore, Md.*

"Having last week given our readers a taste of Hon. Andrew Stewart's speech on the subject of the report of the Secretary of the Treasury, involving the tariff, Mexican war, etc., we have been requested by several to publish it in full, with which request we comply. We regret that we are compelled to divide it; but, without omitting other important matters, we find it impossible to give it all this week."—*Freeman, Fla.*

"Read Mr. Stewart's speech. It is made up of facts and deductions. It is a plain, sensible exposé of the tendency of Mr. Walker's tinkering. Pennsylvania may well be proud that she has in the National Legislature such a champion of her interests."—*The Journal, S. C.*

The foregoing extracts, with others, show that the tariff, or protective policy, has always been a national, and not a local question, always and everywhere, throughout the Union; supported by the Whig and Republican parties, and opposed by the Democratic party, from our earliest history up to the present time.

IN DEFENCE OF THE TARIFF AND DISTRIBUTION.

Delivered in the House of Representatives of the U. S., March 13th, 1844.

Mr. Stewart, of Pennsylvania, rose to inquire of the Chair whether the previous question, which had been called on the engrossment of the bill, would preclude discussion on the question now propounded by the Chair, "Shall this bill pass?"

The Speaker having replied in the negative—

Mr. Stewart said: However unprepared, I am nevertheless glad, sir, of the opportunity thus unexpectedly acquired of saying a few words on this important measure before its final passage. On coming into the hall a few minutes since, I was surprised, sir, to learn that this bill to repeal the Distribution Law, reported by the Committee of Ways and Means within the last hour, had been already read a first and second time under the previous question, and was now on its final passage. Sir, is this fair? is it right, that this bill, by far the most important that has occupied the attention of the present Congress, should thus be hurried through all its stages, and finally passed, under the gag, without amendment or debate? Why this hurry and haste? Why post with such dexterity to this destructive deed? Why is this important measure to be thus despatched in an hour, when days and months have been spent in the discussion of matters of comparative insignificance? The motive cannot be mistaken: its friends are afraid of discussion; they fear the development of facts which must prostrate them before the people; but they cannot escape, sir. They may, by the gag, suppress debate here, but they cannot, thank God, gag the people and the press; they can and will speak out, in tones of thunder, against the doings of this day.

The proceeds of the sales of the public lands of this country belonged to the States of this Union. It is a fund which this Government holds in trust for the people of the States; and a period has arrived in our history when, by the maladministration of this Government, a state of things has been brought about in which the States are involved in debt, a debt which was not only crushing the people of the country under taxation, but was driving some of the States to repudiation and bankruptcy. Is this Government to furnish no relief to the States of this Union? Does it owe no obligations to the States and to the people?

Are we to sit here calmly and see the States and the people of the Union crushed under the weight of direct taxation, see the character of the country disgraced, see repudiation stalking forth throughout the land, and this House and this Government, which had the power to relieve the people from their burdens and redeem this Government from disgrace, do nothing? This was a matter in which this Government was deeply interested. The interest and honor of this Government must be sustained or destroyed with the interest and honor of the States—they are inseparable—we are one people in the estimation of mankind, and share in the same glory and in the same disgrace.

Sir, you will have a surplus in the Treasury, at the end of the year, derived from the existing tariff, if let alone. And what will you do with it? Why not give the proceeds of the land to the States, to which it justly and fairly belongs? If you do not, you will be driven to the necessity of another Distribution Law to divide the surplus revenue among the States.

GENERAL JACKSON IN FAVOR OF DISTRIBUTION.

This policy was strongly recommended and urged by General Jackson, not in one, but in three of his annual messages, and it had been adopted in Congress by a majority of more than four to one, 155 to 38 in the House, and 24 to 6 in the Senate. Yet gentlemen now contend that this measure is not only highly inexpedient, but unconstitutional; and Mr. Van Buren, in his Indiana letter, declares that the people would "stultify" themselves by its adoption—a declaration by which he not only stultifies General Jackson, but himself also. General Jackson, in his first message, advocates the policy of distribution, and says, "the most safe, just, and federal disposition that can be made of the surplus revenue will be its distribution among the States, according to their ratio of representation." In his next message of 1830, he renews this recommendation, and takes up and answers, at great length, and with great ability, all the objections that had been urged against the policy of distribution—the very same objections that are here urged by Mr. Van Buren and his friends, he answered and overturned, in their order, No. 1, 2, 3, 4, occupying several pages of his message, to which he commended the gentleman from Virginia, [Mr. Dromgoole,] who had reported this bill. In his message of 1832, General Jackson again took up and discussed, at great length, the subject of the public lands: he says they ought to "cease, as soon as practicable, to be a source of revenue;" that "the idea of raising revenue from them ought to be abandoned;" that they would endanger the "harmony and union of the States;" and he expressly declares, what is unquestionably true, that these lands were pledged to the General Government to pay the revolutionary war debt, and that that debt being now discharged, the "lands were released from the pledge, and it is in the discretion of Congress," he says, "to dispose of them in such way as may seem to them best." Such are the sound and deliberate opinions of General Jackson; yet Mr. Van Buren, who concurred with him at the time, now says, in his Indiana letter, that the people would "stultify themselves by the adoption of a proposition so preposterous." These are his words—a high compliment to his "illustrious predecessor" —"a preposterous proposition," which, Mr. Van Buren says, no one but a fool would think of, and that "its agitation, he regrets to say, is calculated to degrade the character of the American people in the estimation of mankind."

These, sir, are perhaps some of the developments which gentlemen intended to suppress by the previous question.

Why not give the land proceeds to the States? We are now receiving under the tariff of '42 more revenue than we want; during the last month we have received more than two millions of dollars in the single port of New York. Suppose we receive in all the other ports in the Union no more than is received in New York, and it will amount to four millions per month, equal to forty-eight millions per year. Still gentlemen are not satisfied, and a bill has been reported by the Ways and Means to repeal the tariff of '42, because it has destroyed the revenue, and they have substituted one which they say will increase the revenue. Yes, sir, the *Globe* also, in an editorial article of the 10th of last month, stated that the last Whig Congress had "doubled the expenditures of the Government, and reduced the revenue one-half"—a statement made in the face of official documents showing that the reverse was much nearer the truth. Yes, sir, the report on the finances at the opening of this session shows that the ordinary expenditures during Mr. Van Buren's administration amounted to nearly thirty-four millions in one year, and averaged more than twenty-eight millions; while in 1842 and '43, under a Whig Congress, the average was little over twenty-three, and that the revenue had been increased by the Whig tariff of '42 from less than fourteen millions in 1840 and '41 to more than eighteen millions in 1842 and 1843, and it would be more than twenty-five, and might possibly reach thirty millions the present year. Yet the *Globe* says, in the face of these facts, that the Whigs have "doubled the expenditures, and reduced the revenues one-half!"

From present prospects, am I not justified, sir, in saying that we shall have a large surplus over and above the current expenditures? Why not then give the proceeds of the lands to the States to relieve the people of the indebted States from the load of taxation by which they are now ground down to the earth? This fund justly belongs to the States—in the language of General Jackson, this Government now holds it in trust for the States after the paying of the revolutionary debt, for which it was pledged, and a Court of Chancery, upon a bill filed, would decree this fund to the States on proof of the payment of the debt for which it was pledged. You have no use for this fund, then why, I repeat, sir, not give it to the States to which it rightfully belongs? What better use can you make of it?

Mr. Dromgoole said, pay off the Whig debt with it!

The Whig debt! I thank the gentleman for this suggestion—the Van Buren debt he should have said. Yes, sir, the existing debt was inherited by the Whigs from the gentleman and his party; it was the only legacy Mr. Van Buren had left to his country when he retired from office. He had found the treasury with a surplus of more than sixteen millions of dollars over and above the amount deposited with the States, to which add the proceeds of the bank stock, and the amount he received exceeded twenty-four millions. Well, sir, he not only expended this 24 millions with all the revenues of the Government, but he left the people saddled with a debt of $17,356,998, consisting of treasury notes, unpaid appropriations, and debts outstanding; and this was the debt the gentleman [Mr. Dromgoole] is pleased to call the Whig debt—it is ours, but we got it by descent, it came from that gentleman and his party; but the Whigs could pay it, and would pay it, if gentlemen would let the present tariff alone a few years longer. The Whigs had paid part of it, and would soon pay the whole. But if gentlemen succeeded in reducing the tariff as proposed by the Committee of Ways and Means, to which the gentleman [Mr. Dromgoole] belonged (seven out of nine of that committee were Van Buren men), this debt will soon be again doubled, especially if you superadd the extravagance and prodigality of another Van Buren administration—of which, however, sir, I am happy to believe there is not the slightest probability.

But why, let me ask gentlemen, repeal the distribution law? it is not now in operation, and it cannot operate till all the duties are brought down to 20 per cent. Why repeal it then? unless the Committee of Ways and Means contemplate the reduction of the duties to 20 per cent., for till this is done there can be no distribution under the existing law. But I have another question to ask the committee—if you repeal a part, why not repeal the whole of the law? This law gives to each of the new States 500,000 acres of choice land over and above their distributive share. This part of the law is left unrepealed, and in full force, while all the rest of the States are deprived of all the benefits of this law now and forever. As to the old States the law is repealed, but the new States are left to enjoy the benefits of its provision. Why is this so? This certainly requires explanation, and it was perhaps partly to avoid this also that the previous question has been called.

The revenue plans of the Committee of Ways and Means are wholly unintelligible to me—precisely the same measure is proposed at one time to reduce, and at another time to increase, the revenue; whether there be too much or too little revenue, the same remedy is recommended, a "*reduction of the tariff*—down with the tariff." So these political doctors have, it seems, the same remedy for all diseases. In 1832, when we had a surplus revenue of upwards of $17,-000,000 to relieve the treasury, Mr. McDuffie, then chairman of the Ways and Means, reported just such a bill as this reducing duties, and it was then supported by the present chairman [Mr. McKay, of N. C.] as a measure calculated to reduce the revenue. Now, that honorable gentleman reports a similar bill reducing the duties for the contrary purpose, the increase of the revenue; how the same measure is to have opposite effects at different times I am at a loss to discover, perhaps the honorable chairman can explain it. This bill proposes to reduce the duties to about what they were in 1840 and '41, when the revenue from imports was about fourteen millions of dollars. Now, under the present law (the act of '42) the revenue would probably be about double that amount, yet the Committee of Ways and Means propose to repeal the act of '42, and reduce the duties to about what they were in 1840 and '41, for the avowed purpose of increasing the revenue. This surely requires explanation; I cannot understand it, nor do I see how any body else can. But how, I ask, is a general reduction of duties to increase the revenue? Clearly this could only be done by a corresponding increase of imports. If you reduce your duties one-half, you must certainly double your imports to get the same amount of revenue. The Secretary of the Treasury says we will have twenty millions of revenue under the existing law, and he wants five millions more, and the Committee of Ways and Means, to accomplish this object, instead of increasing the duties one-fourth, reduce them one-fourth; clearly then they must increase imports one-half. Our imports have averaged for some years past about one hundred millions; on this, with the present tariff, the secretary says we will this year have twenty millions of revenue; reduce it one-fourth and we will have but fifteen. To make up this loss, we must import twenty-five millions more goods; and to add five millions (the required amount) to the revenue, we must import twenty-five millions additional, making an increased importation of fifty millions, to get five millions of revenue which is not wanted, and would never be acquired by this measure if it were.

But our present amount of foreign imports, viz.: one hundred millions, is sufficient to supply the demand; how then are you to make room for fifty millions more? This can only be done by destroying fifty millions of dollars of our own domestic productions, to make way for that amount of the productions of foreign industry. We must, according to this financial scheme, not only destroy fifty millions of dollars' worth annually of our productive industry, but we must send fifty millions of dollars of hard cash to foreign countries, to purchase what we now *do* produce, *can* produce, and *ought* to produce at home; and for what? To raise five millions of revenue by taxation, which is not wanted! Now, sir, I submit, is this a wise, is it an American policy? Is it not rather a *British* policy, a plan to reduce the duties and open our ports to the importation of British goods, to the sacrifice and destruction of our own mechanics, farmers, and manufacturers? Yes, sir, and this is to be done by an American Congress, and by the representatives of the American people! Can such an anti-American—such a British system as this, stand for a moment before this free and enlightened people? Pass this bill, sir, take five dollars off bar iron, and still more off iron in all its other forms, and, sir, you will go far to extinguish the fires of every furnace and of every forge in Pennsylvania. By this bill you will strike down your own mechanics—your hatters, your shoemakers, your blacksmiths, your tailors, your saddlers; in short, all your mechanics; you will paralyze and prostrate your glass works, paper mills, tanneries, salt work, collieries, lead mines—your woolen and cotton factories; but above all, you aim a death blow at the American farmers, not only by destroying their home markets, almost the only markets they now have, but what is still worse, you will convert the mechanics and manufacturers thus thrown out of employment into agriculturists, into producers instead of consumers of agricultural productions.

When you double production and diminish consumption one-half, do you not ruin and destroy the farmers of this country? And, sir, allow me to say, that in a country like this, where seven-eighths of the entire population is engaged in agriculture, when agriculture is destroyed, the country itself is destroyed. Agriculture is the great basis and foundation on which every thing else depends; when the farmer prospers, all prosper; when he sinks, all the rest, professional men, mechanics, and all go down with him. It is the great object therefore to take care of agriculture, make this prosperous and the whole country will prosper; and how is agriculture to be made prosperous but by building up and sustaining home markets. It is therefore not for the manufacturers, but for the mechanics and farmers, yes, sir, for the farmers, that I advocate the protective policy. There is one important fact which lies deep at the foundation of the whole subject, to which I am anxious to attract the attention of the farmers and politicians of this country, and it is this, that half, and more than half, of the entire price of the hundred millions of dollars a year of foreign goods imported into this country is agricultural produce raised on a foreign soil, worked up and manufactured into goods, and then sent here for sale; and that the farmers and people of this country send in this way fifty millions of dollars a year to purchase foreign agricultural produce, in the shape of goods, while foreigners take little or nothing from us; our whole agricultural exports to all the world (excepting cotton and tobacco) do not amount to ten millions of dollars a year; thus, sir, we purchase five dollars' worth of foreign agricultural produce to every dollar's worth we sell; this may seem strange, but it is strictly true; I defy contradiction—I challenge investigation. Let gentlemen disposed to contest it select an article of foreign goods, a yard of cloth, a ton of iron, a hat, a coat, a pair of shoes, any thing, "from a needle to an anchor," examine its constituent parts, the raw material, the clothing and the subsistence of the labor employed in its manufacture, and it would be discovered that more than half, often three-fourths, of the whole price is made up of agricultural produce. It is a well known fact that farmers often make hundreds of dollars' worth of domestic goods, cloths, etc., without using a dollar's worth of any thing not produced on their own farms; goods and cloth thus made are therefore entirely agricultural; and are not the same materials used in the manufacture of goods, whether made on a farm or in a factory?

Mr. S. said he had ascertained the fact from his own books kept at a furnace, that more than three-fourths of the price of every ton of iron sold, was paid to the neighboring farmers for their domestic goods, their meat and flour, that clothed and fed his hands; for their hay, corn, oats, etc., that sustained his horses, mules, and oxen, employed about his works. In England, iron is made of the same materials that constitute it here; well, we now import, manufactured and unmanufactured, eight millions of dollars' worth of iron and steel; say only half its value is agricultural produce, thus, then, we send four millions of dollars a year to purchase foreign agricultural produce, converted into iron, and sent here for sale, while our own country is filled with ore and coal, buried and useless, and the produce of our farmers left without markets. Will the farmers of this country submit to such a system as this—openly advocated and adopted to favor foreign industry at the expense of our own? Will they tamely and silently agree thus to be crushed and sacrificed? No, sir, they will not; they will speak out against this unjust and ruinous measure; your tables will soon groan under the weight of their remonstrances against it. I call on them to do so; I call on them to come to the rescue before it is too late.

BRITISH BILL.

The avowed object of this bill is to open our ports to the importation of British goods—to favor foreign farmers and mechanics, and destroy our own. Sir, give the people time to be heard, and this bill cannot pass; let it be discussed, and it can never pass an American Congress. There is one way in which it can pass—send it to the British Parliament, and it will be passed by acclamation. England would give millions to secure its passage. It had recently been stated in an official report, read in the House of Commons, that unless the American Tariff of 1842 was modified and reduced, Great Britain would have to pay the United States cash for their cotton, instead of paying in goods as she formerly had done; and this bill accordingly modifies and reduces the tariff of 1842 to suit the wishes of the British Chancellor, who, while he recommends free-trade and low duties to us, takes special care to adhere to his own prohibitory system. While this bill proposes greatly to reduce the duties on foreign distilled spirits, England exacts a duty of 2700 per cent. on ours; and this is reciprocity! This bill reduces the duties on tobacco and its manufactures, while England demands 1200 per cent. on ours, and actually collects $22,000,000 of revenue annually from our tobacco, equal to the whole revenue of this Government—such is British reciprocity and free-trade. Since the tariff of 1842, the tables with England have been turned; last year the balance of trade with Great Britain exceeded $13,000,000 in our favor, instead of being about that amount against us, as in former years. The imports of specie had in the last year reached the unprecedented amount, as appears by official reports, of more than $23,000,000, most of it from Great Britain. No wonder England and her statesmen were anxious for the reduction of the American Whig Tariff of '42. No wonder her Chancellor exclaims against the tariff, and says it will oblige them to send us specie instead of goods hereafter to pay for cotton. No wonder our country is rapidly recovering from its late depression—that its course is again onward and upward—that its former prosperity is returning—a prosperity it always had and always would have under an efficient protective system, but which it never had and never would have without it. No wonder specie had become abundant—that the banks had resumed —that exchanges had become equalized and interest reduced

—that manufactures had revived—that agriculture was recovering—that the mechanical and every other branch of the national industry was fully and profitably employed. All these were the necessary and undeniable fruits of the existing tariff policy—results seen, felt, and acknowledged throughout the land—yet, in the face of all these facts—shutting their eyes to these great lights blazing up before them—the Committee of Ways and Means have reported a bill to repeal this beneficial act of 1842, and bring us back to the low duties and the low condition of 1840. They have struck a death-blow at this policy—a policy which had vindicated its adoption by all its fruits, which had fulfilled all the hopes of its friends, and falsified all the predictions of its enemies; but shall this blow be unavailing? No, sir, it will recoil and overwhelm its authors. The people who have experienced the benefits and the blessings of this measure, will not abandon it. Even its enemies are now disposed to give it a fair and full trial, and condemn it only when it fails. Then why not, sir, wait till the people have an opportunity to pass upon this question at the approaching elections? They will then settle it one way or the other. If the enemies of the tariff policy prevail, they can and will repeal it; but if you repeal it now, and its friends are successful, it will be immediately restored. Then why not let it abide this result? Let it go to the people, let them decide it, and, for one, sir, I am prepared to acquiesce in their decision. The Committee deprecate agitation; why not, then, let the matter rest. Let the experiment be tried, and if it fails, put it down. Whence the urgent necessity of a change; what interest in the country calls for it; who has demanded it; who has petitioned for this or any other change? No one; but the Committee of Ways and Means say we must have more revenue—more revenue—and how do they propose to raise it? By reducing the duties; and this, my word for it, will result, as it always has resulted, in a reduction of revenue; it is the necessary and natural consequence. This was once the opinion of the honorable chairman of the Committee of Ways and Means [Mr. McKay] himself, and as there is now every prospect of a redundant revenue, I should not be surprised if, before the bill is disposed of, it should be advocated as a measure to *reduce* the revenue, and this report be amended by striking out the words "a bill to *increase* the revenue," and inserting the words, "a bill to *reduce* the revenue." I affirm it as a fact, and here challenge contradiction, that the revenues of the country always have been increased or diminished, as we increased or diminished the duties on foreign goods; and why will this not be the result now? [Here Mr. McKay called Mr. Stewart to order, and said it would be time enough to discuss the tariff when that measure came up for discussion].

Yes, said Mr. S., the gentleman has got a vote to print and circulate 25,000 copies of his report—his speech in favor of his bill—and no doubt he is anxious to suppress any reply; but, sir, I have accidentally got in between two previous questions, and I wish to say a little on the other side, and little it will be compared with the voluminous report of the Committee of Ways and Means, which report, I assure the gentleman, I will take great pleasure in sending to my constituents, who will readily comprehend and appreciate its destructive doctrines. But the gentleman tells me to wait till the tariff comes up for discussion; sir, this may never happen; may not the majority pass that bill, as they are passing this important bill, under the previous question? a majority may take the bill out of committee, and pass it under the gag without amendment or debate; and from the disposition evinced to suppress debate on this occasion, have we not a right to apprehend that the same course will be pursued on the subject of the tariff, which, if passed at all, must be passed under the gag—it will not bear debate.

But, sir, when I was interrupted by the honorable chairman of the Committee of Ways and Means, I was about to say, that if this bill increases the revenue to meet the demands of the treasury, it can only fulfil this office by nearly doubling importations. It repudiates protection, and adopts the horizontal plan; with a few exceptions, it brings everything down to thirty per cent. till the 1st of September, 1845, when there is to be a general reduction of all ad valorem duties to twenty-five per cent. and under, resulting in a reduction of the duties imposed by the tariff of 1842 about one-third, or say one-fourth; then it is manifest that you must import one-fourth more foreign goods to make good the loss of revenue by this reduction, and one-fourth more to raise the additional five millions required, making an increase of one-half, viz.: fifty millions, which must, of course, destroy that amount of our own production; for instance, by this bill one-half the protection is taken off hats; two-fifths off ready-made clothing; two-thirds off shoes; one-half off manufactures of iron; so that the hatters, tailors, shoemakers, and blacksmiths lose one-half of their protection, and the Treasury one-half the revenue; and to make up for this loss of revenue we must, of course, double the importation of hats, shoes, manufactures of iron, and ready-made clothing, destroying a corresponding amount of our own production, as the consumption will continue the same whether the supply be furnished at home or from abroad; three cents is taken off every pound of imported wool costing over seven cents; of course we must greatly increase the importation of wool to make good this loss of revenue.

To understand the injurious operation of this bill upon every branch of the national industry, agricultural, manufacturing, and mechanical, I would suggest to the reader to turn to the table marked "C" in the appendix to the report of the Committee of Ways and Means, where he will see the precise extent to which every branch of industry will be affected by this measure. This report itself will thus furnish the best and most conclusive evidence of the destructive effect of the proposed measure upon American labor, and its beneficial effects upon foreign, and especially British industry; hence he had denominated this a "British bill," because it was calculated to advance the interest of British mechanics, manufacturers, and farmers, at the expense of our own.

But, sir, if more revenue is wanted, why not increase the duties on luxuries consumed by the rich, rather than thus strike down the poor man's labor, and take the bread from the mouth of his children, to make room for the importation of $50,000,000 worth of foreign goods? Is this, sir, an American measure; can it receive the support of an American Congress, or the representatives of the American people? I call on the authors of this ruinous measure to come forth in its defence. I call on them to assign some reason for its adoption. I can readily discover reasons enough why England should desire its adoption, but they are the very reasons why we should reject it; just so far as it benefits them it injures us; this is a contest between foreign and American mechanics, farmers, and manufacturers, for the American market, and the question is, which side shall we take? The tariff of 1842 shuts out the foreigner, and gives the Americans the market; this bill proposes to repeal the tariff of 1842, and give it to the foreigner; to open our ports, and again flood our country with foreign goods, and export money by ship-loads to pay for them; and why? I again ask the committee upon what principle of national policy this measure is sustained?

THE TARIFF DEMOCRATIC—FREE-TRADE MONARCHICAL.

Mr. Dromgoole replied to enable bare-headed people to buy cheap hats!

Mr. Stewart. To enable bare-headed people to buy cheap hats! Sir, let me tell the gentleman if he carries this measure, the poor people of this country would not only go bare-headed, but bare-backed; they would be doomed, like the paupers of Europe, to go half-fed and half-clad. The tariff, sir, is "the poor man's law;" it is this, and this alone, that gives him employment and wages. Just as the tariff goes down, the wages of labor will go down with it. Repeal the tariff—adopt the gentleman's favorite plan of "free-trade," and you will bring down the labor here, in every department of industry, to the level of the labor of the serfs and paupers of Europe. This is certain—it is inevitable. As certain as the law of gravitation—as inevitable as that the removal of an obstruction between two unequal bodies of water, will reduce the one to the level of the other. Repeal the tariff, and what is there to prevent our country from being instantly inundated with the productions of the low-priced labor of Europe? When hatters, shoemakers, blacksmiths, and all must come down and work as cheap as they do, or give up the market! With the present facilities of intercourse by steamships, you might as well attempt to establish higher wages and higher prices on one side of a street than on the other, as to establish and sustain higher prices and wages here than in Europe, under the delusive and Eutopian scheme of "free-trade." But, sir, this scheme would bring in its train other and more fearful consequences. Adopt this scheme, and you will soon bring down and degrade the now free and prosperous labor of this country, not only to the *moral*, but to the *political* condition of the slaves and serfs of Europe. By reducing their wages, you deprive the poor man of the means of educating his children and fitting them to be free. By thus depressing one class of your people, you necessarily elevate another. You divide society horizontally into upper and lower classes—distinctions and titles supervene—jealousies and finally hostilities follow, and liberty itself is in the end swallowed up in monarchy. Such are the political and moral tendencies of every step in the direction of free-trade. The protective policy is, therefore. *democratic* in its character and tendencies, it is a policy which promotes *equality*, not by depressing one class, but by elevating all—by elevating, sustaining, and protecting the labor of your own country against the ruinous and degrading effects of a too free competition with the low-priced and depressed labor of Europe. These are views which belong to this subject, and should not be overlooked or disregarded by those who represent the free labor of this country, and especially by those who make *professions of democracy and love of the people.* Now is the time, and this is the question, to test their sincerity. Those who represent *slaves* may be excused, but those representing *freemen* will be held to a strict accountability.

THE DUTIES ADDED TO THE PRICE, NOT TRUE.

The great and leading objection to the protective policy is, that the duties are added to the price, and paid by the consumers. This objection lies at the foundation of the opposition to this policy; and, if unfounded, this opposition ought to cease. The duty is added to the price; this is the theory. Now, sir, how is the fact; what says experience? All experience proves that this objection has no existence, save in the imaginations of those who make it.

Now, sir, I lay it down as a general proposition, that there never was a high protective duty imposed upon any article, from the foundation of this government to the present day, the price of which has not been in the end reduced—greatly reduced—in many instances to one-half, one-third, and one-fourth of what it had been before those protective duties were imposed. This, sir, may seem to gentlemen on the other side to be a strong declaration; but, sir, I make it deliberately, with a full conviction of its truth, and I challenge gentlemen to disprove it—I defy them to point out a single instance to the contrary. Let them examine, and they will find invariably that wherever the duties have been highest the prices have ultimately come down the lowest, and for a very obvious reason—high duties promote competition, and competition never fails to bring down prices. This effect is invariable and universal; but unfortunately the duties always run up as the prices run down; hence the frightful lists of duties exhibited by the Committee of Ways and Means, amounting to 200, 300, and 400 per cent. When first imposed these duties were but 30 or 40 per cent.; but now, owing to the reduction of prices, they have run up to 200 or 300 per cent. By way of illustration, take the article of glass, on which a duty of $4 a box was imposed at a time when glass cost $12; this was then a duty of 33 per cent.; but now when home competition, induced by this protective duty, has brought down the price to $2 a box, the duty, owing to this reduction of price, is 200 per cent. instead of 33. The same is true of many other articles on which the duty, when imposed, did not exceed 20 or 30 per cent.; but now, owing to reduction of price produced by home competition, they amount to 200 or 300 per cent. When four cents per pound duty was put on cut nails the price was twelve cents per pound, and this duty, of course, was 33 per cent.; but now, when the effect of this protective duty has been to reduce the price of nails from twelve to three cents per pound, the duty is increased to 100 per cent. This is equally true of spikes, rods, wood screws, etc. Again, eight cents a yard duty was imposed on coarse cottons when imported at twenty cents, being a duty of 40 per cent.; but now, when the price has come down to five cents per yard, the duty goes up to 160 per cent.

Sir, I could go on and enumerate more than twenty such instances where the duties, though moderate when imposed, now actually exceed the price of the article; yet we are told that in all cases the duty is added to the price and paid by the consumer! That is, that the consumer pays $4 a box duty on glass that he buys for $2; four cents a pound on nails that he buys for three cents; and eight cents a yard on coarse cotton goods that he buys for five cents. Such are the absurdities in which these stale anti-tariff theories involve their votaries; but suppose what they allege were true in point of fact, and that the duty is really added to the price, the cost of cotton goods being twenty cents when the duty of eight cents was imposed, add the duty, the price would be, of course, twenty-eight cents a yard, and the duty only 28 per cent. instead of 160, as stated by the committee. Hence, if you raise the price fivefold then the duty is quite reasonable, and there will be no objection whatever to its payment. Let the manufacturer, then, run up his price from five to twenty-five cents a yard, and he at once silences all the objections of the Committee of Ways and Means, as this would fix the duty at 30 per cent., just what they want it. But suppose the manufacturer were, to reduce his price to one cent a yard, then the duty, being eight cents, would be 800 per cent. Horrid oppression! Who would submit to pay a duty of 800 per cent.? Who could then refuse to go with the Committee of Ways and Means for reducing such enormous duties?

But the Committee of Ways and Means say that the object of this bill is to increase the revenue by reducing the duties; yet, in the very same paragraph they say that should the revenue be found redundant, to avoid the horrid evils of deposits or distribution among the States, the duties should be instantly *reduced*, so as to reduce the revenue to the wants of the Government; at this time, the committee say, there is not revenue enough, and they propose to *increase* it by *reducing* the duties; but should it turn out that there is too much, then they say *reduce* it by *reducing* the duties. Thus a reduction of duties is alike effectual with the committee for a reduction or for an increase of revenue. Excellent disciples of Dr. Sangrado, who had but one remedy for all diseases, "bleeding and warm water." How such a palpable contradiction is to be reconciled or explained I am at a loss to conjecture.

The committee proceed next to say that it is the true policy of every interest in the country, except manufacturers, to advocate the proposed reduction of duties, and they especially name agriculture. Now, sir, in my opinion the reverse of this proposition is true; agriculture is much more interested in the maintenance of the present protective tariff than the manufacturer, and for the most obvious reasons: high protective duties are calculated to induce increased investment in manufactures. The effect of this is clearly to increase the demand for the raw material and breadstuffs produced by the farmers; and the necessary consequence of this increased demand is to increase the price of everything the farmer has to sell, and, by increasing the quantity, reduce the price of manufactured goods. Thus the protective policy enables the farmers to sell higher and buy lower; while on the other hand increased competition obliges the manufacturer to sell lower and buy his supplies at higher rates; yet it is asserted in this report, and in every anti-tariff speech, that high protective duties are imposed for the benefit of the manufacturer at the expense of the farmer. Now I submit whether practically the opposite of this proposition is not the truth; and whether such is not the necessary and unavoidable result of the great laws of *demand* and *supply*, which regulate and control prices throughout the world.

But agriculture is still further benefited by the protective policy. By increasing manufactures it withdraws a portion of the capital and hands from agriculture and converts them into consumers instead of producers, into customers instead of rivals, thus diminishing the quantity and increasing the demand for agricultural supplies, and at the same time increasing the supply and reducing the price of the manufactured goods which they get in exchange. Thus, in every point of view in which the subject can be considered, the farmer is more benefited than the manufacturer by the adoption and maintenance of the protective policy. By way of illustration, suppose in a village there is one manufacturing establishment of woollen goods, here the surrounding farmers sell their wool and other agricultural supplies; the manufacturer, having a monopoly, regulates his own prices, as well as those of the farmers, he demands what he pleases, and gives what he will. But suppose a high protective tariff on woollen goods is passed, and instead of one woollen factory there spring into existence five or six in this village; the existing monopoly is at once destroyed; there is six times the demand for wool and provisions. This increased demand necessarily increases the price of everything the farmer has to sell, and by glutting the market with six times the quantity of woollen goods, the price is necessarily reduced. Such are the plain and obvious benefits of the protective policy to the farmers; yet politicians would have them believe that they are oppressed and ruined by this policy, which can alone render them prosperous.

And here, sir, it may not be improper to remark, that Mr. Van Buren entirely concurs with the Committee of Ways and Means. In his letter to the Indiana convention he says: "The great body of mechanics and laborers in *every branch* of business, whose welfare should be an object of unceasing solicitude on the part of every public man, have been the greatest sufferers by our high protective tariff, and would continue so to be were that policy persisted in, is to my mind too clear to require furthur elucidation;" but he further says, what is much nearer the truth, that high duties are injurious to the manufacturers themselves, for whose especial benefit we are told by the committee these high duties are imposed. Mr. Van Buren says: "Excess of duties, which tempt to an undue and ruinous investment of capital in their business, is injurious to the manufacturers;" and how—by promoting competition and reducing prices? But is not this for the benefit of the consumers?

But this is not all Mr. Van Buren says against the protective policy—he says, "the period has passed away when a protective tariff can be kept up in this country," that the tariff "increases the poor man's taxes in an inverse ratio to his ability to pay," and that direct taxation is a more equal and just system of revenue than duties on foreign goods. These, sir, are Mr. Van Buren's opinions upon the tariff, as proclaimed to the world in his Indiana letter.

But let us look a little into the details and practical operation of this bill on the great agricultural, manufacturing, and mechanical interests of our country.

In the first place it greatly reduces the duties on wool and woollens of all kinds; three-fourths of the duties and more are taken from coarse cottons and calicoes; lead is robbed of more than nine-tenths of its protection. But Pennsylvania seems to be singled out for destruction. Her iron, her coal, her glass, her paper, her salt, and leather are all struck down together, and we are to go to England for iron, coal, glass, etc. Yes, sir, in 1842 we imported more than four millions of bushels of coal under a duty of $1.75 per ton. This bill reduces it to $1. Of course you must double, and doubtless you will treble the quantity imported; and for what? To increase the revenue. A few days ago Pennsylvania passed a resolution *unanimously* instructing us to go for protection "without regard to revenue." Yes, sir, these are the words, protection "without regard to revenue;" and here we are reversing the rule, going for a bill for revenue without regard to protection; voting for 20,000 copies of a report in favor of this anti-tariff, anti-American, this British bill.

But this bill greatly, very greatly reduces the duties on whiskey, brandy, gin, and wine. We must import whiskey and brandy for revenue, and give the rich their wine at one half the present duty, and they must of course drink double the quantity or we lose revenue. What say you temperance men to this? You must all get drunk on foreign spirits to increase the revenue. Tax the poor by direct State taxation, and let the rich indulge in wine, brandy, silks, and laces at lower rates! No, put the duties high on luxuries, and distribute the proceeds of the land among the States to relieve the poor from taxation. Sir, pass this bill to lighten the burdens of the rich, while you double the burdens, reduce the wages, and destroy the labor of mechanics and the poor, and go home and hear what they have to say on the subject.

The following abstract from table C, in the appendix to the report of the committee, will show the practical operation of this bill upon the mechanical, agricultural, and manufacturing interests of the country.

Names of the articles.	Present duties.	Proposed duties.
	Per ct.	Per ct.
EFFECT UPON MECHANICS.		
Clothing, ready-made by tailors	50	30
Mits, caps, binding, and hosiery	30	20
Umbrellas, parasols, and sun-shades	30	25
Silk hats, bonnets, etc.	55	25
Hat bodies	43	30
Hats and bonnets of vegetable substances	35	25
Children's boots and shoes	60	30
India-rubber shoes	30	20
Clocks	30	20
Untarred cordage	188	30
Iron cables or chains	80	30
Cut and wrought spikes	82	30
Cut nails	43	30
Brass kettles (hammered)	43	30
Japanned, plated, and gilt ware	30	25
Cutlery of all kinds	30	25
Sole-leather	53	25
Calf-skins	37	25
Bricks and paving tiles	25	15
Metal-buttons	30	25
Hard soap	51	30
Chinaware	30	20
EFFECT UPON FARMERS.		
Wheat	35	25
Beef and pork	120	25
Cheese	70	25
Vinegar	54	25
Pearl, or hulled barley	67	30
	Per ct.	Per ct
Whale or fish oil	44	30
Wool costing over seven cents per lb	3 c. per	lb. off.
Linseed oil	43	30
Spirits from grain, first proof	132	42
Brandy, etc., from other materials	180	38
Coal, per ton	$1 75	$1 00
EFFECT UPON MANUFACTURERS.		
Wool, all manufactures of	40	30
Carpetings, treble grain	87	30
Brussels	42	30
Venetian	45	30
other ingrain	46	30
Coarse cottons, (being a reduction of three-fourths)	120	30
Cotton bagging	53	30
Furniture, oil cloth	62	30
other kinds	54	30
Iron, bolts and bars	77	61
railroad	77	31
pigs	72	56
nail and spike rods	56	30
vessels cast	45	30
wood screws	63	30
Steel, cast, shear, and German	36	21
Glass, cut	186	30
window, 8 by 10	62	30
12 by 16	165	30
Lead, pigs, and bars	66	30
Gunpowder	51	30

The 12th section of the bill provides that after the 1st of September, 1845, all the duties above 25 per cent. are to be reduced to that horizontal standard, 25 per cent.

In 1842 we imported more than 4,000,000 gallons of wine, and nearly 2,000,000 gallons of distilled spirits. England imposes 2700 per cent. duty on our whiskey, and we, by way of reciprocity, now propose to reduce our duties on English and Irish whiskey (1,650,000 gallons of which, with other distilled spirits, were imported in 1842) to a mere nominal duty! The duty of twenty-five cents on wheat would also be affected. This bill brings all duties above 30 per cent. down to 30 per cent.—a horizontal tariff, except on a few specific articles; and in one year more it brings the duties down to 25 per cent., discriminating for revenue below that standard. This was bringing it nearly down to Mr. Van Buren's standard, established in his famous Indiana letter. His maximum was 25 per cent. till the debt was paid, and then 20 per cent., discriminating for revenue below that amount, but in no case above it for protection. This was Mr. Van Buren's plan, as laid down in that letter; to which he referred gentlemen who might be disposed to doubt it.

[Here Mr. S. was interrupted by a call to order from a Van Buren man.]

Mr. S. said gentlemen seemed very solicitous about order when their favorite men and measures were assailed, but nothing was out of order when it suited their purpose. Why was not the gentleman from Ohio [Mr. Duncan] called to order, when, on a bill to fix the time of holding the elections, he had introduced a coon, a dead coon, and had dissected it professionally, discussed it scientifically, inside and out; he had introduced all the Whig banners and flags of the campaign of 1840, and displayed them with great pomp, circumstance, and ceremony; and all this, in the estimation of gentlemen and of the Chair, was then perfectly in order?

DISTRIBUTION ADVOCATED.

From recent intelligence, coming in from all quarters, it is now manifest that we shall have a surplus revenue at the end of the year, independent of the proceeds of the public lands. If, then, the tariff yields revenue enough, as I doubt not it will, why not distribute the land proceeds among the States, to relieve their people from oppressive taxation? Pennsylvania, sir, owes a debt of forty millions of dollars, contracted in the prosecution of a stupendous, but ill-advised, system of internal improvement, equally important to Ohio and the whole West, and hence she had claims for assistance on this Government.

[Mr. McKay said, if she had contracted a debt of $40,000,000, let her pay it!]

Sir, if you withhold her share of the public lands, how is she to pay it? Her debt is now increasing, by the addition of $2,000,000 annually, on account of interest. She could pay it by doubling and trebling the present heavy taxation, which now crushes her people to the earth. Yes, double the taxes of Pennsylvania, and it would not pay the interest of her debt, let alone the principal.

As a Pennsylvanian, therefore, I go for the proceeds of the public lands to aid the people of Pennsylvania to pay their debt. Pennsylvania has a clear, legitimate, undoubted right to one-tenth part of the land or its proceeds. The population of Pennsylvania is one-tenth part of the population of the Union; and if we were to distribute the land itself to-morrow among the States of this Union, Pennsylvania would get more than one hundred million acres of the public lands. Would not that be an ample fund in the end to pay off the debt of Pennsylvania thrice told! Now, I claim, *as a Representative from Pennsylvania,* her share of the proceeds of the public lands; and I hope no Representative from Pennsylvania, who looks at the condition of his constituents, crushed under this weight of taxation, of unceasing and increasing taxation, would vote against it. He thought that no gentleman from Illinois, Indiana, Ohio, Louisiana, Alabama, Maryland, Michigan, Mississippi, and other indebted States, some of them more, and others almost as much, indebted as Pennsylvania, in proportion to their population and means, ought, and he hoped none of the Representatives of these States would vote, to withhold from their people their share of the land, and by so doing, rivet taxation on them and their posterity forever. By the terms of the grants or deeds of cession, these lands had been ceded by the States to the Union. And for what? To pay the Revolutionary war debt. And when that was paid, the lands were to go to the States, including the new States, and those which had made the cessions.

What does this Government want with this fund? It has an abundance of revenue, and if we relieve the people of the States from taxation by giving them what they are entitled to—the proceeds of the public lands—do we not relieve the people of these United States? Do we not relieve the people of this Government from taxation, when we relieve the people of the States from taxation? (For the people of the States and the people of the United States are the same people.)

I submit whether it is not right and fair to relieve the indebted States of this Union from the heavy burden of taxation which is crushing their people, by giving them their share of the proceeds of the public lands. The tariff, so far as it operates as a tax upon the people, is the lightest form, and least felt, inasmuch as the payment is entirely voluntary; but the chief burden of taxation in this form is thrown from the people of this country upon the foreigner, who is obliged to reduce the profits and the prices of his goods, in order to get them into market, wherever there is an American price established by American labor.

But, sir, there is another argument in favor of distribution—so long as the proceeds of the public lands come into the Treasury of the General Government, we never can have a firm, settled, established revenue policy. The fluctuations in the proceeds of the sales of the lands in past years, varying as they have from less than $2,000,000 to upwards of $24,000,000 per annum, if they are suffered to remain in the general Treasury, we must raise and reduce the tariff of the country correspondingly. I would take the proceeds of the lands and give them to the States, if for no other reason than to relieve the Treasury from this unsettled policy, and to give the country a firm and established revenue system.

In 1836, the public lands yielded upwards of $24,000,000, a sum sufficient to defray all the expenses of the Government, and of course creating an immense surplus; then we heard the cry of "repeal the tariff—down with the tariff—too much revenue." But in two or three years the proceeds of the lands sank down to less than $2,000,000; then was raised the cry of "up with the tariff." Thus, so long as the proceeds of the lands, this uncertain and fluctuating source of revenue, go into the Treasury, nothing can be settled or fixed in the tariff policy of the Government.

I hope, therefore, the representatives of the indebted States will go with me and vote down this bill to repeal the distribution act, and thus relieve their tax-ridden people from the burdens of direct taxation, and at the same time relieve the Treasury from this source of revenue, which unsettles and deranges not only the finances, but the trade and business of the country. Sir, this measure of distribution is equally important to the non-indebted States; they would receive an equal proportion of the proceeds of the lands, which could be applied to purposes of education or of improvement, or to whatever the wisdom of their people might direct.

This measure of distribution is a measure of relief to the States, and I now predict that we will have two parties in this country—the "*relief party*," going for distribution, and "*the anti-relief* and *tax party*," going for direct taxation. There were only two ways of paying the State debts—distribution or taxation; taxation, unmitigated taxation, now, henceforth, and forever. Which are you for is the question, and gentlemen must meet it. They must either go for distribution and relief, or for taxation and no relief. They have their choice, they must make it and be responsible to the people.

The improvements made by the States, and which had been the great cause of involving them in debt, are highly beneficial to the United States, in connection with the transportation of the mails, the promotion of commerce among the States, and the defence of the country in time of war; and hence, the United States was bound to help pay for them, by giving the proceeds of the public lands.

General Jackson advocated the distribution of the surplus revenue among the States, on this ground. He contends, in his message of 1830, with great truth, that the improvements made by the States, "constitute the surest mode of conferring permanent and substantial benefits on the whole Union." Besides, he contends that the money distributed by the General Government among the States, "would be more judiciously applied and economically expended, under the direction of the State legislatures." Such were some of the arguments urged by General Jackson in favor of this policy which Mr. Van Buren now denounces as a "preposterous proposition,"—the mere agitation of which, he says, is disgraceful to the character of the American people, and which his friends on this floor are now voting down, without a word of explanation or debate. What will the illustrious Chieftain of the Hermitage say to this?

THE WHIG AND VAN BUREN SYSTEMS.

But, sir, we are told that "the Whigs are a party without principles." Sir, are not their principles known and avowed every where? On this subject, the Whig system is this: Remove from the National Treasury that disturbing source of revenue, the Public Lands, and give them to the States to which they rightfully belong, to pay their debts, and relieve the people from taxation. Then regulate the tariff, so as to supply revenue enough for an economical administration of the Federal Government, by imposing protective duties on such articles as we can and ought to supply at home, and revenue duties on luxuries and articles not produced, sufficient to supply the wants of Government. This is the Whig system. Now, sir, what is the Van Buren system? Just the reverse. It is to refuse all relief to the people and the States, by distribution or otherwise; to reduce the tariff, and let in foreign goods to the destruction of our own industry; exhaust the wealth and currency of the country to pay for them; double the expenses of Government, to enrich office-holders and favorites, and leave the Government again as they left it in 1840, after twelve years' administration, impoverished, and overwhelmed with bankruptcies and debts, State and National, amounting to more than $220,-000,000. How was it, sir, during the twelve preceding years, when Whig policy prevailed? Look at the official reports from the Treasury, and you will find, sir, that during that period we paid off $141,000,000 of the war debt, expended $12,000,000 for internal improvements, and left the country with a surplus revenue of more than $12,000,000 a year, a sound currency and universal prosperity; but in 1828 there came a change. The next twelve years was a period of disastrous experiments, resulting in the excessive increase of banks, the ruin of the currency, the inordinate importation of foreign goods, the consequent destruction of agriculture, manufactures, and the mechanic arts, and the involvement of the States and people in a foreign debt of more than $250,000,000, which now hangs like a millstone about their necks. The people could stand it no longer; they determined, in 1840, to have a change—to throw off this incubus—but, by an unforseen event, this was defeated. The period is, however, rapidly approaching when the people will again come to the rescue, and achieve the great object they then had in view.

But we are told, sir, by Mr. Van Buren himself, that this glorious revolution of 1840, was the result of infatuation, folly, and madness, on the part of the people. Sir, is this true? Is it not a foul slander on the American character? Is it not a gross insult to the people, and will it not be so regarded? Sir, that election was the result of a deep and deliberate conviction of the ruinous effects of Mr. Van Buren's policy—effects seen and felt, severely felt, throughout this land. The people saw that nothing but a change—a thorough change—could save the country from hopeless bankruptcy and ruin. That conviction has since been strengthened and confirmed; and the beneficial effects of the Whig tariff of '42, now rapidly restoring the national prosperity, furnish new and powerful motives to stimulate and strengthen the friends of reform. Sir, if you want evidence, look to the unequivocal indications of public opinion throughout the country. Is not the "handwriting upon the wall" in characters so large and legible that "he who runs may read?" In 1840, the people, by the unprecedented majority of 145,-000, pronounced judgment against Mr. Van Buren. Can this be overcome without a change? And where are the changes in his favor? Where is the man who voted against him then, who is for him now? or if there be any such changes, are there not two to one the other way? But, sir, if there were nothing else, the passage of this bill, withholding from the people, in their time of need, their share of the Public Lands, and the attempt to repeal the tariff of '42, and again inundate the country with foreign goods, break down our own farmers, mechanics, and manufacturers, by the passage of this destructive, anti-American, anti-tariff bill, would of itself be abundantly sufficient to condemn *any* party, however popular, with a vast majority of the free, enlightened, and patriotic people of this country.

The people will not permit any man, or party of men, long to trample upon their rights and interests with impunity. I know, sir, they have borne much for the sake of party; they have excused bad actions by the ascription of good motives. But there is a point where "forbearance ceases to be a virtue;" that point has been reached and transcended. The people have decided upon a change, and they will have it. They expressed this determination in 1840—they will repeat it in 1844, with increased emphasis. The decree has gone forth, and is irrevocable. It is seen on every hill—it is heard on every breeze—and felt in every throb of the popular pulse. The hand is upraised, and the blow will follow as certain as the stroke of fate; as well might you attempt to avert the winged lightning or stop the thunderbolt of Jove. The popular will is formed; it is the true and just sovereignty in this land; it must be respected and obeyed. And politicians can no more stay it in its course, or avert it from its purpose, than the tempest-tost mariner can the winds and the waves that overwhelm him.

COMMENTS AND OPINIONS OF THE PRESS.

"We commence to-day, and shall finish next week, the publication of Mr. Stewart's able speech on the bill to repeal the land distribution law. We advise our readers to preserve the number containing this valuable speech, which abounds with useful and interesting matter, and will furnish them a club with which to demolish the flimsy arguments of the locofocos. Read it—study it, and make it your own—it behooves every Whig to be fully prepared to meet the adversaries of Clay and Protection. Mr. Stewart held the locos of the House very uneasy for an hour, and they tried various expedients to put him down, but without accomplishing their object."—*Palladium, Ohio.*

"We learn from Washington that the best judges there have pronounced the speech of Mr. Stewart,—part of which will be found in this paper,—to be the best delivered *on any subject* during the session. A great number of copies have been ordered by different members, for distribution among their constituents, and we cannot doubt that it will do much good. We have looked through it with a view of making extracts, but not finding any part which we could properly omit, we shall give it entire.

"We have seen no production of Mr. Stewart's in which he has displayed more strongly his ability to render the most abstruse subjects intelligible to the most common reader—It is an argument addressed, in fact, to the people, and we venture to predict that no mechanic, or farmer will or can rise from the perusal of this speech, without participating with its author, in his zeal for the 'American system.' The facts are so strong—the arguments so conclusive—the whole so plain and intelligible, all must admit their force."—*Boston Patriot, Mass.*

"All this Mr. S. saw, and with patriotic devotion to the great interests of the American people, he determined to make one more effort to save them; and how that effort has succeeded will be spoken in tones of thunder through the ballot-box next fall, and echoed from Maine to Georgia—from the Atlantic to the Western pale of civilization. Mr. Stewart is, undoubtedly, one of the ablest statesmen of his age. His whole career, since his first entrance into public life, has endeared him, not only to the people of his native state, but to the whole Union."—*Visitor, Balt., Md.*

"Another extract from this gentleman's able speech in defence of the tariff will be followed up by others. The high estimation in which it is held may be inferred from the following paragraph, which we find in a late number of the Washington Whig *Standard*:—

"'We are requested to state that the able speech of the Hon. Andrew Stewart, of Pa., in favor of the tariff and distribution, is still for sale at the office of Messrs. Gideon on 9th street, at $1 per hundred. Fifty thousand copies of the speech have already been issued and disposed of.'"—*The Mail, N. J.*

"We commend the speech of Mr. Stewart, of Pennsylvania, published in this paper, to the attentive perusal of every man into whose

9

hand it may come, be he Whig or locofoco. It is a plain and powerful common sense production, free from all vulgarity and personal abuse; and yet, strange to say, this is the speech which created such a row in Congress, exciting the wrath of that blackguard and bully, John B. Weller, and his dastardly assault upon Mr. Shriver, a gentleman little more than half his weight. We do not know that it will be necessary to publish any more speeches on the subject of the tariff. Mr. Stewart's arguments and facts are unanswerable; and that, perhaps, is the reason why the locofocos were put so completely out of humor during the delivery of his speech."—*Reporter, Penn.*

"On our outside page will be found this able defence of American labor. We commend it to the notice of our readers. It is condensed, brief and to the point. It should be read by every man, woman and child in the country.

"Especially should every farmer make himself thoroughly acquainted with its arguments. Mr. S. shows conclusively the folly of admitting foreign products, and thus breaking down our manufactures, and thus destroy the home market. Again we say, let every one read it."—*The Times, Ky.*

"We ask particular attention to the masterly speech of Mr. Stewart, of Pennsylvania, to which we have devoted a good part of our columns this week. It is a clear and unanswerable defence of the protective policy of the Whig party, and shows to a demonstration what the country may expect should the reins of government again come into the hands of the locofocos. The name of Van Buren 'will rhyme to nothing but ruin,' and with his sub-treasury and down-with-the-tariff policy, it would be ruin and distress indeed. Read it, farmers, mechanics and laboring men—then hand it to your neighbor for perusal, and a correct decision will certainly follow,"—*Courier, Mass.*

"The speech of Hon. Andrew Stewart, a Representative from Pennsylvania, will be found in to-day's paper. We commend it to our readers, assuring them that it is eminently worthy of an attentive perusal."—*The Herald, Ashborough, N. C.*

"On the first page of to-day's paper we publish the first part of a speech by the Hon. Andrew Stewart, on the tariff question, which we wish every reader of the *Register*, Whig, Antimason, Locofoco, Tyler, etc., to peruse with care and attention, giving to the facts and arguments adduced, due weight and consideration. Next week we will publish the remainder. Mr. Stewart takes a plain, practical view of the question, and defends the interests of the laboring people of the United States, against assaults made on them by the Vandal Locos, who wish to reduce them to a level with the poor of the monarchical and despotic government of the Eastern world, with signal ability."—*Banner, Ind.*

"Upon the topics of which it treats, no man is more competent to speak than Mr. Stewart. By the by, we know no one whose uniform adherence to Whig principles entitles him to more favor from the Whig party than Andrew Stewart; and in his selection by the Whig Convention, as the candidate for the office of Vice-President, they would not err. He would, we are convinced, not only prove popular with the Whigs of Pennsylvania, but with all such in other States who have regard for the peculiar interests of the working classes of our country, and the true policy of our Government."—*Herald, Frederick, Md.*

"The following is from the speech delivered by Mr. Stewart before the House of Representatives, in March last. The speech is an unique production, and the facts and arguments contained in it are sufficient to overrun all the force which can be brought to bear upon the subject of protection by the advocate of free-trade, or of a tariff for revenue only."—*Standard, N. Y.*

"We call the attention of our readers to the extracts from the speech of Mr. Stewart, of Pennsylvania, in defence of the present tariff. He handles without gloves the adherents of free-trade and the enemies of American industry. We think it next to impossible for a sane man to read his able exposition of the benefits of a tariff without being convinced of the direful results from a repeal or modification of the present salutary tariff."—*Independent, R. I.*

"A considerable portion of our paper to-day is occupied with the concluding part of Mr. Stewart's speech on the tariff and distribution question. As we intimated last week, the speech is one of the most clear, forcible, and searching papers we have met with for some time. Mr. S. handles his subject as one well acquainted with all its operations and bearings, and shows, it seems to us, conclusively, that the *Whig, Clay, American policy* is the only policy that can ever render our country prosperous and happy, and make her people truly independent, which we wish every reader of the *Register*, Whig, Antimason, Locofoco, Tyler, etc., to peruse with care and attention, giving to the facts and arguments adduced, due weight and consideration."—*Register, Conn.*

"It is a very just remark of the Washington, Pa., *Reporter*, that 'Mr. Stewart may be regarded as the shield of the Whig party on the floor of the House of Congress.' His constant watchfulness over the true interests of the people, and his fearless defence of Whig measures, entitle him to the esteem and gratitude of the whole country. With the bravery of an Achilles, he is ready for every exigency, bearing himself nobly, and to an extent successfully, through every battle."—*Statesman, N. H.*

"If you want your understanding enlightened upon the subject of the tariff, by clear, sound, matter-of fact argument, don't lay this paper down until you have read the speech of the Hon. Andrew Stewart, of Pennsylvania. It is the best tariff speech we have ever read. It should be posted up in every farmer's house, in every shoe-shop, hat-shop, smith-shop, and every other kind of shop and factory from Maine to Louisiana."—*Sentinel, Maine.*

"The extracts from the late speech of the Hon. Andrew Stewart, in another column, cannot be too attentively read and considered. Mr. S. has gained 'golden opinions' in all parts of the country, for the ability he has displayed on this subject. An eastern editor styles him the 'shield and buckler' of the Whig party in the present Congress, and well he deserves the compliment."—*Press, Mo.*

"The following strong and convincing arguments in demonstration of the practical benefits of the Farmers by the Protective System are extracted from a speech made in Congress by the Hon. Andrew Stewart, of this State. They constitute a complete refutation of the attacks made on the tariff in the locofoco papers."—*Star, Ga.*

"As we shall take occasion to refer at some length to the speech in a few days, we will now only say that Mr. Stewart is one of the most industrious and judicious advocates of protection in Congress, and has embodied in his speech all the arguments that can be adduced to strengthen his views on this momentous question. In fact, we intend to lay his speech by, and if we should ever take part in politics again, it will save us the necessity of taxing our patience for 'strong points' in favor of domestic industry."—*Gazette, Nashville, Tenn.*

"The conclusion of Mr. Stewart's able and convincing speech in defence of the Tariff and Distribution, will be found on our first page. We say to the *farmer*, who is inclined to credit the assertion made in Franklin county and elsewhere, that the existing tariff is 'ruinous and oppressive,' to read this speech, and see how their interests are to be sacrificed by the locofoco bill now undergoing discussion in the House. We say to the mechanic, look at the table on the first page and see what 'love for protection' the dear locos have." — *Whig, Del.*

"The Speech of the Hon. Andrew Stewart—referred to by our correspondent—is, by every Whig, at least, who has read it, considered well worthy of the high encomium pronounced upon it by him. That it may be even more extensively read than it has been, we shall endeavor to give it a place in our columns hereafter."—*Messenger, Ala.*

"Our readers will not complain that we have occupied the most of our space to-day, with Mr. Stewart's speech on the tariff. Let every man in favor of home manufactures, 'mark, learn, and inwardly digest' this common sense and unanswerable argument."—*Voice of Freedom, Vt.*

"We have this week commenced publishing Mr. Stewart's speech on the tariff. It is an able speech, and deserves to be read by every friend of American industry, and home protection. Read it, and then hand it to your neighbor, with a request that he may read it, and do with it as you have done."—*Sentinel, Loudon, Va.*

"In my last notice of the proceedings of the House of Representives, I unintentionally omitted giving you any account of the powerful speech of the Hon. Andrew Stewart, of Pennsylvania, on the bill for repealing the Distribution Act, and for reducing the tariff. Every effort was made to prevent Mr. Stewart's obtaining the floor and to gag him, if possible, upon the great and vital question, which its advocates wished to thrust unceremoniously upon the people of this country."—*Journal, S. C.*

PROTECTION OF WOOL AND WOOLEN MANUFACTURES.

DELIVERED IN THE HOUSE OF REPRESENTATIVES OF THE U. S., FEBRUARY 1ST, 1827.

THE bill for the protection of the Woolen Manufacturers having been read a third time, and the question being on its passage—

Mr. Stewart rose in defence of the bill. He supported it on the ground that it was a bill for the benefit of agriculture. In his opinion, no State in the Union had a deeper interest in its success than that which he had the honor in part to represent. In supporting this measure, he regretted to find himself placed in opposition to two of his most distinguished colleagues [Messrs. Ingham and Buchanan], with whom he had co-operated, with great pleasure, in support of the tariff of 1824. That bill was not more important, in his judgment, to the agricultural interest of Pennsylvania than the bill under consideration. What is the object of this bill, Mr. Chairman? It is the encouragement of the growth and manufacture of wool at home, and to prevent its importation from abroad. It is to create a home market for our farmers; a safe and a sure one, which no changes in Europe can affect. It is to prevent the importation of the agricultural produce of foreign countries, to the neglect and ruin of our own. What, he inquired, is the importation of cloth, but the importation of agricultural produce? Is not cloth the product of agriculture? Analyze it; resolve it into its constituent elements, and what is it? *Wool* and *labor*. What produces the wool? Grass and grain. And what supports labor but bread and meat? In Europe it got no more, and scarcely that. Thus cloth is composed of the grass and grain that feed the sheep, and the bread and meat that support the laborer who converts the wool into cloth. And are we to be told that it is the policy of this country, where seven-eighths of the whole population are agriculturists, thus to import annually eight or ten millions of dollars' worth of grass and grain, and bread and meat, converted into cloth, and that, too, from the starving and miserable countries of Europe, while our own are rotting on our hands? Sir, this is the policy we are pursuing, and its continuation is advocated by the opponents of this bill. That the importation of cloth is the importation of agricultural produce, may be regarded as a novel doctrine; and to assert that thousands of tons of *grass* and *corn* are annually transported from Ohio and Kentucky to the Atlantic markets, would be considered as no less strange; but it was not less true. It was transported, not in its rude and original shape, but, like the cloth, in a changed and modified condition. It was *animated,* converted into live stock, cattle, and horses. Each one of these animals carried five or six tons of hay, and fifty or one hundred bushels of corn, for consumption, to the markets of the East, which it is the policy of this bill to sustain and to increase. Hence he contended that it was a bill for the benefit of agriculture. There was no foundation for the objection urged by gentlemen, that it would "tax the farmer and ruin agriculture." This argument had been urged a thousand times against this policy. It was urged against the minimum of twenty-five cents per yard, imposed by the tariff of 1816, upon cotton. This principle was then ably and successfully advocated by his colleague [Mr. Ingham], who, he was sorry to find, opposed it now.

What had been the effect of the minimum duty imposed upon cotton? It had afforded effectual protection in that case, as it would in this. It had established manufactures in this country; and had this taxed the farmer? No. It had the opposite effect; it furnished the country a better fabric, for one half the sum it cost before. This would not be denied. Nor was this all. It had supplied a home market to the Southern planters for 180,000 bales of cotton last year, worth six or seven millions of dollars; and this market was not only permanent, but increasing; thus verifying every anticipation of its friends, and furnishing a most triumphant refutation of every objection urged by its enemies. It furnished facts and experience, in opposition to speculation and theory. And would not similar effects result from a similar policy adopted in regard to wool? Why not? He defied ingenuity itself to furnish a distinction. What was required to convert *cotton* into cloth? Capital and labor. And what was required to convert *wool* into cloth? The same—capital and labor. Then, if the capacity of the country for the production of the raw material is equal in both cases, its capacity for the manufacture of the cloth in both cases must be equal. This could not be controverted. But he contended that the capacity of the country for the production of wool was greater than its capacity for the production of cotton. Cast your eyes abroad over the Union, he said, and scarcely a State is to be found which is not, in a greater or less degree, adapted to the production of wool; yet how few do you find adapted to the culture of cotton?

If this view of the subject, then, said Mr. S., be correct, it follows as an inevitable consequence, that the protection proposed by this bill, so far from taxing agriculture, will have the same effect as that produced in the case of cotton—to diminish the price of the manufactured article, and at the same time furnish a permanent home market, not only for millions of wool, annually, but also for the flour and other agricultural products of Pennsylvania, and the other interior and Western States. Even now, without the benefit of this bill, the New England States imported last year 629,000 barrels of flour from Pennsylvania and the other agricultural States, for consumption in their manufacturing establishments, while all Europe, from whence we purchased and imported more than $60,000,000, took less than 57,000 barrels of our flour—not the one-tenth part of the amount consumed in New England. Then adopt this measure; let our farmers purchase their cloths where they can pay in their own productions, and no longer compel them, by your anti-American policy, to wear foreign wool, and support foreign labor, feeding on foreign bread, when our own fields are lying waste for want of a market for the fruits of our own labor.

There was another view of the subject in relation to agriculture, which he begged leave to submit. The fact seemed to be admitted on all hands, that, unless protection be promptly extended to our woolen factories, they must inevitably sink. The most undoubted evidence is upon our tables, of the determination of some of the most extensive woolen factories in the Union to wind up their business, having suffered a loss of 10 per cent. on their capital during the last year. The capital interested in these institutions is estimated at about $80,000,000. Refuse to pass this bill, and you not only destroy this immense capital, but you also destroy the market it supplies for millions, as your wool, flour, and other agricultural productions, and, at the same time, force this immense capital into agricultural pursuits, and compel the thousands of hands engaged in manufactures to become producers instead of consumers—rivals in agriculture instead of customers: a result alike deplorable to the agriculturist and manufacturer, and by which we may be again doomed to witness, in case of war, the disgraceful and humiliating spectacle of an American Minister applying to Congress to suspend the non-intercourse, to enable us to receive from our enemy *blankets* to cover our soldiers and fulfil our treaty stipulations with the Indians.

But, sir, we are told that this bill will create *monopolies*, and tax with a "monstrous" and "odious" taxation, the farmer, "for the benefit of a few overgrown capitalists." This is the old and often refuted argument, mere assertion, which all the experience of this country had disproved. The tendency of this policy was, Mr. S. contended, precisely the reverse of this theory; it was to destroy monopolies, and to benefit the farmer; it would increase the number of woolen establishments; increase the quantity of the manufactured articles; increase competition; and of necessity diminish the price of the manufactured fabrics, while an increased demand for the raw material, and breadstuffs, would as inevitably enhance their value. For example, the woolen establishment at Steubenville, we are told, consumes annually $50,000 worth of the agricultural produce of the surrounding country; if, by rejecting this bill, you should destroy that establishment, what would be the effect on the farmers? It would not only destroy this market, but greatly increase the quantity of agricultural produce, by converting customers into rivals; consumers into producers of agricultural produce. But suppose, sir, on the other hand, that, by passing this bill, you erect *three* other establishments at Steubenville, or in its vicinity, of equal extent —and Mr. S. had this morning received a letter from a gentleman in that part of the country, stating that he had an establishment which cost him $50,000, ready to go into operation in case this bill passed;—suppose this and two others, of which he had personal knowledge, should go into operation, would this impose an odious tax on the farmer, for the benefit of the manufacturer? Would this create monopolies? No, sir, precisely the reverse; it would diminish the quantity, by withdrawing labor from agricultural production, while it would increase the demand in a threefold degree, and reduce the price of the manufactured fabrics, by an increased production of them. Thus, the price of agricultural produce would be increased by an increased demand; and the price of cloth would be diminished by its increased production. This was the effect of this policy applied to cotton; it would have the same effect if applied to wool. He defied gentlemen to establish a distinction, unless they could reverse the order of nature, and repeal the laws of cause and effect. And this, Mr. S. contended, was the universal, the plain, the practical effect of this policy, wheresoever it had been adopted; and such would be the effects of this bill. It will secure for the farmers of Pennsylvania a market for their wool and flour, to an extent equal to that furnished for the cotton of the South; the opinions of his colleagues [Mr. Ingham and Mr. Buchanan], to the contrary notwithstanding. The farmers of this country understand the subject; they understand their own interest; they look at it practically; they know that the erection of an extensive manufacturing establishment in their neighborhood, for the consumption of their wool and other produce, is no "tax," is no injury to them; but, on the contrary, a great and positive benefit; and gentlemen reckoned without their host, if they expected to convince them by stale theories and metaphysical refinement.

Mr. S. would now dismiss this branch of the subject, on which he feared he had dwelt too long. The argument which seemed to be most relied upon was, that this measure would "destroy commerce." This argument Mr. S. considered as equally unfounded. It was a sound political axiom, that the prosperity of commerce would always be in proportion to the prosperity of agriculture and manufactures. This maxim was universal in its application to this as well as in all other countries. There could be no greater error in political economy, than to suppose the policy which promoted the interest and prosperity of one of the great departments of national industry, would destroy or injure any of the others. The interests of all were so intimately and inseparably blended together, that it was impossible to adopt a policy which would promote the interest and prosperity of one which would not promote the interest and prosperity of all. He asserted it as a general principle, sanctioned by all experience, that the policy which gave successful activity to one great branch of national industry, would soon impart its beneficial and vivifying influence to all the rest. It was like the pebble cast upon the lake, which spread its undulations to the remotest shores. Commerce was properly called the *hand-maid* of agriculture and manufactures; her legitimate office was to carry and exchange the surplus productions of the world. If, by your policy, you destroy your agriculture and manufactures, which are inseparably connected, you will destroy the office of commerce—"Othello's occupation's gone"—and your commerce must sink into a common grave with your agriculture and manufactures; they furnish the daily bread it feeds upon. Look to the history of all times, past and present; it furnishes a strong and unbroken chain of evidence in support of this position. Look to Great Britain. That country furnished an illustrious example. Where will you find so great a manufacturing nation, yet where so great a commercial country as that? And who is so ignorant as not to know that she owes her commercial prosperity entirely to the prosperity of her manufacturing institutions? Destroy her manufactures, and what becomes of her commerce, of her agriculture, of the nation? Sir, it is gone—inevitably gone; she cannot survive the destruction of her manufactures a single day; this was the vital spark which infused life and animation into her whole system; and nothing was more true than the declaration lately made in her Parliament, that a contest for manufactures was a contest for "national existence." What was it, sir, that enabled this little island to maintain a bloody contest of more than twenty years with the colossal power of Napoleon, and finally to triumph on the ever-memorable field of Waterloo? What enabled her during this period to subsidize all Europe, and support an army of 400,000 men? Sir, it was the prosperous condition of her manufactures; by these she wielded a power, derived from labor-saving machinery, equal to 200,000,000 of hands, and thus laid the world under contribution. How will you account for the ability of that nation to raise from her people for the maintenance of this war $7,038,000,000—4,653,-000,000 by taxes, and 2,070,000,000 by loans? Is it not attributable entirely to the prosperous condition of her numerous and immense manufacturing establishments? Yet we are told that manufactures are to "ruin commerce, tax agriculture, and destroy the revenue." As well might gentlemen tell us that bread is destructive to human life; or that the genial sunshine and refreshing showers are destructive to the vegetable kingdom. But suppose for a moment, contrary to all experience, that the establishment of manufactures would injure commerce. Are we to be told that the interests of agriculture and manufactures are to be sacrificed at the shrine of foreign commerce—an interest more favored and more protected than any other in the nation? Are we to be told that we must import grass and grain; import wool, agricultural produce, to keep commerce and navigation employed? With the same propriety might gentlemen advise the Pennsylvania farmer, whose grain is rotting in his barn, to send his wagon to Canada for a load of wheat, for the sake of keeping his team employed!

Mr. S. said it had also been alleged by gentlemen that this measure would greatly diminish the revenue. This he denied; and expressed the opinion that it would greatly improve the revenue. What was lost on cloths, he contended, would be more than supplied by an increased importation of other articles. The only plan to increase your revenue is, by a wise and salutary system of legislation, to increase the prosperity of the country; to increase its ability to purchase and consume foreign productions. Make the people rich and prosperous, and in the same proportion you will add to the revenue; depress the national industry, destroy your agriculture and manufactures, and your commerce and your revenue must sink with them. These he considered as sound principles of political economy, which were invariable and universal in their application. By way of illustration, Mr. S. referred to facts: At the woolen establishment at Steubenville, it appeared there was annually consumed $30,000 worth of imported goods, such as paid the highest rate of duties, groceries, coffee, tea, sugar, etc., paying into the Treasury at least $10,000 per annum. Destroy this, with the thousands of other establishments which contributed in like manner to the Treasury, and what becomes of your revenue? By this destructive policy you dry up the great springs and fountains which now replenish your public coffers; you take away the business and bread of thousands of your people; you destroy their ability to contribute to your revenue by the consumption of foreign goods; they can no longer purchase teas and coffee, silks and crapes, but are compelled to seek a miserable and scanty subsistence by the cultivation of the soil, without a market for the fruits of their labor. It is known that since the tariff of 1824, the manufacturing establishments of New England had greatly increased; and last year, when your aggregate imports were greatly diminished, the imports of Boston were $600,000 more than they were the year before—a fact, which showed most conclusively, that by increasing your manufactures, you not only supply a market for your farmers, but you also increase both your commerce and your revenue, by the increased importation and consumption of foreign commodities.

It was the great increase of the manufacturing establishments in that district of country, that prevented the commerce and importations of Boston from experiencing a decline similar to that felt in every other portion of the Union. But if the manufacture of our cloths should have the effect to diminish the revenue, would gentlemen contend that it would be a wise policy to send millions of money abroad to purchase and import wool and woolen goods, for the sake of adding a few thousand dollars to our revenue? This principle, if followed out, would result in establishing the general position, that, for the sake of revenue, we should import everything, and produce nothing. How long would such a system last? It was as absurd in theory as it would be ruinous in practice.

His colleague urged the oft-refuted argument, that this bill would lead "to frauds and smuggling." Why had it not this effect in the case of cottons, where the duties were as high, if not higher, than those proposed by this bill? It was as easy to smuggle cotton as woolen goods; yet he never heard any complaint on this score. The argument of "frauds and smuggling," however, was one of those general and common-place objections which operate against all duties, and all protection; for what duty was it that might not be as readily evaded by frauds and smuggling as the proposed duty on woolens? This was a standing argument against all tariffs; and he was surprised to hear it come from his colleague, who had always been friendly to the tariff policy.

Other gentlemen contend that the present duties are sufficiently high. This is, however, an argument against fact and experience; our tables are loaded with the most clear and convincing proofs to the contrary. Why they were inadequate, it was not very material to inquire. If it were, the reasons are sufficiently obvious. In the first place, the payment of the present *duties is evaded* by those engaged in the trade, three-fourths of which, at least, was in the hands of British merchants and British manufacturers, who, by false invoices, by importing the cloths in an unfinished state, and by various other false and fraudulent practices, defrauded the revenue, and evaded the duties. But what operated mostly against us—and it was a cause of a *permanent character*—was found to exist in the changed condition of Europe. Lately, when all Europe was in arms, the British supplied the wants of the world, all the world were her customers, and all the world paid her tribute. Since the restoration of peace, the Continental Powers of Europe had turned their attention from arms to the cultivation of the arts—the din of industry prevailed where lately was heard the din of arms—they had everywhere introduced labor-saving machinery; they had become rivals instead of customers; they had guarded themselves against British skill and British capital, not merely by protecting duties, but by whole systems of prohibitions. Russia, in 1823, had enacted a tariff recommended by Count Nesselrode, containing no less than three hundred and forty prohibitions! France, Prussia, and Germany, had pursued a similar policy. These countries have already acquired a degree of skill and perfection, in the use of scientific power, that enabled them not merely to supply their own wants, but to meet Great Britain in the fair and open field of competition, and to supplant her in foreign markets. These evils were increasing; Great Britain cannot long sustain the competition, for the most obvious reason; labor pays in France but the one-third part of the taxes imposed on it in Great Britain; and agriculture being less burdened, of course the means of subsistence were much lower.

The consequence is, that there is no longer a market for British fabrics; her manufactories must go down for want of employment. Labor, says Mr. Peel, in the English Parliament, is compelled to subsist "on a half-pint of oat meal per day." And where is England to find employment for her starving and tax-ridden operatives? where is she to find refuge from impending ruin? *In war*, by withdrawing the attention of Europe from the arts, and again engaging them in arms. England must have war; her manufacturers will be driven to desperation without it. They force their fabrics into our market at a sacrifice, because they can find a market no where else; and thus our woolen institutions must be ruined and destroyed, unless they can labor as low as the starving operatives of England; or unless the aid proposed by this bill is speedily afforded for their relief.

Will gentlemen reject this bill, and withhold this relief?

He appealed to the magnanimity, to the justice of the South, to say whether, after, by the application of the principle of this bill to cotton, by which their planters had secured a home market for six or seven millions of dollars' worth of their cotton annually, and received in exchange the manufactured fabrics at one half of what they before cost them—whether they would now withhold a similar protection from the suffering *wool* and *grain* growers of Pennsylvania, for whom they professed so much friendship? They would obtain by this bill a similar market for their products, which were now excluded from Europe. It was to this protection of this *home* market, *home* consumption policy alone, they could look for relief. He appealed to gentlemen representing the wool-growing, and grain-raising States, would they vote against this bill, and withhold this protection? Would they go home and tell their constituents that, although they had no market for their produce abroad, they should have none at home? That, though their grain was excluded from Europe, still they should be compelled to wear European wool, and support European labor, feeding upon European bread? That they would not protect our own establishments, our own markets, in the Eastern States, which last year consumed six hundred and twenty-nine thousand barrels of flour from the other States, together with wool and other agricultural produce, amounting to at least eight or ten millions per annum? Were gentlemen disposed to adopt such a course?

No country, Mr. S. affirmed, had ever flourished without manufactures, and manufactures had never flourished in any country without protection; in few countries were the protecting duties as low as ours; in most countries they were prohibitory. By this policy France had risen like a phœnix from the ashes of a wasting and desolating war of thirty years; her finances were prosperous and ample; her people industrious and happy; and every branch of her industry protected and successful. Look at all-powerful Russia, surrounding and guarding her industry with a rampart of three or four hundred prohibitions. Look, on the other hand, at the once powerful and proud, but now poor and prostrate Spain, who, by neglecting her own industry, and depending on foreign labor for the supply of her wants, had become dependent, and little better than a colony of France. Look at miserable Ireland and Portugal, dependent on England. In short, history furnishes no example of a nation adopting "the free-trade policy," neglecting their own national industry, and depending upon the industry and skill of other countries for the supply of their wants, that did not finally become dependent and tributary; and shall we not profit by these examples?

The true policy of this country, Mr. S. said, was to make *New* England, instead of *Old* England, the great theatre of our manufactures. They had the capital, and their population had become sufficiently dense to justify its employment in this way. We shall thus create in our own country, an ample market for the consumption of the cotton and sugar of the South, and the wool and flour of the Middle and Western States, which no longer found a market abroad. It will make the great sections of our Confederacy mutually dependent on each other. It will bind and unite them together by the strong ties of interest and intercourse, combining all the elements of National prosperity—agriculture, manufactures, and commerce. These, with a good system of *internal communications*, would render our prosperity perfect, and our Union indissoluble. This constituted what was properly and emphatically called the "American system of policy." It was a system he never would abandon, it was a subject on which he could make no *compromise*. He would be a traitor to the best interests of his country if he did. He would oppose those who were opposed to this system, and he would support those who supported it. His maxim was "*measures and not men;*" a maxim from which he would never depart. This system was intimately and inseparably connected with the best interests of the State from which he came, as he believed it was with those of the whole Union. He was firmly convinced that the adoption of this system alone would enable this nation speedily to attain that proud pre-eminence among the Nations of the earth to which our great advantages, natural and political, gave us a just right to aspire. Regarding the bill under consideration as a part of that system, it should have, through all its vicissitudes, his cordial and unwavering support. He concluded by expressing the hope that the motion to re-commit would not be adopted, and that the bill might pass in its present shape.

SPEECH IN REPLY.

Messrs. M'Duffie, Ingham, Cambreleng, and others, having spoken in reply, and against the bill—

Mr. Stewart again rose, in reply, and said that he had not intended to trouble the House again on this subject; but he felt himself constrained by the remarks just made by his colleague and the gentleman from New York [Mr. Cambreleng], to offer a few remarks in reply. He would vote against the motion of his colleague [Mr. Buchanan] to recommit the bill. Its recommitment at this late hour of the session, he contended, would be tantamount to its rejection. He had voted for the proposed duty on imported spirits, when offered as an amendment by the gentleman from Kentucky, [Mr. Wickliffe;] if offered as an amendment he would vote for it now. If this object, however, were deemed so important, why had not his colleague referred it by resolution to the Committee on Manufactures, while the subject was before them; or why was it not offered by his colleague [Mr. Stephenson] when the bill was in the Committee of the whole, for amendment? He would suggest to his colleague, whether he might not arrive at his object, if it were at all practicable, by having it introduced in the Senate; and if it could not be introduced there, of course, it would be stricken out if introduced here. He, however, differed with his colleague, who had declared that the proposed duty on imported spirits and hemp was more important than the duty on wool and woolens. Their relative importance appeared from the importations of 1825. The importation of wool and woolens that year amounted to about $12,000,000; while the importation of spirits, distilled from *grain*, amounted to only $484,000, and hemp to $431,000; all other spirits amounted to $1,650,000; the whole less than one-fourth of the importation of wool and woolens: hence, he thought himself justified in saying that his colleague had misapprehended the matter when he had supposed the provisions of this bill less important than the objects to which he had referred; but if the motion prevailed, Mr. S. contended, that not only the bill, but also the objects sought by the recommitment, would be lost. For this reason he would vote against the recommitment, the object of which could be attained elsewhere. But his colleague had taken occasion to declare that the bill under consideration would

10

operate injuriously on the interests of Pennsylvania; and, that if Pennsylvania was true to herself, she would vote against this bill. Against this opinion Mr. S. earnestly protested—no State in the Union was more deeply interested in the passage of this bill than Pennsylvania. It was by sustaining and increasing our home manufactures alone, that Pennsylvania is to obtain a market for her productions, now excluded from Europe by absolute prohibitions. Great Britain from whom we purchase about ten millions of dollars' worth of wool and woolen goods, annually, takes in exchange from Pennsylvania, what? Nothing but *cash*. She takes not $50 worth of all her agricultural productions!! Yet we are told if Pennsylvania is true to herself she will oppose this bill; by so doing, in his judgment, she would be false to herself, false to her interest, and false to her uniform principles and policy. What State in the Union had been so uniform, so consistent, so steady and unwavering as Pennsylvania, in maintaining the principles and policy of this bill? None—look at her votes—look at the tariff of 1824, you will find but one solitary vote out of twenty-six against it; wherefore, then, this sudden revolution, this sudden change on this subject; he was at a loss to conjecture.

The gentleman from New York [Mr. Cambreleng] might make long and ingenious speeches, he might deal in stale theories and metaphysical refinements as much as he pleased, but the real question could not be disguised. All admit that there is at this moment a struggle of life and death between the *British* and *American* manufacturers, not for the *foreign*, but the *American* market. The contest is between *New England* and *Old England*, and the question is, which side are we to take? Shall we save seventy or eighty millions of our own capital, and our own markets, for our own people, or sacrifice them for the benefit of *foreigners*, and foreigners who have shut their ports against us? The gentleman from New York [Mr. C.] has called this a "*New England* bill," and from principles of "*patriotism*," he says he is opposed to it. "It is *immaterial*," he says, "to us, whether we get our cloth from Manchester or Boston." This may suit the patriotism of the representative of a city where it is said that three-fourths of the woolen business is in the hands of *British* merchants, and *British* manufacturers; but Mr. S. took his principles from another school. For he had been told in the course of the debate by a gentleman from South Carolina [Mr. M'Duffie] that there are two schools of political economy—one headed by Adam Smith, and the other by Mathew Carey—a British and an American school, and we are warned by that gentleman against giving up the sound doctrines of Smith, for what he is pleased to call the "*Statistical Nonsense* of Mathew Carey." Now, sir, although the views of Adam Smith and other British writers may suit the purposes of the gentlemen from New York and South Carolina, yet they must give me leave to say that I would not give one page of the "*Statistical Nonsense*" of Mathew Carey on this subject, for all the theories of Adam Smith, and their long and learned speeches into the bargain.

The gentleman from New York, after the example of the gentleman from South Carolina, has volunteered a grave lecture to the Pennsylvania Delegation as to the course they ought to pursue. He has told us of the taxes and burdens this bill will impose on the farmers of Pennsylvania, and their wives and daughters; now, sir, I have only to say, that when I want advice upon this subject I will not go to the Representative of the commercial city of New York for it, to Adam Smith, or the British chancellor, Mr. Huskisson. He could assure the gentleman that the Pennsylvania farmers and their wives and daughters understand their own concerns quite as well as he could tell them. Sir, let the gentleman go with me into the interior and western parts of Pennsylvania, amid the ruins of our once flourishing manufactories. Let him ask the farmers what would be the effect of restoring these establishments. Sir, they will inform him that instead of taxing them it will add 100 per cent. to their farms, that it will revive and reanimate every branch of industry, and enable their wives and daughters again to purchase and consume foreign goods, and thus enrich the public treasury. From letters just received by Mr. S. he was informed that several extensive woolen establishments in the West, if the protection afforded by this bill were granted, would again be put in operation and again diffuse their benefits and blessings over the surrounding country. The consumption of foreign goods and groceries, paying the highest rates of duties, at all these manufacturing establishments was immense, and would more than supply all the loss of revenue by the non-importation of woolens. Hence he contended that the universal assumption that this measure would impair the revenue was founded in error. Experience showed that the importations, and of course the revenue received, last year, by the manufacturing cities of the East were greatly increased, while the revenue and importations of other parts of the Union had been greatly diminished. The arguments that this bill will destroy the revenue, destroy commerce, and tax the farmer, are all alike, they are against all experience. The policy which will enrich the country, will enrich your treasury by enabling the people to purchase and consume foreign goods. By promoting the prosperity of one great branch of national industry you promote all the rest.

Sir, the plain question is, shall we abandon our manufactures, and our agriculture, and import *agricultural* productions—wool and woolens from Great Britain, whose policy now compels her people to starve before they dare consume a mouthful of American bread, or American meat, though it were offered to them for nothing? It is made by their laws a penal offence to do so. Sir, this is the question, and gentlemen cannot escape from it. The gentleman from South Carolina (Mr. M'Duffie), adroitly attempts to evade the arguments which he cannot meet by saying that they put him in mind of "the house that Jack built." This is a reply unworthy of that gentleman. It is a reply that any body could make to any argument. It was his (Mr. S.'s) object, and the object of this bill, to sustain the houses the nation had built, which were about to fall by foreign fraud, if not by force, and which it was our duty as American statesmen to defend and uphold.

Sir, we are told that we must buy from Great Britain that she may buy from us. How is this matter? Great Britain buy from us! what does she buy from the Middle and Northern States? Sir, nothing. Great Britain, from whom we bought, in 1825, upwards of $42,000,000 merchandize—$10,682,000 of it wool and woolens, took in exchange of the agricultural produce of all the States north of the Potomac and Ohio an amount less than $500! and yet we are told by American statesmen, gentlemen representing these States, that we must purchase wool (and why not flour too) from Great Britain to induce her to purchase from us! I repeat it, and I defy contradiction, for it is proved by our records, that in 1825 the whole importations into England, Scotland, and Ireland from this country to feed and support their manufacturers did not amount to $200!! Sir, only $151! Of flour, rye, corn, wheat, oats, pulse—and every other species of grain, $88! Of all kinds of animal food—beef, pork, bacon, etc.—$34! And of all kinds of drink—whiskey, gin, beer, cider, etc.—$29! With these facts staring him in the face, the British Minister himself would blush to ask the grain growing States of the Union to "buy from them that they might buy from us." Sir, I would say to him, as I now say to the gentleman from New York, the duties proposed by this bill on British wool and woolens are too low. When Great Britain resorts to prohibition I will countervail her policy by a like resort to prohibition. If she prohibits our flour and provisions, I will prohibit her wool and woolens. We can live as independently of her as she can of us. If she will take but $151 worth of our bread and meat to feed her manufacturers, I will take but $151 worth of her wool and woolens. I will go to New England or Steubenville and buy from those who will buy from me and who will gladly give us cloth in exchange for our provisions and wool. That the cotton growing States of the South should advocate the consumption of British goods is not surprising when we advert to the fact that in the same year, 1825, Great Britain bought more than $30,000,000 worth of Southern *cotton*, and more than $3,000,000 of their *tobacco and rice*, and this single fact explains the whole secret of *their* hostility to this bill. The farmers of the Northern and Middle States must wear English wool, because England consumes Southern cotton! The clamor about destroying the revenue, ruining commerce, and taxing the farmer, was all well enough to fill up a speech. But the gentleman from New York (Mr. Cambreleng) deceived himself if he supposed the farmers of Pennsylvania were to be carried away by such arguments. They were an intelligent class of men who viewed the subject practically, and who could not be deceived in relation to it. Sir, the farmers of Pennsylvania and New York know that it is better for them, and better for the nation, to save the $10,000,000 a year which is now sent abroad for woolens, and to get them at our own manufacturing establishments by an exchange of equivalents, by exchanging wool and flour for cloth. They know, sir, that last year New England imported and consumed upwards of $3,000,000 worth of the flour of Pennsylvania and the other grain growing States with an equal amount of other provisions, while Old England took not a mouthful to feed her half-starved operatives. They know, sir, that the object of this bill is to create and sustain a home market for the consumption of their own agricultural produce which no longer finds a market abroad. They know that if this bill fails these manufactures and this market, with the millions of capital invested in them, are gone—are lost to the nation, and that the British, having thus triumphed over the American manufacturers, will demand whatever prices they please for their goods, when the competition is crushed and put down. And, sir, will the Representatives of these farmers, of these wool and grain growing States, promote this result by refusing this protection? He hoped not—for one, he would not. Other gentlemen might entertain different views, but with his convictions he would feel himself a traitor to the best interests of his constituents if he voted to embarrass or defeat the measure—a measure which he regarded as more important to the *agricultural interest of Pennsylvania* than any other provision that ever had been, or ever could be introduced into any tariff. It would create for Pennsylvania a permanent market for her wool and provisions similar to that furnished to the cotton of the South by the protection extended in 1816, to the manufactures of cotton, amounting to about $7,000,000 per annum. But the gentleman from New York has said that the importation of manufactured cotton was greater since 1816 than for a number of years before. This might be true, and still it proved nothing, for our importations were, we all know, for a long time prior to that period interrupted by non-intercourse, embargo and war.

[Mr. Cambreleng explained by saying he did not confine himself to that period.]—Mr. S. continued. It mattered not, he said: the material fact was not denied by the gentleman, that we now not only supply our own market with better coarse cottons, at half their former price, but actually export large quantities to foreign markets, where we meet the British manufacturer on equal terms, and compete with him successfully. And so it would be with reference to woolens, if adequate protection were afforded by the passage of this bill. He defied gentlemen to show why the same policy which enabled us to supply ourselves and export cottons, would not have the same effect with respect to woolens. When the duties of 1816 were imposed for the protection of cotton manufactures, precisely the same arguments were urged from all quarters against that measure, that we now hear reiterated against this. Gentlemen from the South told us then, as they tell us now, that the duties were prohibitory, that they would destroy the revenue, destroy commerce, tax the whole community, establish monopolies, etc. But experience has proved in that case, as it would in this, that these objections were unfounded. The effects were precisely the opposite of those anticipated—it increased commerce, reduced the price of cottons one-half, and furnished the planters of the South an annual home market for 54,000,000 of pounds of their cotton. These were facts, and facts which could not be controverted or denied.

If the arguments of gentlemen opposed to this bill were well founded it must be a *ruinous* measure indeed—several gentlemen had labored to demonstrate that it would ruin the manufacturers which it professed to relieve, by administering a dangerous and excessive *stimulus* to this branch of industry, that capital would be everywhere attracted to it, that the business would be overdone, the market glutted with woolen goods, that prices would consequently fall below what they now were, and thus the *manufacturer* would himself be ruined by this measure—while other gentlemen, on the same side, contend that it will ruin the farmers, and tax enormously the whole community by *increasing* the price of the woolen fabrics, that it will create odious monopolies, etc., all for the benefit of a few wealthy manufacturers! One gentleman [Mr. Archer], with great ingenuity, had supported in a long and elaborate argument both of those positions, and had succeeded in proving, no doubt to his own satisfaction, that this bill would ruin the manufacturers by *diminishing* the price, and ruin the consumers by *increasing* the price. Mr. S. would not attempt to answer arguments so opposite. They answered each other, and were thus neutralized and refuted.

As to the argument of his colleague [Mr. Ingham], that smuggling would be promoted, it was an argument against all tariffs. The existing revenue duties on teas, coffee, etc., were much higher than the proposed duties on wool and woolens, yet we hear no complaint or objections to them on account of smuggling, though everybody would admit that it was much easier to smuggle tea and coffee than it would be to smuggle wool and woolen goods. The facilities for smuggling woolens, it is said, are great in this country, on account of the great extent of our maritime frontier; and were not, he would ask, the same facilities afforded for smuggling every other species of goods? But he denied that these facilities were as great here as those existing in other nations separated from each other, not by oceans, but by rivers and such other boundaries as separated the States of this Union; yet even with these great facilities for smuggling we see these nations protecting themselves against each other, not by high duties merely, but by absolute prohibitions—prohibitions were common in the tariffs of France, England, Russia, Prussia, and indeed in every country where manufacturers had ever flourished. Some of these tariffs contained more than 300 prohibitions.

Before he concluded, Mr. S. begged leave to say a word in reply to his colleague [Mr. Buchanan], who contended that the commencement of the duties on wool and on woolen goods should be simultaneous, and this was one of the objects of the proposed recommitment. In this also he differed in opinion with his colleague. The only way to create a market for our own wool was to sustain and increase our woolen manufactures by affording them adequate protection and encouragement. To stop the importation of the raw materials at once, would leave them without an adequate supply; when our flocks were sufficiently increased, when the necessary capital had been invested, and when our establishments have got into fair and successful operation, then the duty will, according to the provisions of the bill, fall down upon the foreign wool and exclude it when the country has acquired the capacity to furnish it to the extent required. He therefore thought the postponement of the increased duty on wool for a year or two was a wise and necessary provision—when he expressed this opinion, however, he was far from concurring in the opinion expressed by his colleague [Mr. Ingham], that the whole United States did not furnish at present a supply of fine wool sufficient to make a suit of clothes for each member in this house; on the contrary, he knew of *two flocks* west of the Ohio, which alone furnished wool of the finest quality, fine enough for any member, sufficient, and more than sufficient to furnish each member *five full suits of clothes* annually!

Mr. S. said he would notice one other remark of the gentleman from S. C. [Mr. M'Duffie], and he had done. The Hon. gentleman from S. C. has said that the course I am pursuing in supporting this measure, in his opinion, so injurious to the revenue, was a course calculated to destroy what he is pleased to call my "hobby" internal improvement. Sir, the *tariff policy* is not less a hobby of mine than *internal improvement*—these are hobbies that run together, they pull the same way—they are united, inseparably united. They constituted together the grand "American System," and they must stand or fall together. The tariff was to furnish a market by establishing manufactures at home, to consume the raw materials and breadstuffs of the Middle and Western States which he had already showed were absolutely excluded from Europe by prohibitory laws, and the system of *internal improvement* was to facilitate by good roads and canals the intercourse resulting from this state of things—to facilitate the exchange of the productions of the agricultural States for the productions of the manufacturing States, thus binding the Union together by the strong ties of interest, of intercourse, and of mutual dependence. The South, Mr. S. said, would ultimately have to unite in this great system, when the cottons of Egypt, the Indies, and South America shall have driven them too from the European market; a period rapidly approaching, for gentlemen say they are now compelled to sell at a loss; they, too, will then be advocates of this policy. Sir, it is this *system of national improvement and national protection* which is to elevate this country to the high and exalted rank she is destined to hold among the nations of the earth; it is identified with the future prosperity and glory of the Republic. Sir, it is with these convictions, convictions firm and immovable, that he supported this measure, and should support every similar measure, so long as he held a seat upon that floor. But the gentleman from South Carolina [Mr. M'Duffie] would pardon him if he, in turn, should say to him that he [Mr. M'D.] also had his *hobby*, and that in his [Mr. S.'s] judgment, the course which the gentleman was pursuing was calculated to destroy his *hobby* also.

I [said Mr. S.] have ridden with the gentleman from S. C. on this hobby; but if the gentleman would compel him to go against tariffs and internal improvements, against all those great principles which Mr. S. could never abandon, he should be constrained, however reluctant, to leave him; but he thought the gentleman would fail if he made the effort to give it this direction. They [Mr. M'D. and Mr. S.] had acted together on this subject [Mr. S. was understood as referring to the Presidential question] in 1825, and under like circumstances they would act together in 1829. Mr. S. would always hold himself bound, he said, to carry into effect on this subject the *known will* and wishes of those whom he had the honor to represent, and whom he never would, knowingly, *misrepresent* on this or any other subject. His maxim was "measures, and not men;" he should always support the *measures* he thought *right*, he cared not where they originated, by whom they were supported, or by whom opposed. This was the course he had prescribed to himself—he thought it a correct course, and he would pursue it on all occasions firmly and fearlessly.

[After Mr. Stewart delivered this speech, he left the Democratic and went with the Republican party, which supported his measures—the *tariff* and *internal improvements*—the leaders of the Democratic party having exchanged with the South "measures for men," principles for promotion, Mr. Buchanan getting Secretary of State and the Presidency, Mr. Ingham Secretary of the Treasury, and Mr. Wilkins Minister to Russia, and afterward Secretary of War, and others according to their merits.

When Mr. Stewart returned home, after the adjournment, he made a speech to the people of his district—*overwhelmingly Democratic*—declaring his determination to go for Mr. Adams, and against General Jackson, saying that, with his convictions, if he did not, he would be false to himself, to his country, and his constituents; and if they chose to turn him out for doing so, all right. The Democratic party then took up the Hon. Wm. G. Hawkins, President of the Senate of Pennsylvania, residing in Greene county, which had never had a member in Congress in the district, composed of Fayette and Greene. Yet after an exciting contest, and every effort made to defeat Mr. S., he was elected by a majority of 238—225 in Fayette and 13 in Greene; while Jackson had a majority over Adams of 2800, being more than two to one in his district, a result unprecedented in the history of elections. Mr. S. was afterwards re-elected several times. In 1848, he declined the nomination to Congress, having been nominated by the convention of his district for Vice-President, for which he afterwards received a majority of the votes of the Pennsylvania delegation in the national convention that nominated General Taylor in Philadelphia, and afterwards was recommended to General Taylor, by a majority of the Pennsylvania delegation in Congress, for Secretary of the Treasury, which was declined in consequence of his confinement at the time by severe illness.

To show Mr. Stewart's motives for leaving the *strong* and *joining* the *weak* party in his district, we copy from "Niles' Register," vol. xxxii. page 412, a few of the concluding paragraphs of the speech he made to his constituents after his return home.]

SPEECH AT UNION TOWN, PA.

JULY 4, 1827.

At the celebration of Independence, at Union Town, the following toast was drunk:

Our Representative in Congress:—His untiring zeal in support of the "American System," in protecting and defending our interests from the assaults of our enemies, "foreign and domestic, open and insidious," entitles him to the thanks of his constituents, and the gratitude of his country.

After the cheering which followed this toast had ceased, Mr. *Stewart*, the Representative of the Fayette and Greene district, rose and addressed the meeting in a speech of considerable length, from which we make the following extract:

At peace with the world, the foreign relations of our country present no questions of doubtful policy of difficult determination; but the attention of American statesmen is at this time principally attracted to the great and important subject of establishing a wise and permanent system of *internal* policy, adapted to the present situation and exigencies of our country: a system, having for its object the development of our vast resources, and the improvement of our internal condition on the one hand; and on the other, to countervail the restrictive and prohibitory policy of other countries towards us, by extending equal and adequate protection to every branch of the national industry, to agriculture, to manufactures, to commerce. A system providing for a just and equal expenditure of the public revenue throughout the whole country from which it is drawn, by everywhere building up proud, and permanent, and glorious monuments of internal improvement, facilitating "internal commerce among the several States," the north with the south, the east with the west, uniting and bringing them together by strong and indissoluble bonds; promoting their defence in war, and their prosperity in peace. In short, a system dispensing its benefits and its blessings alike to all, shedding joy and gladness over this free and happy land—and what system is to accomplish this? I answer, that system to which you have just referred—the *American System*—which the next Congress will be called upon to adopt or reject. On this great question, so interesting to us all, the parties in Congress are nearly equally divided. The contest will, therefore, be obstinate and protracted. Pennsylvania holds the scale between the north and the south: if she is faithful to herself, to her best interests, to her uniform principles and policy, all will be safe; otherwise, all will be lost, and the country left in its present unimproved, dependent, and embarrassed condition. The south, and the *opposition* generally, you will again find arrayed in solid column against this system of policy.

If the present administration and its friends support, as they do, this system of policy, am I required by any of you to desert it, and join the opposition? If they support the Chesapeake and Ohio Canal, as they did—only one member in the six New England States voting against the bill, which passed on this subject—am I also to desert this favorite measure of yours, and join the opposition in opposing it? If they advocate appropriations to repair and extend the Cumberland road, must I join the opposition on this subject, too, lest I may be called an *administration man?* Who among all my constituents, would require me to pursue such a faithless, unprincipled, and dishonorable course? No, gentlemen, so far as this policy and these measures are concerned, I am an *administration man,* and should merit the just reprobation of every honest man in the community if I were not.

Gentlemen, I have no interest to promote separate from yours. From the present administration I never have and never will ask any favor personal to myself: I aspire to no higher situation than that which I derive from the kindness and favor of the people of this district; a favor and kindness already extended far beyond my deserts. In my public course, (if I know myself,) I have had but one object, and that was to promote the true interests of my constituents; these interests I have endeavored to understand. I have marked the movements of men and the progress of events with reference to those interests, when the best opportunities were afforded of forming a correct judgment, and I am free to say the result has been a firm and settled conviction, that, to promote your interest, and the interests of my country, I must support the policy of the present administration—the policy of the "American system"—it is the policy of Pennsylvania and of the nation; calculated alike to promote our prosperity, independence, and happiness, and to accelerate our rapid and onward march to greatness and to glory.

Believing, on the other hand, as I do, that it is the great and primary object of the opposition to arrest these measures, and to prostrate the system of policy, so important to us all, I shall resist their efforts; I should be base and recreant if I did not. I care not by what wiles, or with what weapons, they wage war against these measures—I care not what *names* they may assume, or with what *names* they may be associated—I care not with what mighty political instruments they may aim the mortal blow; for one, humble as I am, I will attempt to ward it off though I may fall beneath it. I have no wish, politically, to survive the downfall of these measures.

This course, gentlemen, may not be trimmed to the popular breeze; it may not tally with the present state of popular opinion; yet it is a course which accords with the great and true interests of the country, and, sooner or later, it will receive the sanction of the public approbation. Already has the course of the opposition alarmed many of our most distinguished and clear-sighted statesmen; it has opened the eyes of the farmers and manufacturers to a true view of the subject, and a just sense of their danger. The next session of Congress will remove the mask, and disclose the true aim of their batteries to every eye unblinded by prejudice. Pennsylvania, ever faithful to herself and the country, will stand erect in the hour of trials: she will never abandon her republican colors; she will not commit political suicide by uniting with any party of men in opposing her best, her dearest, her most vital interest. Patriotism, principle, policy, all unite their voices, to forbid it, and their admonitions will neither be unheard nor disregarded.

Gentlemen, I will detain you no longer. Called up by the kind expression of your approbation of my *past* conduct, I felt it my duty to give you this frank and full disclosure of the course which a sense of public duty requires me to pursue in *future:* it looks, you perceive, to measures, and not men; it is the course pointed out by principle, and I will add, by patriotism, and which I must follow at every hazard. By it I may forfeit your favor and confidence, but no earthly consideration can tempt me to betray your interest.—I offer you as a sentiment:

"*The American System,*" and its friends throughout the Union.

ON THE TARIFF.

DELIVERED IN THE HOUSE OF REPRESENTATIVES, U. S., ON THE 8th OF APRIL, 1828.

MR. STEWART rose and said, he had been deprived by sickness of the advantage of hearing most of the discussions on the subject now under debate; he was still much indisposed; but the deep interest which he felt, in common with his constituents, in this measure, forbade him to be silent.

[After receiving the bill and suggesting a variety of amendments he intended to offer reducing the duties on the raw materials, and increasing them on the manufactured goods, he proceeded to say :]

There was one cardinal principle which lay at the very foundation of the protecting system, which had been wholly lost sight of by the committee, that was, to keep the duties higher on the manufactured articles than on the raw material, otherwise the foreigner would always find it his interest to work up the raw material at home, and thus oblige us to purchase and pay for, not only the raw material, but the labor employed and the provisions consumed in its manufacture.

If one or the other must be imported, nothing can be more evident than that it is much better for the farmer that we should import the raw material than to import the manufactured article, and for this plain reason; if wool, hemp, flax, etc., were imported raw, it would be worked up by American labor, feeding on American bread and meat; but if worked up into cloth in England, we lost this market for both. Our imports of *woolen goods*, Mr. S. said, amounted on an average to from 8 to 10 millions of dollars a year, while our imports of *wool* amounted to less than half a million. The committee have told us that the wool used in making a yard of cloth is equal to one half its value, so that in $8,000,000 of cloth, there is 4,000,000 of dollars' worth of wool, and the balance of its value mostly consisted of agricultural produce, provisions, soap, tallow, wood, teazles, fuel, etc.; all these must be paid for by those who purchase and consume the cloth. A practical manufacturer had furnished him, Mr. S. said, with the cost of the component materials of a yard of cloth, the result was, that more than three-fourths of the whole price was made up of agricultural productions. Thus, in a yard of cloth worth $4.00,

There was of wool	$2 00
Provisions, fuel, soap, tallow, etc.	1 15
Profits, etc., etc.	85
	$4 00

Thus the American farmer who purchases five yards of British cloth, worth $4.00 per yard, actually pays for $10.00 worth of British wool, $5.75 of British bread, meat, fuel, soap, etc., and $4.25 only for profits, making in $20.00, $15.75 for foreign agricultural produce, while his own is rotting on his hands for want of a market, and this was the ruinous and absurd policy we are pursuing; sending 8,000,000 of dollars to England every year to purchase woolen cloth, more than three-fourths of which actually went to pay for wool and other agricultural productions, and the same thing was in a greater or less degree true in relation to twenty or thirty millions of other manufactured goods imported, viz: $4,000,000 of hemp and flax goods; $8,000,000 of cottons; $5,000,000 of iron and its manufactures, etc. These, if manufactured at home, would create a market for that amount of American labor and capital, instead of being sent abroad. This vast sum would be kept at home to enrich our own country, and reward our own industry.

This was the evil: will this bill afford a remedy? In his opinion it would not; with proper amendment it might; as it now stood it was a delusion alike destructive in its tendency to both the farmer and manufacturer.

Look at its provisions, you will find it to be a bill for the destruction, and not for the protection of American manufactures. What is the real state of the case? The American manufacturers are engaged in a struggle of life and death with the British. They say without aid they must go down; and we in fact now see them tottering to their fall. They call upon their country—they call upon us for protection. They ask for relief, and the bill offers them not protection, but additional burthens. They ask "for bread, and we give them a stone." This was not mere assertion; let gentlemen look into the bill; what does it propose? It proposes to increase the taxes 100 per cent. on the wool, flax, and hemp, purchased by the manufacturer, without giving him any corresponding protection; and this is done under the specious and delusive pretext of protecting the farmers. The farmers are not to be thus deceived; they understand their own interest too well; they want no double duties of this kind, unless also granted to the manufacturers; they want a market—a home market, created by home manufactures; they see plainly enough, that if the manufactures are destroyed, their market is gone; they have no foreign market; they can have none: their reliance, their sole reliance is on the markets at home. The idea that the interests of the farmer and manufacturer are at variance, was all a delusion; the same destiny awaits them—they must rise or fall together. Their fortunes are embarked on the same sea, and in the same vessel; they must sail triumphant before a prosperous breeze, or sink together in a common grave. They are bound together by ties, which no friendly hand will ever attempt to sever; and the labored efforts now made to create jealousies between them, had no friendly origin; it proceeded either from a misapprehension, or a disregard of their true interests.

The bill proposes to raise the present duty on coarse wool, of a species not produced in our own country, from 15 to 150 per cent., and for this enormous increase of duty on coarse wool, what additional protection is offered to the manufacturer, who is already sinking under the weight of foreign competition? Only $3\frac{1}{3}$ per cent! Thus an increase of more than 100 per cent. is proposed, to keep out half a million dollars' worth of wool, and $3\frac{1}{3}$ per cent. to keep out eight millions of dollars' worth of woolen goods. We thus exclude a handful of raw wool, and import in its stead ten times as much made up into cloth, and all for the protection of the farmers! From such protection they might well exclaim, "Good Lord, deliver us."

The bill next proposes to raise the present duty on hemp and flax, from $35 to $60 per ton, equal to about 100 per cent. But there is not one cent of protection proposed on a single article manufactured of hemp or flax, except sail duck. Now it was a known and admitted fact, that the water-rotted hemp used for sails and rigging, was not produced in this country; the consequence is, that you compel the manufacturer to pay nearly double the present duty for his hemp, while he gets not a cent of additional protection on his manufactured goods. The consequence would be his immediate and utter destruction. Then what becomes of the farmer? Where is the market for his hemp and flax? And where his market for grain and provisions? It is gone, destroyed by this ruinous system of legislation, and instead of importing raw hemp, to be manufactured by American labor, subsisting on American grain and provision, we will import the manufactured goods; for who would be so stupid as to import hemp, charged with a duty of sixty dollars per ton, when he could import it in a manufactured state, at a duty of 25 per cent.?

Next the bill very properly proposes to raise the duty on bar iron, if hammered, to twenty dollars and if rolled at thirty dollars per ton. But no increase is proposed on manufactures of iron, except 10 per cent. on a few specified articles. Thus the duty on bar iron will be about 50, while the duty on manufactures of iron is only 25 per cent. What would be the effect? Would this exclude iron? No; it would be imported in a manufactured state! Even now, without this additional temptation to fraud and evasion, the British are in the habit of getting their bar iron welded together in the form of hoops, calling it "wagon tire," and thus bringing it under the denomination of "manufactured iron," by which means they get it in at about fifteen dollars, instead of thirty dollars per ton. This shows the propriety of the rule, that the duty on manufactures should always be higher than the duty on the raw material, for it was surely better, if the foreign article must be imported—to import it in its raw state, and employ our own labor in converting it into articles for use, rather than to have this done abroad, by which foreign labor and foreign agriculture would be encouraged instead of our own.

These were some of his objections to the bill in its present form, and he now gave notice, that with a view to remove these objections, he intended to move several amendments, the object of which would be to give protection to the manufacturer, by making the duties on manufactured goods correspondent to the duties imposed on the raw material; he would therefore move in the first place, to give a progressive increase of 5 per cent. per annum on woolen manufactures, until it arrived at 50 per cent., so as to correspond with the proposed increase of the duty on wool; still leaving it the advantage over cloth of seven cents per pound, specific duty equal to about 30 per cent. on common wool. The second amendment he proposed, would be to add a progressive duty of 15 per cent. to the present duty on all manufactures of hemp and flax. This would raise the duties in the end to 40 per cent., which would fall considerably short of the proposed duty of sixty dollars per ton on the raw material. Next he would ask the committee to add a like increase to the present duties on all manufactures of iron and steel, by which these duties would also be raised to 40 per cent. The propriety of these amendments would be obvious by adverting to the present state of our importations, to which the committee, he thought, had not sufficiently attended.

1st, As to woolen goods, we import about ten millions dollars a year, while of wool we import less than half a million.

2d, Of manufactures of hemp, and flax, we import about four millions dollars, and of raw hemp and flax, little more than half a million.

3d, Of manufactures of iron, we import about three millions dollars a year, and of bar-iron, about one and a half; it was therefore evident that the great evil consisted in the importation of the manufactured goods, and not of the raw material. This was the great error in the bill, that while it proposed heavy duties on the raw material, it gave no protection to the manufactured article. The committee were all anxiety to exclude a few pounds of wool, while they permitted the importation of twenty times the amount in a manufactured shape. The bill would betray the farmer, whom it affected to favor—it would tempt him by this high duty on wool, to increase his flocks, while it would destroy even the existing markets, and leave him without any. This would be the plain and practical operation of the bill in its present shape, and it was proper that the people should know it in time to avoid it.

There was no country in the world as exclusively engaged in manufactures as Great Britain; her manufactures were the main stay of the nation, they were the great source of her immense revenue, the grand pillar that supported her agriculture, and the aliment that fed and sustained her extensive commerce. There the manufacturers pay an excise annually to the government, of no less than $138,000,000, while the whole revenue of this government amounted to about twenty millions. It was stated by writers of reputation and authority, that their consumption of agricultural produce amounted to $1,408,000,000 per annum; in that country where the policy of protecting and supporting manufactures is perfectly understood, what is the system adopted? It is precisely the reverse of that recommended by this bill; instead of putting duties on the raw material, they have taken them off to the last farthing. After the restoration of peace in Europe in 1816, when those countries turned their attention from war to the cultivation of the arts, when in consequence of this, Great Britain found her foreign markets greatly diminished, and herself in fact struggling with powerful rivals, what did she do? Look at her legislation—we see her ministers recommending the repeal of every duty which imposed a burden on her manufacturers; when we, in 1816, extended protection to our cotton manufactures, she reduced soon after her duty on raw cotton, from a penny half penny per pound, to 6 per cent. *ad valorem.* When we protected woolens in 1824, she immediately defeated the whole of our protection by reducing the duty on raw wool, from six pence sterling, to one penny per pound; and now when the American and British manufacturers are engaged in a struggle of life and death, a struggle for the American market—what a contrast does the policy of the two countries present? We see Mr. Huskisson coming forward in Parliament, with a bill to repeal all the duties affecting the manufacturer—to repeal even the penny a pound on wool, while our committee recommend an increase of 20 per cent. *ad valorem,* with a specific duty of seven cents per pound, equal to more than 100 per cent. of increase on coarse wool. Mr. Huskisson reduces the duty on hemp and flax, we increase it—he reduces the duties on all kinds of dye stuffs, indigo, etc., expressly for the purpose of favoring the manufacturers, who, he says, can no longer go ahead in the race of competition, unless every pound of burden is taken off them—do we follow his example? No, sir, whilst Mr. Huskisson takes the last feather off the back of his old and experienced coursers, to run against the Americans, what does our committee of manufactures propose? Do they propose to lighten their burdens also? No, sir, they propose to throw bags of sand upon their backs, then crack the whip, cry clear the way, a fair race. With such inequality it is impossible that we can maintain the competition, our establishments must inevitably go down unless some additional protection is afforded to countervail the effect of these heavy duties imposed on the raw materials. We have heard the highest eulogies pronounced on Mr. Huskisson, for his liberal and enlightened policy, by gentlemen opposed to the tariff; they tell us that while we are imposing heavy duties in this country, Mr. Huskisson is taking them off, and thus "freeing trade of its shackles." Do gentlemen deceive themselves, or do they wish to deceive others? True, Mr. Huskisson recommends the repeal of duties, but for what purpose? Not to leave the manufacturer without protection, but to increase his security. He begged gentlemen to look at Mr. Huskisson's speech of 1824, which had been so much admired, as a powerful defence of the principles of "free-trade." Sir, it is anything else. In the very first sentence of this profound and elaborate speech, Mr. Huskisson distinctly announces his object, which was, he said, to repeal the duties levied on the importation of "*materials* employed in some of our principal manufactories;" he then proceeds in detail to recommend the reduction of duties on wool, iron, copper, lead, etc. In consequence of the high duties on these raw materials, foreigners could undersell them, and he states the fact, that "extensive orders received at Birmingham, had been transferred to the continent, because the British manufacturer could not fill them on the terms required, in consequence of the high duty on the raw material;"—he then proceeds to recommend a reduction of the duties on a great variety of articles used by the manufacturer, descending to the most minute and trifling items—indigo, logwood, madder, shumach, verdigris, fustic, etc., etc.; these duties, he says, operate "as a premium, to encourage the inhabitants of other countries to do for themselves, that which, greatly to our own advantage, we should otherwise have continued to do for them;" and he held himself at liberty, he says, "to propose a still further reduction of these duties, should this be found insufficient to enable the British manufacturers to preserve their foreign markets;" and concludes this branch of the subject with a general provision, fixing the duties on all raw materials unspecified, 30 per cent. lower than on manufactured goods. As to wool, Mr. Huskisson says, "the duty is now one penny per pound on all foreign wool. It has been stated to me, that even this rate of duty presses heavily upon the manufacturers of *coarse woolens*, in which we have the most to fear from foreign competition, and that considerable relief would be afforded by reducing it to one half penny per pound."

Mr. Huskisson, it is true, proposes to reduce the duties

on some articles of manufacture, but it is expressly on the ground that they are so firmly established that the protection is no longer necessary; for instance, as to cotton, he says, "it will not be denied that in this manufacture we are superior to all other countries, and that by the cheapness and quality of our goods, we undersell our competitors, in all the markets of the world, open alike to us and to them —I do not except [he continues,] the market of the East Indies, (the first seat of the manufacture,) of which it may be said to be the staple, where the raw material is grown, where labor is cheaper than in any other country, and from which England and Europe were, for a long time, supplied with cotton goods; now, however, British cottons are sold in India, at prices lower than they can be produced for by the native manufacturers. If any doubt could possibly remain, that they had nothing to fear from foreign competition, especially in their own markets, it must vanish, when I state the fact, that we exported last year, £30,795,000 sterling, of cottons, [equal to $138,000,000,] yet such has been the fear of jealous monopoly, and such the influence of old prejudices, that in our book of rates, the duties, will the committee believe it?" exclaimed Mr. Huskisson, "stand at this moment, (1824,) at £75 per cent. on certain goods, on others at £67 10*s*., on a third class at £50 per cent."

"It is impossible," he says, "not to smile at the discriminating shrewdness which made these distinctions, and which could discover, that with a protection of £67 10*s*., more was necessary to make the balance incline on the side of the British manufacturers, in the market of his own country. These absurd duties, and absurd distinctions attach alike upon the productions of our own subjects in the East Indies as upon those of other countries."

Here we see Mr. Huskisson proposing to reduce the duties on cottons; and why? Because they are no longer necessary, they had acquired such perfection as to fear no competition, still he retained a duty of 10 per cent. Was it candid or fair in Mr. Huskisson, thus to ridicule "the discriminating shrewdness" of those wise statesmen, who went before him, and provided those duties? 67½ per cent., he sneeringly says, was deemed necessary to protect the domestic manufacture of cotton, and yet he himself had but just stated the reason why these duties were necessary at the time of their adoption; it was to protect the British manufacturer against the Indies, from whence, he says, they were then supplied with cotton goods, where the raw material was grown, and where labor was cheaper than in any other country. Hence it was necessary then to adopt these "*absurd*" duties of 75 and 67½ per cent. to protect the infant manufactures of England, against the old establishments of India, in the same manner precisely that it is now necessary here, to protect our infant manufactures against the old establishments of Great Britain. And, sir, I have no doubt the time will come, and it is not perhaps distant, when we too will no longer require these protecting duties; when we will be able to export to all the world, and when Mr. Huskisson will find it necessary, again to resort to these 67½ per cent. duties, to exclude American cottons as his ancestors had to do, to exclude those of India. I repeat sir, it was neither candid nor respectful in Mr. Huskisson, thus to denounce as "absurd and ridiculous," what he well knew was indispensable, and laid the foundation of their present prosperity. But his motive is not entirely concealed; these duties having answered their purpose, and being no longer necessary, are repealed; for the sake of what? The example to other countries; that they may be induced, he says, to follow our example, and abandon the protecting system; and what then? Why England would have the undisputed possession of the market; and he judged correctly as to the effect, for gentlemen on this floor have caught the bait, and are actually referring to this very speech of Mr. Huskisson, as evidence that the protecting policy is abandoned in England, and we, they say, should follow this bright example.

But what does Mr. Huskisson himself say as to his object; can any one who will examine the subject, fail to see through his policy? He says, "Let foreign countries look on and see our course, and I have no doubt when the government of the continent shall have contemplated for a few years longer the happy consequences of the system in which we are now proceeding, *that their eyes will be opened*." Yes, sir, their eyes will be opened. "They will then believe," says Mr. Huskisson, "but at present they do not, that we are *sincere* and *consistent* in our principles." No doubt, sir, very sincere in reducing duties no longer necessary. "They will then *imitate* us," he says, "in our present course, as they have of late been adopting our cast off systems of restrictions and prohibitions. That they have hitherto suspected our *sincerity* and looked upon our *professions* as LURES to ensnare them, is not very surprising, when they compare those professions with those codes of prohibition which I am now endeavoring to pare down and modify to a scale of moderate duties." These were Mr. Huskisson's own declarations; and if he could succeed by such means in inducing us to arrest our tariff, and to put our foot in the trap he has so artfully set for us, we would deserve the fate that would await us. But in conclusion, Mr. Huskisson takes special care to assure the Parliament that all the reductions he proposed were "*right and proper in principle,* and calculated to afford encouragement and assistance to their manufactures;" which was, in fact, the legitimate end and object of every tariff.

After all this, gentlemen tell us that Mr. Huskisson and Mr. Canning have yielded to the liberal system of free-trade, and that we should follow their example. They were repealing the duties imposed by Edward and Elizabeth, by Pitt and Fox, duties that protected and raised the British manufacturing skill and industry to its present unexampled height; constituting the foundation and basis of the power and the glory of the British empire; and now, when they have acquired such skill and power, perfection and extent, that they are fairly beyond the reach of competition, her ministers cry out to those who are wisely following their footsteps to wealth and independence, stop! you are wrong! you are wrong to follow the examples of our ancestors which you see us now discarding, and adopting in their stead, the new and glorious theory of free-trade. It is unwise and unmanly to resort to artificial regulations to protect yourselves against us; we are willing to meet you in the open field of fair competition. Yes, sir, the giant may well tell the stripling to lay aside the pistol, and meet him in the open field with the weapons which nature's God had supplied. Well might Napoleon dispense with arms when he had conquered the world; and well might Mr. Huskisson recommend free-trade when it would make the world tributary to England.

Mr. S. said he would now proceed to notice some of the few arguments which he had had an opportunity of hearing on this subject, advanced by his colleague [Mr. Stevenson] and Mr. Wright, of New York, who had framed this bill. In the first place they attempt to sustain it as a measure for the benefit of the farmers, and endeavor to array the farmers and manufacturers against each other. The attempt of the latter gentleman to misrepresent the report of the Secretary of the Treasury, and to show that the secretary wished to protect the manufacturer at the expense of the farmer, was uncandid and illiberal; it was utterly unworthy of the gentleman from New York. No impartial man, he affirmed, could read that able and luminous report without rising from its perusal with a full and thorough conviction, that it was the great object of the Secretary of the Treasury to advance the interests of agriculture as well as manufactures. Yet, the gentleman boldly asserts, that the secretary wishes to protect the manufacturer at the expense of the agriculturer of the country. Surely, if the honorable gentleman would take the trouble to read the whole of the secretary's report, he must be satisfied that he had done him great injustice, and he hoped he would have the magnanimity to acknowledge it. In the next place, his colleague [Mr. Stevenson] had said, that the protection extended to manufactures greatly exceeded the protection received by the farmers, and by way of illustration, he says, that the duties received on cloth last year, amounted to $3,000,000, while those on wool amounted to only $105,000; could his colleague be serious in urging such an argument? Everybody knows that the duties received was evidence of the amount of importation, and not of the amount of protection afforded. The bill proposes to raise the duty on wool 100 per cent., amounting to prohibition. Next year, if the bill passed in its present form, there would probably be no wool imported, and, of course, no duties. So that, according to his colleague's argument, there would then be no protection at all on wool, though the duties were actually raised 100 per cent.!! This was the plain and inevitable result of the gentleman's argument. This fact showed, however, another circumstance, not unworthy of notice, viz.: that the importations of cloth amounted to thirty times more than the importation of wool, and that there was fifteen dollars' worth of wool imported, worked up into cloth, to one dollar's worth imported in a raw state; and that, therefore, it was fifteen times more important to our farmers to exclude the cloth than the wool, which was exactly the opposite of the conclusion at which the gentleman wished to arrive.

The next argument offered by his colleague to justify the low rate of duty proposed on coarse woolens, was equally unfortunate. The object was, the gentleman said, to spare the farmers, the poor men, and the Southern slaves. Spare the farmers, how? by compelling them to purchase their clothing from Great Britain. The poor man would prefer American cloth, which he could procure in exchange for his own labor, to giving cash to the British, even though he got it at a lower rate. But the argument that the duty would raise the price to the consumer, was an argument against all experience; protection had, in the end, always lowered the price, as it would do now; and no real friend to the policy of protecting our national industry would use such an argument. The only sound rule upon this subject, he said, was this: that duties imposed upon imported articles which could not be produced at home, alone operated as a *tax*, while duties imposed upon what we can produce at home, always brought down the price in the end. Such always had been, and such always would be the result. In selecting objects for protection, there were four things to be considered.

First. The *capacity of the country* to produce the article to the extent required. *Second.* To encourage the manufacture of that which induced the greatest consumption of *agricultural produce. Third.* Of that which employed the greatest amount of *labor-saving machinery.* And *fourth.* Of those things for which we have now to pay *cash* to countries taking none of our produce in exchange. These were the proper objects of our attention, and among them he would number *manufactures* of *wool*, of *cotton*, of *hemp*, of *flax.* These manufactures were alone to be effectually protected by excluding the manufactured goods. You may shut out the raw material, but it will answer no purpose if you still admit the manufactured article, which must always bring the raw material with it. It was the introduction of foreign manufactures that carried off our currency by ship loads; it was this that exhausted and impoverished our country; and it was here that the remedy should be applied. To attempt to cure the evil in any other way was mere political *quackery*, it was a deception upon the country; to impose heavy duties on wool would never lead to its consumption; you must increase the ability of the manufacturer to purchase and consume it; and this was alone to be accomplished by granting him increased protection and encouragement.

But his colleague, as well as the gentleman from New York, [Mr. Wright,] had contended, that inasmuch as some of the manufacturers examined before the Committee had said, that under like circumstances they could manufacture in this country as cheap as they could in England; and then assuming that the only difference was in the price of wool, which they stated at about 60 per cent. against the American manufacturer, they endeavored, by a very long and labored argument, to prove that the protection afforded by this bill was equal to the difference in the price of wool. But could it be possible that gentlemen would attempt to persuade this house, and the American people to believe, that the American manufacturer required protection only against a difference in the price of wool? he did not intend to labor this point with the gentleman, but he would briefly direct his attention to some other circumstances which, he trusted, they would consider not altogether unworthy of consideration.

In the first place he would ask, was nothing required to protect the American manufacturer against the evasions, the frauds and perjuries which were known and admitted to be practised every day by the foreign importer, who, being in most cases the foreign manufacturer himself, he of course fixed the cost of his goods at what he pleased, and paid duty accordingly; it being the foreign *cost*, and not *value*, that governed the duties. This was a bad regulation, and he intended to submit an amendment to correct it, by fixing the value in the *American* ports, and not the cost in the *foreign* country. This was the practice in Great Britain and all other countries as far as he knew, and he saw no reason why it should be departed from here. The effect of this regulation had been to throw more than three-fourths of the woolen business into the hands of foreign merchants and manufacturers; the American merchant being obliged to pay the duties honestly according to the prices actually paid as proved by his invoices.

In the next place he would ask gentlemen if nothing was required to protect the American manufacturer against the constant efforts of our foreign rivals to break them down by throwing vast quantities of goods into the market? was nothing required to counteract the effects of the premiums and bounties which were paid by the government in Great Britain to their exporters? was nothing required to sustain the infant and rising institutions of our own country, struggling for existence against the immense capital, the skill, the experience, the combined power of the old and long-established institutions of Great Britain, exerting every nerve to strangle them in the cradle? In such a contest it did seem to him to be unworthy of American Statesmen, called upon by the cries of their suffering fellow-citizens, to look on with cold indifference, and gravely debate about a cent or two of additional protection. Sir, as Americans, in such a case we should extend the hand of assistance promptly and freely. We have millions and hundreds of millions at stake. If these institutions go down for want of protection, who will again be found willing to risk his capital in so hazardous an enterprise? when will we see these institutions again rise from the dust? where will our farmer then look for a market for his produce? where will the thousands of manufacturers thus thrown out look for employment? Was it possible, in such a crisis, when half the States of this Union had sent us their memorials, when our tables groaned under the loads of petitions daily presented from all parts of the country, calling upon us to protect the American against the British manufacturer—was it possible to sit here deliberating, day after day, week after week, and month after month, to determine whether we will save these establishments or not? For the character of the country he hoped not; he hoped an adequate protection would be granted, and granted promptly.

There was one other consideration which rendered increased protection necessary at this time. Since the restoration of peace in Europe, many of the continental powers have turned their attention to the erection and encouragement of manufactures, and instead of being customers have become powerful rivals of Great Britain. The natural effect has been, to throw thousands of the British manufacturers out of employ, who, of course, become paupers. The government was, therefore, compelled to support them at an expense of about twenty-five millions of dollars a year. To reduce the amount of this expense, the government agreed with the manufacturer, that if they will keep them employed, the government will pay one-half, one-third, one fourth, or one-fifth of their wages, the manufacturer paying the balance; hence, the British manufacturer having a considerable portion of the wages of his hands paid out of the poor rates, was enabled to undersell the American manufacturer. If gentlemen would place the Americans on an equal footing in this respect, by paying their laborers, they would not be troubled for further protection. These were some of the reasons which rendered additional protection necessary, and which showed that the difference in the price of wool was not the only thing against which protection was required, as had been contended by his colleague [Mr. Stevenson] and the gentleman from New York.

Much had been said about the Harrisburg convention and American System, they had been often, and he thought unnecessarily introduced into this debate, and made the subjects of much censure, and unmerited abuse. The Harrisburg convention represented the feelings and sentiments of a large majority of the people of this nation; they had assembled from half the States of this Union; and for talent and patriotism, in his opinion, they were inferior to no convention of men, that had ever assembled on a similar occasion, in this or in any other country, and he regretted that their recommendations had been so little attended to by the committee of manufactures.

As to the "American System," language furnishes no term of reproach or abuse, that has not been applied to it; it had been called a system of robbery, of oppression, and of injustice, which ought and should be resisted. This was strong language, to say the least of it, and he hoped the feeling in which gentlemen indulged would pass away with the occasion; he could not forbear to express his regret at seeing his colleague [Mr. Stevenson] joining the enemies of the tariff in this hue and cry against the American System. He calls this system a "cant phrase," and a by-word. Mr. S. said he entertained very different views upon this subject. "The American System," which he understood to mean the policy of protecting domestic manufactures, and promoting internal improvements, he considered as constituting a system of national policy, which lay at the foundation of the present contest for political power. The great question to be decided was, whether the American System was to be established or put down; this was the true question at issue, and it was in vain to disguise it—it could not be disguised in this house, and it could not be much longer disguised in this country. The line had been already so often and so distinctly drawn, that every one must see and understand it; the contest was no longer between federalists and democrats, but between the *friends* and *enemies* of domestic manufactures. Already we see the forces not only marshalled in this house, but throughout the nation on this great question. A majority of the States of this Union have pledged themselves by solemn legislative resolves, to support the one side or the other. On the one side we see most of the Southern States, Virginia, North Carolina, South Carolina, Georgia, Alabama, Mississippi, Tennessee, etc. On the other side we see New Hampshire, Vermont, Connecticut, Massachusetts, Rhode Island, New York, Pennsylvania, Delaware, Ohio, Indiana, etc. The enemies of this policy, fearful of the result, if this be made the question in the Northern and Middle States, have artfully endeavored to divert public attention from it, by holding out the idea, that the contest is between the old *federal* and *democratic* parties. The absurdity, however, of this must be apparent when we advert to the fact, that there are not more than twenty-eight federalists in both Houses of Congress, and these about equally divided on the Presidential question. It was therefore evident, that the old party names had nothing to do with the present contest. The division of parties now stood on new ground, and must be determined on new principles; the fate of the American System was the question to be determined, and it became every man to take his stand on the one side or the other. Mr. S. said he had no hesitation as to his course, he would support the men who supported these measures, which he regarded as connected with the lasting prosperity of this country. There was, however, another and an opposite system to the one just mentioned, called the British System—a system, which made every merchant and storekeeper in this country a collector for British merchants and manufacturers. The British merchants and manufacturers import their goods, sell them at auction, receive the amount, duties and all in cash; for the duties (about one-third of the whole amount) they give bond without interest to the government, payable in six, eight, and twelve months, which, in three voyages will be more than equal to the whole value of the original cargo. Your country merchants who purchase these goods carry them into every part of the Union, sell them for cash, return to the Atlantic cities to give it again to the British merchants and manufacturers for a fresh supply; and thus the country was impoverished and exhausted. This was the true source of the distress and embarrassment so universally complained of, and such were the effects of the British System, as contradistinguished from the American System. His colleague had said, however, that too much prosperity weakened, while adversity strengthened the bonds of our Union. If this were true, the gentleman's plan would certainly perpetuate the union by keeping us in poverty; but he denied the soundness of the argument, he maintained the reverse of this proposition, a system which would grind down the people, would weaken their attachment to the government, which was after all the only genuine cement that was to preserve this noble edifice from falling to pieces. Strengthen the attachment of the people to the laws and government, and you will strengthen the bonds that bind us together.

Several gentlemen, Mr. S. said, had referred to a statement made by him at the last session on this subject; it had also been noticed in many of the public prints, and had called down upon him the severe animadversion of the authors of the celebrated Boston report. The statement he had made was, that in 1825, Great Britain did not take more than $500 worth of the agricultural produce of all the States north of the Ohio and Potomac to feed her manufacturers. This had been contradicted, and reference had been made to the commerce and navigation of that year, to show that $108,000 worth of flour had been exported in that year to Great Britain; so it appeared by the custom-house books. But who was so ignorant as not to know, that not a pound of this flour ever went to Great Britain:—it was impossible according to the existing laws of Great Britain. During the whole of that year, and for a long time before, the British corn laws were prohibitory, and did not admit the importation of a single pound of flour, or a bushel of grain, from any foreign country; of course no part of this flour could have entered into her consumption. What other productions of the farmers of this country were exported to Great Britain in that year? If gentlemen would take the trouble to examine, they would find that all the productions of animals, meat of all kinds, butter, cheese, beef, pork, bacon, etc., exported in 1825 to Great Britain, amounted in all to *thirty-four dollars;* and of beer, porter, cider, spirits, molasses, sugar, etc., the amount was *thirty-six dollars.* So that, instead of $500, it appears at the utmost extent, her importation of grain and provisions of all kinds from the United States, in 1825, could not have exceeded $70; and he would no doubt be safe in saying seventy cents; for doubtless this $70 worth of bacon, beef, pork, beer, cider, spirits, etc., was consumed by the sailors long before it reached its port of destination.

It might be asked, what became of the $108,000 worth of flour? This was easily explained; we know that very often cargoes shipped to Great Britain never go there; part of a cargo may be disposed of at the port for which the vessel clears out, and part in another country, for instance: the cotton part of a cargo might be sold in England, and the flour which could not be sold there might be carried to France, Spain, or some other country. Vessels, it is well known, often clear out for *Cowes* (a port on the British coast,) *and a market.* These vessels merely touch at this port to ascertain the state of the foreign markets and regulate their ulterior destination accordingly. Yet the whole cargo of every vessel cleared out for "*Cowes and a market,*" was entered at our custom-houses as exported to Great Britain; hence our exports to Great Britain appeared much greater than they really were; this accounted for the $108,000 of flour apparently exported to Great Britain in 1825. Mr. S. therefore contended, that instead of $500 there was not $100 worth of American provisions of every kind sent to Great Britain in the year referred to; and yet we are required to purchase from Great Britain, that she may purchase from us. Could such a course of policy as this find an advocate in any of the grain growing States of the Union? Our commerce with Great Britain was on a much more favorable footing before the Revolution. Whilst colonies, she admitted our productions in exchange for her manufactures, as she now did from her other colonies. As soon as we achieved our independence, she commenced her system of exclusion, which she has systematically maintained ever since; and now enforces with so much rigor, that recently an American merchant was prohibited from selling to the manufacturer who supplied his cargo, a few barrels of damaged flour as *sizing*, on the ground that it would be a violation of their corn laws. In referring to the early history of our commerce with Great Britain, Mr. S. said, he found a fact which confirmed the statement he had just made, it was this: that for six years before the Revolution, viz., from 1768 to 1774, our imports from Great Britain averaged about $10,000,000 per annum, and our exports $8,000,000, leaving a balance against us of only $2,000,000 a year; and for six years after the Revolution, viz., from 1783 to 1789, though we continued to purchase the same amount from her, she took less than $4,000,000, only half the amount she received from us before, leaving a balance of nearly $6,000,000 a year against us. So far, therefore, as our commerce is concerned, it would have been better if we had continued colonies, unless we return "measure for measure," when she ceases to take from us, cease to receive from her. The balance of trade with Great Britain was now more than $7,000,000 against us; exclude cotton, and it will be more than $25,000,000 a year against us. No wonder our cities and the nation were drained of their currency. Such was, and such must continue to be the ruinous effects of our present system. In seven years, from 1795 to 1802, the aggregate balance of trade against the United States, with all the world, amounted to $106,-976,367; of this amount, the balance with Great Britain, alone, amounted to $106,118,104, leaving for all the rest of the world a balance of less than half a million against us. This showed how effectually we were made tributary to Great Britain, who took little or nothing from the north, but the money we got in our trade with other countries. From 1801 to 1811 (ten years), the accumulated balances against us in our trade with Great Britain amounted to the enormous sum of $220,000,000, as appeared from Pitkins' Statistics. From 1793 to 1800, the whole of the exports from Great Britain, to all the countries of Europe, only amounted to $36,000,000, a year; while her exports to the United States alone, during the same period, amounted to upwards of $41,000,000 a year, being $5,000,000 more than all Europe put together; yet she excluded our productions by absolute prohibition. She will not permit the importation of a barrel of our flour, though offered for fifty cents. This showed the wisdom of other countries, and the folly of ours in strong relief. By this policy of excluding the productions of other countries, and protecting her own industry against all competition, Great Britain had been enabled to sustain a war for twenty-five years with the colossal power of Bonaparte, when he swayed the sceptre of almost entire Europe. Her people were thus enabled to sustain an annual burthen, amounting to nearly $300,000,000, while it prostrated this country to raise, during our late war, $11,000,000 a year by taxation. Such was the effects of encouraging domestic manufactures. It was by her manufacturing establishments Great Britain laid the world under tribute. It was her manufactures that filled her exchequer, by the payment of excises, amounting to $138,000,000 a year! It was these establishments that raised her excises in twenty-five years to the vast sum of $4,625,000,000, while her imports amounted to less than $1,700,000,000, leaving a balance of $2,925,000,000 in her favor, equal to $117,000,000 a year!

It was these establishments that sustained her agriculture, furnishing her farmers with a market to the amount of $940,000,000 a year for grain alone, independent of meat and other provisions, wool, hemp, flax, etc., amounting no doubt to a much greater amount! It was these establishments that sustained her all-powerful navy; that clothed her armies; that supported and nourished her unbounded commerce, a commerce that traversed every sea, and whitened every ocean, bringing back its rich returns, and pouring a constant shower of gold into the lap of that favored land. Such were the effects of manufactures there, and such, he contended, would be their effects here, if properly protected and sustained by the Government. By means of these establishments, Great Britain wielded a scientific power, afforded by labor-saving machinery, equal to 200,000,000 of hands; she thus employed 200,000,000 of slaves—slaves not requiring overseers and masters; not requiring to be clothed and fed; not requiring to be tasked, and kept in motion by the lash; but sustained and impelled by water or steam. Aided by this machinery, one man was able to pay for the labor of 200 farmers. They purchase our cotton, say $20,000,000 a year; with this they make the world tributary to them, to the amount of hundreds of millions. What she receives from us, she makes the basis of her national wealth; what we take from her we consume; it is made the basis of no wealth, but like "the baseless fabric of a vision, leaves not a wreck behind." Our commerce with Great Britain, he therefore contended, was not an exchange of equivalents; it might be assimilated to our exchange of beads and gewgaws, for the furs and paltries of the Indian tribes.

Mr. S. said he would now notice a few of what might be called the standing arguments of the enemies of the protecting system. If we look to the numerous memorials from all the Southern States, in opposition to the tariff; if we look to the arguments urged in and out of the House; if we look to the late report of the committee of ways and means on the subject, it will be found that the whole of the opposition rests upon three or four bold assumptions. If we grant the premises thus assumed, the conclusions against us are irresistible; but if the premises are shown to be false, then the whole superstructure must tumble to the ground. He therefore proposed for a moment to examine the premises on which this opposition was mainly founded; in the first place it is asserted, that we have no constitutional power to pass a tariff for the protection of domestic manufactures; secondly, that this policy is destructive of the revenue; thirdly, that it is destructive of commerce; fourthly, that it is oppressive and ruinous to agriculture, and, fifthly, that it is "taxing the many for the benefit of the few." First, then, as to the constitutional power, Mr. S. said he considered it too clear to admit of argument. The Constitution expressly declares, that Congress shall have power "to lay and collect taxes, *duties, imposts,* and excises, to pay the debts, and provide for the common defence and general welfare;" and the Government had accordingly acted upon this clear ground, from the foundation of the Government up to the present day, and the right to impose duties for the protection of manufactures was not only expressly asserted in the acts of the first Congress, but had been reasserted by every executive, and by the most eminent and distinguished statesmen, in support of this position. He begged leave to read a few extracts from the messages of the several Presidents on this subject.

General Washington, in his first message, delivered January 8, 1790, says: "The advancement of agriculture, commerce and *manufactures,* by every proper means, will not, I trust, need recommendation." Again, in his message of October 25, 1796, he says: "Congress have repeatedly, and not without success, turned their attention to *manufactures,* and the object is of too much importance not to secure a continuance of their efforts in every way that shall appear eligible;" he also recommends to Congress the establishment, by law, of agricultural societies, to grant "premiums, *pecuniary aids,* etc."

In the messages of Mr. Adams and Mr. Jefferson, we also find the subject of manufactures frequently recommended to the favor of Congress. Mr. Jefferson, in his letter to Benjamin Austin, Esq., in 1816, uses this strong and emphatic language: "To be independent for the comforts of life, we must fabricate them ourselves—we must now place the *manufacturer* by the side of the *agriculturalist.* The grand enquiry now is, shall we make our own comforts, or go without them, at the will of a foreign nation? He therefore who is now against *domestic* manufactures, must be in favor of reducing us either to a dependence on that nation, or be clothed in *skins,* and to live like *wild beasts* in dens and caverns—I am proud to say I *am not one of these, experience has now* taught me that manufactures are as necessary to our *independence* as our comfort;" and expresses his determination to wrest this weapon from foreign hands, by purchasing nothing foreign when the domestic article can be had, without regard to *price*.

Mr. Madison, in his message of 5th November, 1815, recommends to Congress, "The just and sound policy of securing to our *manufactures* the success they have obtained, and are still obtaining, etc." And in his message of 15th February, 1815, he says: "There is *no* subject that can enter, with greater force and merit, into the deliberations of Congress, than a consideration of the means to preserve and promote the manufactures which have sprung into existence, and attained an unparalleled maturity throughout the United States, during the period of the European wars. This source of national independence and wealth, I *anxiously* recommend to the prompt and constant guardianship of Congress." In his message of 5th December, 1815, his recommendations on this subject are equally strong and emphatic, and says that by proper protection and encouragement "our *domestic manufactures* may, at an early day, not only furnish a source of *domestic wealth*, but also of *external commerce*." These recommendations are repeated and reinforced in his message of December 3d, 1816.

Mr. Monroe, in several of his messages, strongly recommends the subject of manufactures to "the *systematic* and *fostering* care of Congress," and especially in his message of December, 1819, he makes a very strong appeal on this subject.

Mr. Adams, in his first message to Congress, of December, 1825, has also recommended the protection and encouragement of *manufactures* and *agriculture* to the favorable consideration of Congress.

Thus we have the express recommendations of every executive since the foundation of the government, to which he would add the opinion of Mr. Hamilton, contained in his masterly report on this subject, made as Secretary of the Treasury to Congress; he says: "A question has been made concerning the constitutional right of the government of the United States to apply this species of encouragement; but there is certainly no good foundation for such a question.

"The National Legislature has express authority, 'to lay and collect taxes, duties, imposts, and excises, to pay the debts, and provide for the common defence and general welfare,' with no other qualifications than that, 'all duties, imposts, and excises shall be *uniform* throughout the United States; that no capitation or direct tax shall be laid unless in proportion to numbers ascertained by a census or enumeration taken on the principles prescribed in the constitution;' and that 'no tax or duty shall be laid on articles exported from any State.' These three qualifications excepted, the power to raise money is plenary and indefinite, and the objects to which it may be appropriated are no less comprehensive, than the payment of the public debts, and the providing for the common defence and general welfare. The terms, 'general welfare,' were doubtless intended to signify more than was expressed or imported in those which preceded; otherwise numerous exigencies incident to the affairs of a nation, would have been left without a provision. The phrase is as comprehensive as any that could have been used; because it was not fit that the constitutional authority of the Union, to appropriate its revenues, should have been restricted within narrower limits than the 'general welfare;' and because this necessarily embraces a vast variety of particulars, which are susceptible neither of specification nor of definition.

"It is, therefore, of necessity left to the discretion of the National Legislature to pronounce upon the objects, which concern the general welfare, and for which, under that description, an appropriation of money is requisite and proper. And there seems to be no reason for a doubt, that whatever concerns the general interests of learning, of agriculture, of *manufactures and of commerce, are within the sphere of the national councils, as far as regards an application of money,*" etc. So much for the question of constitutional power; if gentlemen could overturn the opinions of those who made the constitution, and have administered it ever since, of course no opinion of his could be of any avail.

The second ground assumed by the opponents of the tariff is, that it will destroy the revenue; some say to the amount of four, and others, eight millions, we had precisely the same predictions, from the same gentlemen, as to the effect of the tariff of 1824. But unfortunately for their characters as prophets, instead of diminishing, it has increased the revenue, and such will be the effect of this and every other tariff, properly framed. The revenue would always be in proportion to the prosperity of the country, this was an invariable rule; it would always be in a ratio corresponding with the ability of the people to purchase and consume the productions of other countries, and although the tariff might lessen the importation of some articles, it would increase the importation of others, in a corresponding degree; besides a diminished quantity would yield an increased revenue, owing to the increase of the duties imposed. Manufactures destroy the revenue! he would ask gentlemen if the manufactures of Great Britain destroyed her revenue? It was her manufactures alone that sustained her revenue, and without them the nation would be bankrupt in a single year; this could not be denied by any one at all acquainted with the financial condition of that country. The whole net revenue of Great Britain for the last year (1827), as stated by Mr. Peel in the House of Commons, a few months since, was £49,581,000 sterling, equal to $220,000,000, and of this at least $128,000,000 was the product of the excises levied on her manufactures, which exceeded the whole amount of our revenue for the last six years!! Destroy the manufactures of Great Britain, and her commerce, her revenue, and her agriculture, sink together in a common grave. Manufactures constituted the main pillar of the British Empire, they drew to her coffers the wealth of the world; by these she subsidized Europe, by these she raised a revenue from her people of more than $250,000,000 a year, during her struggles on the continent; while the United States would have been bankrupt by an attempt to raise a tithe of this amount. She was the most manufacturing, and we the most agricultural nation in the world; compare our financial resources, take one of the years of our late war, say 1814, when every thing was taxed, land, carriages, watches, stores, distilleries, etc., etc., yet the whole amount of our revenue, in that year exclusive of loans, amounted to $11,500,000 only, and our loans to $23,000,000, making $34,500,000, while Great Britain raised during the same year (1814), by taxes, $301,000,000, and by loans $245,000,000, making in all $546,000,000, when we were bankrupted by an effort to raise $35,000,000, and two-thirds of it by loans, bearing six and seven per cent. interest; this showed what kind of foundation there was for the assertion, that the protection of manufactures would destroy our revenue.

The third objection was, that the tariff would destroy our commerce; this was about as well founded as the objection just examined. The manufactures of Great Britain, every one knew, furnished the aliment that fed and sustained her immense commerce; employing 20,000 vessels and 150,000 seamen. We were told in 1824, that the bill then passed was the stone that would sink the last ship beneath the wave, and the gentleman from New York [Mr. Cambreleng] then told us it would destroy $30,000,000 of commerce and $7,000,000 of revenue; what was the result? These predictions, like the rest, turned out to be visionary; instead of destroying, it greatly increased our commerce, as was apparent, from an examination of our exports and imports, for three years before, and three years after the passage of that bill. For three years before the tariff of 1824, our imports amounted to $241,000,000, and our exports to $221,000,000, leaving a balance of $20,000,000 against us. For three years after the tariff (viz. from 1824 to 1827) our imports amounted to $261,000,000, and our exports to $257,000,000, leaving a balance of $4,000,000 against us; thus our commerce was increased in this short period $20,000,000, and the balance reduced from $20,000,000 to $4,000,000; here are practical results, opposed to theory and speculation. We are now told the same thing, and such would again be the result, if the bill passed with the necessary amendments, which he trusted it would receive before its final passage through both houses. It was unnecessary to say more on this branch of the subject, and he would turn his attention to another prominent objection to this policy, which although entirely unfounded, had been so often repeated, that it became a sort of settled maxim among many of our political economists; the maxim was this: that the tariff-policy was "taxing the many for the benefit of the few;" give gentlemen their own premises and they can prove anything, but the premises here assumed, happened to be untrue, as was clearly proved by the following table, showing the amount of duties now imposed on certain articles, the prices formerly paid for them, when imported, and the prices now paid, when supplied at home.

	Present duties.	Former cost when imported.	Present cost when made at home.
Indian Cotton Goods	30 pr. ct.	20 cts. pr. yd.	9 cts. per. yd.
English "	25 "	25 "	13 "
Nails	5 cts. lb.	16	7 cts. pr. lb.
Glauber Salts	2 "	10	3 "
Copperas	2 "	6	3 "
Refined Saltpetre	3 "	10	7 "
Window Glass	$3 a 4 box.	$15 00 box.	$5 00 per box.
Bed-ticking	25 pr. ct.	50	25 cts. per yd.
Satinet	33 1-3	1 50	30 "
Negro Cloths	32 1-3	50	37 "
Broad "	33 1-3	6 00	3 00 "
Cotton Yarn, No. 16	25 pr. ct.	1 00	30 "
Cheese	9 cts. lb.	15	6 cts. pr. lb.

One-third less than the duty, so that if the price would fall, by repealing the duties, as is contended, cheese would be worth three cents less than nothing!!

Since the tariff of 1824, there is not an article embraced in it, the price of which has not been greatly reduced; cotton bagging had fallen from 37½ to 25 cents per yard, wool and woolens, on which the duties were greatly increased, have fallen at least 33⅓ per cent., etc., yet gentlemen gravely insist, with these facts staring them in the face, that protecting duties will raise the price, and tax the many for the benefit of the few!! The above facts, however, furnished a complete refutation of these absurd notions and idle theories, so often repeated.

Mr. Stewart said he would, in conclusion, beg the attention of the committee to the only remaining objection which he proposed now to notice. It was this, that "the protection of domestic manufactures operated injuriously upon the farmers and agriculturists of the country." This constituted one of the standing and leading grounds of objection to the policy he was advocating, and indeed it had been favored by his colleague [Mr. Stevenson], who had talked much of the tax which the duty on woolens would impose upon the farmers, etc. In the first place, it would be proper to consider what the present condition of our agriculture was; to see what effect manufactures had had on agriculture in other countries; and what had been, and would be, their effects here.

During the general war in Europe, which continued to prevail, with but few months' intermission, from 1793 to 1815, a period of nearly twenty-three years, having an abundant foreign demand, a great portion of our labor and capital was of course attracted to agriculture, so that in 1810, when the census was taken, it appeared that seven-eighths of our whole population was engaged in the cultivation of the soil; this demand was, however, suddenly arrested and cut off by the restoration of peace in 1815, when the powers of Europe abandoned war and returned to the cultivation of the soil; the effect was, that our exports of flour fell, in five years, from seventeen millions of dollars to less than four! and all our other agricultural exports, except cotton, tobacco, and rice, fell off in a corresponding proportion. At the close of the war, in 1814, Great Britain took from us nine millions of dollars' worth of cotton, and about six millions of flour and provision; last year she took twenty-five millions of cotton, and not a single barrel of flour; it was excluded by absolute prohibition; twenty years ago we exported more than double the quantity of flour, grain, and other provisions that we export now; in 1806, it amounted to more than twenty millions, in 1826 to less than ten, while in 1820 the exports of cotton was less than thirteen millions, and in 1826 more than thirty, so that whilst our foreign market for grain and provisions had fallen off more than one-half, the market for cotton had more than doubled; this might be sport for the South, but it was death to the Middle and Western States. The South says, "Let us alone," we are doing very well; while the Northern, Middle, and Western States cry out for protection; having no foreign, they must seek a home market, in home manufactures. By referring to our commerce and navigation for the year 1826, it would be seen that the total exports of domestic productions from the State of Pennsylvania, having twenty-six representatives on this floor, amounted to only $3,158,711, while those of South Carolina, with but nine representatives, amounted to $7,468,966; our exports of cotton had increased within the last eight or nine years from 81 to 203,000,000 of pounds, while the imports into three of our Northern cities last year had exceeded their exports by $24,208,758; this showed, in a strong light, the great advantages enjoyed by the Southern cotton-growing States over the Western and Middle grain-growing States; and yet gentlemen from the South threaten resistance, a separation of the Union, and God knows what all, if Pennsylvania and her sister States of the North attempt to relieve themselves by establishing domestic manufactures, to consume their wool, grain, and other provisions, instead of sending their last dollar to import them from Great Britain, who refuses to take a dollar's worth of anything from them in return. He would appeal to the magnanimity and to the justice of the gentlemen from the South, and ask them if they could reconcile it to their own consciences, thus to force so great a portion of their fellow citizens to remain in poverty and dependence on a foreign power acting so unjustly towards them. These States having the power to relieve themselves, would be false and faithless to themselves and their posterity, if they did not exert it; and, instead of resisting, he thought their brethren of the South should lend them a helping hand—they would ultimately find a surer and a better market for their cotton in New England than they would find in the mother country.

But Soutnern gentlemen appeared apprehensive, that if we take less of British manufactures, she will take less of their cotton, and this idea in fact lay at the foundation of all the violent opposition to this policy in the South; no doubt this was a sincere and honest opinion, but he considered it entirely erroneous. He believed that the South was not dependent on Great Britain for a market, but that Great Britain was in fact dependent upon the South for a supply of cotton, an article which constituted the basis of her national wealth; she could obtain an adequate supply nowhere else. If this raw material was withheld for a single year, the effect would be ruinous; her manufactures of cotton alone amounted to $300,000,000 a year; but how, he would ask, would Great Britain undertake to exclude our cotton, even if she had the disposition to do so? Not by duties; this would be taxing her manufacturers, who, after being relieved to the last cent, could scarcely maintain the competition in the markets of South America. So far from increasing, she had been compelled to repeal the whole of her duties on raw cotton; this was done not to favor us, but to sustain her own manufactures. The British consumption of cotton at present was about 162,000,000 of pounds, and of this 125,000,000 was American, amounting to 77 per cent., and this proportion is rapidly increasing—a few years ago, less than half her supply was American; our cotton is, in fact, better and cheaper than that of any other country, and so long as it is so, Great Britain will find it her interest, and finding it her interest, she will take it in preference to any other. Her manufacturers, left free to choose for themselves, will always purchase from those offering them the best and cheapest article, without inquiring whether they took British manufactures or not; so that the fears entertained by Southern gentlemen are visionary and unfounded; no country in the world could rival our Sea Island cotton, and it was to the manufacture of the finer fabrics the British attention was now mostly directed. The best India cotton would not bring more than 14 or 15 cents, while it was stated by a gentleman in South Carolina, that a planter had even this season, when the price was unusually low, sold his Sea Island cotton at $1.43¾ per pound; with this there could be no competition, therefore they had nothing to fear from any part of the world. Gentlemen in the South had, in 1824, when the tariff was under debate, expressed the same apprehensions. We were then told, as now, that if the bill passed, Great Britain would cease to purchase their cotton, that she would exclude it, etc. The bill passed, and what had been the result? the very next year she took nearly double the quantity she had taken the year before; in 1824, she took but 282,773 bales; in 1825, she took 425,195 bales. If such were the effect of the tariff on the cotton trade, it would be well for the South if we passed the tariff every year; thus the predictions of the enemies of the tariff had been happily defeated in every instance. They told us in 1824 it would destroy the revenue; it had increased it. They told us it would raise the prices of goods; they had fallen more than 30 per cent. They told us it would destroy the British market for our cotton; it had increased nearly 100 per cent. These prophecies are again repeated every day, and with no better reason; the results would again prove them false prophets, and the gentlemen themselevs, as friends of their country, ought, as he had no doubt they would, rejoice in the disappointment of their own gloomy foreboding.

As to the effects of manufactures on the agriculture of the country, he would make but a few additional remarks; and in the first place, he laid it down as a general principle, established by the experience of all countries, that agriculture had always flourished in proportion to the number and extent of manufactures.

Great Britain was admitted on all hands to be the greatest manufacturing nation in the world, and the United States the most agricultural. In England, only one-third of the people were engaged in agriculture; in the United States, according to the census of 1810, seven-eighths were engaged in this employment—in Great Britain, the consumption of grain alone produced in that small island, not as large as some of the States of this Union, was equal to $18,000,000 every week, more than double our exports of flour and grain of all kinds to all the world. If she would take one week's supply from us, we would be satisfied.

To show the beneficial effects of manufactures on the value and productions of land, he would contrast the United States and Great Britain, one being the most agricultural, and the other the most manufacturing nation in the world, which he thought would place the matter in a just and clear light:

	No. employed in agriculture.	Whole population.	No. of acres.	Value per acre.	No. of acres t each person.
In England	1-3	15,000,000	32,000,000	$241	2
United States	7-8	12,000,000	646,000,000	4	53
Ireland	2-5	7,000,000	20,500,000	180	3
Virginia	9-10	1,000,000	41,000,000	5	41

Here was exhibited, by a few facts, the most conclusive and irresistible evidence of the powerful influence of manufactures in sustaining agriculture. In England, where nearly two-thirds of the people were manufacturers, land was worth on an average $241 per acre, while in the United States, where not more than one-eighth of the people were employed in manufactures, the land on an average was not worth more than $4 per acre; other causes, it was true, had their influence, but this was the most important and influential.

The gentleman from Virginia [Mr. Randolph] had given us a description of the miseries of Ireland, a people who, he said, "lived on the potatoe, the whole potatoe, and nothing but the potatoe," who he described as the *lazeroni* who were reduced to the "minimum and pessimum of human existence." Let the gentleman, however, for a moment compare the resources of that country with his own native State, the ancient dominion, and perhaps he would not think so contemptibly of the Irish. In Ireland two-fifths of the people only were engaged in agriculture, yet they exported more grain and flour than the whole United States put together, though it was not half as large as the State of Virginia. If the gentleman would look at the exports of Ireland in the year 1823 he would find that her exports of flour and grain amounted to $9,000,000, while the whole exports of the United States of these articles amounted to only $6,500,000, leaving a balance in favor of Ireland of $2,500,000. In the same year her exports of animals and animal productions was $16,500,000, while those of the United States amounted to only $2,500,000, leaving in her favor a balance of $14,-000,000, which made an excess of grain and animal food exported more than the United States of $16,500,000, about $3 to one. Her exports of butter alone amounted to $8,500,000, while our whole exports of flour, grain, meat, provisions, spirits, etc., amounted to only $9,000,000 to all the world! Yet her population was not half, and her territory not one-thirtieth part ours. There they had less than three, and here we had more than fifty acres to each individual; there only two-fifths, and here nearly seven-eighths were engaged in agriculture; yet their agricultural exports of grain and provisions amounted, in 1812, to more than double those of the whole United States. After this statement of facts, which the gentleman could not controvert or deny, how, he would ask, would old Virginia, as to resources, compare with Ireland, the land of the "*lazeroni?*" This was the effect of manufactures and of persevering industry. But this was not all. By referring to the financial history of Ireland, the gentleman from Virginia would also find that the people of Ireland actually paid more revenue into the Exchequer every year than was paid by the people of the United States; and if he would look back to the year 1814, during our war, when every nerve was strained in this country, and taxes were imposed on almost everything, with all our exports we were able to raise only $34,500,000, and $23,000,000 of this by loans, while Ireland raised in the same year $82,000,000, more than double that of the United States, $39,000,000 of which was raised by taxes, and $43,000,000 by loans. Such were the facts which history furnished; and however humiliating they might be to our pride, it was proper that we should look at them, inquire into the causes, and correct the ruinous and paralyzing policy which had led us to these extraordinary and painful results. The remedy, he thought, was easy and obvious; it was at home—cherish and protect our own industry—protect it against all foreign competition, in short, put the country on its own resources instead of looking abroad for what we ought to and can furnish at home. This is the true secret of the system that enabled great Britain to stand under a burden which we could not sustain for a single hour. Look at her enormous debt of $3,775,000,000, contracted during a war of nearly twenty-three years, waged against the colossal power of Napoleon, the interest of which alone amounted annually to more than five times the whole revenue of the United States. Great Britain adopted none of the maxims of our Southern anti-tariff politicians, who contend that we should "buy where we can buy cheapest." She compels her manufacturers to consume British bread, and no other, though it were offered to them for nothing. So far as free-trade will make other nations tributary to her, she is willing to adopt it, but no further. This was the part of wisdom, and he hoped yet to see this nation adopt a similar policy.

Why was the price of agricultural produce high during the late war? Why was money plenty? And why did industry everywhere enjoy ample reward? The reasons are obvious: it was because a part of our surplus agricultural laborers were drawn off to another theatre of action, and thus became consumers instead of producers, customers instead of rivals; and because British manufacturers were then excluded, and the millions of dollars before sent abroad were kept in active circulation at home. Wretched, indeed, must be that policy which makes war a blessing and peace a curse to the country.

Mr. S. said he had examined the bill under consideration with all the attention of which he was capable, and which his situation had permitted, and he thought the burdens which the bill, as reported, would impose on the manufacturer, would not be compensated by corresponding benefits. He trusted, however, it would be so amended as to benefit the country, benefit the farmers, and save the manufacturers from the ruin which impended over them, and which must soon and certainly fall upon and crush them, unless shielded and protected by the strong arm of Government. Mr. S. said he would detain the committee no longer, he had exhausted his own strength, and no doubt their patience; and after thanking the House for the attention with which he had been heard, he took his seat.

NOTE.—The amendments Mr. S. advocated were mostly adopted, and the bill as passed the highest and best protective tariff ever enacted, with but six votes against it in all the Western and Middle States, New York included, and eighty votes in said States for it.

THE ORIGIN OF THE COMMON SAYING, "I ACKNOWLEDGE THE CORN."

During the debate on the tariff of 1828, when Mr. Stewart first undertook to demonstrate to the American *farmers* and *laboring men* that they were every year sending millions of dollars in *coin* to Europe to pay for *foreign agricultural* produce, converted by *foreign* labor into goods and sent here for sale, thus enriching foreign farmers and laboring men, instead of retaining these millions at home to enrich themselves; a farmer, he said, who goes into a store and buys a hundred dollars' worth of foreign cloth, lace, iron, everything, what does he pay for? *Agricultural* produce, *wool, flax*, or *hemp*, and the *bread, meat*, and *vegetables* consumed by foreign labor while converting them into cloth. A yard of lace worth $6 is but $6 worth of foreign farm and garden produce, consumed by some poor man or woman, whilst making the lace, and who got barely what they eat for their work, and that is what you pay for when you buy the lace. To say that a lady carries $6 worth of bacon and beans, cabbage and krout round her neck, converted into lace, may seem strange, and it would be equally strange to say that Western farmers in Ohio and Kentucky send their *hay, grass, corn*, and other grain to New York and Philadelphia to pay for foreign agricultural produce, converted into goods.

Here Mr. Wickliffe, of Kentucky, interposed, and said "there never was a ton of *hay* or a bushel of *corn* or grain of any other kind sent from Kentucky to Philadelphia or New York."

"Will the gentleman, then, tell us," said Mr. S., "what they do send?" Mr. W. replied, they send horses, cattle, hogs. Very well, then, how much grass, grain, hay, and other produce does a farmer put into the skin of a horse worth $100? Just $100 worth, which, thus animated with life and legs, carries this $100 worth of produce to Philadelphia and New York, with the owner on top of it (a laugh). And how much of like produce does a fat ox worth $50 carry to the Eastern market? Just $50 worth. And how much does a fat hog worth $10 carry? Just $10 worth of *corn*. Here Mr. Wickliffe sprang to his feet and exclaimed, amid much laughter, "*Mr. Speaker, I acknowledge the corn.*" This went into the papers, and it is said gave rise to the common saying, "*I acknowledge the corn.*"

CONTRASTING THE REPUBLICAN *PROTECTIVE* TARIFF OF 1842, WITH THE DEMOCRATIC *FREE-TRADE* TARIFF OF 1846, AND SHOWING THE EFFECTS OF THE POLICY OF THE TWO PARTIES GENERALLY UPON THE REVENUE AND PROSPERITY OF THE COUNTRY.

DELIVERED IN THE HOUSE OF REPRESENTATIVES, U. S., ON THE 11th DAY OF JUNE, 1848.

[*Extract from Speech.*]

THE President and secretary both repeat, that the tariff of 1846 has not only greatly increased the national prosperity, but that it has actually increased the revenue $8,000,000. Now, so far from this being true, it clearly appears from the secretary's own showing, that the revenue would have been $7,202,657 more, had the tariff of 1842 continued in operation. So that instead of gaining $8,000,000, we have lost more than $7,000,000 of revenue by the tariff of 1846—a blunder of more than $15,000,000 in a single year!

Now, for the facts I refer gentlemen to the first pages of Mr. Walker's last three annual Reports on the Finances; they will there see it stated that, in the fiscal year 1845, the revenue from customs was $27,528,112—that in 1846, the revenue was $26,712,667—producing an average amount of revenue, under the tariff of 1842, of $27,120,389. Whereas, in 1847, under Mr. Walker's great revenue tariff of 1846, he himself states that the revenue from customs is but $23,747,864—nearly three millions less than in 1846, and nearly four millions less than in 1845. Yet we are told, in the face of these official facts, that the tariff of 1846 has increased the revenue $8,000,000. But this is not all; by referring to the secretary's late Report on Commerce and Navigation, (not yet printed,) it will be seen that the dutiable imports in 1847 were $10,365 404 more than in 1845.

under the tariff of 1842; and had it been still in force, this excess, at 32 per cent., (the average of the duties under the tariff of 1842,) would have yielded $3,416,429 of revenue, which, added to the excess of revenue received in 1845 over 1847, $3,786,228, makes the sum of $7,202,657 more revenue under the tariff of 1842, had it remained in operation, than has been received under the tariff of 1846. Now what becomes of the secretary's $8,000,000 of increased revenue? Instead of $8,000,000 *plus*, his tariff of 1846 is $7,000,000 *minus*. Or to prove it in another and simpler form, Mr. Walker says the average of duties under the tariff of 1842 was 32 per cent., and under the act of 1846, they are 22 per cent.—consequently, the revenue upon the same imports must be one-third less. So that instead of $23,-747,864, the amount received under the existing law, we should have received, under the tariff of 1842, one-third more, viz.: $31,663,812. These are mathematical results, derived from Mr. Walker's own reports, and there is no escape for him or his defenders. I call on them to deny it, if they can. But besides all this, Mr. Walker, in his annual report last winter, page 1, estimates the receipts from customs for the fiscal year 1847, at $27,835,731; he has received, he says, but $23,747,864—four millions less than his estimates. Yet the President and secretary both boast that the tariff of 1846 has more than realized their expectations. Now, if $4,000,000 less than their estimate equals their expectations, then they must have, for the purpose of deception, deliberately made their estimate $4,000,000 more than they expected to receive. Can the secretary explain this? I hope he'll try, but I predict he will not.

But Mr. Walker contends that the tariff of 1846, having greatly increased the export of domestic products, has, as a matter of course, brought in a corresponding increase of imports and revenue. But has the tariff of 1846 increased the amount of domestic exports? I say it has not, and I shall prove it by Mr. Walker's own figures. I shall show conclusively that the only increase of exports has been in breadstuffs and provisions, required to prevent starvation, and would have been taken to the same extent, and paid for in the same way, without regard to our tariff, or anything of the kind. Now take the export of domestic products for ten years, from 1835 to 1845, and deduct therefrom the amount of breadstuffs and provisions, and it will be found that the annual export of domestic products, exclusive of breadstuffs and provisions, was $91,813,589; then take the export of domestic products during the last fiscal year, under the tariff of 1846, viz.: $150,637,464, and deduct the breadstuffs and provisions, $65,906,273, and it leaves of everything else but $84,720,191—more than $7,000,000 less of domestic exports last year, exclusive of provisions and breadstuffs, than the average of the preceding ten years; yet, in the face of these facts, furnished by his official Report on Commerce and Navigation, he gravely tells the American people that free-trade and the tariff of 1846, and not the famine in Europe, have produced the great increase of exports and imports. The report not being printed, I cannot refer to the pages from which I derive these facts, but they are accessible to gentlemen who wish to inquire.

Next as to the *modus operandi,* the plan by which the President and secretary attempt to make it out that they have received more revenue under the tariff of 1846 than was received under that of 1842. How is this done? It is done by cutting up the years; taking a few months of one year, and a few months of another—fivĕ months under the tariff of 1842 and seven under the tariff of 1846. Now everybody knows that the tariff of 1846 was passed in July, and did not go into operation till December; during this period of four or five months, imports paying duties were almost entirely arrested. The fact being that the duties would in a few months be greatly reduced, a very large amount of goods, which would have come in and paid duty according to the then existing tariff of 1842, were withheld till the duties came down. They were piled up in warehouses, or kept in bond till the tariff of 1846 and low duties took effect; besides, goods which had paid heavy duties were re-exported, and the duties withdrawn from the Treasury, to be returned when the duties came down—thus a pipe of brandy, for instance, which, under the tariff of 1842, had paid one dollar per gallon duty, the owner, by re-exporting it with a drawback of the duty, and re-importing it immediately after the tariff of 1846 took effect, reducing the duty nearly one-half, would clear forty cents a gallon; thus robbing the tariff of 1842, and giving its revenue to the tariff of 1846. During this period of five months, of course little revenue, in comparison, was coming in, though the country was still nominally under the tariff of 1842. Now these are the months which this very candid secretary takes for his estimate of the produce of the tariff of 1842. As soon as the reduced tariff of 1846 went into operation, all these goods, which had been held back waiting for the reduced duties, were at once poured in, and in pours revenue by millions. The goods and duties withdrawn from the tariff of 1842 now return under the tariff of 1846; and these are the months which this truth-seeking secretary takes, as showing the comparative product of this model tariff, contrasted with five months of the tariff of 1842, giving a little over $7,000,000 for five months; when, for two years before, the revenue had exceeded an average of $27,000,000! And this is put forth as a fair comparison. He might as well compare the strength of a giant and that of a child, by putting down what the giant could lift when on a sick bed and in his last hours, and what the child could lift in the vigor of health, and under a sudden and violent excitement. Would this be a very satisfactory way of proving that the child was stronger than the giant? Yet the comparison would be just as fair.

The next thing the learned secretary attempts to prove is, that under low duties more revenue is always obtained than under high duties. To show this, he selects ten years' income under high tariffs, and ten years under a low one. He selects ten years, from 1832 to 1842, under the compromise bill, for his *low* tariff, and ten years, under the high tariffs of 1824 and 1828, with two years under the tariff of 1842, as the *high* tariff period. Now, I assert that in these very years, his own figures prove that we got $82,000,000 more under the high tariff than we did under the low. For the proof, I refer gentlemen and the secretary to his own official Report on the Finances in 1845, page 956. Here you have his own report. Take it down, gentlemen; I desire you to make a minute of what I state, for what I say I can prove. I hope the ex-chancellor of the exchequer [Mr. McKay] will pay special attention to these statements. I say, on Mr. Walker's own showing, that under the ten years of low tariff the receipts were $214,885,858, and that under the high tariff years the receipts were $297,842,215. The difference in favor of the high tariff is $82,956,356—$8,295,635 per year; and yet the secretary and the President say that all experience proves that low tariffs give the most revenue! I refer (said Mr. S.) to date, book, and page. Let them look at it. I want Mr. Walker himself to look at it. I suppose when he sent us his report, with all these confident statements, supported by figures too, he thought it would answer its purpose. He owes it to his character for truth and candor to come out and admit or deny this statement, or authorize some friend to do it for him on this floor. Will it be done? We shall see.* Here are the tables taken carefully from Mr. Walker's report:

Revenue, for ten years, under low tariff, from 1833 to 1842.		Revenue for ten years, under the high tariffs of 1824, 1828, and 1842.	
1833	$24,177,578	1825	$31,653,871
1834	18,960,705	1826	26,083,861
1835	25,890,726	1827	27,948,956
1836	30,818,327	1828	29,951,251
1837	18,134,131	1829	27,688,701
1838	19,702,825	1830	28,389,505
1839	25,554,533	1831	36,596,118
1840	15,104,790	1832	29,341,175
1841	19,919,492	1844	29,236,357
1842	16,622,746	1845	30,952,416
	$214,885,853		$297,842,211
			214,885,853
Difference in favor of high tariffs, in ten years			$82,956,358

Loss of revenue, in ten years, under the low tariff, $8,295,635 *per annum.*

THE COMPARATIVE EFFECTS OF HIGH AND LOW TARIFFS ON EXPORTS AND IMPORTS—BALANCE OF TRADE, ETC.

The Secretary affirms that the balance of trade is always in our favor under a low tariff; that our exports exceed our imports, and that the exports of breadstuffs and provisions are especially increased. Now I say that, deducting the imports during the ten years of high tariffs, selected by the secretary for comparison, from the imports during the ten years of low tariffs, and it will appear that the balance against the country under the low tariff was $401,976,076—equal to $40,197,607 a year; and, deducting during each period the goods re-exported, the balance against the country would be increased to the sum of $423,455,724. And how had it been paid? By $200,000,000 of State bonds sent to Europe to pay for goods, a mercantile debt of nearly an equal amount, resulting at the end of the low duty period,

* No answer was ever given, or explanation made or attempted.

in 1840, '41, and '42, in repudiation and bankruptcy, State, National, and individual, throughout the land. Yet we are told by the President and Secretary that low duties produce prosperity, National and individual, and especially the prosperity of the farmers and laborers—of the "toiling millions," "the voters"—those who control the policy and measures of Government. Yes, sir, these are the very men they would thus deceive and ruin. Here are the tables of exports and imports, taken from Mr. Walker's Annual Report on the Finances, dated December 3, 1845, page 956:

Imports in ten years under low tariff or compromise bill.		Imports in ten years under the high tariffs of 1824, 1828 and 1842.	
1833	$108,118,311	1825	$96,340,075
1834	126,521,332	1826	84,974,477
1835	149,895,742	1827	79,484,068
1836	189,980,035	1828	88,509,824
1837	140,989,217	1829	74,492,527
1838	113,717,404	1830	70,876,920
1839	162,092,132	1831	103,191,124
1840	107,141,519	1832	101,029,266
1841	127,946,177	1844	108,435,035
1842	100,162,087	1845	117,254,564
	$1,326,563,956		$924,587,880
	924,587,880		Excess of imports in ten years of low tariff, $401,000,000. Equal to $40,000,000 a year against the country.
	$401,976,076		

Yet we are told that low tariffs always favor the country and promote the national prosperity.

But this is not all. Take the exports from the imports during these ten years of low duties, and it will be found that the debt against the people of the United States in favor of foreigners is, $176,166,242. What a sum of national prosperity is here exhibited! But there was another very important fact he wished here to bring to the attention of the House and the country—it was this: that, during eight years of the highest tariffs, of 1824 and 1828, *one hundred and three millions* of surplus revenue were applied to the payment of the public debt, and that during a corresponding period of eight years of low duties under the compromise bill, after wasting $40,000,000 of surplus revenue, a debt of about $40,000,000 was contracted; showing a failure of revenue to meet expenditures, under the low duties, of about $80,000,000 in eight years; and it further appears, that after the tariff was raised, in 1842, there were paid in the four years of its existence nearly $40,000,000 of public debt; and now, since the repeal of the tariff of 1842, and the restoration of low duties, the revenue has again run down, and the national debt is again running up at the rate of $40,000,000 or $50,-000,000 a year. Here are facts that speak volumes as to the effect of high and low tariffs on the revenue and national prosperity. What a commentary is this on Polk and Walker's theory of low duties producing high revenue, and high tariffs producing low revenue!

Such is the evidence in favor of Mr. Walker's position, that low tariffs always turn the balance of trade in our favor. Such are the happy effects of his policy of free-trade. Low tariffs always have been, and always will be, the ruin of the country. Let any man look at the scenes of general distress which always have followed this insane policy; the ruin of flourishing establishments, the multiplication of bankruptcies, the advertisements of sheriffs' sales, the destruction of credit and confidence, the prostration of enterprise, the stagnation of trade, and general condition of discontent and misery which have invariably succeeded the adoption of these false and visionary theories, and he will find one of the best criterions to judge of their political soundness. And such, I say, will always be the consequence of a repetition of the experiment. Mr. Walker says that they never have followed. I say they always have. Their whole theory is a mistake, and practice will ever so prove it to be; and when it is put forth in the very face of facts which every intelligent man knows, it is difficult to resist the conclusion that there is an object to be attained by misleading the public mind.

Again: The secretary asserts that low duties have always been accompanied by a greatly increased export of breadstuffs. And he attributes the sudden augmentation in those exports during the last season, not to the famine in Ireland, and over the South of Europe—not at all; but solely to his model tariff of 1846! That is what has done it all. Low duties, not starvation, have induced the people of the old world suddenly to eat Indian meal, and call out for American flour and American beef. But I wish to ask him—and I put the same question to Southern gentlemen in this House—if this reduction of duties is the thing which has produced so large an export of breadstuffs, pray why had it not, in this same degree, increased the exports of cotton and tobacco? The export of cotton under this model tariff of our model President has been less by $4,000,000 than the average exports of ten years past (from 1835 to 1845), less of tobacco by a million and a half—less of manufactures by nearly $2,000,000—less of the productions of the forest—less of almost every thing but breadstuffs and provisions. How is this to be accounted for? Dr. Walker's specific of '46 has a double operation—purgative as to breadstuffs and provisions, but astringent as to everything else. Who can doubt that famine, and nothing but famine, has produced this greatly increased exportation of breadstuffs? *

But what produced this falling off under this beautiful free-trade policy? Was that, too, the fruit of the tariff of 1846? Why has there been no increased exports of cotton? Southern gentlemen, cotton-growers, how is this? And you, ye tobacco-growers, how comes it that, under Mr. Walker's patent machine to increase exports, the export of tobacco has fallen off a million and a half? What say you to that? Was this the happy effect of the tariff of 1846? The secretary tells us that the starvation in Europe has had little or nothing to do with the consumption there of our breadstuffs; nothing whatever. Well, the starvation has ceased, breadstuffs are down, and now the redoubtable Mr. Secretary Walker is like to be caught in his own trap! I tell you that in a few weeks more the corn laws in England, sliding scale and all, will be in full operation. They were merely suspended, not repealed, during the famine; and now, when the famine is over, and Mr. Walker is caught in Sir Robert Peel's trap, the corn laws go into full effect on the first day of March next, and then exports cease, the revenue falls off, and Mr. Walker will have to appeal to us to restore the tariff of 1842, to replenish his empty sub-treasury, and feed his starving armies and officers, civil and military, at home and abroad.

Referring again to the low tariff period, from 1833 to 1842, under the compromise bill, and the high tariff period, from 1817 to 1832, the secretary says, "The average exports of breadstuffs and provisions were much larger in the years of low, compared with high duties." Indeed, he repeats

* Congress passed a bill to send provisions to relieve the starving people of Ireland.

this over and over again, that the "export of breadstuffs and provisions was much greater under low than high duties," which he says "the *tables of the Treasury clearly prove.*" Now, I propose to examine these tables, and will "clearly prove by them" just the reverse of the secretary's position, to an extent that will astonish the secretary himself, if he can be astonished at anything. I will show that, during four years of the period referred to, under the tariff of 1828, the highest tariff we ever had, we actually exported to Great Britain more than *one hundred times* as much breadstuffs and provisions as we did during four years under the low duties of the compromise bill.

[*Mr. Holmes* said, you mean, I presume, one hundred *per cent.*, not one hundred *times* more.]

I mean, said Mr. S., what I say, *one hundred times* more.

[*Mr. Holmes*—Please, give me the facts.]

Mr. S.—I will, and I want you to take them down—examine them at your leisure, and disprove them if you can; here are the facts taken from the annual Treasury Reports on "Commerce and Navigation," carefully revised by an officer of this House. I refer to Great Britain, not only because she is our principal customer, but because Mr. Walker has referred particularly to our exports of breadstuffs to England, and says, we must take more of her goods, or "she will have to pay specie for our breadstuffs, and not having it to spare, she will reduce the price of cotton." But here is the table from Mr. Walker's report which he would give to the gentleman from South Carolina [Mr. Holmes] for his special attention.

Four years under high tariff of 1828.	Imports from Great Britain.	Exports of breadstuffs to Great Britain.	Four years under low tariff, Comp'se bill.	Imports from Great Britain.	Exports of breadstuffs to Great Britain.
1829	$27,000,000	$1,777,124	1835	$66,000,000	$28,917
1830	26,000,000	1,606,738	1836	86,000,000	1,684
1831	47,000,000	5,578,592	1837	52,000,000	1,402
1832	42,000,000	541,787	1838	49,000,000	62,626
	$142,000,000	$9,504,241		$253,000,000	$94,629
Average p. year.	$35,500,000	$2,376,050		$63,250,000	$23,657

Thus it appears, from Mr. Walker's own official documents, that during four years of our highest tariff—the tariff of 1828—we took about half as many goods from Great Britain, and she took one hundred times as much of our breadstuffs as she took during four years of our lowest tariff. Yet, Mr. Walker repeats, over and over again, that our export of breadstuffs has always been greater under low tariffs than under high tariffs, and refers to Treasury tables to prove it! Has Mr. Walker looked at these reports? Does he know what they contain? He surely does not, or he never would have ventured upon such statements as these. Here it is seen that, in 1836, we took 86,000,000 of dollars' worth of goods from Great Britain, and she took 1684 dollars' worth of breadstuffs from us in payment! Yet Mr. Walker says in his report of 1845, page 13, that we must take more English goods, otherwise "the increased sum England will have to pay for our breadstuffs we will not take in manufactures, but only in specie, and not having it to spare, she brings down, even to a greater extent, our cotton." 86,000,000 of British goods will not pay for 1684 dollars' worth of American breadstuffs, and the balance England will have to pay "in specie, and not having it to spare," will bring down the price of our cotton! Is not this "cool" —is it not wonderful?

But Mr. Walker says the farmers are particularly benefited by free-trade and low duties; the dear farmers—"the toiling millions"—the "voters"—who control the affairs of Government; these, he says, are the men most benefited. Benefited by what? By importing, as in 1836, 86,000,000 of dollars' worth of British breadstuffs, raw materials and labor combined in the form of British goods, in exchange for 1684 dollars' worth of breadstuffs taken from us! What makes foreign goods? *Agricultural produce and labor*—nothing else. The raw material and provisions constitute more than half of the value of all foreign goods, and the balance of the price is made up of the wages of labor and profits of capital; these are the elements, and the whole of the elements, of price; and this is, in fact, what the American farmer pays his money for when he buys foreign goods —foreign agricultural produce, and foreign labor—while American farmers are left without a market for their wool and provisions, and their money sent to import it, in the form of cloth and other articles, from abroad. Is this not true to the letter? Yet this, we are told, is the policy to favor American farmers!

Mr. Walker talks much of breadstuffs. His report is stuffed with breadstuffs, "*ad nauseam.*" It was a fact susceptible of the clearest proof, that from the day of our independence to the present hour, we have imported twenty dollars' worth of breadstuffs in the form of goods from Great

Britain, to one dollar's worth she has taken from us in their raw form. What proportion of the price of goods was made up of the breadstuffs consumed by the labor employed in producing the raw materials, and afterwards in converting them into goods? Take a ton of iron, or a yard of silk, it was all labor—labor from the ore to the anchor, from the worm and leaf to the finished ribbon—all labor. And what did this labor get? It got what it eat—breadstuffs—bread, and hardly enough of that; and this is what we pay our money for when we buy foreign goods. Taking this view of the subject, Mr. Brown, a distinguished British writer, has lately said, that "Great Britain exports more agricultural produce than any other nation in the world"—exported in the form of goods. Now, he wished to inquire, what part of the value of foreign goods consisted of breadstuffs; he believed one-half would be a fair calculation, but to prevent cavil, say one-eighth. And what follows? It follows mathematically, that in 1836, under Mr. Walker's low tariff, we imported from Great Britain, in the form of goods, *sixty-three dollars and eighty-three cents* worth of British breadstuffs to *every cent's worth* she took from us in its raw state. Here are the facts; and Mr. Walker, who is great at figures, can make the calculation for himself. In 1836, we imported 86,000,000 of dollars' worth of British goods, and she took 1684 dollars' worth of our breadstuffs—that is $510.68 worth of British goods to one cent's worth of our breadstuffs. Now, assuming that one-eighth part of the price of goods is made up of the breadstuffs consumed by the labor employed in their manufacture, and it will amount, as stated, to sixty-three dollars and eighty-three cents' worth of breadstuffs imported from Great Britain in 1836, to one cent's worth that she took from us; and yet Mr. Walker says, we must take more British goods, otherwise she "will have to pay us specie for our breadstuffs, and not having it to spare, she will not pay as much for our cotton!" What a financier—what a statesman is this, whose report is proclaimed by his friends to be "the greatest production of the age." He reduces duties one-half to increase the revenue. And how? By doubling our imports of British goods, made up of British agricultural produce and British labor, to favor American farmers, mechanics, and workingmen—"the toiling millions." No wonder his report was printed by order of the British House of Lords, of which Mr. Walker speaks with so much pride and exultation. And the gentleman from Illinois [Mr. McClernand] is in ecstasies with the Report; and he too tells us of the wonders the tariff of 1846 has done for his constituents, and for the farmers and grain-growers of the West; free-trade, low duties, and British goods, are the very thing for them. Now, he wished to tell the gentleman one thing, and he hoped he would take it down and examine it—it was this: that under the low tariff in 1836, his constituents (assuming that they consume goods and export breadstuffs in proportion to the rest of the people of the United States) purchased and consumed 373,000 of dollars' worth of British goods, containing 46,000 of dollars' worth of breadstuffs, being one-eighth of their value, to every seven dollars' worth of breadstuffs Great Britain took from them; this result was produced by dividing the whole amount of imports of goods and exports of breadstuffs by 230, the number of Representatives on this floor. To show that these calculations were correct, he would furnish the following table, which he commended to the careful examination and consideration of the farmers and grain-growers of the United States, taken from Mr. Walker's report.

YEARS.	Amount of imports from Great Britain.	Am't of breadstuffs imported in goods estimated at ⅛ of their value.	Am't of breadstuffs exported to Great Britain from U. S.
UNDER HIGH TARIFF.			
1829	$27,000,000	$3,375,000	$1,777,124
1830	26,000,000	3,250,000	1,606,738
1831	47,000,000	5,875,000	5,578,592
1832	42,000,000	5,250,000	541,787
Total	$142,000,000	$17,750,000	$9,504,241
Average of 4 years..	35,500,000	4,437,500	2,376,060
UNDER LOW TARIFF.			
1835	$66,000,000	$8,250,000	$28,917
1836	86,000,000	10,750,000	1,684
1837	52,000,000	6,500,000	1,402
1838	49,000,000	6,125,000	62,626
Total	$253,000,000	$31,625,000	$94,629
Average of 4 years..	63,250,000	7,906,250	23,657
1836	$86,000,000 Goods imported.	$10,750,000 Breadstuffs imported.	$1,684 Breadstuffs exported.

THE EFFECT OF LOW DUTIES AND FREE-TRADE ON LABOR AND PRICES.

Thus it appears that the learned secretary's facts and his theories are always at war. His utopian schemes look exceeding well till his facts are brought to bear upon them, then they vanish into thin air. Unfortunately for Mr. Walker, ingenuity cannot overcome truth, for "truth is mighty and will prevail." To show the contradictory character of Mr. Walker's reports, he would here cite a few out of a great many instances.

In one part of his report the secretary boasts of the happy effects of the tariff of 1846, in reducing taxes, lightening the burdens of the poor, of the "toiling millions." In some instances, he says, they have been reduced from 100 and 200 per cent. down to 20 and 30. On bar iron the duty had been brought down from 75 to 30 per cent.—from $25 to $10 per ton; on the poor man's coal, the duty had been reduced from 67 down to 30 per cent.—more than half the tax had been taken off foreign coal; now, this all looks very well for the consumers of iron and coal, but after a while he comes to speak of another class of the "toiling millions;" the voters of Pennsylvania, who make iron and dig coal; and now hear what this consistent secretary tells them. He tells them that the tariff of 1846 is the very thing for them; he congratulates them on the fact that "coal and iron are in greater demand, are bringing *better prices* than before the the repeal of the tariff of 1842;" these are his very words. Now, how the tariff of 1846 can at the same time reduce the prices of iron and coal to favor *consumers* and raise them to favor *producers*, is a theory I cannot understand—it is an up and down, yes and no operation, which will puzzle the ingenuity of the secretary himself to explain. But, then, he has another, and a worse difficulty to explain. The object of the tariff of 1846 was to increase the revenue. Now, what has been its effect? It has destroyed more than half the revenue arising from these very articles, without benefit to any body but the *foreign importer* who sells us his iron, according to Mr. Walker, for a "better price," pays ten dollars instead of twenty-five into Mr. Walker's empty sub-treasury, puts the fifteen dollars as additional profits into his pocket, which, under the tariff of 1842, he would have paid into the treasury. Now the same thing may be said of coal—instead of a duty of six cents a bushel, the foreign importer now pays less than three, sells his coal at a "better price," and fobs the difference. Who then does Mr. Walker's tariff benefit? The foreigner, and the foreigner only, at the expense of the American treasury and the American people. Salt was another article illustrating the folly of low duties, the effect of which was to destroy revenue and increase prices; the prices are increased by diminishing home supply, and giving the foreigner the control of the market, and the revenue is reduced by the operation. Nearly three-fourths of the duty was taken off salt to favor the poor—the result is, that foreign salt has raised 25 per cent., and the treasury has lost three-fourths of the revenue. And yet Mr. Walker insists that his tariff favors the poor and increases the revenue! The same thing is true in an infinite variety of similar cases, which he had not time now to particularize; he would, however, refer to one or two, for the benefit of the South—the cotton-growers, the great admirers of the tariff of 1846. Now how has it affected these gentlemen? The duty had been greatly reduced on cotton-bagging; this checked the domestic supply, and the price, I am credibly informed, has increased from twelve cents per yard, under the tariff of 1842, to twenty cents under the glorious free-trade tariff of 1846. The treasury getting less, and the consumer paying more; the price of the cotton itself has been reduced nearly one-third, amounting to a loss on the cotton crop of $20,000,000. Cotton, under the tariff of 1842, brought ten cents per pound, it is now down to seven, and still declining. The sugar business, I am told, has fared even worse than the cotton. Mr. Walker is himself obliged to admit that the cotton interest has suffered; and what Southern interest has not? The injury is universal, and the suffering must soon become so. The famine and the potato had saved, for the moment, the North and West; but that over, and the floods of foreign goods will soon sweep away their last dollar. Such always has been and always will be the effect of low duties. Nothing but *war* and *famine* have saved this administration; it is now the daily bread it feeds upon; destroy the war at home, and the famine abroad, and it cannot survive an hour.

Before leaving this topic, he wished to make one other remark, it was this: that it appeared from the treasury reports, that the imports of iron, coal, salt, etc., had been very little increased, so that the treasury had actually lost more than half the revenue on these articles, amounting to several millions of dollars, which was so much clear gain to the foreign importer, while Mr. Walker's "poor people" had been obliged to pay more for these necessaries of life, imported from abroad, than they had to pay under the oppressive and much abused tariff of 1842, when produced at home.

But there is another position taken by Mr. Walker in favor of the free-trade theory, which I cannot let pass unnoticed. Mr. Walker distinctly avows it to be his purpose and his policy, to prevent "the substitution of rival domestic products" for similar foreign goods. This purpose was more than once avowed by Mr. Walker in his celebrated report of 1845. It is his declared policy to put down the productions of American industry, American "rival products," and give the American market to our foreign "rivals." And these are the principles and the policy openly avowed by an American Secretary, and sanctioned by an American President—to prefer the productions of *foreign* to those of American industry—to send away of our money, $50,000,000 more than was required under the tariff of 1842, to get the same amount of revenue. And why send this fifty additional millions to support and enrich foreign labor, instead of our own? Why destroy the markets for fifty millions of the productions of *American* agriculture and *American* labor combined, and supply its place with the productions of *foreign* agriculture and *foreign* labor? I demand a reason for preferring foreign to American productions. I ask our President and Secretary, why they prefer foreign hats, shoes, boots, coats—everything they eat, drink, and wear—to those of American manufacture? Why they prefer foreign sugar, salt, iron, and coal, when our resources are abundant and inexhaustible, and our labor ready and willing, with proper protection and encouragement, to bring them forth? But no! This must not be permitted. "Domestic rival products" must not, says Mr. Walker, be substituted for those of foreign countries, and especially for those of England; for, says Mr. Walker, if we don't take more British goods, "England will have to pay specie for our breadstuffs, and not having it to spare, she will bring down the price of our cotton." No wonder this report was printed in the House of Lords; and its author would appear much better advocating such doctrines before the House of Lords, than before our American Congress. They were British doctrines—not American; and they must be so pronounced by every true American heart. Yet we are told, that Mr. Polk is "the model President," and Mr. Walker, the "model" Secretary; and a pretty pair of "models" they are. [A laugh.] Queen Vic. would surely grant a patent for such "model" *American* statesmen as these. But let them look out. Old Rough is coming, with his check shirt and home made coat, tc pitch all these miserable models and British doctrines overboard, to go where they belong.

But, sir, Mr. Walker's ostensible object is revenue. He reduces duties to increase revenue, and this can only be done by increasing imports in a greater ratio than the reduction of duties—for instance: he has reduced the duty on hats from 50 to 30 per cent.; on shoes, from 45 to 30 per cent.; on ready-made clothing he has reduced the duties from 50 to 30 per cent.; on smith work, from 61 to 30, making an average reduction of more than 40 per cent. on these articles. This will, of course, diminish the revenue 40 per cent. unless the imports are increased in the same proportion. Now, why import two-fifths more shoes, hats, clothing ready-made, and blacksmith work from abroad, and throw our own mechanics out of employment, to beg or starve, and give our money to foreigners by millions, without adding a cent to the revenue—robbing American industry of its just rewards, and giving it to foreigners; and this is the way Mr. Walker favors and supports American labor, the "toiling millions?"

A DIALOGUE.

Suppose Mr. Walker calls to settle with his hatter on the Avenue, Mr. Tod, saying, "Sir, I am sorry to leave you, but I must get my hats from England hereafter, to enable her to pay me a high price for cotton; but remember, sir, I am a great friend to the 'mechanics and workingmen,' and particularly to the 'voters;'" would not Mr. Tod be very apt to tell him that he would vote for those who supported American industry and American mechanics, instead of foreigners, and would he not be very likely to receive the same kind of comfort from his tailor, shoemaker, blacksmith, and all?

Suppose Mr. Walker next addresses the iron, the woolen, the cotton, the paper, the glass, and other manufacturers of the United States, saying, "gentlemen, you must cease to substitute your 'domestic products' for foreign goods; and to compel you to do so, I have taken off more than half the duty levied by the tariff of 1842 on the foreign 'rival products.'" But why, they may say, Mr. Walker, thus destroy American capital and American labor, giving our money and our market to foreigners? Why send millions of money abroad to purchase foreign wool, and other agricultural produce—breadstuffs, and raw materials in disguise—

fashioned into goods, which we can better supply at home, made of American agricultural produce, and saving millions and hundreds of millions of dollars to fill up the channels of circulation at home, making our own, instead of foreign countries prosperous? "Well, there is some force in this. But gentlemen," says Mr. Walker, "I reduce the duties to increase the revenue. How will you answer this, gentlemen?" The answer, sir, is plain; these low duties never did, and never will increase revenue. The revenue has always gone up and down with the duties, they being the source of revenue. In this country, where the revenue is a *voluntary*, and not a *compulsory* contribution, by the people to the Government, the way to make a rich treasury is to make a rich and prosperous people. Send your money abroad, break down and impoverish your own citizens, and you, of course, impoverish your treasury. When do people purchase and consume rich goods, paying high duties? When they have the ability, when they are prosperous. When do they abstain? When they are poor, and without money. If you wish, sir, to enrich your exchequer, give *protection* and *prosperity* to your own people, as the one is always the consequence of the other. "But, gentlemen," says Mr. Walker, "I have another reason for reducing duties, it is to favor the 'poor—the toiling millions'—by reducing the price of their goods." Well, sir, how is this? Have you done it? You tell us that you have, by the tariff of 1846, reduced the duties on iron, coal, salt, and many other leading articles, more than one-half, and yet you yourself tell us in your late official report, that the prices of these articles are now higher, under the tariff of 1846, than they were before the repeal of the tariff of 1842! Can you explain this? "Well, gentlemen, not exactly—not at this moment." Well, sir, will you allow us to do it? "Certainly, gentlemen, certainly, if you please." Well, sir, by destroying protection, and opening our ports to foreigners, you alarm capital—you check investments—you break down competition, and you, of course, diminish supply and increase prices. "Demand and supply regulate prices." Give protection, increase your machinery, start new factories, stimulate competition, increase supply, and you reduce prices. This, sir, is a law of trade, as certain in its operations as the ebbing and flowing of the tides. "Well, gentlemen, I am not *practically* acquainted with these matters. I am a cotton-grower, I wish to make money plenty, and prices high abroad where I sell, and make it scarce and prices low at home where I buy; I want to sell in a high, and buy in a low market. I have not now time to discuss this question further. I am very busy, I must go to the Treasury, but I beg you to believe that I am the special friend of the American mechanics, workingmen, and particularly *the voters*. Good-bye, I must be off."

But Mr. Walker has not only reduced the duties on the productions of American mechanics, but he has reduced still more the duties on the luxuries of the rich. Among the rest, he has reduced the duty on foreign brandy and spirits distilled from grain nearly one-half; and this, too, is done to increase the revenue. We must, therefore, import and drink double as much brandy and spirits as we did under the tariff of 1842, otherwise Mr. Walker will lose revenue. Yes, sir, import and consume double as much brandy to get the same amount of revenue. Instead of reducing, he should have doubled those duties, and if he and his friends will drink foreign liquors, let them pay for them. But Mr. Walker's revenue has gone down, and he now calls on Congress to make up for the loss of revenue on brandy, fine cloths, and other luxuries, by taxing the poor man's *tea* and *coffee*. Let him restore the duties on the rich man's brandy, and other luxuries, and then talk of taxing tea and coffee, and not before; and till he does this, he will never succeed in perpetrating this outrage on the American people.

Knowing that low duties always invite excessive imports, resulting in a large balance of trade against the country, ending in bankruptcy and ruin, Mr. Walker undertakes to show that an unfavorable balance of trade is of no importance; that the balances against us have been frequent and heavy. Yet, he says, our country has survived and prospered.

But does not Mr. Walker know that excessive imports, and an unfavorable balance of trade, are always followed by the exportation of specie, with all its disastrous consequences?

Mr. Walker might as well tell a farmer in Pennsylvania, who sold his whole crop to a merchant from whom he got all his supplies for his family, that it made no difference to him whether, at the end of the year, the balance was in his favor or against him. A nation is a family upon a large scale, and the same principles of industry and economy that secures wealth and prosperity to the one, will secure it to the other. The great error, on this point, consists in the assumption of a fact that is not true—that the foreign goods we purchase are to be re-sold, whereas they are imported for *consumption*, and are consumed, and the balance against the country has to be paid in cash.

I must hasten on—but I cannot omit to notice, for a moment, one of the greatest absurdities of this extraordinary report. Mr. Walker gravely tells us, that our domestic products amount to $3,000,000,000 a year; of this we exported last year $150,000,000, the balance being required for the supply of the home market; but he says, that by adopting low duties, we might increase our exports and imports to $900,000,000, and our revenue to $90,000,000 a year. This he makes out by *supposing*, against all experience, that foreign countries would take from us three times as much as they now do; but *supposing* what has always happened, that by *low duties* you break down and paralyze your own national industry, export your specie, involving the country in ruin and bankruptcy, destroying both exports and imports, then what? Instead of $900,000,000, your exports and imports will sink down to less than $250,-000,000, the ordinary amount. But Mr. Walker goes further still; he says, by adopting absolute and unqualified free-trade, resorting, of course, to *direct taxation* for revenue —levying the taxes on the *American people* instead of *foreign goods*—Mr. Walker says we would "measure our annual trade in imports and exports by *thousands of millions!*" Who can but smile at such insanity run mad. Mr. Walker might measure his imports by "*thousands of millions*" if he had money to pay for them, but when he tells us that the whole of the specie in the United States does not exceed $90,000,000, not enough to pay for one month's imports under his "free-trade" system, how long would it last? His "free-trade" engine would blow out before it got fairly under way. Our imports may depend upon ourselves, but our exports depend upon the disposition of foreign countries to purchase; and they will not purchase from us when they can supply themselves. If Mr. Walker can devise a plan to create a famine or the potatoe rot in Europe, he may, to some extent, carry out his theory, but not otherwise. We can purchase as much as we please while we have money or credit; but like the reckless spendthrift, when these are gone, we must quit, and go to work, or starve. There is but one way in which Mr. Walker's plan of making our imports and exports amount, under "free-trade," to "thousands of millions," and that is the plan, no doubt, he has in view. That is, to export our ore and coal to England, and bring it back in bar iron, axes, hoes, shovels, needles, and anchors. Export our wheat and corn, and bring it back in flour; or what is worse for us, and better for them, worked up in costly manufactures. Send them our hogs, and bring them back in Bologna sausages. Send them our raw hides, and bring them back in leather, shoes, gloves, etc. Send them our wool at fifty cents per pound, and buy it again at ten times that amount, in cloth—paying, not only for the wool, but for the foreign labor, and the profits of foreign capital employed in its manufacture. Send ten dollars' worth of raw material, and buy it back with the addition of one hundred dollars paid to foreign labor for working it into goods, while our own labor is left without money and without employment. I see it stated, that one dollar's worth of iron, made into main-springs of watches, is worth $20,000; and this is all labor and its subsistence.

Such is Mr. Walker's theory of "free-trade" carried out to its practical results—this, he says, would give employment to all our ships. Yes, sir, and with the same propriety he might advise a western Pennsylvania farmer to load his wagon with wheat, and take it to Kentucky to be ground, and bring back his flour, to keep his team employed—what would the farmer say to Mr. Walker's proposition?

THE DEGRADING EFFECT OF "FREE-TRADE" ON LABOR AND WAGES.

But, sir, I wish to present another, and a more important view, in connexion with this subject of "free-trade," which Mr. Walker regards as the greatest blessing that could be bestowed upon the people of this country, and especially upon the laboring people—the "toiling millions" as he calls them—in whose prosperity and welfare he seems to take such especial interest; he speaks of increasing their "comfort, education, and intelligence," of "enhancing wages of mechanics and toiling workmen," blessing them with increased prosperity.

Now, I undertake to say, and to demonstrate, that just the reverse of all this would be its consequences; and I submit the matter to the enlightened judgment and decision of the American people. I say that, instead of enhancing wages and increasing the "prosperity, comfort, education, and intelligence" of "the toiling millions," it would degrade them in every department of industry, to the miserable condition of the pauper and serf-labor of Europe, subsisting themselves and families on a shilling a day.

Break down the walls of protection, repeal the tariff, open your ports, establish free-trade, and let in the products of foreign twelve and a half cents a day labor, and American labor must quit work and give up their markets till our money is all gone; then our mechanics and workingmen must come down, and work as cheap as they do. Is not this inevitable? And these are the blessings Mr. Walker has in reserve for the dear people, "the voters," "the toiling millions." Mr. Walker says in his Report, that "freight," with steam and modern improvements, amounts to little or nothing; that *duties* are the only thing that prevent foreigners from taking free and full possession of our markets, and in this he is right for once; they will take possession of our markets till American labor, mechanics, and all, come down and work for a shilling a day. Is not this perfectly clear? Can it be doubted or denied? For illustration: suppose in Baltimore manufacturers and mechanics hire workmen at twenty-five cents a day, and here in Washington they pay a dollar, will not the Baltimoreans send down their goods, hats, shoes, clothes, everything, undersell the hatters and others here, and must they not either give up business, or bring their labor down to the Baltimore standard? They may buy as long as they have money, but when their money is all gone, they must work cheap or starve. The only difference between Europe and Baltimore is the "freight," which Mr. Walker says is now but a slight impediment to imports. Such would be the ultimate effects of "free-trade" on American labor.

The great object and office of a tariff is to protect high and prosperous labor against the ruinous effects of free competition with low-priced and depressed labor. Low labor wants no protection against high labor, but the high must be protected against the low, or by free competition be brought down to its level. This result follows just as certainly as the removal of a wall which separated two unequal bodies of water, would bring the one down to the level of the other. Proclaim "free-trade," open your ports to the productions of the pauper and serf-labor of Europe, working for ten cents a day, and what follows? In pour their goods, and out pours your money; goods come in and money goes out, till it is all gone; then we must make our own hats, shoes, and clothing, or go without. And this is the way in which Mr. Walker, his "model President," and the advocates of "free-trade," would increase the wages, and promote the "comfort, education, and intelligence" of the American people—by degrading them to the condition, *moral* and *physical*, and, in the end, the *political* condition, too, of the paupers and slaves of foreign despots. How could American freemen live on a shilling a day? How could they educate their children, who would be obliged to work from the cradle to the grave? Unfitted to be free, they would become subjects and slaves. Depress one class, and you of course elevate another—put down the many and you build up the few—first you establish a nobility, and next a king. I submit, would not such be the tendency, if not the end of "free-trade," carried out to its final results? Yet this is "*democracy*," the modern "progressive democracy," as preached and practised by Polk and his party.

But this is not all. The duties levied on foreigners to protect our laboring men, furnish nearly the whole revenue for the support of Government. But establish "free-trade," and you not only release the foreigner and his goods from all taxation, but you transfer the burdens to your own impoverished people—you appoint swarms of tax-gatherers to harass and plunder them—to sell their last cow, and take the last bite of bread from their children, to support your wars, your standing armies, tax-gatherers, lords, princes, and pensioners. The revenue collected from protective duties heretofore levied on foreign goods was felt, not as a burden, but as a blessing and benefit in the protection and prosperity it gave to the national industry; but repeal these duties, paid by foreigners for the privilege of selling their goods in our markets, open your ports, crush your labor, inundate your country with foreign productions, and then resort for revenue to *direct taxation*, and you convert a blessing into a bitter curse. But, thank God, the remedy is in the hands of the people! I leave Mr. Walker and free-trade with "the voters," the "toiling millions," to settle the matter in their own way.

Mr. Walker says, "it will soon become an axiomatic truth, that all tariffs are a tax upon labor and wages"—on *American* labor. A small mistake; if he had said a tax upon *foreign* labor, for the protection and encouragement of *American* labor, he would have been right. This is a small blunder. He will no doubt revise and correct in it his next essay on the beauties of "free-trade."

But Mr. Walker boasts that his report of 1845, published in England by order of Parliament, "accelerated, if it did not produce the repeal of the corn laws." This is another blunder. The corn laws were only suspended till Mr. Walker repealed the odious anti-British tariff of 1842. That accomplished, and the famine over, the corn laws go into operation again on the 1st of March, sliding scale and all. But Mr. Walker says he has not only converted Great Britain, but he has staggered all Europe. Hear him! Hear him! "France, Russia, Germany, Austria, Italy, Prussia, Switzerland, Holland, Belgium, Denmark, Sweden, and even China have moved, or are *vibrating* or *preparing* to move, in favor of the same great principle;" another blunder, these nations, or most of them, so far from relaxing, are increasing or strengthening their protective systems, wherever their markets are likely to be invaded by foreign manufactures coming into competition with their own. But who told Mr. Walker they were "vibrating or preparing to move?" They may *vibrate* a little, to amuse Mr. Walker, and induce him to take our duties off their goods, and he has done it. And what have they done? Nothing—nothing at all. They are "vibrating," but their tariff vibrations all go up instead of down, while they laugh at Mr. Walker's simplicity.

But, above all, I beg you to protect and cherish your national industry; to protect and sustain it against the efforts of its enemies, *foreign* and *domestic*, to break it down. Labor lies at the very foundation of the national prosperity. Labor, in every department—in the fields, in the workshops, in the factories—cherish it and preserve it as the great element of your national wealth and independence. When labor prospers, all other interests prosper. When labor is depressed, all other interests must suffer and sympathize with it.

What is all other capital compared with the capital of labor? Estimate your labor at one-tenth of your population, say 2,000,000 of laboring men; if they earn but $180 per year, this is equal to the interest of a capital of $3000 per annum at 6 per cent., which, multiplied by 2,000,000, the number of laborers, makes our *labor capital* equal to *six thousand millions of dollars;* and this is the great element of power and wealth and prosperity that Mr. Walker would sacrifice and degrade to the wretched

[NOTE.—The last pages of the only remaining copy of this speech in pamphlet form are destroyed.]

To show that the facts stated by Mr. Stewart in this speech were never contradicted or denied, we refer to the following incident:

Shortly after the close of the tariff debate, Mr. Stewart and Judge Bayley of Va., were competitors for the floor; when the Speaker was about to assign the floor to Mr. Bayley, Mr. Stewart said he had a point to make, in which he felt confident the chair and the house would sustain him; all would recollect that at the close of his speech, on the tariff, the gentleman from Va., Mr. Bayley, rose and pledged himself to answer this speech *before the close of the debate*, or forfeit his right to ever speak again upon this floor. He has never answered or *attempted* to answer it, nor any one else, and he has therefore forfeited his right to the floor. The chair recollecting the fact, sustained the point, and amid roars of laughter, assigned the floor to Mr. Stewart.

COMMENTS AND OPINIONS OF THE PRESS.

"We have just perused this admirable and triumphant refutation of Mr. Secretary Walker's free-trade doctrine. The famine in Europe which created a great demand for our breadstuffs enabled the advocates of the free-trade policy for a while to deceive those who look merely upon the surface of things, by attributing this exportation all to a low tariff. While this exportation temporarily saved the country from the ruinous effects of the tariff of 1846, the loco papers have been shouting with tones of exultation—'where's the ruin?' Mr. Stewart shows that this increase of the exports of breadstuffs is in no degree owing to the repeal of the tariff of 1842, but to the famine. The export of cotton has been less by four millions of dollars than the average exports of the last ten years, and tobacco a million and a half. If this reduction of the tariff has caused an increase of exports, why has it not extended to some other articles than breadstuffs?

"But a change is already felt—starvation is ceased—already our cities begin to feel that there is a 'pressure in the money market.' The *Argus* and some other papers may for a while continue to throw out the inquiry, 'where's the ruin?' But this will be only for country consumption where the trouble is not yet seriously felt. Mr. Stewart says that on the first of March next, the corn laws of England will be again in full operation—that they were merely suspended during the famine—and then Mr. Walker will be caught in Sir

Robert Peel's trap; exports will cease, the revenue fall off, and Mr. Walker be obliged to call for a restoration of the tariff of 1842 to replenish his empty treasury and to feed his armies and officers at home and abroad, military and civil.

"We look upon this speech as a complete and triumphant refutation of the long and visionary report of Mr. Walker."—*Standard, N. Y.*

"The following is from the speech delivered by Mr. Stewart before the House of Representatives, in March last. The speech is an unique production, and the facts and arguments contained in it are sufficient to overrun all the force which can be brought to bear upon the subject of protection by the advocates of free-trade, or of a tariff for revenue only."—*Gazette, Va.*

"We commend to the attentive perusal of our readers, the speech of Mr. Stewart. We consider it a most valuable production. Mr. Walker and his famous report are minutely dissected, and their deformities fully exhibited. It is the best exposé of the relative bearings of a high and low tariff we recollect to have seen. Let none be deterred from reading this speech, because of its length. Commence it, and you will finish it."—*Mail, N. J.*

"The conclusion of Mr. Stewart's able and convincing speech in defence of the tariff will be found on our first page. We say to the *farmer*, who is inclined to credit the assertion made in Franklin county and elsewhere, that the existing tariff is 'ruinous and oppressive,' to read this speech and see how their interests are to be sacrificed by the locofoco bill now undergoing discussion in the House. We say to the mechanic, look at the table on the first page and see what 'love for protection' the dear locos have."—*Gazette, Ky.*

"It is a very just remark of the Washington, Pa., *Reporter*, that 'Mr. Stewart may be regarded as the shield of the Whig party on the floor of the House of Congress. His constant watchfulness over the true interests of the people, and his fearless defence of Whig measures, entitle him to the esteem and gratitude of the whole country. With the bravery of an Achilles, he is ready for every exigency, bearing himself nobly, and to an extent successfully, through every battle.'"—*Whig, Mo.*

"Mr. Stewart, of Pennsylvania, has made an able and practical speech in favor of Western improvements and in vindication of Whig principles.

"He replied to the labored arguments and erroneous statements of Jameson, Kennedy and Ficklin, with much effect. With a 'pencil of light,' he delineated the whole American system as the very foundation of our national prosperity. Next week we shall make copious extracts from this admirable speech; we have read it with much pleasure and profit. It is a plain exposition of Whig principles."—*Statesman, N. H.*

"The excellent speech of this *first rate* representative in the Congress of the United States, occupies a very large space in to day's paper, but, as it is a very interesting document, both as regards the questions discussed and the able manner in which they are handled, we doubt not that our readers will be pleased with its publication. We ask for it, on the part of all intelligent and honest men, an impartial perusal.

"Since ever Mr. Stewart has occupied a place in the councils of the nation, he has evinced a degree of devotion to the interests of the country, unsurpassed, and exhibited such a profound knowledge of its institutions and the policy that should govern it, that he has gained for himself, from one end of the Union to the other, a reputation of which any man might be proud."—*Register, Ind.*

"The Hon. Andrew Stewart, the talented Whig Representative in Congress from Fayette county, well known as a distinguished advocate of the tariff policy, attacked the President's Message in the House, on Wednesday last, and it is said, 'entirely demolished its free-trade arguments.'

"The speech of Mr. S. is spoken of as able and conclusive, so much so that no champion of the Administration from the free states attempted a reply. The only one who offered was of Tennessee, a roaring locofoco free-trade man, Johnson, who after blustering awhile and endeavoring to rebut the arguments of Mr. Stewart, was finally silenced, being met in a way he little expected. We shall publish the debate when received."—*The News, Miss.*

"We this week make some valuable extracts from the speech of Andrew Stewart, Esq., member of Congress from Fayette county, Pa., on the subject of the tariff, to which we would direct the attention of all into whose hands this number of our paper may fall. That is the grand rallying point, and the one to which we desire most to see all eyes directed. If we had nothing else in view, the honor, the prosperity, and the perpetuation of the free institutions of our country should prompt us to urge the protective policy."—*Sentinel, Conn.*

"We particularly ask attention to the speech of the Hon. Andrew Stewart, member of Congress from Pennsylvania, to Mr. Walker, the Secretary of the Treasury. As yet, we confess, we have not given the ponderous report of the Secretary any more than a casual reading, a glance at its leading points—not that we do not consider it of any importance, but because we have not had time to digest its crude and monstrous propositions. Under the peculiar circumstances of the country, and from the position of the parties, we are disposed to attach more than usual importance to this document; and we had determined to give it a patient reading, with a view of expressing freely our opinions upon it. When about to do so, the speech of Mr. Stewart met our eye, and we transcribed it from the columns of the *National Intelligencer*, with a hearty approval of its manly spirit. It is pungent in its language, and unanswerable in its arguments and deductions. If this is a foretaste of the gauntlet Mr. *Walker* has to *run*, he will have occasion for all the haste he can conveniently make to get beyond the lash of the friends of protection.

"But for the present we hand Mr. Walker over to Mr. Stewart, and we beg the friends of the country—the friends of protection—those who would save the poor man from the *mercies* of the demagogue, to read and see how a small man can be used up on his own ground."—*Ohio State Journal.*

"Mr. Stewart's speech *on the tariff of* 1842, and on Mr. Secretary Walker's free-trade report, delivered a few weeks ago in Congress, is published in this paper. The space it occupies could not be better filled. Plain and practical, it can easily be comprehended by the intelligent reader. It is to the point, and exposes forcibly the anti-American policy which has been so industriously promulgated by President Polk and his Secretary of the Treasury; and therefore we trust that every one into whose hands this paper may fall, will give it a careful and honest perusal."—*Republican, Ill.*

"There never was more truth and humor put into a brief compass than in the following pithy extract from the recent speech of Hon. Andrew Stewart, of Pa., in the U. S. House of Representatives. It describes that miserable thing, *Polkism,* with the faithfulness of a daguerreotype :

"'But this administration goes by the rule of contrary; their theories and their measures are always at war. When they preach economy, I look out for extravagance; when they flatter the people as the true sovereigns of the land, then comes a veto; when they cry peace, then look out for war; when they say democracy, look out for aristocracy; when they denounce paper money, look out for treasury notes; when they say 54° 40′ or *fight,* look for "*slink out,*" and 49; when they say *no conquest,* look out for *all of Mexico.*'

"It is said that no speech yet delivered in Congress has been so largely subscribed for as Mr. Stewart's, 50,000 copies having been already sent out."—*Herald, La.*

"We have placed upon the opposite page the speech of Hon. Andrew Stewart of Pennsylvania, on the subject of the tariff. It needs no comment but such as every sensible reader will make for himself. We commend it to the friends of James K. Polk, whose election was advocated on the ground of his especial friendship for 'Protection to the farmer and mechanic.'"—*Register, Vt.*

"Mr. Stewart of Pennsylvania has made an able and practical speech in vindication of Whig principles.

"He replied to the labored arguments and erroneous statements of Jameson, Kennedy and Ficklin, with much effect. With a 'pencil of light,' he delineated the whole American system as the very foundation of our national prosperity. Next week we shall make copious extracts from this admirable speech; we have read it with much pleasure and profit. It is a plain exposition of Whig principles."—*Whig, Tenn.*

"We publish the entire speech of Mr. Stewart, of Pa., in favor of Western improvements and the protective tariff policy, in this day's *News.* It exhibits, in a clear and plain manner, the course of the two political parties upon these important and vital questions. Let every Farmer, Mechanic—every *Western* man—read it with attention. This speech of itself is worth the subscription to the Ohio *News* for one year, to any Western man."—*News, Ohio.*

The Raleigh (North Carolina) *Star* publishes the speech of the Hon. Andrew Stewart, of Pennsylvania, in defence of the tariff, and calls attention to it in the following language:

"Let no one fail to read the able and interesting speech of Mr. Stewart, in to-day's *Star* on the tariff. It uses up Mr. Polk and Secretary Walker most effectually."

"The speech of the Hon. Andrew Stewart on our first page should be read by every citizen who has a vote at the next Presidential Election. Its *facts* exhibiting the past official conduct of General Cass, its exposition of his inconsistencies upon matters of civil policy, and its unanswerable argument against locofoco measures and policy in general."—*Telegraph, Harrisburg, Pa.*

"The following strong and convincing arguments in domonstra tion of the practical benefits of the farmers by the protective system are extracted from a speech made in Congress by the Hon. Andrew Stewart, of this State. They constitute a complete refutation of the attacks made on the tariff in the locofoco papers."—*The Freeman, R. I.*

"On our first page will be found an able speech on the tariff, by *Mr. Stewart*, of Pennsylvania. *Farmers, Mechanics and Laboring men*, read it, and remember what you read."—*Gazette, Ga.*

"We this week publish the able and interesting speech of Mr Stewart, of Pa., on the tariff. Whigs read it and commit to your memory—honest locos read it and reflect."—*Star, S. C.*

IN FAVOR OF WESTERN IMPROVEMENTS AND THE TARIFF.

DELIVERED IN THE HOUSE OF REPRESENTATIVES, U. S., JANUARY 16TH, 1844.

MR. STEWART, of Pa., said, that although he was not from a Western State, yet the State from which he came was as deeply interested in the improvement of the navigation of the Western waters as any State in the Union. These great rivers were, in fact, but extensive feeders of those great lines of improvement connecting the Atlantic and Western States, made by Pennsylvania and Maryland at an expense of some $50,000,000, constituting a debt which now rested with mountain weight upon their people. These State works were alike national in their character and their benefits, and ought to have been made by national means, and would have been so made, with all the other great works of internal improvement which had involved the States of this Union in a foreign debt of $200,000,000, had that great "American system" of policy been continued, which had just been denounced in such emphatic terms as "an imposition—an exploded humbug," by the gentleman from Missouri [Mr. Jameson], Mr. Kennedy, of Indiana, and Mr. Ficklin, of Illinois, and over the "explosion" of which they had exulted in so much triumph. True, it had been exploded, and the prosperity of this country from its deepest foundations had been involved in the explosion. It had thrown back this great nation a century from the point where it would have now been, had that "explosion" not occurred; and had involved the States (and among the rest the States represented by these gentlemen) in debts and embarrassments, from which (if this denounced system was not speedily restored) they would not recover for a century to come.

THE EFFECT OF THE VAN BUREN SYSTEM ON THE INTERIOR AND WESTERN STATES.

Mr. S. affirmed, and could demonstrate, that by adopting Mr. Van Buren's system, the whole of the great interior and

Western States would be now, henceforth, and forever, excluded from all participation in the benefits of the disbursement of the ample revenues of this Government, amounting to some twenty or thirty millions a year. Without the power of internal improvements (a power which Mr. Van Buren expressly denied), where, he would ask these gentlemen, is the object? He called on them to point their finger to a single one in the interior and Western States on which any portion of the national revenue could be constitutionally expended. Look at the great heads of appropriation. Where are your navy and army, for which seventeen millions are this year required? Where your forts and fortifications; your light-houses, buoys, and beacons; your seawalls, breakwaters, and harbors; your custom-houses, foreign intercourse, surveying, and Indian departments? Were any of these in the interior? None—not one. These were the objects on which the revenues of the Government had been expended, poured out like water, and, without this power, must continue to be expended, now and forever. The people of the great interior and the West were thus doomed to be tax-payers, "hewers of wood and drawers of water," as they had been for the seaboard. Their money, like their vast rivers, might continue to flow in ample streams to the Atlantic; and by denying this beneficent power, you blot out the sun which alone could exhale and carry back, in refreshing showers, any portion of these vast contributions to the interior sources from which they come. Draw a line five miles from the seaboard, the external boundary of the United States, and he believed he would be safe in saying that there had not been expended, out of three hundred millions, as much within this circle since the explosion of "the whig system" by the Maysville and Wabash river vetoes, as had been expended, first and last, in the erection of these buildings for the accommodation of Congress; and even that amount, small as it was, must (according to Mr. Van Buren) have been expended in violation of the Constitution.

How gentlemen who advocated these appropriations, and represented the interior and Western States, so deeply interested in the policy of internal improvements, could, consistently with "their principles," support Mr. Van Buren, who expressly denied their constitutionality, he was at a loss to imagine. [Here Mr. Wentworth inquired by what authority Mr. S. charged Mr. Van Buren with denying this power.] Mr. S. said, on the authority of his own signature, not once, but repeatedly; and, for the gentleman's information, he would read a paragraph from Mr. Van Buren's letter of the 4th October, 1832, to a committee at the Shocco springs, North Carolina, where, in answer to a request for his opinion on the subject of internal improvements, he says: "The broadest and best defined division is that which distinguishes between the direct construction of works of internal improvements by the General Government, and pecuniary assistance given by it to such as are undertaken by others."

"The Federal Government," says Mr. Van Buren, "does not, in my opinion, possess the power first specified; nor can it derive it from the assent of the States in which such works are to be constructed." He afterwards expressly approved the veto of the bill subscribing stock to the Maysville road, which was of the second class of works specified above; and he also approved of the veto of the bill for the improvement of the navigation of the Wabash river; and, upon the same principles, were he now President, he would be bound by his oath to veto this very appropriation. Yet gentlemen advocate this measure with great zeal and ability, and he fully concurred in all they said in its favor; but how could they, at the same time and in the same breath, advocate the election of Mr. Van Buren to an office in which he would be obliged to veto this appropriation if it passed? This was the dilemma. The gentleman from Missouri [Mr. Jameson] has told us that the Whigs are "a party without principles," and that his party had principles, and that they will "stand or fall by them." Now, the gentleman must give up his man or his principles—he cannot support both; they are antipodes. Which will he do? He says they will stand by their principles—very well! This they may do; but with the man they are sure to fall. The Whigs, the gentleman says, are the "fag ends of all parties;" they live in "glass houses." He has talked very learnedly about "coons, hard cider, cider-barrels," etc., and informs us that the Whigs have been weighed in the balance and found wanting—a small mistake. It was Mr. Van Buren who was, in 1840, weighed in the balance and found wanting; and he would now predict that in 1844 he would be found much lighter than he was then, because the effects of his principles and measures had been severely felt, and were now better understood by the people. But these were small matters. He would now give his attention to something more important. Whilst denouncing the "American system," which had been called the Clay system, reference had been made to the antagonist system—the Van Buren system, which, in 1830, had been established on its ruins. This was a great question; it lay at the very foundation of the national prosperity, and he was glad of the opportunity now presented of calling public attention to it.

THE VAN BUREN AND WHIG SYSTEM CONTRASTED.

What were these two opposite systems of national policy? And what had been their effects on the country? To understand this, it was necessary to refer to a few historical facts, which he would do very briefly.

The great object of the American system was the protection of American against foreign industry by a protective tariff, and the disbursement of the surplus revenue (which always had, and always would, result from such a tariff) for the improvement of the internal condition of the country. The collection of revenue for one great object—national protection, and its disbursement for another equally important object—national improvements. In ten years this system had paid off more than one hundred and twenty-five millions of war debt, and left in 1832, when that debt was discharged, an annual surplus of about eighteen millions of dollars. Now, was it not manifest that if this policy had been continued, and the surplus annually applied to internal improvements by direct appropriations and subscriptions of stock to works of a national character, made under State authority, the amount expended since 1832 (allowing no increase of revenue from the increase of wealth and population), would have now amounted in the aggregate to more than two hundred and fifty millions of dollars, and would have accomplished all, and more than all, the States have since done, without involving this Government or the States in one dollar of debt?—promoting, at the same time, a just and equal expenditure of revenue in the interior and Western States, in the execution of a great system of improvements, which, for defence in war, would be vastly superior to forts and fortifications, by promoting rapid concentration and movement. And if war never occurred these improvements were worth all they cost for the peaceful purposes of facilitating and cheapening intercourse among the States—the transportation of the mails, and of uniting and binding together the distant parts of our extended country in the strong and enduring bonds of interest and intercourse. Such would have been some of the happy fruits of this "exploded American system." He well remembered that, in 1824, the Committee on Roads and Canals, of which he was then a member, seeing the period of the final payment of the public debt rapidly approaching, when a large surplus revenue would be left unemployed in the treasury to crush the tariff and destroy the country, with a view to prepare for that event in time, a bill was reported laying the foundation of a system of internal improvement coextensive with the whole country, to absorb this surplus of eighteen millions a year, after the payment of the public debt, by organizing a board of internal improvement to survey all the great lines of internal communication, and have maps and plans of the whole, with estimates of their costs, in readiness, when the debt was paid, on which to expend this surplus. This bill was passed with the powerful aid of the distinguished senator from South Carolina [Mr. McDuffie]; and six years thereafter, when these surveys and estimates, under the direction of Mr. Calhoun, were nearly completed, and the public debt nearly discharged, a bill for the subscription of stock in the Maysville road—a link in a great chain of communication proposed to connect the Ohio river with the Gulf of Mexico—was passed, and this was the occasion seized on by Mr. Van Buren, as he would show, to break down this whole system, and thus force back upon the treasury this enormous surplus, which could be in no other wise expended, and thereby break down the tariff, destroy our manufactures, ruin agriculture and the mechanic arts, inundate the country with foreign goods, and export all the hard money in the country to pay for them, and throw upon the States the burden of making these works of internal improvement, which they were moreover tempted to undertake by the promise of the distribution among them of this annual surplus of eighteen millions of dollars. But the first distribution of forty-five millions had not yet been paid over when Mr. Van Buren was elected President, and who immediately called an extra session of Congress, recommended the repeal of the law, and withheld from the States more than nine millions of dollars, the fourth instalment of the first distribution. The States thus tempted having commenced their systems of improvement, were obliged to go on, still hoping for the promised aid, until they found themselves involved in a debt of two hundred millions, which this Government was bound in good faith to pay out of the proceeds of the public lands, or the surplus revenue, which would again result from a protective tariff if that policy were again adopted and adhered to.

Now, was it not clear that if the Whig system had been maintained, and the annual surplus of eighteen millions had been applied to internal improvement since the payment of the debt, in 1832, all the works made by the States would have been accomplished, and much more, without debt or embarrassment of any kind? He would now prove that Mr. Van Buren had himself contrived the whole plan of breaking down this system, which would ere now have elevated this country to a point of prosperity and power without a parallel, and had substituted his own destructive system, which had crushed this great nation, in spite of all its youthful energies, down to that degraded condition, struggling amid bankruptcies, and repudiation, State, national, and individual, in which it was found when the last Whig Congress assembled, and from which that Congress had succeeded in partially relieving it by passing the tariff of 1842, and thus restoring the protective policy. To prove that Mr. Van Buren was, in fact, the author of all this mischief, he referred to his letter to Sherrod Williams, of Kentucky, dated at Albany, the 8th of August, 1836, in which he says, that although he doubted the constitutional power of Congress to distribute the surplus revenue among the States, yet that he had "favored the idea as the only means of arresting internal improvements by the General Government;" that General Jackson had concurred in this opinion, and he had accordingly recommended this plan of distribution—not in one, but in two messages, in which all the objections now urged by Mr. Van Buren's friends against it were fully and satisfactorily answered; and he would commend this message to the attention of gentlemen now opposed to distribution. They would find this policy most ably advocated and defended in General Jackson's annual message, dated 7th December, 1830, in which the fear was expressed that Congress would appropriate the money to local objects; and, to avoid this, he recommended that it be given to the States, that they might appropriate it to national objects.

COMPARATIVE EXPENDITURES OF THE VAN BUREN AND WHIG ADMINISTRATIONS.

When Mr. Van Buren came into power he found the treasury with a surplus of $25,748,463; from which deduct unavailable funds and amount deposited with the States, and it still left an available surplus of upwards of sixteen millions of dollars; to which add proceeds of bank stock, etc., sold, upwards of eight and a half millions, making about twenty-five millions of dollars of surplus funds; yet with all this, and more than thirty-one millions a year of revenue, he left the treasury more than eight millions of dollars in debt, besides outstanding claims and debts amounting to several millions more. On the other hand, Mr. Adams, when this exploded and denounced American system was in operation, with six millions a year less revenue, paid off in four years upwards of forty-five millions of dollars of the war debt, and left a surplus of about six millions in the treasury when he retired. During Mr. Adams's administration, when like appropriations were made for internal improvements, the whole expenses of Government amounted, on an average, to about twelve and a half millions a year, while, during Mr. Van Buren's administration, they were increased to an average of more than thirty millions per year, and in one year to more than thirty-seven millions, nearly three times the amount expended by Mr. Adams. This was the "economy and reform" of Mr. Van Buren's administration, and it was the benefits and blessings of this system gentlemen seem so anxious to have restored. [Order, order, from both sides.] These were "spoils" worth having; and no wonder they were somewhat impatient to have them again; these were facts which he was prepared to establish by official documents; and such was the difference between the Van Buren and the American or Whig systems? [Here was a general call to order, and much confusion.] As this seemed to be an unpleasant topic, Mr. S. said he would turn his attention to something else.

WHAT THE LAST WHIG CONGRESS HAD DONE FOR THE COUNTRY.

Several gentlemen had inquired what the last Congress—the Whig Congress—had done for the country. If in order, he would tell them: They had restored the national prosperity by restoring the protective policy. The beneficial effects of the Whig tariff of 1842 were already seen, felt, and acknowledged throughout this country; it had revived manufactures, created new markets for the farmers, and had given employment to laborers everywhere; it had turned the balance of foreign trade from about twenty millions, the average balance for the last ten years against us, to a very large balance in our favor (with Great Britain alone the balance last year was $13,604,000 in our favor), resulting in the importation of twenty-two millions of specie, which had found its way into the banks, enabling them to resume specie payment; thus restoring a sound currency, and reducing the rate of interest from 4 or 5 per cent. per month to 4 or 5 per cent. per annum. And whilst it had conferred all these benefits and many more upon the country, it had at the same time increased the revenue from customs, as appeared by the late treasury report, from $12,496,834 in 1840, to $18,176,720 in 1842, and an estimated revenue from customs of twenty millions for the current year (and he had no doubt it would exceed by three or four millions this estimate), making an increase of revenue in 1842 over the year 1840 of more than six millions and a half of dollars. Yet the Globe and Mr. Van Buren's friends here are crying out, "reduce the tariff to increase the revenue;" when we had too much revenue the cry was, "reduce the tariff to reduce the revenue." So, whether we have too much or too little, the remedy was the same; reduce the tariff! reduce the tariff!! This was the great panacea, the Van Buren nostrum, to cure all diseases. [Here was another general call to order.] Mr. S. said he was but answering the inquiry, "What had the late Whig Congress done for the country?" He was showing the important fact that they had done more for the country than had been done for the last fourteen years—that they had lifted the country up from the degraded and prostrate condition in which Mr. Van Buren had left it, and if gentlemen did not wish this question answered they ought not to have asked it.

But this was not all the Whig Congress had done for the country. By the introduction of economy and retrenchment, they had reduced the expenditures of Government from $26,394,343, the amount appropriated for 1841, to about twenty-two millions last year. It had revived the policy (wholly abandoned by Mr. Van Buren) of improving the navigation of the Western waters, and had appropriated

$150,000 to these objects. [Here Mr. S. was interrupted by the inquiry, where is the evidence that Mr. Van Buren had abandoned this policy?] Where is the evidence? Here in the records of this House. In the last two years of Mr. Van Buren's administration the estimates of the officers in charge of these works were withheld by the secretary contrary to his uniform practice, and contrary to his duty, unless ordered so to do by the Executive. But Mr. Van Buren had not only withheld the estimates, and thus stopped the appropriations for these objects, but he had actually sold the snag-boats and tools on the Cumberland road, as the end and final winding up of all these operations; and whilst he thus withheld every dollar from the interior and the West, he more than doubled the expenditures of Government. [Here was another call to order by Mr. Cave Johnson and others—sustained by the Chair.] Why had the gentlemen not called his friend from Missouri [Mr. Jameson] to order when he applied all sorts of epithets to the Whigs—called them the "fag ends"—a party without principles, bank and anti-bank, tariff and anti-tariff, abolition and anti-abolition? This was all in order. He had told us that for "principles the Whigs had substituted coonery, coons, coon-skins, hard-cider, cider-barrels, canoes, and carousals." They had promised much and performed nothing. These were the gentleman's words, as reported; yet this was all in order—perfectly in order. But to show in reply what the Whig principles were, and their effects, was all out of order. Be it so. And as it was out of order to say anything against Mr. Van Buren, he would have to submit and pass to something else.

LOOK TO TARIFF AND RETRENCHMENT FOR MEANS.

It had been asked by several gentlemen, where was the money to come from to make these improvements? If in order, he would answer the inquiry. He would, in the first place, adhere to the present protective tariff, which would soon yield an ample surplus, by making the people prosperous, and furnishing them the means to purchase and consume foreign imports; the revenue would always be in exact proportion to the ability of the people to purchase and consume foreign goods. And in the next place, he would get the money for their Western improvements by retrenching the expenditures on the seaboard, on the army and navy, and forts and fortifications. The increased expenditures for the war and naval departments had been enormous, and ought to be greatly reduced. The average expenditures for the war and navy departments during Mr. Adams's administration amounted to only $7,750,000 per year; during Mr. Van Buren's administration they had increased to $16,872,000 per year, and this year there are required upwards of seventeen millions! In these branches there ought to be a reduction of five or six millions at least. He would never vote for duties on tea or coffee, or otherwise tax his constituents to keep up these enormous and useless establishments—useless, and worse than useless. In peace and in war a good system of roads and canals, with the citizens, soldiers, and volunteers, rapidly concentrated and moved without fatigue to any point where their presence might be required, was a more efficient and available system of defence for such a country as this than all the forts and fortifications and standing armies that could be raised. For this he had the authority of the most distinguished men that ever graced the War Department of this Government—and among them Calhoun, Cass, and Spencer, whose reports on this subject were most able and conclusive. With the railroads since constructed from this city, North and South, what hostile foot could have ever profaned this capitol? Before the enemy could have got out to sea from Baltimore, the forces from Boston, New York, Philadelphia, and Baltimore could have been concentrated, with all their munitions of war, at this point for its defence. Of what use were your forts? The enemy went round them and captured and burnt your city almost without resistance; and with the present improvements in the West, Upper Canada would have been taken without a struggle. He would therefore take from the army and navy and from forts and fortifications enough to make all these Western improvements without increasing the expenditures of the Government or the burdens of the people.

The claims of these Western rivers to the fostering care of the Government were peculiar and imperative. These rivers were the internal concerns of no State in the Union; they were external to all the States—they were boundaries; like the Atlantic, they washed the shores of many States, but passed through the territory of none. No State, therefore, ever had, or ever would appropriate a dollar for their improvement; hence they must be improved by the Government, or remain forever as they now are. The subject would, he hoped, be referred to a select committee, or the Committee on Roads and Canals, and not to the Ways and Means, who have, we are informed, refused to appropriate one dollar to internal improvements of any kind, no doubt on constitutional grounds, as two-thirds of that committee were friends of Mr. Van Buren, who denied the power, as had been shown.

THE CONSTITUTIONAL POWER CONSIDERED.

How any constitutional lawyer could deny to this Government the power to improve rivers and make roads and canals, he had always been at a loss to comprehend. This power was just as clear, and sustained on precisely the same grounds, as the power to erect a fort, improve a harbor, or to purchase a mail-bag. The Constitution gave Congress no express authority to do any of these things; they were incidental to the power of defence—of "regulating commerce" and "establishing post-offices," which powers necessarily carried with them the means of their own execution; but the express authority was given to Congress to pass all laws necessary and proper to carry into effect these powers. Hence the power to defend the country gave Congress the right to purchase cannon and erect forts as the means of defence. Now, if a railroad or a canal was found to be as available for defence as a fort, had they not as good a right to adopt it? Who could doubt it? The Constitution says, "Congress may regulate commerce with foreign nations and among the States." What right have you to build a ship or improve a harbor? The Constitution is silent upon the subject. It is because you have the power to regulate commerce with foreign nations. And was it not manifest that you have precisely the same power to regulate commerce among the States by improving rivers or harbors, or other means equally appropriate to this end? Most clearly. To have specified in the Constitution all the means, would have been to make a code and not a Constitution.

You have whole systems of legislation in relation to the transportation of the mail? Whence the right to pass all these laws imposing fines and forfeitures? It could only be sustained as incidental to the power conferred on Congress "to establish post-offices and post-roads." Now if roads were as necessary to transport the mail as coaches and contractors, mail-bags, etc., has Congress not the same right to construct them as means to accomplish this end? Certainly it had. Thus each grant of power carried with it, as a necessary and indispensable incident, the means of its own execution. The military power carried the right to construct military roads; the commercial power, commercial roads; and the post-office power, post roads. Without the right to adopt means these grants of power would be idle and nugatory. When it is proposed to construct a road or canal, the question for Congress to consider is, whether it is necessary and proper as a means of executing any of the constitutional powers of Congress? Defence in war, commerce in peace, or the transportation of the mail, if its fitness to any of these ends was admitted, the question was settled, and this right to construct it was undoubted. This was briefly his view of the constitutional power of Congress over the whole subject, and it was fully sustained by Chief Justice Marshall in the opinion delivered in the case of McCulloch and Maryland.

THE TARIFF AND PROTECTION.

Many gentlemen, and the gentleman from South Carolina [Mr. Holmes] among the rest, had introduced the tariff into this discussion. That gentleman, addressing himself to the Western members, had suggested that if they would go with him to destroy the tariff he would support an appropriation for the Mississippi. As a Western man, he rejected the gentleman's proffered aid. He would not consent that the gentleman should drive a dagger deep into their vitals, even though he might be willing to vote a pittance to pay their funeral expenses. He was utterly opposed to the introduction of the gentleman's wooden horse in the West. He wished none of the gentleman's help on such conditions. He would say to him, "*timeo Danaos et dona ferentes.*" If that gentleman could pour out the whole resources of the Government into the West it would be no compensation, not the tithe of compensation, for the injury the repeal of the tariff would inflict upon that great agricultural country.

He deeply regretted to see that the representatives of some of the Western States on this floor were now nearly unanimous against the protective policy, where formerly (as the journals would show) they were unanimously in its favor. The Western people and their interests were the same now as then. Whence this change? It was obviously political. These States were now represented by the political friends of Mr. Van Buren, who had recently declared in a letter to the editor of the Richmond *Enquirer* that he was opposed to the late protective tariff "both in its principles and details." They must therefore either abandon the protective policy or abandon Mr. Van Buren; and it seems that they have determined to adhere to the man and abandon the cherished policy of the West, without which they never can be prosperous; and this, upon some proper occasion, he would endeavor to demonstrate.

He could not forbear, however, to notice briefly some of the arguments urged by gentlemen from the West against the protective policy, and especially by the gentleman from Missouri [Mr. Jameson], who had spoken last, and who had but substantially repeated the objections urged by Mr. Van Buren and others. In reply, he would submit very briefly some facts and general reflections, to which he invited the sober and dispassionate attention of the Western farmers, who could not long be imposed upon by stale theories in opposition to well-known and ascertained facts.

In the first place, the gentleman from Missouri [Mr. Jameson] has told us that the foreign market was everything and the home market little or nothing; "that one-third of the State of Missouri could furnish surplus agricultural produce enough to supply all the persons engaged in manufacturing in the East."

2. That the Western farmers were robbed and plundered by the protective tariff for the benefit of the Eastern manufacturers.

3. That the effect of the protective policy was to "increase the price of everything the farmer has to buy, and reduce the price of everything he has to sell."

4. That the protective duty was always added to the price of the goods and paid by the consumer, whether the goods were of foreign or domestic origin, "for the manufacturer always puts up his goods to the full amount of the duty;" and thus (he says) the Western farmer is obliged to pay from 30 to 200 per cent. duty to the Eastern manufacturer.

5. That the "protective policy creates and cherishes monopolies."

Now, these comprehend all the great and substantial objections urged against the protective policy, condensed into a single view. They covered the whole ground, and they were all contained in Mr. Van Buren's letter of the 15th February last to the Indiana convention, and repeated in almost every anti-tariff speech in and out of this House.

He proposed to take up each of these stereotyped objections, and to show, not by theories and assertions, but by ascertained and admitted facts, that they were not only false and unfounded, but that exactly the reverse of each was the truth; and he would confidently submit the matter to the judgment of every farmer and every man in the country, who would give the facts a calm and dispassionate consideration.

Now, sir, as to the first proposition: Is the foreign market for our agricultural produce everything, and the domestic market little or nothing? By referring to the census of 1840, it would be seen that the agricultural productions peculiar to the States north and west of the Potomac, Ohio, and Mississippi—to wit: grain of all kinds, flour, meat, fruit, animals, animal productions, etc.,—amounted to more than $1,000,000,000, while the exports of these articles for the last ten years to all the world amounted, on an average, to only $8,500,000. Now, if the manufacturers and the mechanics throughout the United States consumed only one-tenth part of these agricultural products it would amount to one hundred millions; yet the home market was nothing! And one-third of the State of Missouri could furnish a surplus more than sufficient to supply all the Eastern demand! Now, he affirmed, and the gentleman's own premises would show, that there was more than eight, and he might say ten dollars' worth of agricultural produce raised on the soil of Great Britain and sent to Missouri for sale and consumption to one dollar's worth of agricultural produce sent from Missouri to Great Britain. This might seem strange, but it was true, not only of Missouri, but of all the other Middle and Western States.

FOREIGN IMPORTS—AGRICULTURAL PRODUCE—VIEWS FOR FARMERS.

Now, he presumed, it would be admitted—it could not be denied—that one-half, and more than one-half, of all the goods imported from abroad, was strictly agricultural produce, consisting of the raw materials and breadstuffs, the subsistence of labor worked up and manufactured into articles of use. Well, the imports from England in 1842 were

$33,446,499; one-half being agricultural produce, would make $16,723,249. Missouri contained one-forty-fifth part of the entire population of the United States, and the gentleman says consumes foreign imports in proportion to her population. She therefore consumed of the agricultural imports from England, in 1842, $371,622 worth. Our exports of all the agricultural productions of the Middle and Western States, flour, grain, meat, fruit, animals, and animal productions to England amounted, in the same year, to $2,021,307—Missouri's share of which, according to her population, would amount to $44,918; so that Missouri has bought $371,622 worth of English agricultural produce, and sold to her only $44,918 worth!—less than one-eighth part. But is it true that one-half of the value of all foreign goods imported is agricultural produce? This is an important question, and one which he was anxious that the farmers of this country should thoroughly understand. It had not heretofore received due consideration, and he was anxious to impress it upon the public mind. Take cloth, glass, iron, everything—analyze them, resolve them into their elements, so to speak, and you will find that much more than the half of their value or price is made up of agricultural produce. In a yard of common cloth, take the wool (itself nearly half its value), the bread and meat and other articles composing the subsistence of the labor employed in its manufacture, with other subordinate ingredients, and you will find that three-fourths of its value is derived from the produce of the soil; farmers often make in their own families woolen goods for consumption and sale to the amount of hundreds of dollars, without purchasing a dollar's worth of anything not produced on their own farms. Is not this cloth, then, made up entirely of agricultural produce? And is not all cloth composed of the same materials, whether made in factories or on farms? If, then, the farmer purchases foreign cloth, does he not, in fact, purchase foreign agricultural produce converted into cloth, while his own produce is, to use the language of the gentleman, "rotting on his hands for the want of a market?" How, then, can Western representatives contend that it is better for their constituents to send their hard money (for England takes no other kind) to purchase agricultural produce in the shape of goods in preference to establishing manufactories and markets at their own doors, and keeping their money in active and profitable circulation at home? Will you foster the interests of British farmers in preference to our own? In a contest between the British and American farmers for the American market, he asked gentlemen from the West which side they would take? The protective tariff is the American side—the opposite is the British side: which side will you take? This is the true question at issue, and it can neither be disguised nor evaded. [Here was a general call to order by the anti-tariff men.] Mr. S. remarked that what he had said in respect to cloth was equally applicable to iron, glass, and indeed every species of manufactures. He had himself made iron, and he knew, as a matter of personal observation and experience, that when he sold his iron he paid eight dollars out of every ten of the whole price to the neighboring farmers for grain, etc., to feed his horses, oxen, and mules; and bread, meat, and domestic goods, to clothe and feed his hands. Four-fifths of the whole value of iron was therefore strictly and truly agricultural produce; and the representatives of farmers, with Mr. Van Buren at their head, wished to go to England to buy iron, four-fifths of the value of which was British agricultural produce, in preference to sustaining those great markets for the farmers—the iron-works of our own country.

Our importations of foreign goods for consumption (deducting re-exports) amounted, upon an average, for the last ten years to $114,399,434 per year, one-half being agricultural, the result is that we have imported from abroad annually into the United States, for sale and consumption, $57,199,717 worth of agricultural produce, the growth of a foreign soil, whilst our whole exports of the agricultural products of the Northern, Western, and Middle States, have fallen short of $8,500,000, on an average, for the last ten years. Was this a sound system for a country in which seven-eighths of the entire population were employed in agriculture? But there was another view which showed the great value and importance of manufactures to the farmers, to which he wished to call their special attention. It was this: In 1842 we exported $8,410,694 worth of domestic manufactures, one-half of which (and he might safely say two-thirds) was the produce of the farmers converted into goods, and thus sent abroad for sale, making an exportation of agricultural produce, in the shape of goods, to the amount of five millions and upwards; and this year, he had no doubt, the amount of domestic manufactures exported would be more than ten millions of dollars, exceeding the whole exports of grain, flour, meat, fruits, animals, and animal productions—and this, too, in a form not to affect injuriously the prices by overstocking the foreign market with agricultural produce in its raw and unmanufactured condition. In this way Great Britain was, in fact, the greatest exporter of agricultural produce in the world—not in its rude and original form, but by doubling its value by the addition of labor and profits. In 1841 her exports of manufactures amounted to the enormous sum of $230,000,000—making her exports of agricultural produce, in this form, $115,000,000. The products of her labor-saving machinery were equal to the results of the labor of eight millions of men. This was the great element of wealth in England, as it was and would be here and everywhere. Destroy the labor-saving machinery of Great Britain and she would be bankrupt in a single year. By this she laid the world under contribution, and enabled her people to pay $250,000,000 of revenue annually. So much for the relative value of the foreign and home market for agricultural produce, and the effect of the protective policy on the interest of the farmers.

THE EFFECT OF PROTECTION ON PRICES.

The next proposition of the gentleman from Missouri [Mr. Jameson] was, that "the effect of the protective policy was to increase the price of everything the farmer has to buy, and reduce the price of everything the farmer has to sell."

Now, does not all experience, as well as the well-known laws of demand and supply, clearly prove that precisely the reverse of this proposition is the truth? The effect of the protective policy, it is admitted on all hands, is to build up and increase the number of manufacturing establishments, and thereby to increase the demand for the raw materials and breadstuffs produced by the farmer, and thereby increase (not diminish) the price of everything the farmer has to sell; and, by increasing the number of manufacturing establishments increase the quantity of manufactured goods, and thereby reduce (not increase) the price of the goods which the farmer has to purchase. Hence, by increasing the demand, you increase the price of everything the farmer has to sell; and, by augmenting the quantity, reduce the price of everything the farmer has to purchase. Such was the well-known operation of the great law of demand and supply, universal and invariable in its results.

Besides, by increasing manufactures, you withdraw a portion of the labor employed in agriculture, and employ it in manufactures—making customers and consumers of those who were before rivals in the production of agricultural supplies. And these results were not only theoretically, but they were practically true. He saw it stated this morning in a paper from that gentleman's [Mr. Jameson] country that wheat had recently risen fourteen cents in the bushel, and that pork was selling for double the price it brought just before the passage of the late protective tariff. And on the other hand, he affirmed it as a fact, he defied contradiction, and invited gentlemen to the scrutiny, that there was not a single article of any sort or kind which had been highly protected, (which we had the capacity to produce, and had succeeded in producing), that the price had not been invariably reduced by the home competition, stimulated and excited by protection to less, often to one-half, one-third, and one-fourth part of the price paid for the same article when exclusively imported from abroad. He would refer to coarse cottons, for which everybody knows we paid fifteen and twenty cents a yard before they were manufactured here, which are now bought (of better quality made at home and paid for in produce) at five and six cents per yard—glass, for which we paid, when imported, $12 per box, is now made at home for $2 per box. This is the way prices are increased, and the farmers are "robbed and oppressed," in the language of the gentleman, by the protective policy; this is the way this gentleman's constituents are fleeced of "half their hard earnings by the Eastern manufacturers." Now he defied the gentleman to put his finger on a single article in the whole tariff on which high protective duties had been levied, that had not in time been reduced, and very greatly reduced in price by domestic competition—and yet, in the face of these facts, the gentleman stands up and gravely repeats this stale and threadbare theory, "that protective duties increase the price of everything the farmer has to buy, and reduce the price of everything he has to sell."

THE DUTY ADDED TO THE PRICE—NOT TRUE.

Next, the gentleman tells us that "the duty is always added to the price and paid by the consumer, on both foreign and domestic goods; for the domestic manufacturer, he says, always raises his goods by the amount of the duty;"

and this theory is also advanced by Mr. Van Buren in his letter to the Indiana convention, before referred to. Now let us see how this theory will bear the test of a practical examination. The consumer has to pay the duty to the manufacturer; this is the universal theory. Now, if the gentleman would turn to the tariff he would find that the duty on the lowest priced cotton goods was upwards of eight cents per square yard; these goods were sold to the gentleman's constituents in Missouri for six cents, and often less than six cents per yard. Now, if the gentleman would go home and undertake to convince the simplest old woman in his district that she was obliged to pay the Eastern manufacturer eight cents a yard duty on a yard of coarse cotton, which she bought for six, he would undertake a task in which, with all his eloquence and ingenuity, he would utterly fail. The duty on glass was $3 per box, a duty imposed when foreign glass was imported and sold at $10 and $12 per box; now it was selling in his country for $2.50 per box; the duty on nails had been five cents per pound, imposed when the price was ten or twelve cents, now they are made and sold for four cents. Such were the fruits of the protective policy by which the price of glass had been reduced from $10 to $2.50, and nails from twelve to four cents per pound; and the same was true of paper, type, hardware, and an infinite variety of articles. Now, if the gentleman would go home and tell his constituents the honest, plain, common-sense farmers of Missouri, that they had to pay $3 duty on a box of glass which they could purchase for $2.50, and five cents a pound duty on nails which they purchased for four, they would laugh in his face. Yet he has just gravely asserted that "the duty is always added to the price by the manufacturer, and is paid by the consumer." Now, with such facts before him, he thought it might puzzle even a Van Buren man to believe Mr. Van Buren himself, who had asserted this same thing in his Indiana letter, where, perhaps, the gentleman had got this idea.

The gentleman next says that the protective policy creates and cherishes monopolies. Now, if to increase competition (the admitted effect of this policy) was to create and cherish monopoly, then the gentleman was right; but if to promote competition was to destroy monopoly, then the gentleman was wrong. In this, as in all the other cases, the reverse of the gentleman's proposition was true. Protection promoted competition, and thereby destroyed monopoly. This was too clear to admit of illustration or argument.

His time was nearly out, and in conclusion he would say that he advocated the protective policy, not as a policy calculated or intended to advance the interest of the manufacturers at the expense of any other class; on the contrary, he regarded it as a policy eminently calculated to advance the welfare and prosperity of agriculture.

AGRICULTURE WAS THE GREAT OBJECT OF THE PROTECTIVE POLICY.

It reduced the price of manufactured goods by promoting competition, while on the other hand it enhanced the price of agricultural produce by increasing the demand and diminishing the supply, by withdrawing a portion of labor from this great department of industry, and employing it in the consumption instead of the production of agricultural supplies. It was therefore for the benefit of the farmers, and not the manufacturers, he advocated this policy.

Agriculture was the great parent of production; it was the great fountain of national wealth and prosperity. In this country, where seven-eighths of the entire population were employed in agriculture, it might be emphatically said that the "farmers produced all and paid all;" and at the ballot-box they were all powerful. He hoped they would for once make common cause; that they would unite in one great vigorous effort to advance their own interest—the interest of the nation; to protect and defend their own great American markets against the efforts of foreigners to occupy them, by breaking down our protective policy, and inundating our country with their agricultural produce, manufactured and worked up into goods, and thus sent here for sale, while their own ports were hermetically sealed against our productions by prohibitory duties. He appealed to the farmers of the great West—he implored them to come to the rescue—to defend and maintain their own great American interests, by electing men to this House and to the Executive Government who would take the American side against foreigners in this great struggle now going on for the American market. The remedy was in their own hands, and it was their own fault if they failed to apply it. If they failed, they themselves would be the sufferers. The great American Whig system had been tried, fully tried.

In 1816 we passed a protective tariff, which, with the tariffs of 1824 and 1828, had paid off (principal and interest) of the war debt, in 1832, $229,000,000. It had furnished a sound and uniform currency; it had rendered the whole country eminently prosperous in all its interests, agricultural, manufacturing and commercial; and just at the time this war debt was paid off, and the surplus of eighteen millions a year, derived from the protective policy, was about to be applied to the construction of those internal improvements, which had since involved the States in a foreign debt of more than $200,000,000, there came "a frost, a killing frost;" this American system of policy was, in the language of gentlemen, "exploded," and the Van Buren system, introduced by Mr. Van Buren himself, then prime minister, established on its ruins. In a few years the expenses of Government were doubled, and almost trebled; internal improvements arrested and transferred to the States; the protective tariff repealed and the country ruined; agriculture, manufactures, and commerce went down together; and individuals and governments, State and national, involved in one common scene of bankruptcy, repudiation, and deep disgrace. Such were the clear and undeniable fruits of the Van Buren policy, and such was the admitted condition of things in 1840, when the people, who had forborne till "forbearance ceased to be a virtue," rose in their might and resolved to throw off this ruinous system and return to the system that had rendered them prosperous; by one united and vigorous effort they had succeeded for the moment by the election of Harrison and a Whig Congress, who had partially restored the national prosperity by the tariff of 1842; but all their high hopes and bright prospects were struck down by the death of their chief, and the succession of a man who is now an adherent of the Van Buren system. Thus, sir, the popular effort of 1840 to restore the Whig system had been defeated and postponed; but, thank God, the time is approaching, and is at hand, when the people would again come up with redoubled vigor and energy to the rescue. They were defeated in 1840, but in 1844 they would succeed, as he hoped and believed, by a still more triumphant majority, because the ruinous effects of the Van Buren system, and the beneficial effects of the Whig policy, were now more clearly seen and better understood. This was a contest for measures, not for men—men were nothing, measures and principles everything; much for weal or for woe depended upon the result; the fate of the country, he believed, was involved in the issue. Shall the country get up and again advance in a career of prosperity under new auspices, or fall back into the wretched and deplorable condition in which Mr. Van Buren left it in 1841? This was the great question at issue—a question which touched the interest of every man in this country deeply and vitally, and in reference to which he could neither be indifferent nor silent.

Against Mr. Van Buren personally he had said nothing—he had nothing to say; it was to his measures and principles he was opposed. He firmly believed before God that the re-election of Mr. Van Buren would be the greatest calamity that could befall this country. Under this solemn conviction he felt it to be his duty to avert this calamity if he could. It was a duty from which he could not be diverted nor driven by any species of intimidation here or elsewhere. It was a high duty he owed to his country and his constituents, and he would be false to them and to himself if he failed, on all proper occasions, firmly and fearlessly to perform it.

MR. STEWART'S DEFENCE OF HIMSELF AGAINST THE ABUSIVE ATTACK OF MR. WELLER.

[Mr. Winthrop moved that the gentleman from Pennsylvania [Mr. Stewart] have leave to speak a second time; and the yeas and nays being demanded, the yeas were 152, nays 18. So leave was granted.]

Mr. Stewart returned his cordial thanks to the House for this manifestation of its kind disposition towards him, and for the present opportunity of explanation. He had been about to say, when up before, that he made no personal attack on any one, nor any allusion of a personal or offensive character; he had entered only into general remarks, and that in answer to those of other gentlemen on the great questions of public policy which divided the country. For this he had been assailed in the manner which all present had heard, and which it was not necessary to characterize, because it sufficiently characterized itself. He said that every gentleman on that floor would bear witness that, during the course of discussion, both in Committee of the Whole and in the House, different gentlemen, the gentleman from Indiana [Mr. Kennedy] and from Illinois [Mr.

Ficklin] had spoken of "the exploded American system," and had denounced it as leading to the most destructive effects on the public prosperity. The gentleman from Missouri [Mr. Jameson] followed in the same strain, and, speaking of the Whig party, took occasion to characterize it as the "coon party;" a party without principles; the fragments of a party; the fag ends of all parties; as weighed in the balance and found wanting; and had spoken of the Whig policy as now utterly exploded. After all this, what had Mr. S. done? He had only replied to these charges, first made by other gentlemen, and, in so doing, had endeavored to vindicate the policy of the Whigs, and to show that it had been productive of very great blessings and benefits, and had rendered the country prosperous. On the other hand, he had spoken of what was usually known and spoken of as the Van Buren policy, and had set its effects in contrast, endeavoring to show the practical consequences of both systems on the welfare of the country, and to make it appear that the latter policy had plunged the country in debt, and stricken down the interests of agriculture and manufactures. He considered these as legitimate subjects to be brought up in reply to what had been said on the other side. The gentleman from Missouri, [Mr. Jameson] had said that, unlike the Whig party, Democracy had principles for the eye of the world, and principles it would stand or fall by. Mr. S., in reply, had a perfect right to speak of those principles, according to his views of them, and this he had done; but in all the remarks he made he had indulged in no personal allusion to the member from Ohio, or to anybody else. To that member he was a stranger, and always would be. He had made no allusion to him. He had endeavored to show that the opposite line of policy was injurious. In so doing, he acted on a great principle of public duty, in endeavoring to ward off from his country the introduction again of a policy which, as he believed, had operated to weaken and destroy the foundations of the public prosperity.

After he had made an argument resting on these principles, the member from Ohio, at a very early hour, immediately after the reading of the journal, rose in his seat before Mr. S. was in the House and made a violent personal attack upon him, and such a one as Mr. S. would not here characterize, as he could not while restrained by the rules of parliamentary decorum. All the House had heard it. In that attack he had charged Mr. S. with having made a "stump speech," as having violated all propriety, as having spoken in a manner unworthy of a man, and had concluded with moving the previous question.

[Here Mr. S. quoted several passages from Mr. Weller's speech, especially that in which he pledged himself to disprove all Mr. S. had said about Mr. Van Buren, or take the brand of falsehood on his own forehead; and, if he did, then to fix it on the forehead of Mr. S.]

Now, as Mr. S. had made no personal allusion whatever to the gentleman—no, the member from Ohio—but had spoken only on matters of general interest to the House and to the country, he would ask of every candid and fair man whether it was his duty to sit in silence under such a charge against him? The personal attack was perfectly unprovoked, and it was made in terms such as Mr. S. could not suitably characterize without violating the rules of order; they characterized themselves. Thus assailed, what had been his course? On the first opportunity in which he could get the floor he alluded to these remarks, he had quoted the report of them, and had then added that he was prepared to sustain all the charges he had made to the very letter; and thereupon he had gone into the proof from public documents and Mr. Van Buren's own letters. Mr. S. appealed to all who had heard him to say whether he had not made out, fully and substantially, the truth of every single charge. He would submit that question to the recollection of every gentleman on that floor. And there he had left the subject. He made no remark of a personal nature. All he had done was to remove the brand of falsehood from his own brow and let it rest where it might. He could not have said less.

The member on the next day, in reply to these remarks, in which there had not been one word of personality to any gentleman in that House, and after sleeping on the matter, came into the House and accused Mr. S. some ten or twelve times of "falsehood," of "lies," of having uttered "falsehood No. 1," falsehood No. 2, No. 3, No. 4, 5, 6, 7, 8, and 9. This was an easy way to answer an argument or get out of a difficulty; but would such an answer satisfy an intelligent and enlightened community? Would they not infer that no better reply could be made? The member had admitted the facts but denied the inferences, as to the withholding the estimates for these Western improvements; and this, in his polished language, is lie No. 1. Next, he [Mr.

S.] had expressed the opinion that from Mr. Van Buren's principles, as he had read them, he would be bound to veto the proposed appropriation were he now President; and this was lie No. 2. Next, Mr. S. had expressed the opinion that the tariff of 1842 had promoted the national prosperity; and this was designated as lie No. 3; and so on with all the rest. Now, how easy would it be to retort these vulgar epithets. The member has said that my speech had been made "one hundred times on every stump in the West." These were his very words; and what was this? Truth, of course. Now, Mr. S. here reaffirmed every position he had before taken, and held himself ready to establish by the most indisputable testimony the truth of every one of them. He appealed to that House to say whether the member had disproved, or in the least impaired, one of them. He should avail himself of a proper occasion to prove this; and such a day would come. He here pledged himself before that House and before the country to make out the most perfect demonstration of all that he had asserted. The member from Ohio did not once deny that Mr. Van Buren had withheld the estimates for the Cumberland road; he had only denied the inference of Mr. S. from the fact that the secretary had acted under his instructions. He admitted the estimates were withheld, but denied that the President had given his secretary any instructions to withhold them. Now, the member could no more prove that Mr. Van Buren did not instruct the secretary to do it than Mr. S. could prove that he did. Neither of them was present. But Mr. S. had inferred that as it was the secretary's official duty to report the estimates, and as he had always previously done it, he could not on that occasion have avoided doing it unless acting under Executive instructions. What Mr. S. said was a matter of inference, and not an assertion of fact at all. There had been some little difficulty as to a date, and as to whether he had withheld them a few days or a few months, more or less. And what difference did that make as to the general fact? There was one thing about which the member had triumphed very confidently: he said he would prove, and he did prove, that Mr. Van Buren did sign bills making appropriations for works of internal improvement. Certainly he did; nor had Mr. S. ever denied it. What he said was that Mr. Van Buren denied the power of this government to execute works of internal improvement; and not only so, but that even the consent of the States could not confer upon it the power. And for this he had shown Mr. Van Buren's own words. If the member had proved that, after avowing this principle, Mr. Van Buren acted afterwards in utter inconsistency with it, that was a matter between the member and his candidate. If he could prove, and did prove, that Mr. Van Buren acted against his own faith, and violated his oath of office, that was the member's own affair.

Mr. S. knew very well that Mr. Van Buren's friends could show that he held very different opinions at different times. Mr. S. could have shown the gentleman more than that: he could have shown him that Mr. Van Buren voted in favor of putting turnpike-gates upon the Cumberland road to tax the free citizens of Pennsylvania for travelling over a highway in their own Commonwealth; but President Monroe had vetoed the bill as unconstitutional, thus putting down an unconstitutional law for which Mr. Van Buren had deliberately voted. This was a greater violation of the Constitution than the other case. Latitudinous as Mr. S. was held by some to be on the interpretation of the Constitution, he could not go that, and he voted against the bill. Mr. S. might further have proved that Mr. Van Buren voted for the tariff of 1828, and about twenty times against the reduction of the high duties imposed by that bill. Mr. S. had voted against the high duties in the tariff of 1828, and for their reduction. Extravagant as his notions were said to be, he could not go the length Mr. Van Buren had gone, though that gentleman had said he was now against the existing tariff, both in its principles and details. If in these things he was inconsistent with himself and his own avowed principles, Mr. S. could not help it. Mr. S. insisted, then, that he had fully established all the charges he had brought.

There had been some dispute as to what the building of this Capitol had cost; the member from Ohio had stated that it cost but a little over a million. Mr. S. understood that to build it at first and repair it after it was partially burnt, had cost between three and four millions.

He pledged himself to prove every position he had taken; he reaffirmed every one of them fully, to vindicate himself in the course he had pursued, and wipe off from his brow that brand of falsehood the member was so anxious to fix upon it, let it rest where it might.

Mr. S. went on to say that it did seem to him that if, when a member of that House discussed, in an orderly parliamentary manner, questions relating to the generally policy of the country and the Government, deprecating such as he deemed to be destructive in their tendency, he was to be interrupted by cries of "falsehood" and "lies," the freedom of debate was gone. If such a state of things was to be tolerated the members might as well return at once to their constituents; their rights were gone; and there was nothing in our institutions any longer worth preserving. If they could not retain personal respect enough for each other to observe personal decorum in debate; if that House of the people's representatives was thus to be degraded and disgraced by low, vulgar, billingsgate abuse, the liberties of that body and of the country were gone. The people themselves, by the acts of their representatives, would be degraded in the face of the world, and popular government and popular institutions would fall into disrepute and become a reproach.

These disgraceful scenes enacted in this hall would degrade the character and weight of this House, and destroy the high and commanding influence which it always had exerted in the administration of the affairs of this Government. This is, emphatically, the people's House, where they speak and act through their immediate representatives; those who destroy its character and influence, destroy the just power and influence of the people themselves, and thereby strike a blow at the very heart of freedom. He protested against such a condition of things.

[*Mr. McConnel* (interposing). And I protest against your slandering the majority of this House.]

Mr. Stewart resumed. He should notice no such interruptions. But he did say that so long as interruptions of this kind, and such as had repeatedly broken in upon his former remarks, were to be permitted, and a member, while attempting to discharge his public duty, was to be put down by cries of liar and villain, the freedom of debate was gone, and the rights of the minority sacrificed. He never would descend to follow such examples; he should do his duty on that floor firmly and fearlessly, nor was he to be driven from it by any such attacks. He was told that he could go out of doors to explain; but his constituents had not sent him to that House to engage in fisticuff fights, or carry public measures by force of battle. He would not descend to such a course. On that principle he might encounter every blackguard in the street who was brutal enough to assault a man who gave him no provocation. He should not descend to a personal contest with persons of that sort here any more than he would there.

He hoped to see this whole state of things reformed; but whether it should be reformed or not, if the character of that House was to be degraded, it should not be by any act of his. He should not be deterred from pursuing the even tenor of his way, and discharging his duty by any such assaults, personal as they might be, or abusive as they might be. He was sent there to discharge a responsible public duty, and he should discharge it. He should, on all proper occasions, attack the policy of the last administration, now gone out of power; and he should continue to do this because he believed in his heart and conscience and before heaven that the policy of the man who was at the head of that administration was such as, if persevered in, must break down the country and involve it in hopeless debt, embarrassment and ruin, while he believed as sincerely that the tariff was the only measure which had in any degree lifted it up from the prostration where the Van Buren policy had left it. Under that conviction he felt that he had a duty to perform, so far as his efforts might go, viz.: to prevent the country from again coming under the influence and sway of such a man; for should he again come into power Mr. S. would be ready to despair of the republic. All her great and vital interests must be prostrated. These were his firm, religious convictions in the matter; and, deeply feeling them, he could not sleep in peace upon his pillow did he not exert what little influence he might possess to avert from his country so great a calamity.

He thanked the House for the indulgence accorded to him in the opportunity thus afforded to put himself right before the House and before the country. He submitted it to the House to judge whether he had done anything to justify the attack which had been made upon him. He appealed to gentlemen opposed to him to say whether it was not all fair to reply to attacks openly made upon the Whig party, as being a party without any principles, and as having been weighed in the balance and found wanting. He had felt called upon to vindicate those with whom he acted from such accusations. This he had done, and this was all he had done. He could not vindicate it in any other way. He could not stoop to a contest of fisticuffs, or any other species of personal contest. He was not a fighting man; but if he were, he could not fight all who had here assailed him.

He would conclude by telling gentlemen around him, one and all, that he was not to be silenced by any abusive course; that he was not to be deprived of his constitutional freedom of speech; that he should go on firmly and faithfully to discharge the high duty he owed to an enlightened, free, virtuous, and honorable constituency; but he should always do this in a manner as decorous as the rules of that House could require. He never would follow the example which had been set to him. He deeply regretted the only error which in this case he had committed—an error which he hoped the House and the country would forgive, and which he certainly never should repeat, viz.: the noticing, in any shape or form, remarks which fell from the member from Ohio.

IN FAVOR OF THE TARIFF OF 1824

Delivered in the House of Representatives of the U. S., April 9th, 1824.

Mr. Stewart said, he regretted that the motion now submitted, to reduce the proposed duty on iron, compelled him to depart from the determination he had formed, not to trouble the House with any remarks of his, upon this subject. But when he saw, in this motion, a blow aimed at the vital interests of those whom he had the honor to represent upon this floor, it would be a culpable dereliction of public duty in him to remain silent. He did not intend, however, he said, to enter upon the discussion of the general principles of the bill, further than was necessary to meet and obviate the arguments which had been employed by gentlemen who had supported the proposition now under consideration.

The objections urged by the honorable gentleman from Massachusetts [Mr. Fuller], who first addressed you, are in substance these—That the proposed increase of duty on iron would impair the revenue—injure the farmer—tax all classes of the community—destroy the business, and increase the burdens of commerce and navigation—prostrate the navy—create monopolies—shut the ports of Russia against our produce—and all for the benefit of a few overgrown and wealthy iron masters. This, Mr. S. said, he believed was a fair and full statement of the grounds of opposition assumed, not only by the honorable gentleman [Mr. Fuller], but also by his colleagues [Mr. Webster and Mr. Reed] as well as the gentlemen from South Carolina and Virginia [Messrs. M'Duffie and Randolph].

In the first place, Mr. S. said, it would be proper to inquire into the nature of this proposition, fraught with such direful consequences. It was, he said, nothing more nor less than a proposition to add 37 cents a hundred to the existing duty on bar iron, equal to $7.40 per ton,—not a protecting, but a mere revenue duty.

The quantity of iron consumed in the United States was

estimated at 45,000 tons per annum. During the existence of the embargo, non-intercourse, and war, which created a necessity for the domestic manufacture of this article, capital to a large amount was invested, iron works sprang up in almost every part of the country, and the home supply was soon equal to the demand. However, peace was soon restored, which again let in the foreign article. Still our infant establishments maintained the unequal contest successfully, until Congress interposed, not to protect but to destroy them; and by the iniquitous tariff of 1816, which increased the duties upon sugar, etc., nearly 100 per cent., reduced the duty upon iron from 32 per cent. to $9 per ton. This gave the death blow to the American manufactures. They sunk one after another—the importations increased regularly every year, until they rose from 3000 to 33,787 tons per annum, leaving about 12,000 tons for domestic production; and the importation of pig iron had also increased from 104 tons to 3000 per annum. But, sir, we are told by the honorable gentleman from Massachusetts [Mr. Fuller], that the Russians (from whom we get the most of our iron) are poor, and if we don't buy their iron, they cannot buy our produce. The gentleman feels no regret for the fate of the American manufacturer, who is thus destroyed—the American laborer, who is thus left without employ and without bread—the American farmer, who is thus left without a market for his produce; but his sympathies are all alive for the poor serfs and cossacks of his imperial majesty, the Emperor of all the Russias, lest they should starve for want of our produce. But, sir, do they take our produce for their iron? No, sir; they are not such fools as to follow our example, and take from us what they can produce at home. Sir, they take almost nothing but your cash. How stands the account? Last year we imported from Russia to the amount of $2,258,797; while the amount of domestic produce exported to Russia amounted to only $51,635; leaving a balance to be paid in cash, of $2,207,162. So much for the often-repeated argument that we must buy from Russia, or Russia would not buy from us. We give at the rate of $44 for their produce, and get back *one* for ours. Such a policy as this would ruin any nation. No wonder that, with such a system, our currency was reduced in three years from $110,000,000 to $45,000,000: no wonder that our stocks, and everything transferable, were remitted to Europe to pay an unfavorable balance of trade: no wonder that agriculture, commerce, and manufactures, were all alike struggling for their existence. If there is, however, continued Mr. S., any article we ought to manufacture above all others, an article for which we should be independent of the world, he contended that it was *iron;* it was equally necessary in *peace* and in *war;* it was intimately connected with the defence of the country, as much so as powder and ball. Our country, he said, abounded with ore, with coal, provisions, everything necessary for its manufacture, and the raw material was useless for any other purpose; the capital was already vested, and labor unemployed, which wanted but the vivifying touch of governmental patronage and protection, to spring at once into successful operation, saving millions to the nation, affording a market to the farmer, and employment to labor.

But, we are told by the gentleman from New York [Mr. Cambreleng], that our iron is not so good as the imported—that it is not suitable for the manufacture of cannon. And, sir, is it come to this? Are we to depend on Europe for our cannon?—Is this nation, boasting of its independence, to look to Europe, to the Holy Alliance, for the means of national defence? He disputed the fact of inferiority. The cannon, as well as those who manned them, during the late war, were purely *American;* and where, sir, is the evidence of their inferiority? He fearlessly affirmed that neither the metal of our guns, nor the metal of our men, were ever surpassed. He would appeal for proof to the splendid achievements on the plains of Bridgewater and New Orleans,—to the glorious deeds on Erie and the ocean.

Mr. S. then went on to reply to another objection urged by his colleague [Mr. Breck], who said we must wait till we acquire capital and skill. We must not go in the water till we have learned to swim. These, he contended, were in existence, and it was the object of this measure to put them in motion. During the war there was no want of either *capital* or *skill.* Though they were put down at present, by an unwise and ruinous policy, yet he hoped, by the adoption of this measure, they would be resuscitated. If his colleague, he said, wished to create capital and skill, the only way to arrive at his object was to pass this bill. He would wait forever, if he withheld protection and encouragement, which was the breath that gave being, life, and motion, to industry, capital, and skill, in every country where they were seen to prosper. Gentlemen might ransack all history, ancient and modern, and they could not find a single instance to the contrary. The gentleman from South Carolina [Mr. M'Duffie], continued Mr. S., has contended with more ingenuity than force, that the country could not furnish the article in question, and that the only effect would be to increase the duty which operated as a tax upon the whole community, without benefiting the manufacturer—he also contended that it would impair the revenue. Mr. S. said he could not comprehend how the tax on the imported article could be *increased*, and the revenue *diminished:* both positions he contended could not be correct—the duty and the revenue were the same. If the duty was increased on an article imported, the revenue must, of necessity, be increased in the same proportion. But it appeared that the effect of a measure on the revenue did not depend on the *nature* of the measure itself, but upon the *source* from which it originated. A bill was reported during the last Congress, by the Committee of Ways and Means, in which (according to the recommendation of the Secretary of the Treasury) a duty of $20 per ton was proposed on iron, not for protection, but to increase the revenue. *Now*, when the same duty is recommended by the Committee of Manufactures, together with fifty or sixty other items of that revenue bill, at the same rate of duties, we are told it will ruin the revenue. So that the same duties when proposed by the "Ways and Means" will *improve* the revenue, which, when proposed by the "Manufactures," will *destroy* the revenue, and lead to direct taxation. Such arguments might do to frighten and alarm the people; but, for his part, he did not believe there was any witchcraft in the word "manufactures," which could thus change the effect and operation of this measure. He had no doubt but that this bill would greatly promote the prosperity of the farmers and manufacturers, and, at the same time, add several millions per annum to the revenue. The true plan to increase the revenue, according to his judgment, Mr. Stewart said, was by a wise policy to increase the wealth and resources of the people who pay it. Cherish and sustain your own industry; rely upon your own means; develop and bring into activity your own vast resources; keep your money at home; buy less, and sell more: in short, make a rich and prosperous people, and you will make a rich and flourishing treasury—depress the people, and the revenue would sink with them. The revenue derived from imposts, he contended, would always be in proportion to the ability of the people to purchase and consume foreign products; those who now merely raised bread enough to live upon, would, if employed in manufactures, be able to consume tea, coffee, sugar, and other articles, which paid an enormous revenue to the public treasury.

To illustrate this, he would, with the permission of the House, refer to a few facts which fell within his personal knowledge and observation. In the county in which he resided, during the late war, and at its close, there were, in successful and prosperous operation, some twenty or thirty iron works, of different kinds, employing, perhaps, fifty persons each, and saving to the nation from ore and coal (which now remains buried and useless,) nearly $500,000 a year. Attached to many of these works, were found *stores* of foreign goods, supplying the workmen and others, to the amount of, say $2000 per annum, mostly groceries, tea, coffee, sugar, etc.—of which nearly one-half of the whole price went into the public treasury, in the shape of duties. Since the restoration of peace, and the repeal of the protecting duties in 1816, these works, he said, had been mostly abandoned, their owners were ruined and insolvent; the miserable hands were turned adrift without employment; the farmer, who then received from fifty to eighty cents per bushel for his grain, was now unable to get half that amount; the government had lost the thousands of revenue derived from the sale and consumption of foreign goods; and commerce and navigation had lost the profits of their importation. The nation was impoverished by the annual loss of millions of money, which now went to support and enrich the farmers and manufacturers of England and Russia, instead of our own, who were suffering for want of a market. Land, and its produce, property of every kind, had depreciated more than 50 per cent., producing the most heart-rending scenes of distress, embarrassment, sacrifice, and bankruptcy, among those who lately enjoyed the most cheering and flattering prospects. Sir, upon what principle can such policy as this be justified or defended? He put it to honorable gentlemen to say, whether they could look on such a scene with indifference; whether they could reconcile it to their consciences, to give a vote which would withhold protection from their suffering fellow-citizens, who were struggling with the boors of Russia and Sweden? He hoped the protection would be granted: if not for the sake of the manufacturer, he asked it for the sake of the farmer —for the sake of the revenue—for the merchant—for the nation: it was demanded by everything *American*—by every proud and patriotic feeling.

But, sir, we are told by the honorable gentleman from Virginia [Mr. Randolph], that this duty on iron will oppress the poor; that it will tax the farmer, who, having no market for his corn, cannot buy iron, and "will be compelled to plough his fields with a crooked stick." Sir, the object of this bill is to give to our farmers a market. Iron works consumed immense quantities of grain, and would gladly give iron in payment; whereas, in Europe, they refuse our grain, and require cash. He could safely assert, upon the best evidence, that there were single manufactories in the United States, which consumed, annually, more of our grain than both England and France put together, from whom we purchased to the amount of thirty or forty millions a year. He would refer the honorable gentleman to the farmer himself:—ask *him*, whether the erection of manufacturing establishments in his neighborhood will injure his farm, or his business? whether it will compel him to "plough with a crooked stick?" But, says the gentleman, it will oppress the poor, and tax all classes. Let gentlemen, before they pronounce the proposed addition of thirty-seven cents a hundred on iron oppressive, look to some of the existing duties. By the existing tariff, which is too sacred to be touched or altered, you impose duties, varying from 50 to 180 per cent. on tea, coffee, sugar, salt, etc., articles consumed by the poor, while many of the most refined luxuries, jewelry, etc., pay but 7½ per cent. According to the existing duties, the poor man who buys $50 worth of sugar, tea, and salt, a year, pays $25 of taxes into the treasury; while the rich man, who buys $50 worth of jewelry, pays but $3.75. A more iniquitous system of taxation never existed in any country: yet it must not be touched! A duty of a few cents on iron, for the purpose of encouraging the manufacturer at home, was pronounced by the gentleman from South Carolina [Mr. M'Duffie] an intolerable tax; while a duty of 120 per cent. on tea, which could never be raised here, was not worth the gentleman's notice at all; it excited no uneasiness whatever. But we are referred by gentlemen to the remonstrances from our chambers of commerce. Sir, and who compose these chambers of commerce? He was credibly informed, that a majority of them were

British merchants and persons connected with British merchants and manufacturers. No wonder, sir, that *they* complain; that *they* remonstrate against any alteration of a system of policy by which they have been enabled to grow rich at our expense—which has rendered this nation more *dependent* and more completely *tributary* to Great Britain than we were when *colonies;* a system which favored foreigners, and destroyed our own merchants, which gave them almost the entire supply of our market. It was a fact, of universal notoriety, that more than two-thirds of all the goods imported from Great Britain were imported on account of British merchants and British manufacturers; who, if let alone, with the facility of our *auctions*, and the benefit of our system of *credits*, by which we *loaned* to British merchants, out of the pockets of our people, more than five millions a year, without interest, they would soon succeed in driving the American merchant completely from the ocean. No wonder, then, that *they* should remonstrate against any change in such an admirable system, by which they receive from us more than thirty-four millions a year. But the British minister, it is said, has remonstrated with the Secretary of State against the increase of duty on iron! The British minister has remonstrated! And are we so humbled? Must we ask the British minister whether we may employ our own people to make our own iron? Sir, does Great Britain ask *us* whether she may exclude *our* produce from her ports? Such a suggestion there would meet with merited contempt. These remonstrances against the measure were, with him, Mr. S. said, so many arguments in its favor. It would benefit us in the same proportion that it would injure them; our loss was their profit, and our profit would be their loss.

The honorable gentleman from Massachusetts [Mr. Webster] has made a most pathetic appeal to the House on behalf of "*commerce and navigation*," which he represented as struggling for its existence, scarcely able to keep its head above water. If you impose this duty on iron, the honorable gentleman says, you throw the last stone to sink the ship. What! $7.40 a ton upon iron ruin commerce and navigation!!—an interest which had experienced more favor than any other in the nation; which was owned and directed by men of great wealth and capital, ruined by a trifling duty on iron! It was impossible. To build a ship of 100 tons burden, only 4 tons of iron was required, upon which the whole increase of duty would be only $29.60. So that

$29.60 on each vessel of 100 tons burden, was to "sink the ship," ruin commerce, and destroy the navy. He had a better opinion of our commerce, and our navy, than to suppose they were to be seriously affected by a matter of this kind. But, sir, with what propriety can commerce complain, when a slight protection is asked by the manufacturing interests of the country—foreign commerce, which has ever been the favorite of government; which has been protected at the expense of every other interest in it—not only by fleets and navies, but by discriminating duties, equal to 600 or 700 per cent.? An *American* coasting vessel, of one hundred tons, for instance, making twelve entries a year, only pays $6 duty, while a *foreign* vessel, of the same size, and for the same entries, pays $600. An American vessel, of three hundred tons, engaged in foreign trade, making five entries per annum, would pay only $90 duty, while a foreign vessel, under like circumstances, must pay $750. But, sir, permit me to remind the honorable gentleman from Massachusetts [Mr. Webster] of some of the other burdens and taxes, to which the farmers and manufacturers of this country are subjected, for the benefit and protection of *foreign commerce*. Sir, for what was the late war declared? Was it not emphatically for the protection and defence of "*free-trade and sailors' rights?*" A war which had involved this nation in a debt of more than $100,000,000; had filled this land with widows and orphans; a war in which the farmers and manufacturers had suffered every privation; in which they had freely and bravely fought, and bled, and died, for the defence of "*free-trade*," against foreign aggression; and now, when they ask a trifling duty, to protect them against foreign competition, equally destructive to them, they are gravely told that it cannot be afforded, lest it may injure commerce and navigation! But sir, this is not all. Are we not called upon, almost daily, in this House, to appropriate millions after millions of the public money to erect light-houses, buoys, and beacons, along the coast, for the protection and benefit of "foreign commerce;" to support ministers, consuls, and agents, throughout the civilized world; for the regulation and protection of our "foreign commerce;" for the erection of forts and fortifications, for the defence of our harbors, dock yards, and commercial cities; for the support and maintenance of fleets and public ships to guard and protect our foreign commerce throughout the world; and, he understood, it in some instances cost the government more money to protect our merchants (especially in the Baltic) than the whole of the commerce was worth? Look, sir, at the enormous expense of sending abroad fleets to distant seas, to suppress the pirates that annoy our foreign commerce. And who pays these immense expenditures? Not the merchants, but the farmers and manufacturers of this nation. And when *they*, the farmers and manufacturers, ask, in turn, that their interests may be protected, not by duties of 600 or 700 per cent.—not by war, nor by forts, nor lights, nor fleets, nor navies—not at the expense of millions of the public money, but by a mere act of legislation; what, sir, is the reply of the friends and champions of commerce and navigation, this highly favored interest? They gravely tell us, that *we* don't need protection; they cry, "let us alone; you will injure the revenue, tax commerce, and destroy the carrying trade." Might not these replies be retorted, when the merchants claim protection? Might *they* not be told, that the protection *they* sought would diminish the revenue, tax the farmer and manufacturer? Might they not, moreover, be asked, what great and signal service the foreign merchants had rendered this country, to entitle them to such special favor? Look at the ruinous balance of trade against us. But he would not recriminate; he was willing to extend every reasonable aid and protection to commerce; but he, at the same time, thought that *this* was not the only interest in the country; he thought there were other great and important interests in the nation, entitled to equal favor.

But commerce was represented as being on the decline, as well as agriculture and manufactures. This was, he considered, a matter of course. Commerce was the offspring of agriculture and manufactures; where there was neither agriculture nor manufactures, there could be no commerce; they must rise and fall together. The only legitimate business of commerce was to distribute and exchange the surplus productions of labor. If, by a wise policy, you restore your agriculture and manufactures to their former prosperity, commerce will revive; and soon again will it be seen to spread its white bosom to the prosperous breeze. But even if this measure should have the effect of lessening the *foreign* carrying trade, still we would be more than compensated by the increase of internal commerce and the coasting trade. But, would it be seriously contended, that we should import what we do not want, for the sake of employing *foreign* commerce? Was it consistent with sound policy, to import our iron from Russia, when we could produce it at home, merely to employ commerce? As well might it be contended, that we ought to export our flour to England, and have it manufactured into bread, and re-imported, to keep commerce and navigation employed!! And this would not be more absurd and ruinous than much of the system now in operation.

Mr. S. begged leave here to notice another argument, which had been urged, not only against the duty now under consideration, but against the bill generally: it was this:—that the proposed measure would operate injuriously on the farmers; that it was "taxing the many for the benefit of the few." The effect, Mr. S. contended, would be directly the reverse: it would benefit the farmers much more than the manufacturers. To simplify his views on this point, he said, he would confine them to a single county, in which he would suppose there to be, at present, a single manufacturing establishment, employing one hundred hands, consuming $10,000 worth of grain and other agricultural productions, and making $20,000 worth of the manufactured article; and then suppose that, by the operation of this measure, there should spring up in this county, ten new and rival establishments, of equal extent, you thus withdraw one thousand hands from agricultural employment, and make them consumers instead of producers; you give the farmers an increased market to the amount of $100,000; and you save $200,000 a year, in one county, which is kept in profitable circulation at home, giving life and activity to every branch of industry, instead of being sent to support the industry of England, who, by her existing laws, will not suffer her people to consume a pound of our flour, even if it were offered at fifty cents a barrel!! This, Mr. S. contended, was the plain and obvious tendency of the great measure under discussion. And which, he begged leave to ask, was the more benefited, the farmer, or the manufacturer? Undoubtedly the former. The increased market and increased demand for his produce, necessarily increased the price; while the increased competition among the manufacturers, and the increased quantity of the manufactured article thrown into the market, as inevitably diminished the price; so that the farmer would get more for his grain, and give less for his manufactured goods. Yet, with these plain results before us, it was still gravely urged upon the House, by almost every honorable gentleman who had opposed this bill; it was a principal ground

17

of opposition, that it would "ruin the farmers, tax the many for the benefit of the few, create monopolies, enable the rich manufacturer to extort from the people," etc., while, in fact, its real tendency and effect was, he contended, precisely the reverse.

But, Mr. S. said, there was another and still stronger view of this subject, in relation to its effects upon the interest of the farmer and agriculturist. It was a fact (however strange it might appear), susceptible of the clearest demonstration, that this nation, almost entirely agricultural, instead of exporting, actually imported agricultural labor, from the poor and wretched countries of Europe, to the amount of $20,000,000 or $30,000,000 a year. He did not mean to say that it was imported in its rude and original shape; but it entered into the composition of manufactures; and, thus altered and modified, was imported and consumed among us. Sir, of what is your imported cloth composed? your imported iron, spirits, hemp, linen—in short, almost everything? Count the cost of the raw material, the wool, hemp, flax; then add the price of the provisions, the bread, meat, fuel, etc., consumed by those employed in the fabrication of the manufactured articles, and you will find that one-half, nay, two-thirds of the price of our imported goods consisted of agricultural labor, and went to support and sustain the farmers of foreign countries, of England, France, and Russia—while our own, shut out from Europe, and shamefully abandoned at home, were left without a market, and without a motive to industry. With an almost unlimited extent of fertile territory, abounding with the finest soil and most delightful pastures, we were importing even *grass* from foreign countries in the shape of tallow and wool. Last year we had imported vast quantities of both; 4,000,000 pounds of tallow, equal to the product of 80,000 cattle. And was it wise in this nation, where 83 per cent. of the whole population were employed in agriculture, to import $20,000,000 or $30,000,000 worth of agricultural produce every year, in the shape of manufactures from abroad, and most of it from England, whose territory was not much larger than some of our States, and where the proportion of agriculturists was not equal to one-third of her population? The immense sums thus sent to Europe, he argued, were *worse* than thrown away; for the amount was not only *lost* to the country, but it introduced the labor and industry of other countries to paralyze and destroy our own. He compared it to the money expended by an individual in the purchase of spirituous liquor, or other deleterious drugs, the use of which impaired the health and ruined the constitution; in both cases the loss of the money was the smallest part of the evil. These being the effects of the present system on the farmers, any change would be to them desirable —it might be for the better, it could not be for the worse.

The Hon. gentleman from Massachusetts [Mr. Webster] has been pleased to denounce the restrictive policy as unwise and injudicious. He, Mr. S., would respectfully ask the honorable gentleman to point to the country that, neglecting the protection and encouragement of its own industry, and depending on foreign labor and skill for the supply of its wants, was not ultimately ruined. *History furnishes,* he said, no such instance. Look at miserable Poland, Italy, and Portugal, adopting the free-trade policy. Look at wretched Ireland, dependent on England. Look at the once flourishing, but now degraded, Holland, sinking like ourselves, under the deleterious influence of the free-trade system. He also referred to the once powerful and proud, but now poor and prostrate Spain. She, when self-dependent, relying on her own internal energies and resources, was feared and respected by the most powerful nations on the continent; but since, like us, she had opened her ports to foreign nations, and become dependent on foreign labor, foreign capital, foreign industry and skill, for the supply of her wants, all the wealth of her South American provinces, the rich mines of Peru and Chili, could not save her; she had sunk, under the withering influences of this wretched and ruinous system, to her present abject and degraded condition. And, were it not for the cheapness of our government, the freedom of our institutions, the wars in Europe, which gave us a market, and the great and unparalleled advantages, natural and political, that we enjoy, this country too would have long since sunk under our present unnatural, anti-American, and destructive system of policy. But, sir, look for a moment, on the other hand, to the condition of those nations with inferior advantages, protecting, by high duties and prohibitory laws, their own people, and their own industry, against the injurious effects of foreign competition. Look at France, rapidly rising, like the Phœnix, from the ashes of a wasting and desolating war of thirty years; her finances prosperous; her revenue ample; every branch of industry protected, prosperous, and successful; excluding even England, who had so recently placed the Bourbons on the throne. Look at all-powerful Russia, guarding herself against foreign competition by a perfect system of prohibitions, selling us iron, etc., to the amount of between $2,000,000 and $3,000,000 a year, and taking in return less than a fortieth part in the produce of our soil, and the balance in *cash*. It is true, sir, that, in 1820, Russia determined to try our system of free-trade, of "buying where she could buy cheapest." But mark the consequence. She soon found herself on the brink of ruin, and quickly retraced her steps. In less than two years the Russian Minister, Count Nesselrode, declared, in his official report, that this policy compelled Russia to pay a "*ruinous tribute*" to England, France, Prussia, and Austria, who "*remained faithful to their prohibitory systems.*" "Agriculture," he says, "without a market, industry without protection, languish and decline; specie is exported; and the most solid commercial houses are shaken," etc. Accordingly, in 1822, Russia re-enacted her tariff; not like ours, proposing mere revenue duties, but one which contained no less than 340 *prohibitions;* and, in January last, a few months since, this Russian tariff underwent a "judicious revision," by which the number of prohibitions was greatly increased. And finally, look, sir, at Great Britain, the most illustrious instance that the world has ever furnished of the complete triumph of the protecting policy. But, we are told that England prospers *in spite* of this system. As well might it be said, that men live in spite of the bread they eat; that the grass grows in spite of the rain and sunshine; or, that the globe we inhabit performs its splendid course in spite of the agency of that Being "who rides in the whirlwind and directs the storm." Sir, England extends ample protection to every branch of her industry—agriculture, manufactures, and commerce. England is dependent on England alone; she buys nothing that she can produce, and produces everything that can be bought. By the use of labor-saving machinery, England, with a population of 14,000,000, wields a manufacturing force equal to 220,000,000 of hands; one boy, in an English factory, can produce as much as will purchase the produce of fifty American farmers; one pound of cotton is so manufactured as to purchase 2000 pounds—thus, ten cents is made equal to $200 by the addition of labor, principally of machinery. Her cotton manufactures alone are estimated at $224,000,000, while the raw material costs less than

$25,000,000; her agricultural produce (upon a territory comparatively limited, and of inferior soil) is estimated at $487,000,000 a year, while our whole agricultural exports (exclusive of cotton and tobacco) are less than $12,000,000—not equal to the support of 250,000 manufacturers, at $50 a head. Sir, what is it that enables Great Britain to lay the world under contribution? What enabled her to subsidize all Europe? to support an army of 400,000 men? to sustain for nearly thirty years, an exhausting, bloody, and desolating war, with the colossal power of France, and finally enabled her to triumph on the ever-memorable field of Waterloo? Was it not the wealth derived from her manufactures? What was it, he asked, that enabled her, during that period, to raise 7038 millions of dollars, 4653 millions by taxes, and 2070 millions by loans; whilst her people, notwithstanding these tremendous burdens, enjoyed an unusual degree of prosperity? Was it not attributable to her flourishing manufactures? And how was it, that *now*, in time of peace she could raise, and her people could pay, with ease, and without a murmur, $252,000,000 of revenue per annum; $119,000,000 of which arose from the excise on twenty-five articles of manufacture!—while it would convulse this nation to its centre, to raise, in the same way, one-twentieth part of the amount. Sir, were we not ruined in our resources, and prostrate in our power, by a petty war of two and a half years duration? The revenue paid by the people of Great Britain, in one year, was equal to half the whole amount of the expenditures of this government for thirty years. Since the late war she had reduced her taxes $28,000,000 a year; and, after defraying her enormous expenditures, and paying $135,000,000, the annual interest of her national debt, she had left an efficient annual sinking fund of twenty-two millions and a half. And whence did she derive these immense resources? Trace them to their origin, and you will find it resulted from the protection and encouragement afforded to her national industry—to her manufactures; which, at the same time, afforded a market for her farmers, and employment for her commerce. In Great Britain, without manufactures, neither agriculture nor commerce could be sustained; they were to them the breath of life—the daily bread they fed upon. The opposition to this measure, Mr. S. said, springs from two sources:—The *commercial interest* on the seaboard, and the *cotton and tobacco planting interest* in the South. The first, from an unfounded, though sincere apprehension, that it would diminish the business, and increase the burdens of *commerce and navigation;* the second, from an apprehension, no doubt equally sincere, but equally unfounded, that, if we cease to purchase from Europe what we can and ought to make for ourselves, Europe will cease to purchase *their cotton and tobacco,* which now constituted three-fourths of the whole agricultural exports of this Union. These two powerful interests had hitherto governed this nation, and dictated its policy. The interior and the West, until lately, constituting but a small part of the great concern, of course, had to submit; but having now arrived at the age of *discretion,* they claimed a right to participate in the administration of the government. They were opposed to the present ruinous system of policy, which was predicated on a state of *war* in Europe. While all Europe was in arms, when kings, abandoning all other pursuits, were contending in fields of blood for kingdoms, crowns, and diadems, the United States, enjoying an unbounded market, grew rich at their expense. But Europe had changed in her condition; instead of universal *war,* there is now universal *peace;* millions of men had exchanged the sword for the plough; had quit war and gone to work; instead of consumers, they had become producers; instead of customers, had become rivals—and our produce was not only excluded from Europe, but the rival commodities had, in many instances, followed us to our own shores. During the last year, even wheat, potatoes, oats, etc., had been imported in considerable quantities; and it had become necessary to protect ourselves, by duties, against these importations; and even this (the proposed duty of twenty-five cents on wheat) had been opposed by the honorable gentleman from Massachusetts [Mr. Webster], on the ground that the importation of *foreign wheat* gave additional employment to our *mills,* and increased the business on our canals. Our own iron works were also to be abandoned, to import our *iron* from Russia, for the sake of employing our "*commerce and navigation!*" This, he said, appeared to him to be about as wise as it would be in a Pennsylvania farmer, who, having a mill on his own farm, yet carried his grain a hundred miles into Virginia, to have it ground, for the sake of employing his wagon and horses! Would it not be better for the farmer to sell his wagon, or employ it in some other way? And so he would say to the merchant.

But, sir, look at the effects of this policy—this system of *free-trade*—"Buying where we can buy cheapest;" look to what it has brought this once happy and prosperous land. With a government the cheapest, the freest, and the best upon earth; with a country possessing every advantage of climate, situation, and soil; yet filled with monuments of misery and wretchedness, of general embarrassment, bankruptcy, and ruin—*Peace* brought no relief to the farmer—none to the manufacturer: to them it brought no blessings; to the country at large it presented a cheerless prospect—of agriculture depressed, manufactures ruined, and the energies of the nation relaxed, broken, and prostrate. And even *commerce*, we are told by the honorable gentleman from Massachusetts (Mr. Webster, though he contends that the country was never in a more prosperous condition), is "scarcely able to keep its head above water." Sir, all the great interests of the country are at the lowest point of depression; they are struggling for life—sinking with agriculture, the basis and foundation of all, into a common grave. And why was this land of freedom, this home of liberty, thus clouded and o'ercast with this dark gloom and despondence, without a ray of hope to lighten or cheer the long vista of futurity? There was no war, no famine, no plague, no taxes in the land: could the cause then be doubtful? Did it not evidently result from our present ruinous system of policy? Was it not because the national industry was unprotected?—because we looked to Europe, instead of our own *people*, our own *resources*, for the supply of our wants?—because we buy from abroad almost everything we eat, and drink, and wear? Look at the national currency, reduced, says the Secretary of the Treasury, in *three years*, from one hundred and ten to forty-five millions of dollars—all gone, together with the evidences of the public debt, *government*, *canal*, and *bank* stocks, to pay *part* of the debt due to foreign merchants and manufacturers; to whom, it was estimated, that we were still in debt $92,000,000 of dollars: more than double the whole currency of the country. Our *imports increased*, and our *exports diminished*. In 1815 and 1816, our imports amounted to the enormous sum of $244,000,000, and our exports to only $134,000,000. Property of almost every kind, and in almost every part of the country, with which he was acquainted, depreciated more than 50 per cent.; the migration of *foreign skill and capital* into the country checked;

eight millions of dollars of revenue lost by the surrender of public lands; sales stopped, and the price reduced to $1.25—the manufacturing establishments, erected throughout the country during the war, abandoned and dilapidating, insolvencies, sales, and sacrifices, had become common and familiar matters of every day's occurrence; while all the efforts of *state legislation* to administer relief had proved unavailing: the *disease* was beyond their reach; it was *national,* and required a *national remedy.* That remedy, he said, was contained in the bill under consideration, and he hoped to see it speedily and successfully applied. It was true, it had been called by the gentleman from Virginia [Mr. Garnett] a "*bitter pill;*" he believed, however, that the *best medicines* were not always the most *pleasant;* and it was certainly better to take even a "*bitter pill,*" than perish. But it certainly could not, with propriety, be pronounced *bitter*, since the honorable Speaker [Mr. Clay] had just thrown in such a vast quantity of *molasses.*

The strong ground, however, on which this measure was met and opposed, was, that it would operate injuriously to the interests of the *sugar, cotton,* and *tobacco* planters of the South; that it would increase the price of the coarse fabrics with which they clothe their slaves, etc. This argument takes for granted the *fact* in controversy; a *fact* which he could not admit—viz., that this measure would *enhance the price* of the article manufactured. This he denied; and insisted that *New England* could, and would, manufacture the raw materials of our own country, *cheaper* than could be done in Europe, after they were transported three thousand miles, encountering all the expenses of shipping and re-shipping, excises, imposts, etc., to which they were thus subjected. When it was proposed to increase the duty upon coarse cottons, this same objection, that it was "taxing the many for the benefit of the few," was echoed in newspapers, speeches, and memorials, from Maine to Georgia. The duty was nevertheless imposed; and what has been the result? Coarse cottons, of *superior quality,* are now manufactured in this country, for one half the price formerly paid to Great Britain; and now, instead of importing, we exported, last year, to the amount of $545,000 worth, to foreign countries, after supplying the home consumption, amounting to many millions; which were saved and distributed among our own farmers and cotton growers, instead of going to Europe to reward foreign industry, instead of our own. The same result had attended every industry that had received adequate protection—leather, nails, wood, umbrellas, shoes, boots, hats, etc.; and, from estimates made, it appeared that we saved by the manufacture of *shoes, boots,* and *hats,* alone, upwards of thirty-four millions per annum. He therefore felt warranted by uniform experience, in the opinion, that the articles proposed to be protected by this bill—cotton, iron, coarse woolens, hemp, etc., —would ultimately, and at no distant period, be furnished *cheaper* of American than foreign manufacture. If there was any certainty in the laws of *cause and effect,* this result was inevitable. But the establishment of manufactories of cotton, etc., would not only afford a market for grain and other provisions, but also for the *cotton* of the South; for the time might come, and was perhaps not distant, when the planters of the South might share the fate of the farmers of the western and middle states. They, too, might be deprived of their European market; which might be interrupted and cut off, not only by *war,* and the many other vicissitudes that interrupt the intercourse between nations, but it was a fact of serious import to the South, that the culture of cotton was rapidly extending itself, not only in the *British Islands,* but also in *Egypt* and *South America.* Since 1818, the price had fallen, as appeared by the English prices current, from 28 to 7 cents a pound; our flour had also, owing to the glut of the market, fallen from $8 and $10 a barrel, to $4.50; and tobacco, from $185 to $75 per hogshead. These were some of the effects of a *general peace* in Europe, and they furnished powerful arguments in favor of the abandonment of a policy subject to such ruinous vicissitudes; and pointed out the necessity of adopting a permanent system of *American* policy, which should extend protection and encouragement to *American* industry, and look to *American* means for the supply of *American* wants; and, if there was any nation under the sun, capable of supplying *all* its own wants, he contended it was this one. It was as inconsistent, he said, with our *interest,* as it was incompatible with our *honor and independence,* to look to the crowned heads of Europe, the *Holy Alliance,* for either the means of national *defence* or national *subsistence:* our fathers had achieved their independence in vain, if it was thus to be compromised and "sold for a mess of pottage." What did we not suffer during the late war, for want of necessary supplies? It cost you at least 100 per cent. more to clothe a soldier, than it does at present. And the humiliating spectacle was presented to the world, of an American minister applying to Congress to suspend the non-intercourse, to enable us to get from our *enemies, blankets,* to fulfil our treaty stipulations with the Indians!! This state of things soon *forced* into existence every variety of manufactures. Millions of capital were promptly invested, which relieved the nation. But, as soon as peace was restored, Congress, by an act of the most flagrant injustice, instead of extending protection to those who relieved them in the hour of need, *repealed the duties,* and enabled the enemy to crush them at once, by throwing into our market a supply of goods equal to *two years'* consumption: the customs that year (1816) amounted to thirty-six millions; whereas, in 1820, (four years afterwards,) they amounted to but twelve millions. In 1815 and 1816, our imports, he repeated, amounted to two hundred and forty-four millions: and our exports to only one hundred and thirty-four millions. Great Britain thus, by a single blow, did more to prostrate and destroy American *wealth, independence,* and *power,* than she could have effected by a *ten years' war.* We were thus at once reduced to our former *dependent, colonial,* and *tributary* condition. But, he hoped the period had now arrived, when these shackles, forged and riveted by foreign hands, were to be broken asunder; when this nation, taking a high, a dignified, an independent stand, summoning forth her own boundless resources, should tell the kings of Europe, that she would no longer "*pay them tribute.*" When the South and the West would look to *New England,* instead of *Old England,* for a market and supply for an exchange of equivalents—thus strengthening the bonds that unite us, by the strong ties of interest and intercourse.

And, in conclusion, he would beg leave to appeal to the liberality, the magnanimity, the *patriotism,* of the enlightened representatives of the *South,* who, under an ample protection, were basking in the sunshine of prosperity; and he would ask them, in a spirit of frankness and conciliation, whether they could reconcile it to their consciences to withhold the trifling protection offered in this bill, to the suffering farmers and manufacturers of the *interior* and the *west?* He would appeal to the distinguished representatives of the *sugar planters* of Louisiana, who, with a protecting duty of three cents a pound on sugar, were rapidly acquiring unbounded wealth and princely fortunes. He would also appeal, with the same friendly feelings, to the liberality, nay, he would say, to the *justice* of the gentlemen from the North, who so ably represented, upon this floor, the interests of "commerce and navigation," *the favored few*, and he would ask them, whether, while *they* were protected and defended, not merely by enormous *discriminating duties*, but also at the expense of *millions of the public treasure*, at the expense of the best *and richest blood of this country*, they would turn a deaf ear to the calls of the farmers and manufacturers, the *great mass* of the community, for *protection*, not by the *sword* or the *purse* of the nation, but by a simple act of *legislation*, by the passage of this bill. Sir, said Mr. S., I hope and trust the protection they ask will be granted, and granted by the votes of some of the gentlemen, at least, to whose *liberality*, to whose *justice*, to whose *patriotism*, he had appealed. He hoped the present destructive system of policy would now be abandoned; and, upon its ruins there would arise a system of *American policy*, protecting and cherishing *American* industry; a policy which, in his conscience, he belived would alone save this nation from ultimate *bankruptcy*, and raise it to that proud pre-eminence among the nations of the earth to which the distinguished advantages derived not only from *the valor of our forefathers*, but from *nature, and* from *nature's* GOD, gave us a just right to aspire.

EXTRACTS FROM SPEECH IN OPPOSITION TO THE PROPOSED REPEAL OF THE TARIFF OF 1828, AND IN REPLY TO MR. M'DUFFIE OF S. C., WHO REPORTED THE BILL, AND OTHERS.

Delivered in the House of Representatives the 5th of June, 1832.

Mr. Stewart having moved to strike out the whole of the free-trade bill reported by Mr. M'Duffie, and to insert one of nineteen sections, which he offered as a substitute; and having stated at some length the principal points of difference between the two bills, proceeded to say:

That he regarded the question involved, as decidedly the most important that could possibly occupy the attention of the people of this country, and of their representatives here assembled. It involved not only the prosperity and welfare of the nation at large, but of every individual in it. The question was, whether the agriculture, manufactures, and commerce of this country should be prostrated or upheld; whether we should rely on our own vast resources, or return to a worse than colonial dependence on Great Britain; whether our farmers and mechanics were to be sacrificed, to make way for the productions of the soil and workshops of England; whether we should pull down the walls erected by our predecessors, to guard and protect our national industry, and thus inundate our country with foreign goods, export our specie, and renew the melancholy and desolating scenes of 1817, 1818, and 1819, which followed the reduction of the duties in 1816; or, whether we should firmly maintain our protective system? A system which has vindicated its adoption by all its fruits, fulfilled all the hopes of its friends, and falsified all the predictions of its enemies; a system under which the country had risen to its present high and palmy state of public prosperity. In short, he said, the contest was now between the British and the American farmers and manufacturers, for the American market; and the question is, which side shall we take? This is the real question at issue, and it can neither be disguised nor evaded.

If the British Chancellor had sent us a bill to flood our country with British manufactures—destroy American and build up British industry—make us again dependent and tributary, and crush a great and growing rival, he could not have devised a better plan than that proposed by the Treasury Department. What would he propose? The very thing here recommended; to reduce the duties, and thus remove the obstructions to the importation of British goods. England would give millions to secure the passage of either the bill reported from the treasury, or that by the Committee of Ways and Means. The chairman of the Committee of Ways and Means [Mr. M'Duffie] had frankly avowed his object; it was to destroy American, and make way for British manufactures—to increase the importation of British goods, and the exportation of American specie. So, that, money becoming plenty in England, prices would rise, and, consequently, cotton would command a better price; and on the other hand, money becoming scarce in the North, prices would fall, and they would obtain their supplies at a cheaper rate; in other words, his object was to enrich England, by importing her goods, and impoverish this country, by sending our money to pay for them.

The gentleman frankly admits, however, that it is better for the American farmer to pay even higher prices for American manufactures, because he gets a higher price for his produce in exchange. But this wont do; we must consent to destroy our manufactures, give up our agriculture, and send our money to England, to induce her to give "two cents a pound more for cotton." And if our manufactures and mechanic arts are destroyed, what odds? It is an easy matter, the gentleman says in his report, for "a hatter or a shoemaker to take up some other trade!!!" What other trade, when all are alike destroyed? Can he beg? No, for all would be beggars. But they have an alternative left; and what is it? To go, hat in hand, to some southern nabob, with his thousand slaves, and his six hundred votes, and beg leave to hoe corn, at six pence a day, among his negroes!! Yes, sir, this is the result of the system of policy proposed for our adoption; and if we do not promptly agree to it, South Carolina, we are told, will not remain in the Union five months!! If these are her only terms of compromise, I say, for one, let her go. But, no, sir; she will not go, if she is wise. She is more indebted for security, against dangers that lurk in her own bosom, to this Union, and to its dreaded power, than any State in it. The people of South Carolina cannot shut their eyes to the perils of such a step, though some of her advisers may. She will pause, I trust, and pause long—before she commits this fatal suicidal act. Let her look for a moment at the consequences of such a step, to the present and all future generations—to the cause of liberty throughout the world; let her look to her own situation, and to her own resources—to her means of prosecuting a war against this government; for resistance to the law must result in civil war—this was inevitable. It was proper and right, therefore, that she should first calmly and dispassionately review the whole ground. Where are her army and navy, her men and money, to contend against the united energies of this powerful Union? For, let it be remembered, this Union will remain unbroken, though rebellion may, for a short season, raise her black and bloody standard within its borders. Such things have happened more than once in the brief history of our government, and never with so little cause as now exists in the South. During a period of extraordinary pecuniary distress, the people of Western Pennsylvania had resisted the tax-gatherers, sent by this government to sell their last cow, and the bread from the mouths of their children—still they yielded at once when force was threatened. But where is the tax-gatherer now? Such a thing is unknown under this government. No people under heaven enjoyed so many blessings, with so few burdens, as this people. No man is coerced to pay a cent for the support of government; our revenue is derived from duties levied upon foreign goods, and paid partly, as he would show, by foreigners, and partly by those who chose, voluntarily, to purchase and consume them. Wherefore, then, this perpetual clamor about robbery and plunder, resistance and rebellion? Where are the burdens and oppressions, complained of? They existed only in the dreams and imaginations of gentlemen; they were but shadows, which a moment's cool reflection would forever dispel. These things surely could never produce resistance—there was nothing to resist; but resistance, if it should come, would be put down, as it always had been, without bloodshed, and without difficulty. He hoped, therefore, to hear no more about "glorious rebellion;" it was not a fit argument to be addressed to this House, or this country. We come here to listen to reason—not threats. This was not the language of conciliation; he would never be driven from the discharge of his duty by threats like these; he would not compromise with treason, or concede anything to a spirit of rebellion. To yield to such a spirit, was putting everything to hazard; its demands would only be increased by concessions. The more we yield, the more will it demand, until it ends in resistance. Such a spirit must be met at once with justice, with firmness, and with decision; this was the only true course, and, he hoped, it was the course that would now be adopted. But, sir, it must be admitted, on the other hand, that there are many gentlemen in the South who are disposed to approach this subject in a different spirit, and with a view to its amicable and satisfactory adjustment; to such he was disposed to make every concession that could be made, without absolute ruin to the country in which he lived, and the people he had the honor to represent; hence, he had proposed the bill now under consideration. This bill proposed an annual reduction of duties on everything, except certain specified articles, of 10 per cent. per annum, for two years in succession, and to admit negro clothing free of duty. It contained, however, compensating provisions in the reduction of duties on unprotected articles; guards against frauds; the regulation of the value of the pound sterling; the prompt payment of duties; and the omission of the one dollar minimum. Such was the general outline of the bill he had proposed; it was proposed in a spirit of compromise and concession, and, in that spirit, he hoped it would be accepted.

But it was due to himself to say that it was entirely different from the bill he would have proposed, had he been left free to take the course which the real interests of the country required, without reference to the discontent prevailing in the South. The payment of the public debt presented the most glorious opportunity of elevating this country to the highest point of national prosperity and national greatness; but this glorious opportunity, with all its benefits, must be yielded to the unfounded prejudices of the South.

The course which the interests of this country demanded, and which, under other circumstances, he would have proposed, was to reduce the revenue, by repealing the duties on what we cannot produce, and increasing those upon what we can; to give ample protection, or none at all. The reverse of the course now proposed was the true one: instead of reducing the duties, as proposed by the Secretary of the Treasury, on wool, and woolens, cotton, glass, salt, leather iron, and their manufactures, he would increase them gradually, at the rate of five per cent. per annum, until the market was completely secure to the American farmer and manufacturer; he would thus encourage the investment of capital, and the acquisition of skill; he would extract wealth from the rich mines of the mountains; cover the hills and valleys with flocks and herds; fill the country with smiling villages, and have us become in fact, as well as in name, a free and independent people. He would put the country upon its own resources for what it can and ought to produce, instead of importing it; stimulate domestic instead of foreign industry; diversify labor, promote competition, break down monopoly, increase production, diminish prices, create markets for agriculture, save the millions now sent abroad. The only effectual way to reduce the revenue was to diminish imports by increasing duties. The idea of reducing revenue by increasing imports (the source of revenue) involved an absurdity on the very face of it. But why import wool and woolens? What country, under heaven, possessed such a capacity for their production? And, with proper encouragement and protection, the day was not distant when we would export woolen, as we now do cotton goods. Why not? Is not our capacity for the production of wool greater than for the production of cotton? If we can succeed in converting one into cloth, at the lowest price, why not the other? Why is the cotton manufacture so successful? The reason is obvious; because it received protection by the minimum introduced by Mr. Calhoun, into the tariff of 1816, whereas woolens were left without protection until 1824. The one manufacture was sixteen years old, and the other only eight. Woolens, however, for the time, had advanced more rapidly than cottons. The supply of woolens was now estimated at forty millions per annum, while that of cottons did not exceed twenty-eight; and he would hazard nothing in the prediction, that, if the present protection be continued on woolens, as long as it had been on cottons, we should not only save the thirteen millions of dollars, now sent abroad, but would soon export woolens, and undersell the British, on equal terms, in the foreign markets of the world, where they now acknowledge our superiority in the cotton manufacture, by counterfeiting our marks—a fact notorious, and admitted by all.

Bad as was the bill reported by the chairman of the Committee of Ways and Means [Mr. M'Duffie], yet, in two respects, at least, he thought it decidedly preferable to that of the Secretary of the Treasury. The first was, that, by reducing the duties to 12½ per cent. it would effect a reduction of the revenue, while the secretary's would increase it. The second advantage was, that this project, if adopted, would arrest all our manufactures at once, and bring the country immediately back to a high protective tariff; while that of the Treasury Department would only protract a ruinous struggle, and more effectually destroy the manufacturer in the end; it would also delay the return of the country to a sound and enlightened system of protecting policy. The duties, in neither of these bills, amounted to protection. Anything short of this was alike destructive. Where 40 per cent. was required for protection, thirty was no better than five, except for revenue. There was no civilized and enlightened country on earth that neglected to guard and protect, by adequate regulations, its own industry. No government ever neglected it without incurring immediate ruin; and that protection must always be graduated to the state of the national prosperity; high prosperity and high labor required high protecting duties; impoverished countries, where labor was low, required less. The idea of "*free-trade*" was now universally exploded; it had no advocates in the world, except a few enthusiasts in our Southern States; it was found to be an *ignis fatuus* that had always led its followers to certain destruction—beautiful in theory, but ruinous in practice. The Emperor Alexander of Russia, some few years since, captivated with this theory, had relaxed, for a season, his high system of protection; but soon his prime minister, Count Nesselrode, in an official report, informed him that the effect of the reduction of duties had been there what it would be here; it had, he said, made Russia pay a "ruinous tribute to England and France, who remained faithful to their prohibitory systems; agriculture," he stated, "was without a market; industry, without protection, languished and declined; specie was exported, and the most solid commercial houses were shaken." He, accordingly, recommended a tariff, containing no less than one hundred and forty prohibitions, which was adopted, and the country was restored to its wonted prosperity.

The effect of free-trade, even if universally adopted, would be to reduce the most prosperous country to the condition of the most depressed. But should any nation be so infatuated as to adopt free-trade, while others adhered to the restrictive policy, it would fall an immediate sacrifice—a miserable victim to its own folly and rashness. The protection of every country must be in proportion to its prosperity. Nothing was clearer than that high-priced and prosperous labor required high protection against low-priced and depressed labor. If, in two contiguous territories, enforcing protection, the one highly prosperous, and the other greatly depressed—in the one the productions of labor being high, shoes and hats, for instance, commanding two dollars—in the other, where money was scarce and labor low, they were sold for one dollar—suppose, then, these two countries adopt "free-trade," what will be the effect? Would not the low-priced productions of cheap labor, cheap hats, cheap shoes, cheap every thing, flow into the prosperous country, paralyzing its industry, and drawing away its money, until the money being thus transferred from the rich to the poor country, the depressed would become the prosperous, and prosperous the depressed nation? Such would be the effect of free-trade between this country and Europe, even if they were willing to adopt it. Our laborer must work for six pence per day, or yield the market to the paupers of Europe. But how much more ruinous if we relax and they adhere to their restrictive policy? The reduction of protection would reduce the price of labor in this country just as certainly as the removal of an obstruction, which separated two ponds of unequal elevation, would depress the one to the level of the other, or depress the higher in proportion to the reduction of the wall of separation. Hence, he contended that this was a most important contest. It was a contest to uphold the labor of this country on the one hand, and to press it down on the other; not one kind of labor only, but every kind—agricultural, manufacturing, and mechanical. The question was, whether we should employ and cherish our own industry, and circulate our money at home, or send it abroad to import wool and woolens, iron, hats, shoes, every thing, from foreign countries? Labor is the foundation of national prosperity; it is the great parent of all production. Depress labor, and you depress the nation. Labor would prosper or decline precisely as you increase or diminish protection. Let gentlemen withdraw protection, and flood our country with foreign goods, export our money, and prostrate and paralyze all the laboring classes in the fields and the workshops; and let them go home and tell their constituents that they prefer British to American productions, unless they would work as cheaply as the paupers of England, the serfs of Russia, or the slaves of the Indies; let them go, go, and ask their suffrages, and receive their answers. This might do in the south, where labor had no voice—where the master votes for his slaves; but it would not satisfy the hardy, independent, and enlightened yeomanry of the Northern, Middle, and Western States. The effect of this system of free-trade was to divide society horizontally into upper and lower classes—into nabobs and paupers; rich men and beggars; princes and dependants; that was the legitimate result of the system. It was nothing to the employer that labor was depressed. It was nothing to the consumer, who lived upon his income, upon the interest of his stocks, his mortgages, and bonds, that labor went supperless to bed: his income remained the same, though he paid his laborers but six pence a day. Mr. S. said he knew the sufferings and the toils of labor; he had himself labored for years in the field and in the workshop. It was to the laboring people he was indebted for every thing. He stood here their representative and advocate; and, when he deserted them, he hoped that heaven would desert him. The day had not yet come, he trusted, when the aristocracy were to rule this country. We had heard much during the debate, about the will of the people. The will of the majority had been stigmatized as "the most odious tyranny—worse than the mob, more despotic than a Turkish Divan." He would notice these remarks directly. He supported this system of policy from views widely different from those avowed by many gentlemen. He legislated not for the benefit of the manufacturers, but the farmers of the country. It was the farmers, in fact, who were most benefited by this system of policy. Gentlemen talked of this as a system to sustain and enrich overgrown manufacturing establishments. This was all a delusion. The existing establishments are not to be benefited in the end, though, for the moment, they might be relieved from the injurious effects of foreign competition. This system, he said, while it destroyed foreign competition, called into life and activity competition at home; which, however beneficial it might be to the country at large, was not calculated to increase the profits of capital already invested, no more than the establishment of half a dozen new stores, taverns, hat or shoe factories, in a village, would be calculated to increase the business and the profits of those who already enjoyed the monopoly. To illustrate his view of this part of the subject, he would suppose a case of common occurrence—the case of an interior town, in which there was a single woolen factory, where the neighboring farmers sold their wool, and bought their supply of cloth. The manufacturer, having no competition, regulates both his own prices and those of the farmer. But suppose, in consequence of the encouragement afforded by a high tariff, half a dozen new factories should spring up in this town, producing six times the quantity of cloth, and creating a demand for six times the quantity of wool and provisions, would not the increased production of cloth soon glut the market, and reduce the price? while the increased demand for all the productions of the farmer, would as certainly increase his prices and his profits. He would enjoy the double advantage of receiving more and paying less. This was the plain and practical operation of the protective policy. It was the farmers, after all, who enjoyed its benefits to a much greater extent than the manufacturers. Hence he called upon all who represented the farming and agricultural interests of this country, to rally round, to sustain, and support this system, so essential to their prosperity and welfare. In support of this view of the subject, he begged leave to mention a single additional fact, stated to him by a highly respectable merchant and manufacturer, then present. It was this: That, before the manufacture of cotton goods had succeeded in this country, he sold to the farmers foreign cottons at 40 cents per yard, and received butter at 10 cents per pound. That now he sold them better goods, of his own manufacture, for 10 cents a yard, and gave 20 cents a pound for butter, and for other productions in the same proportion. That then he got two pounds of cotton for one yard of cloth, and now he gave two yards of cloth for one pound of cotton. Such was the effect of this system in favor of both the farmer and the cotton planter, whose true interest it most evidently was, not to destroy, but to increase, by every means in their power, the manufacturing spirit of this country, to stimulate competition, enlarge the capital, and increase the production of manufactured goods, thereby reducing the price of all they purchased, and increasing the price of all they had to sell. Mr. S. appealed to the cotton planters themselves, to say whether such was not the plain and practical operation of the system; and, if so, whether they were not bound, by every principle of self-interest, as well as of liberal and enlightened policy, to support it.

On the subject of taxation, Mr. S. thought there was much misapprehension. Some gentlemen contended that the duties are paid by the producer, others by the consumer; when, in fact, they were paid (to a great extent) by neither. Duties levied on articles not manufactured or produced in this country, he admitted, were paid (so far as the price was enhanced) by the consumer; but duties levied on articles extensively manufactured in this country, were taxes levied upon and paid into our treasury by foreigners. This was perfectly plain and evident. For the sake of illustration, select any article you please, now manufactured extensively in this country, the price of which was known and established, then increase the tax, say 10 or 20 per cent. on the foreign rival production, this could not affect the price established by the manufacturers here. The foreigner must sell at this price, and, of course, pay the duty himself. Take the case of hats, shoes, cloth, iron, glass, or anything else of American manufacture, having a fixed market price; glass, for instance, is manufactured here, at five dollars per box. Then, suppose we add one dollar per box to the duty on foreign glass—a cargo is imported and sold—it can bring no more than five dollars per box. Who then pays the duty? Clearly the foreigner. The American consumer pays no more for his glass after the tax, than he did before it was imposed; he still gets glass at five dollars, the duty being deducted from the profits of the foreign manufacturer; and what was true with regard to glass, was true with regard to everything else. That such had been the practical operation, was established, beyond all doubt, by the foreign invoices filed in the custom house. He had taken the trouble to examine into this matter, and gentlemen would there find the fact proved beyond all doubt, that immediately after the increased duties, imposed by the tariffs of 1824 and 1828, took effect, the prices of the foreign articles on which they were levied, fell in the foreign market precisely by the amount of the duty. The price in the American market remained the same. How did this occur? The importing merchant told the foreign manufacturer that an additional tax was imposed in the United States, but he could get nothing more on account of the duty, and he must, therefore, deduct it from the price, otherwise he could not purchase. The deduction was made accordingly, as was proved by the invoices to which he referred. Immediately after the tariff of 1828, the invoices showed a fall of four dollars and forty cents a ton on foreign hammered bar iron, and seven dollars on rolled, precisely the amount of the increased duty; and the same thing had occurred in relation to cloths, prints, and many other articles. And what is the plan proposed by the Secretary of the Treasury? It is to repeal these taxes, thus imposed upon foreigners, and thereby enable them more effectually to break down and destroy the manufacturers of this country, to flood our country with foreign goods, export our specie, and prostrate every branch of the national industry. The effect of this system was to lighten the burthens and increase the profits of foreign industry, and ruin and depress our own; and it is for us to say whether we will adopt this system; whether we will take the side of the American or the foreigner, in this mighty struggle for the American market.

He now came, Mr. S. said, to an argument of great importance. It, in fact, lay at the foundation of all the opposition and clamor against the tariff policy. He referred to the assertion, made upon all occasions, that the duty is added to the price, and therefore operated as a tax upon consumption. If this assertion should prove to be unfounded in point of fact, as he hoped to be able clearly to show, then, there being no addition to the price in consequence of the protecting duty, of course there could be no grounds of complaint. Now, so far from the duties levied for protection adding anything to the price, he hesitated not to affirm, and he challenged gentlemen to the scrutiny, that high protecting duties had never failed in a single instance to diminish the price, and the reduction of the prices of articles highly protected, had been much greater than on other articles of the non-protected class. And this reduction of price, he also affirmed, had been universal, wherever adequate protection had been afforded. He defied gentlemen to point out a single exception; yet, in the face of these facts, it was asserted that the duty was added to the price! To illustrate his argument on this point, he would mention a few out of a long catalogue of articles which he held in his hand. The duty on coarse cotton goods had been increased 125 per cent.; the price had fallen from twenty-five to six cents a yard, and instead of importing the article, we now not only supply our own consumption, but actually export it to the amount of nearly two millions of dollars per annum. On many grades of woolens, the duty had a few years since been increased on some articles 100 per cent., and the price had fallen to less than one-half its former amount. Our market was already supplied; and if the protection was continued, we should soon export woolens to a greater extent than we now do cotton goods. The duty on window glass had been increased nearly 100 per cent.; the price had consequently fallen from fourteen to four dollars per box; the importation had entirely ceased, and exportations had already commenced. The same might be said of cut nails, shot, lead, chemical preparations, and an almost infinite variety of articles, many of which were now actually bought at our factories for less than the amount of the duty! Yet, sir, we are gravely told, in the face of all these facts, that the duty is added to the price, and that the consumer has to pay it. The man who purchases American calico in Philadelphia for six cents per yard, has to pay eight and three-quarter cents a yard duty!! This was the result of the argument, and the gentleman from New York [Mr. Cambreleng], had proved it by figures, as clearly as that two and two make four. He would not fatigue the committee with a further enumeration of articles; but, when gentlemen daily and hourly asserted the fact that the duty operated as a tax by increasing the price, he hoped they would at least produce some single instance to prove it. But, if gentlemen failed to prove the truth of this assumption, that protecting duties increased prices, the whole clamor and noise about taxation, robbery, and plunder, was false and unfounded, and all the fine and flowery speeches built on this foundation must go for nothing—they vanish into thin air, and,

"Like the baseless fabric of a vision, leave not a wreck behind."

The whole ground of complaint against the tariff was entirely removed. Assumptions against facts, and theories against experience, would not do; something more than these was required to satisfy an intelligent people.

But the fact that a reduction of price followed an increase of protection, was not now more certain than the cause that produced it was obvious. Protection increased competition, competition increased production, and increased production never failed to produce a diminution of price. This was an invariable and unviversal rule, as certain and unerring in its operations as the ebbing and flowing of the tides. Competition was the great agent that worked out these wonderful results. A better illustration of the truth of this proposition could not be found, than was afforded by the familiar fact, that abundant crops always produced low prices, and short crops high ones.

The first section of the Treasury Bill, adopted by the Committee on Manufactures, proposes a total repeal of the tariff of 1828. He was at a loss to see how gentlemen who had voted for that law (and the Secretary of the Treasury, Mr. McLane, was himself one of the number) could now advocate its repeal. Four years ago gentlemen passed this law; they held out the promise of protection to the country; they invited capital to engage in manufactures; they encouraged the farmer to increase his flocks; they told him he should have protection. Capital had been tempted by these promises and inducements to go to work; millions had been invested in woolen, in iron, cotton, and various other branches of manufacture. They are just now getting under way, struggling into life against a powerful rival, when this proposition like a clap of thunder in a clear sky, comes to ruin and destroy them. The gentleman from New York [Mr. Hoffman] who had just resumed his seat, was of the number who voted for this law which he is now about to repeal, and thus sacrifice those who were deceived and deluded by the promised protection of the act of 1828. It was saying to them as the veiled prophet of Korassan said to his deluded followers, when he threw off the veil and doomed them to destruction:

> "There, ye wise saints, behold your light, your star,
> Ye would be dupes and victims, and ye are."

How such a course of policy could be justified and defended, he was at a loss to conjecture. By the act of 1828, gentlemen said to the manufacturers, build up. By this, they say, pull down. Though an action for damages could not, perhaps, be sustained against the gentleman from New York [Mr. Hoffman], yet there was at least ground for a pretty plausible declaration, and he did not know that juries might not be found who would award damages.

Numerous laws had been passed by the mother country, before the Revolution, making it a highly penal offence to erect forges and factories in this country. Those laws were mild and just compared with this kind of legislation. Those laws deceived nobody. They were prohibitory, preventive, and prospective in their operation. They warned the people against investing their money in manufactories. But this system of legislation was deceptive, retrospective, and destructive. It first invited capital to engage in manufactures, and then passed an *ex post facto* law to destroy it. It was inviting the citizens to do a meritorious act, and afterwards punishing him with the utmost severity. This was worse than the Roman tyrant, who concealed the law so as to entrap his people. Such a system was more abandoned in principle, and more destructive in its effects on the Northern and Middle States, than would be a law to emancipate all the Southern slaves; yet who would dream of proposing such a measure, and what a flame would it not produce throughout the Union? But if the people of the manufacturing and grain growing States will not consent to be sacrificed to make a market for British goods, the South will destroy the Union! And must we yield to threats like these? He hoped not. Look for a moment at the importance of the home market for agriculture. The quantity of land in cultivation in the United States he had seen estimated at 350,000,000 of acres; if valued at $10 it would amount to $3,500,000,000. The annual productions of land are supposed to be equivalent to its value. If this was correct, then the annual productions of land in the United States would be $3,500,000,000. Of this the whole was consumed at home, except the miserable amount $47,000,000; and of this pittance, $32,000,000 was cotton, tobacco, and rice; leaving the whole of the agricultural exports north of the Potomac to all the world at $15,000,000!! Yet gentlemen seem disposed to destroy the immense home market by opening our ports to British goods. Agriculture lies at the foundation of the national prosperity. When it prospers, all prosper; when it declines, all suffer. He appealed to the observation and experience of every one for the truth of this remark. This, he affirmed, was the grand thermometer by which the degree of national prosperity was always ascertained.

The American people had long been taught to look forward to the period of the final extinguishment of the public debt as to a glorious jubilee; when the nation, released from this thraldom, would be left free to adopt a system of policy which, while it would render us independent of foreign countries, would at the same time awaken to new activity and life all our energies and all our resources, improving our internal condition, facilitating internal commerce, and rendering this free government, as it should be, the wonder and admiration of the world. But, sir, if the payment of the public debt is to be made the occasion of adopting an opposite system—of arresting the progress of internal improvement; of prostrating our manufactures; paralyzing our agriculture; depressing and degrading the free labor of this country; demoralizing its character, and breaking down its lofty, noble, and independent spirit; if such was to be the result, and he verily believed such would be the effect of the system now proposed by the Treasury Department, then he said the payment of the public debt would be converted into the most blighting and withering curse that ever afflicted any people.

What is the true course of policy now to be adopted? Ask an enlightened American statesman, and he will tell you. Select from this long catalogue those articles which we can and ought to manufacture, and for which we ought to be independent of the world—wool, woolens, iron, cotton—which paid, in 1831, fourteen millions of revenue. Cut off this revenue by a gradual increase of the duties, running them up to the point of ultimate prohibition, encourage capital to go to work, stimulate industry, elicit your resources, promote competition, increase production, save your money, supply yourselves, and finally, supply the world with these articles, as you will do, if you are wise. This was the only true course to reduce the revenue, and, at the same time, advance the national wealth and independence. It would not only have this happy effect, but it would tend more than any other thing to strengthen the bonds of our national union; it would bind together the distant parts, by the strong and enduring ties of interest and intercourse. Our manufactures would naturally spring up in the populous and comparatively sterile regions of the North. The fertile valleys of the West would afford ample and profitable employment to agriculture. The South would still grow the rich products of cotton, tobacco, sugar, and rice; the capital of our cities employed in commerce, the handmaid of agriculture and manufactures, would carry away the surplus of each, and bring back equivalents from abroad. Added to this, a judicious and extended system of internal improvement, uniting the remote sections of our common country, the North with the South, the East with the West, facilitating and cheapening the exchange of their respective productions, destroying distance, promoting social intercourse, diffusing intelligence—in short, making our country not only the admiration of the world, but the very perfection of everything that the aspirations of the enthusiast, or the prayers of the patriot, could ask or desire. The money expended on internal improvements might be invested as stock in companies incorporated by the States, the proceeds re-invested in other works, producing and re-producing their kind, until all was accomplished, when our country would present a scene of unparalleled happiness, prosperity, and power—the revenue arising from these works, paid with pleasure, and, for a full equivalent in the end, might be adequate to all the demands of government. Such a system, in peace, would not only be a source of countless benefits and blessings, but, in war, it would constitute at once the most abundant source of revenue, and powerful system of defence. The physical force of the country could be concentrated, by means of railroads, canals, and steamboats, with the rapidity of thought, either to repel invasions from abroad, or [pointing to the South] to suppress insurrections at home.

Such would be the system of policy which he would adopt, were he free to pursue the course which patriotism and public policy so clearly indicated. But, he repeated, all this must be sacrificed and given up as a peace offering to the South. But even this was spurned. Concessions on the one side seemed but to swell demands on the other. If we surrender our plan of reducing the revenue, by excluding imports, and adopt the opposite, then we are required to regulate the reduction so as completely to sacrifice our interests. This was not compromise: it was dictation on the one side, and submission on the other; and I, for one, said Mr. S., if gentlemen are not disposed to meet us in the spirit of mutual concession and amicable adjustment, will make strict right and justice my guide, and let consequences take care of themselves.

Mr. S. said, he had now presented his general views of this subject, and after a brief reply to some of the arguments of the chairman of the Committee of Ways and Means [Mr. M'Duffie] would trespass no longer on the time and attention of the committee.

In the first place, that gentleman has been pleased to denounce, in the most unmeasured terms, the people of this country: such a philippic against the will of the majority I have never before heard. He has not hesitated to declare, that the "will of the majority is the veriest despotism on earth; that any other tyranny was preferable to this; worse than the worst revolutionary times in France." That the "majority had no more moral sense than a mob;" that "a Russian despotism was preferable to this, because one tyrant could be satisfied, the people never." That he "would prefer living under any tyranny, rather than under this inexorable tyrant—'King Numbers, King Demos,' or in other words, a government of the people." Now, he submitted to the gentleman, whether this was proper language to be used here, by one representing a portion of the people of this country, whether free or not free; was this the language of compromise and conciliation—was this the tone in which to ask for concessions? What was the inevitable result of such doctrines? If the majority is not to govern, who is? If the people are to be put down, who is to be put up? We must have some government. It results in what the gentleman seemed to desire: the substitution of one tyrant for many; his majesty the king, for their majesties the people. Such sentiments, Mr. S. said, he was astonished to hear uttered here; and the more astonished to hear them come from such a source. It was not long since he heard pronounced from that same gentleman, standing in the same spot, one of the most splendid and eloquent eulogiums upon the people; upon the will of the majority; upon their purity, patriotism, and public virtue; and he had heard the gentleman then, with as much admiration and delight, as he now heard him with mortification and regret. He begged leave to call the gentleman's attention to a single sentence of that patriotic and eloquent appeal. The gentleman then said, "The people are essentially patriotic; with them, selfishness itself is public virtue. By the laws of moral necessity, they are obliged to will their own happiness." Such were the sentiments of the gentleman then; they did him honor; they were the sentiments of every American; of every friend of his country and its free institutions. He hoped they were still his sentiments, and that these declarations were but the ebullitions of temporary excitement.

The gentleman from South Carolina [Mr. McDuffie] has been pleased to denounce the tariff as a system of plunder, imposed upon the South by New England for her especial benefit. A New England system! Sir, is this so, or is not the reverse nearer the truth? Let us look into this matter for a moment. Before the late war, the capital of New England was engaged in commerce; Southern gentlemen then controlled the policy of this country; they were the majority; they had power; and how did they use it? Their motto, with regard to New England, as avowed by one of their distinguished leaders on this floor, was "*Delanda est Carthago.*" The commerce of New England was accordingly destroyed: non-intercourse, embargo, and finally war, swept it, as with the "besom of destruction," from the bosom of the deep. She remonstrated, but submitted to her fate. Her capital was forced from commerce to manufactures. This, the wants of the country rendered absolutely necessary; and how was she protected?

After the restoration of peace, in 1816, the duties were reduced one-half, except on a few articles, among which was coarse cottons. The country was inundated with foreign goods; our manufacturing establishments were destroyed, and the imports became so excessive that the balance of trade against us in two years rose to the enormous sum of $111,000,000, bringing in its train the desolating scenes of 1818, 1819, and 1820. He need not describe them; they could never be forgotten. Manufactures being thus destroyed, by this outrageous policy, New England was driven back again to commerce. And what next? Why, sir, in 1824 a general tariff was adopted for the encouragement and protection of manufactures, and their capital had again to be transferred from commerce to manufactures. This, with another measure of the same kind, in 1828, constituted what the gentleman is now pleased to call the "New England system of plunder." Who were the authors of this system? Certainly not New England. Look at the journals, and gentlemen would find that, so far from New England being the author of this policy, it was forced upon her by others. The vote of the six New England States, on the tariff of 1824, stood fifteen for and twenty-three against it. In 1828, their vote stood sixteen for and twenty-three against the tariff; making, together, thirty-one for and forty-six against these two measures. In Pennsylvania, New York, Ohio, and the Western States, the vote was, on the tariff of 1824, for it, seventy-eight, against it, nine; and on the tariff of 1828, for it, eighty, against it, six; making fifteen against, and one hundred and fifty-eight for those two acts.

Yet, in the face of these facts, we are told every day that this policy of protection is a New England system of grinding oppression on the South. Now, sir, this system has been literally forced upon New England by New York and Pennsylvania, and he hoped gentlemen would not pass over

Pennsylvania to abuse New England for what we had done. Sir, we covet the censure of having been the authors of this system, which has contributed so much to advance the prosperity, happiness, and independence of this country. We are proud of the odium, nay, the glory, of having established this system; and it would be base and dishonorable to sit silent in our seats, and hear New England abused on account of measures we have adopted; and, although Pennsylvania and New York had forced this system on her, New England did not talk of resistance or rebellion, but, in a spirit of patriotism, acquiesced in the will of the majority; she had conformed to what seemed to be the settled policy of the country; she had vested her capital, under the protection promised, and shall we now desert her? Shall we violate our pledge? Shall we shamefully and perfidiously sacrifice those great Eastern markets for our agriculture?—a measure alike destructive to them and to us, and for what? In the delusive hope of silencing the unfounded clamors of the South. He hoped not. Pennsylvania was unanimous in adopting this policy, and he hoped she would be unanimous in maintaining it; he hoped for the same unanimity here that was found on a recent occasion in her State Legislature; he hoped she would exhibit no "dough faces" on this question; he hoped she would never sacrifice her policy and her principles to conform to the wishes of any administration, no matter who might be at its head. To factious opposition he was as much opposed as any man on that floor, as his votes would prove, and to them he appealed; he had voted uniformly upon all political questions, under the present Administration, with a majority of his colleagues, who would not be suspected or charged with being opposed to the present Chief Magistrate; but on all great and vital questions of public policy, he never would surrender his principles, or the interests of his constituents, to conform to the views of men in power.

In the next place, the gentleman [Mr. M'Duffie] draws a most melancholy picture of the depressed condition of the South, of their deserted fields and desolated towns, of the impoverishment and dismay that overspread the land. Now, if all this were true, the tariff had not the slightest agency in producing it; for the true causes, if the facts existed, gentlemen must look to the increased production of cotton at home and abroad. Since 1819 the production of cotton in the South had increased four-fold—from 87,-

000,000 of pounds in 1819, to 375,000,000 in 1831, of which 228,000,000 were produced in the new States, where little or none was produced in 1819. But was the picture true, or was it not the mere creature of the gentleman's own excited imagination? In opposition to this theory he would state one or two facts for the consideration of the gentleman, who had represented New England as growing rich and powerful at the expense of the South. Look at this fact, sir. By the late apportionment bill, the seven tobacco and cotton growing States, south of the Potomac, have gained no less than seven new members on this floor, while the six New England States had actually lost one. Yet, in the face of this fact, we are gravely told that the people are deserting the South, and seeking more prosperous climes, while population, in fact, was rushing to the South with unexampled rapidity.

The people of New England were seen daily quitting their homes, endeared by a thousand ties, and emigrating to the South, leaving their friends and relatives; leaving a free for a slave country; leaving a healthy for a sickly climate; risking their lives in a country in every way uncongenial to their feelings and their habits; and why? To make their fortunes in the South. The facility of acquiring wealth in that region presented these powerful attractions; but who ever heard of a Southern man going to New England to make his fortune? They went there occasionally to spend a few thousand dollars at the Saratoga and Ballstown springs, which they would scarcely miss. But let a Southern planter go on to a Pennsylvania or a New England farm, and he would starve. What was the fact? The Southern nabob did not even supervise his own labor; it was managed by overseers. While he rioted in luxury and ease, the Pennsylvania and Northern farmer was up and in the field, from daylight until dark—not with his slaves, but his sons, and oftentimes his daugthers too; and, with all, they made but a scanty subsistence. Could they afford to ride in their carriages, and visit the springs with all the pomp and splendor of Southern magnificence? Yet, gentlemen from the South come here and tell us we are rioting in wealth, acquired at their expense! That they are depressed; and that we must consent to sacrifice our industry, import our wool, our hemp, iron, everything from England, and send our last dollar to pay for it, to induce England to take a little more of their cotton; and, if we don't consent thus to bow down and degrade ourselves to a condition of poverty and dependence worse than slavery itself, why, forsooth, they will dissolve the Union! And what then? He would not say what then might be the condition of the South. But it was a question worthy of their own serious consideration. Now, sir, unless gentlemen could show that men were in the habit of exchanging a prosperous, free, and healthful country for one poor and depressed, he hoped they would say no more about the desolate and deserted condition of the South, and the prosperous and flourishing state of the North. The reverse was the truth, as the march of population, that unerring vane that always indicated the direction of the prosperous gale, proved beyond all doubt. The South was growing with unparalleled rapidity, while the North was declining in population and political power. This fact could not be controverted.

But the gentleman undertakes to account for this supposed prosperous condition of the North, and the depressed condition of the South, by saying that Northern labor "went to elections and *clamored at the polls.*" Now, sir, this is a topic which the gentleman ought not to have introduced into this discussion; he regretted its introduction; but, since it had been introduced, he would say a word or two in reply. The gentleman ought to have recollected that, if Southern labor did not clamor at the polls, it nevertheless had its representatives on this floor. Yes, sir, three-fifths of the Southern slaves are represented here. Take away the votes given by Southern property—by Southern slaves—and you reduce the representation of the Southern cotton growing anti-tariff States nearly one-third. Yes, sir, nearly one-third of the whole of the Southern delegation represents property. In South Carolina, according to the late census, four of her nine members on this floor were the representatives of property. Yet, the gentleman talks of Northern labor clamoring at the polls!! The gentleman himself, with his one hundred slaves, and sixty votes, denounces the majority as King Numbers; King Demos. Might we not retaliate, and call hard names? Why should a Southern planter, with his one thousand slaves, have as many votes as six hundred Northern freemen, who might each possess an equal amount of property? Why not, with equal justice, suffer our manufacturers to vote for three-fifths of their spindles and their looms, or other laboring machines?

What, allow me to ask, does the South give for this immense political power? Nothing at all. Why? Because this very system of raising revenue from duties levied on foreign imports, instead of direct taxes, entirely relieves the South from the payment of the equivalent, in the increased amount of taxes which they agreed to pay as a consideration for this concession. When the constitution was formed, the revenue was raised by contributions levied on the several States, according to their representation in Congress. The South, always fond of political power, proposed to the less ambitious North that, if they would agree to give three-fifths of their slaves representatives in this House, they would consent to pay taxes in the same proportion. To this proposition they assented, and the matter was so arranged in the constitution. No direct tax is now collected. The whole revenue is derived from duties on imports, whereby the South is relieved entirely from the consideration they were to give for this political power. Yet, with all these advantages, they complain, and threaten to resist the right of the majority to govern!!

But, to save appearances, the gentleman is driven to the necessity of asserting a new and extraordinary principle—a new discovery in political science. It was this: that the producer pays the taxes; that he who buys an article, makes it. Hence, he infers that British manufactures, purchased and imported into the South, are American manufactures, just as much as if they were made in the United States. "There cannot," says the gentleman, in his report, "be a more palpable and delusive error, than the vulgar notion that imported manufactures, purchased with the agricultural staples of this country, are foreign productions. They are as strictly and exclusively the productions of American industry, as if they were manufactured in the United States." They make these manufactures, the gentleman says, not with looms and spindles, but with ploughs and hoes. He that buys an article makes it: this is the argument. But it proves too much. Follow it out, and what does it prove? It proves clearly, that, as England buys Southern cotton, she produces it, and is, therefore, a cotton growing country; or, rather, our Northern merchants purchase it, and, therefore, they are cotton planters. But the South, also, purchases New England cotton and woolen goods, therefore they manufacture them, and become *particeps criminis* in this infamous business of manufacturing! It also proves, that, if the gentleman himself, on his way to his lodgings, should call and buy a pair of shoes, he becomes a shoemaker, for he who buys a thing makes it; he buys a hat, and he is a hatter; cloth for a coat, and he is a woolen manufacturer; pays the tailor for making it, and he is a tailor; thus, when he arrives at his lodgings, he finds that, according to this theory, he has, in this short space of time, and for this trifling sum, actually become a hatter, a shoemaker, a woolen manufacturer, and a tailor; in short, that he is "Jack of all trades, but, unfortunately, master of none." Such is the obvious and inevitable result of the gentleman's argument.

But the gentleman further contends, that exports and imports must correspond, and hence he infers that, if we do not import and consume British goods to the amount of $30,000,000 a year, she will not buy more than that amount of their cotton. This Mr. S. considered an unsound position. When the British manufacturer went into the market to purchase his supply of cotton, he took the cheapest and the best he could find, without inquiring in what country it grew, or what was the state of the trade of that country. But, even if the position were correct, what would follow? It would follow, as an unavoidable consequence, that if it were not for the consumption of imports in the Northern, Middle, and Western States, the South would lose at least two-thirds of their present market for cotton, tobacco, and rice. Of the $40,000,000 of Southern exports, the North and West consume and pay for at least $26,000,000. Thus, by dissolving the Union, the gentleman from South Carolina, upon his own principles, will deprive the South of two-thirds of their foreign market for cotton, besides losing the Northern home market, worth at least $10,000,000 per annum. Exports and imports must correspond, says the gentleman. Well, how does this matter stand? In 1830, the whole imports south of the Potomac amounted to about $2,000,000; their exports to $30,000,000: while, north of the Potomac, the imports were $61,000,000, and the exports $20,000,000. Hence, it appears that the South are the exporters, and the North the importers; the South the sellers, and the North the buyers. We, of the North and West, therefore, are tributary—"hewers of wood and drawers of water" for the South. But, with all this, they are not content—we must be degraded to the condition of abject slaves; and if we object, they will dissolve the Union! Sir, it is the South, and not the North, that is most benefited by the

Union. It is the Northern merchant who buys the Southern cotton, and makes sale of it at home and abroad. It is the Northern manufacturer who furnishes their supplies cheaper and better than they ever got them elsewhere. By a dissolution of the Union, the South would suffer as much as the North; the interests of all are united; they must stand or fall together. We must cherish and sustain each other. By taking away our protection, the South

> "Takes that which naught enriches them,
> But makes us poor indeed."

He was surprised to hear the gentleman from South Carolina speak of the advantages of our trade with Great Britain, and of the liberality of her policy toward us. The balance of trade with England last year, against us, amounted to upwards of $11,000,000, and the export of specie to England, in that period, had amounted to more than half that sum, producing universal embarrassment and distress in our mercantile community. The pressure had been so great that the specie in the United States' Bank had been reduced, in a few months, more than one-half—sent to England to make up this unfavorable balance. Great Britain received less than $60,000 of all the grain and bread stuffs of this country, while we received $30,000,000 worth of her manufactures. And this was the liberality which had been so highly eulogised! She excluded our produce by absolute prohibition, and by duties, amounting to four and five hundred per cent. This was British "free-trade!"

The gentleman from South Carolina appeared to be indignant at some remarks which he had found in Niles's Register. Now, he thought gentlemen who were continually threatening resistance, nullification, and a dissolution of the Union, should be the last to arraign others for intemperate language. When Southern gentlemen declare their determination to dissolve the Union, Mr. Niles, the gentleman says, insultingly exclaims: "*let them go.*" And was this not what they desired? Did they wish to be restrained? Such sentiments, the gentleman says, merit the "reprobation of every friend to the *harmony* of the Union!!" He was happy to hear the gentleman speak well of the harmony of the Union—one sentiment, at least, in which he entirely concurred with that honorable member.

In conclusion—the gentleman from South Carolina [Mr. M'Duffie] has painted, in the most glowing colors and fascinating forms, the glorious advantages to the South of a dissolution of this Union. But was there not another side to this picture? and to this he begged gentlemen to turn their calm and dispassionate attention. Before they took this fearful plunge let them look over the precipice on which they stand into the yawning gulf beneath. On the other side of this picture was written, in flaming capitals: "*treason, rebellion, civil war,*" with all its fearful consequences. Let it be remembered, that no State can go out of this Union until it has conquered all the rest. When one State is gone, no two remain united. We have heard of the benefits of destroying this Union: but what will be its cost to those who may attempt it? From imaginary ills they fly to "others that they know not of."

They now complain of taxation! But what will be the taxation necessary to raise and sustain armies and navies to contend against this Government?—a Government which now, with fond and parental affection, guards and protects the South. But taxation would be the smallest item in the frightful catalogue of their calamities. There is still another leaf in this book, to which gentlemen should look. And can they behold it with indifference? It is the page on which posterity will write the epitaph of the authors of the destruction of this happy and glorious Union; of those who should involve us in all the horrors of civil war; who should arm father against son, and brother against brother; who should destroy this bright and glorious example—the only free Government on earth.

How deep and how loud would be their denunciations, how bitter and how blasting would be the curses with which posterity would brand the memories of those men! And will not their sentence be just? Where will they look for extenuation or excuse? Taxation! it is imaginary, not real. All contributions here are voluntary, not compulsory. No people under heaven are half so lightly taxed, or half so highly blessed. In other countries the people are taxed twenty times the amount, to support despots; imposed, not by themselves, but by arbitrary power. Compared with this country, in England taxation was as 18 to 1; yet they submit, and we rebel. Will not the people of the South look at these facts, and pause before they do the fatal deed that must seal forever their own destruction? In this Union the gentleman from South Carolina had everything to hope: his name might go down to posterity among the most distinguished men of the age: his talents might adorn its highest offices, to which he had a just right to aspire; and much as I may differ with that gentleman, said Mr. S., both as to men and measures, yet such is my opinion of his talents and his worth, that I would rejoice to see him at this moment filling the highest of the executive departments of this government, or the highest of its diplomatic stations. That gentleman may be carried away by momentary excitement; still I cannot doubt his attachment to this Union, which I trust he will never sacrifice to imaginary evils. The blessings of this government, and the value of this Union, I have never heard so forcibly urged, or so eloquently portrayed, as by the gentleman from South Carolina himself; and I cannot in conclusion, better express my own feelings, than by repeating the very words uttered by that gentleman in concluding an able and eloquent speech on another occasion, when he said: "The liberty of this country is a sacred depository—a vestal fire, which Providence has committed to our hands for the general benefit of mankind. It is the world's last hope; extinguish it, and the earth will be covered with eternal darkness—but once 'put out that light, I know not where is that Promethean heat that shall that light relume.'"

I appeal to the gentleman—I ask him, is he prepared to destroy that "sacred depository," the Union and the liberties of his country; is he prepared to extinguish, in fraternal blood, that "Vestal fire committed to his hands by Providence, for the benefit of mankind;" is he prepared to destroy "the world's last hope;" to put out and extinguish forever, that great and glorious light of liberty and union now blazing up to the heavens, illumining the path, and cheering the onward march of the friends of freedom throughout the world, and thus to "cover the earth with eternal darkness?" Is he prepared for this?—I pause for a reply.

COMMENTS AND OPINIONS OF THE PRESS.

"We commence to-day the publication of the speech of Mr. Stewart, on the subject of the tariff. As this is a subject of such vital importance to the people of this section of the country, we are sorry our room will not permit us to publish more of the speeches that have been delivered, pending the interesting discussion which has so long occupied the attention of the House. The speech of Mr.

Stewart, however, contains a comprehensive view of the whole ground of debate. He enters into an examination of the several bills presented to the House, and shows that the duties recommended by either of those bills, are entirely inadequate for protection. He exhibits and enforces such a system, as in his opinion is necessary to sustain the manufacturing and agricultural interests of the country. We were particularly pleased with the just indignation with which he treated the threats of the nullifiers of the South, and his assertion that notwithstanding he was willing to give up something on terms of concession, he was determined to yield nothing to intimidation. As much as he would deplore the withdrawal of any of the States from the Union, he would prefer it to an abandonment of the interests of the country, and suffer the minority to rule the majority. He calls upon the friends of the tariff to remain united in sustaining a policy which is absolutely necessary for the continuance of our present prosperity, and appeals to the South, by their love of liberty, and of country, to pause, and reflect, before they strike the fearful blow which must at once prostrate this fair fabric, which was reared and cemented by the blood of our ancestors, and blot out forever 'this great and glorious light of liberty,' which is now illumining the world.

"There are few members in the House better acquainted with the details of the tariff than Mr. Stewart, and none have manifested greater zeal in advocating and supporting it. He considers it, as it really is, a subject of great importance to his constituents, and has, therefore, used every exertion to sustain it. His late speech we consider as one of his most able efforts in defence of the system, and notwithstanding its great length, we have no doubt the interest which our readers generally take in the subject will ensure it a general reading."—*Philadelphia Gazette.*

NOTE.—The above is selected from among many others.

LETTER TO THE HON. JAMES G. BLAINE, SPEAKER OF THE HOUSE OF REPRESENTATIVES, ON THE TARIFF.

[THE ARGUMENT CONDENSED.]

SIR,—Permit an old personal friend to address to, and through you to others, a few brief reflections on the subject of the tariff, now under discussion in the House over which you so ably preside.

First—It seems to me, sir, that there is a *disputed fact* on which the whole theory of free-trade, with all the speeches on that subject depend for support, that ought to be settled before the debate can properly proceed. The fact, or rather assumption, is this, that all *protective*, as well as revenue, duties are "*added to the price of the domestic as well as foreign goods, and paid by the consumer.*" This has always been denied—the proof repeatedly called for, but never furnished, because, upon examination, the reverse was found to be the truth.

If Mr. Kerr and his friends assert the disputed fact, that the duties are added to the price and paid by the consumer, are they not bound to prove it? Suppose these learned lawyers went into court with a disputed claim and demanded a verdict without proof, would not judgment go at once against them? And what better right have they to demand judgment in your court, where the laws are made, than in a court where they are administered? If it be true that the duty is added to the price, the proof is accessible by reference to all of the prices current ever published, showing the prices of the goods when the duties were first imposed for their protection, and then the prices afterward, as manufactures and home competition have progressed; and why has not this proof been produced? Simply because in attempting to do so they discovered that instead of increasing prices the effect of *protective* duties was to *reduce* them, thus obliging these gentlemen, according to their own theory, to go for protection to reduce taxation.

To settle this disputed question, whether protective duties in the end increase or reduce prices, let Mr. Kerr send a resolution to the Secretary of the Treasury to furnish the *prices* of *home* manufactures, when the duties were first imposed for their protection, and the prices since, from time to time, as the supply has been increased by home competition, experience and skill, which Mr. Young, the able Chief of the Bureau of Statistics, can soon supply, and thus settle now and forever this important question of fact, upon the truth of which the free-trade theory, speeches and all, depends entirely for support.

By reference to the debates of 1828, '32, '44, '45, and '46, it will be seen that it was then proved, by the prices current and by mercantile books, that protective duties levied on articles we successfully manufactured at home had in the end, by the investment of capital, competition, and increased supply, invariably caused a reduction in the prices of such goods; yet, in the face of these established facts, gentlemen went on then, as now, reiterating every day this false theory, on which their whole case depended, that *protective* duties are added to the price and paid by the consumer.

Revenue duties levied on articles we do not produce, it is true, are often added to the price and paid by the consumer; but *protective* duties levied on articles we can and do successfully manufacture at home have always in the end caused a *reduction* in price, by an increased supply resulting from home competition, improved labor-saving machinery, skill, experience, etc. The *immediate* effect, however, of a high protective duty, by excluding foreign supply, is temporarily to increase the price by diminishing the supply; but this very increase of price hastens its reduction by attracting capital from other less profitable employments, thereby increasing home competition and supply, and, of course, in the end reducing the price. It is admitted that this effect may sometimes be interrupted by temporary causes—war, famine, depreciated or redundant currency, extraordinary demand, etc.; but these exceptions do not impair the general truth of this theory.

Now, sir, this whole matter is controlled by one great law, generally ignored, *the law of demand and supply*, a law that regulates the price of all the necessaries of life with as much certainty as the law that regulates the ebbing and flowing of the tides. Whatever *increases* the *supply*, *reduces* the price, and whatever *reduces* the *supply*, *increases* the price.

Hence it follows that the *ultimate* effect of protective duties is to reduce prices by increasing home competition and supply.

In the debates of '44—'46 it was shown that in 1816, there was a duty of about seven cents a square yard imposed on cotton goods then selling at twenty-five and thirty cents per yard, by a bill reported by Mr. Lowndes and advocated by Mr. Calhoun, of S. C., and that afterwards a duty of $4 per box was put on glass, three and a half cents per pound on nails, etc., which at the time of the debate appeared to be selling, cotton for six cents a yard, glass at $3½ a box, nails at three and a quarter cents a pound, etc. Yet it was still contended, then as now, that the duty was added to the price and paid by the consumer. That is, that the consumer who bought a yard of domestic cotton for six cents, paid seven cents duty; on a box of glass he bought for $3.50 he paid $4 duty; on a pound of nails he bought for three and a quarter cents, he paid a duty of three and a half cents. These facts were not denied, but the theory had to be maintained, that the duty was added to the price, or all their speeches about taxation, oppression, etc., would have vanished into air.

Now I have a few questions to put to Mr. Kerr, the able and astute leader of the free-trade party, which I hope he will answer in the speech he has promised to make when the Ways and Means report the tariff bill to the House. Now Mr. Kerr, in a speech a few days ago, estimated the home manufacture of iron at $202,000,000; wool at $176,000,000, and cotton at $170,000,000, making together $548,000,000. Then suppose Mr. Kerr, who boasts that he is free-trade from the crown of his head to the soles of his feet, succeeded in his efforts to reduce the duties on iron and woolen goods below the point of adequate protection, and thus destroyed $378,000,000, the present home supply, he says, of iron and woolen goods. What would be the effect of this on the prices of these articles in the markets of the world? Would they not be doubled? How many millions of American capital would it destroy? How many millions of tons of ore and coal, now being developed, would it leave useless in the ground? How many thousand working men, now profitably employed in making this $202,000,000 worth of iron, would it throw out of employment, and how many millions would it take out of the pockets of our farmers who now supply the bread, meat, vegetables, hay, oats and corn, consumed by the men, women, and children, horses and mules, employed in making this iron at home, by sending this $202,000,000 to Europe to purchase that amount of foreign coal and ore, bread, meat, and grain, worked up there as here into iron, to be laid down as rails over the richest mines of ore and coal, and the most productive land in the world? Thus robbing our farmers of their markets, our laborers of employment, and our country of its money to enrich foreigners at our expense. Are not such the legitimate results of free-trade? Are not such the benefits and blessings it would, if carried out, confer upon America's farmers and working men?

Mr. Kerr also estimates the home manufacture of woolen goods at $176,000,000. Is not the wool considered one-half the value of the cloth? And is not the other half principally made up of the wages and subsistence of labor? And is not this what you pay for, when you buy the cloth? Why then give to foreigners $176,000,000 for woolen goods, which, under favor of *protection*, is now retained in our own country, and distributed among our own people? And is this not equally true of all other goods brought from abroad in competition with American Manufacturers? And if not, please point out the exceptions.

Is not *inadequate* protection worse than none, as it encourages American manufacturers to struggle on until they are totally ruined? Whereas if all protection were withdrawn at once, they would if possible save their capital by transferring it to some better employment?

I also ask Mr. Kerr, whether the consumer pays any part of the duty on articles where American competition has established an American price in the American markets? Suppose the price of American pig iron is established in New York by home competition at $50 a ton, the present price—take off the duty, and will not the foreigner continue to sell his iron for $50, the American price? then add $10 to the duty, must he not pay this $10 into the treasury, and still sell his pigs at $50, the established American price? He can't get more, and he wont take less. So whether the duty is high or low, on or off, the consumer gets the iron at the same price. Again, do not protective duties not only sustain our wages at home, but are they not now lifting up the down-trodden labor of Europe, where every day it is demanding higher wages, threatening to go to the United States where it can get two or three times the amount, and must not the capitalist submit to the demands of labor or loose it?

Again, we ask, is not the common idea that either protection on the one hand, or free-trade on the other, is the true policy of all nations alike an absurdity? What can be more clear than that in the commercial intercourse between two countries, in one of which labor and its productions are high, and in the other low, protection is always the true policy of the high priced and free-trade of the low priced country? as between the United States and Europe. Would not free-trade open our ports to the free importation of their goods and the exportation of our money until our money was all gone? Then would not our prosperous labor have to come down to their degraded level—make our own shoes, hats, caps and clothes, or go without them?

Mr. Kerr and others have repeated over and over that protective duties favor the rich monopolists at the expense of the farmers and laboring men. Now I submit to the candor and good sense of Mr. Kerr and others, whether just the reverse of this is not true.

Suppose in some village there is a single woolen or other factory owned by some rich monopolist who dictates the wages of labor and the price of wool and other produce in his neighborhood. Then suppose, by a highly protective tariff you build up two or three other competing woolen mills in this village, requiring two or three times as much labor, two or three times as much wool and provisions, and producing two or three times as much cloth, would this not favor the farmer and the laborer by increasing the price of the produce of the one, and the wages of the other, at the expense of the rich monopolist, who would thus have to pay more for what he bought, and take less for what he sold, thus destroying monopoly by building up competition, the only thing that can destroy it?

By doubling the duty on pig iron, would not the first effect be to raise the price by shutting out the foreign supply and thereby causing such a rush of capital into this highly profitable business as soon to increase the home supply by home competition to such an extent as not only to supply ourselves, but Europe also with pig iron, our capacity for its production being unlimited, while theirs is becoming every day more and more exhausted?

I would be glad to know what answer Mr. Kerr and his friends would have to make to these questions should they meet with them in debate.

Protective duties should be *specific*. *Ad valorem* duties not only promote frauds and undervaluations, but what is worse, going up and down with the price of foreign goods, they take away protection when foreign goods are low and protection is needed, and give higher protection when they are high and protection is not so much required.

But why destroy American manufactories by free-trade? Why give foreigners a monopoly of labor-saving machinery? Why compel our people to work the plough and hoe against the spindle and the loom, by the aid of which latter one woman can pay for the labor of fifty men in the field?

To the non-producers it matters not how low the productions of labor are, which they purchase and consume, nor to the rich monopolist, how low the wages of labor he has to pay; but to productive labor the great and only source of national wealth, embracing more than three-fourths of our entire population, protection is life and free-trade is death. Let free-trade strike down productive labor and the blow will be felt by the nation through its every nerve.

Will the free-trade Democrats permit me to ask them why, in the Senate and House, they go against reducing protective duties on articles extensively produced in their own districts —iron in Pennsylvania, coal in Maryland, salt, sugar, etc., elsewhere? Is it not because they consider these protective duties a good thing? And if good in their own districts and States, why not equally good in others? Are not the votes therefore of these free-traders against reducing protective duties for the benefit of their own constituents, a virtual confession of judgment in favor of protection? Or do they so vote because *protection*, as Senator Morton said a few days ago, is a *party* question, as was proved on Mr. Cox's motion to reduce the duty on pig iron, when every Democrat outside of Pennsylvania voted for the reduction except two, one in Michigan, the other in Kansas; and is not this likely to be the great, if not the only, issue in the approaching presidential campaign, all the other issues having been surrendered and given up by the "new departure?" Can the Republicans desire a better issue?

When was our country ever more prosperous than it now is under the present protective tariff? Go where you may, you see its rich fruits springing up in the greatest profusion. Furnaces, factories, iron, cotton, woolen mills, with railroads being everywhere constructed to carry and distribute the mineral and agricultural productions, resulting from the protective policy, to their appropriate markets, reducing internal taxation, paying off, with unnecessary rapidity, the national debt, and filling the treasury to overflowing, the revenue from customs, where not paid by the foreigner, being a *voluntary* contribution, paid by those only who prefer foreign to American goods—thousands who use American productions only paying not one cent into the national treasury. Why then interrupt this general prosperity by this constant and injurious free-trade clamor and agitation? Why thus check this onward and upward national progress by filling the country with anxiety, trepidation, and alarm? Let Congress repeal the direct taxes, take the duties off tea and coffee, and leave the protective tariff as it is, and thus entitle themselves to the gratitude and the thanks of the whole country, now reaping everywhere the rich rewards of this wise system of Republican policy. But I must stop. There is no end to this subject.

In endeavoring to express in a few words what pages would be required to elucidate, I fear I have sacrificed clearness to a desire for condensation; but these brief suggestions are intended, in fact, merely as hints, to be improved and elaborated by abler and younger minds.

Yours very respectfully,

EIGHTY-ONE YEARS.

HON. JAS. G. BLAINE, *Speaker, etc.*

UNIONTOWN, PA., *April* 10*th*, 1872.

INTERNAL IMPROVEMENTS—CUMBERLAND ROAD BILL.

DELIVERED IN THE HOUSE OF REPRESENTATIVES, U. S., JANUARY 27th, 1829.

[Extracts from Speech in favor of Internal Improvements.]

MR. STEWART expressed his regret that gentlemen had deemed this a fit occasion to draw into discussion all the topics connected with the general power over the subject of internal improvements. If repeated decisions, and the uniform practice of the government could settle any question, this, he thought, ought to be regarded as settled. The foundation of this road was laid by a report made by Mr. Giles, the present governor of Virginia, in 1802, and was sanctioned the next session by a similar report, made by another distinguished Virginian [Mr. Randolph], now a member of this House—it was the offspring of Virginia, and he hoped she would not now abandon it as illegitimate. Commenced under the administration of Mr. Jefferson, it had been sanctioned and prosecuted by every President, and by almost every Congress, for more than a quarter of a century.

His colleague [Mr. Buchanan], who had opened the debate on this subject, seemed to regard the bill with more alarm than the people of the South did the tariff. He had denounced it as a most daring and dangerous usurpation of power, as tending directly to consolidation or separation; as even worse than the sedition law; as alike destructive to the rights of the States, and the liberties of the people. He had, indeed, conjured up a most frightful picture. He had himself called it a "spectre," true: but it was one of his own creation; "a spectre" at which he says even the federalism of former days would have "shrunk back with horror." He had, therefore, felt it his duty to sound the tocsin of alarm—he had exhorted the friends of state-rights to rally their forces—he had appealed to Virginia, whose voice, he said, had awakened some of her slumbering sisters, and kept alive the wholesome doctrine of state-rights; and of this school, he too, it seems, has become a sudden, and of course, zealous disciple. He had, however, taken but one step—he must take another, and that was to deny also the constitutionality of the tariff: this he might do at the next session; and then, and not till then, could he be admitted into full communion; he must go the whole or nothing.

The gentleman has, in fact, distinctly informed us in his speech, that the politicians of this country are hereafter to be divided into two great parties; the one in favor of "federal power, and the other wedded to state-rights;" in other words, those who advocate and those who deny the power of this government to protect domestic manufactures and promote internal improvements. These are the subjects, and the only subjects, over which the power of this government is now warmly resisted. These were the great points of controversy, and he agreed with his colleague that every man must take his stand on the one side or the other. The issue was made up. These measures must be abandoned or sustained. The power exists or it does not, there was no half-way course. If it existed in the one case, it existed in the other; they were kindred measures, and in his opinion, would stand or fall together. After the public debt is paid, which must occur in a very few years, why, you will be asked, impose a tariff of duties, when there is no object on which you can expend the revenue? These subjects were inseparably connected; they constituted one system of policy; it was against this system, that the party "wedded to state-rights" were directing their efforts, and it was this system that its friends were now called upon to defend and uphold.

Mr. S. appealed to the representatives of the interior and the West—without internal improvements, he inquired, what they were ever to expect from the ample expenditures of this government? They must bear their full share of the public burdens, pay their full share of the public revenue, without the possibility of participating in its benefits—the whole would go to the seaboard. In the interior and the West, they had no forts and fortifications, no ships and navies; no sea-walls, dock-yards, lighthouses, buoys and beacons. He affirmed, without fear of contradiction, that from the foundation of the government to the present time, the whole civil expenditures of the government, for all purposes except internal improvements, in the whole Union, twenty miles from the tides of the ocean, had not been equal to the expenditures on a single fortification!! Deplorable, indeed, must be their condition without this power—it amounted to a positive exclusion of the interior and the West, from all participation in the benefits of the public expenditure. Their wealth, it was true, like their vast rivers, would continue to flow in uniform and never-ceasing streams to the ocean, bearing to it their ample contributions. But, by destroying this power, you blot out forever that sun which alone could take up a portion of this great deep, and return it in copious and refreshing showers, over the vast region from which it was drawn, to invigorate and replenish the numberless fountains from which it originally flowed.

Without roads and canals, of what avail was it to the people of the West to possess a country, abounding with all the essential elements of wealth and prosperity—of what avail was it to have a country abounding with inexhaustible mines of coal and ore; to possess a fruitful soil and abundant harvests, without the means of transporting them to the places where they were required for consumption? Without a market, the people of the West were left without a motive for industry. By denying to this portion of the Union the advantages of internal improvements, you not only deprive them of all the benefits of governmental expenditure; but you also deprive them of the advantages which nature's God intended for them. Possessing the power, how, he asked, could any representative of the interior or western portions of this Union vote against a policy so essential to the prosperity of the people who sent him here to guard their rights, and advance their interests?

With these remarks, he would proceed to examine the question of power.

The right of this Government to construct such roads and canals as were necessary to carry into effect its mail, military, and commercial powers, was as clear and as undoubted as the right to build a post-office, construct a fort, or erect a lighthouse. In every point of view the cases were precisely similar, and were sustained and justified by the same power.

The 8th section of the 1st article of the Constitution, enumerated in a few brief sentences all the great powers and ends of this Government, and among the rest was found the power "to establish post-offices and post-roads," "to declare war," "provide for the common defence," "to suppress insurrections and repel invasions," "to regulate commerce with foreign nations and among the several states," ending with the *express grant* of the power "*to make all laws neces-*

sary and proper for carrying into execution the foregoing powers." Without this last power the Constitution would have been a dead letter—the Government could never have gone into operation. The *means* to be employed in carrying into effect the powers conferred upon this Government were not indicated—their selection was of necessity left to the sound discretion of Congress, with this single qualification, that they should be "necessary and proper" means to attain the end proposed; the degree of their necessity was also left for Congress to determine. This doctrine was established by the Supreme Court, and laid down as their unanimous opinion by Chief Justice Marshall, in the case of McCulloch against the State of Maryland (4th Wheaton, 421). "The sound construction of the Constitution," says that enlightened judge, "must allow to the national legislature that discretion with respect to the *means* by which the powers which it confers are to be carried into execution; which will enable that body to perform the high duties assigned to it, in the manner most beneficial to the people—let the *end* be legitimate; let it be within the scope of the Constitution, and all the means that are appropriate; which are plainly adapted to the end; which are not prohibited; but consist with the letter and the spirit of the Constitution, are constitutional." "Where the law is not prohibited, and is really calculated to effect any of the objects entrusted to the Government, to undertake here to inquire into the *degree of its necessity*, would be to pass the line which circumscribes the judicial department, and tread on legislative ground."

The power, said Mr. S., "to establish post-offices and post-roads," involves the power and the duty of transporting the mail, and of employing all the means necessary for this purpose; the simple question then was this—Are roads necessary to carry the mail? If they were, Congress had expressly the right to make them, and there was an end of the question. Roads were, he contended, not only necessary to carry into effect this power; but they were absolutely and indispensably necessary—you cannot get along without them; and yet we are gravely told that Congress have no right to make a mail road, or repair it when made! That to do so would ruin the States and produce consolidation—ruin the States by constructing good roads for their use and benefit—produce consolidation by connecting the distant parts of the Union, by cheap and rapid modes of inter-communication. If consolidation meant to confirm and perpetuate the Union, he would admit its application; but not otherwise. But we are told that the *States* will make roads to carry the mail—this was begging the question. If the States would make all the roads required to carry into effect our powers, very well; but if they did not, then we may, undoubtedly, make them ourselves. But it was never designed by the framers of this Constitution, that this Government should be dependent on the States for the means of executing its powers: "its means were adequate to its ends"—this principle was distinctly and unanimously laid down by the Supreme Court in the case already referred to: "No trace," says the Chief Justice, "is to be found in the Constitution of an intention to create a dependence of the Government of the Union on the States for the execution of the powers assigned to it—its means are adequate to its ends. To impose on it the necessity of resorting to means it cannot control, which another Government may furnish or withhold, would render its course precarious; the result of its measures uncertain, and create a dependence on other Governments, which might disappoint the most important designs, and is incompatible with the language of the Constitution." *And* this was in perfect harmony with the constant and uniform practice of the Government.

Mr. S. begged gentlemen to turn their attention for a moment to the statute book, and see what the practice of Government had been: what had been already done by Congress in virtue of this power of "establishing post-offices and post-roads." In 1825, an act had been passed, without a word of objection, which went infinitely further than the bill under consideration. His colleague [Mr. Buchanan] was then a member of this House, and, no doubt, voted for it. His eloquence was then mute—we heard nothing about State rights, spectres, and sedition laws. This bill, regulating the post-office establishment, not only created some thirty or forty highly penal offences, extending not only over the Cumberland Road, but over every other road in the United States, punishing with the severest sanctions, even to the taking away the *liberty* and the *lives* of the citizens of the States, and requiring the State courts to take cognizance of these offences and inflict these punishments. This was not all; this act not only extended over all the mail roads; but all other roads running parallel with them, on which all persons are prohibited, under a penalty of fifty dollars, from carrying letters in stages or other vehicles, performing regular trips; and authorizing too, the seizure and sale of any property found in them for the payment of the fines. The same regulations applied to boats and vessels passing from one post town to another. Compare that bill with the one under debate: this bill had two or three trifling penalties of ten dollars, and was confined to one road of about one hundred and fifty miles in extent, made by the United States, while the other act, with all its fines and forfeitures, pains and penalties, extended not only to all the mail roads in the United States, but also to all parallel roads; yet no complaint was then heard about the constitutionality of this law, or the dreadful consequences of carrying the citizens hundreds of miles to be tried—under it no difficulty had ever been experienced, and no complaint had ever been heard. There had been no occasion for appointing United States justices, and creating federal courts, to carry this law into effect, about which there was so much declamation on this occasion: this was truly choking at gnats and swallowing camels. To take away *life* by virtue of the post-office power for robbing the mail, is nothing; but to impose a fine of ten dollars for wilfully destroying a road which has cost the Government millions of dollars, is a dreadful violation of State rights! An unheard of usurpation, worse than the sedition law; and went further towards a dissolution of the Union than any other act of the Government. Such were the declarations of his colleague; he hoped he would be able to give some reason for thus denouncing this bill, after voting for the act of 1825, which carried this same power a hundred times further than this bill, both as regards the theatre of its operation and the extent of its punishments.

With respect to military roads and canals, Mr. S. begged leave to say a few words. The Constitution has conferred upon this Government the power to *declare war and provide for the common defence;* with the express right of employing all the means necessary for this purpose; they therefore had the undoubted power to purchase cannon, build forts, provide all the munitions of war, define and punish offences, not because they were mentioned in the Constitution, but because they were necessary and proper means for the national defence. Were not roads equally necessary, nay, in many cases even more necessary for this purpose? Without roads your cannon and other munitions would often be useless and unavailing. In a country like this, Mr. S. contended, a good system of roads and canals, opening easy communications from the centre to the extremes of the Union, constituted the most powerful and efficient system of defence. In a country relying for defence and protection, not upon standing armies, but upon the citizen soldiers, scattered over an immense continent, whatever facilitated the rapid concentration and rapid movement of the physical force of the nation, to the places where its presence might be required by the public exigencies, was of the utmost importance. As a means of national defence, he contended that a system of interior canals, extending from the north to the south, from Boston to St. Mary's, by which our armies and munitions of war could always be ready to meet and repel the enemy—moving *pari passu* with them, would be vastly more important and successful as a means of defending our extended and exposed Atlantic border than all the forts and fortifications that could be erected at any expense. Forts were fixed and immovable; they could not be transferred to the point of attack: if the enemy came to them they might repel him, but not otherwise. Compare them in time of peace: forts and fortifications were a burden of constant and never-ceasing expense, a standing army must be kept up to garrison and keep them in repair, while roads and canals, equally efficient in war, were in time of peace worth more than they cost, in the facilities they afforded to internal commerce, and as bonds of union between the distant parts of our common country. More than this, if the funds for their erection were invested as stock, as in the case of the Chesapeake and Delaware and the Dismal Swamp canals, in addition to all these advantages in peace and war, they would be a never failing *source of revenue*—a source which war would not dry up but would increase, by the vast increase of coasting trade it would force upon them. Hence, Mr. S. contended, that as a means of national defence, roads and canals were more important than forts and fortifications; and if so, as the right of selecting the means of defence belonged expressly to Congress, their right to construct roads and canals for this purpose, was, of course, more clear and undoubted, than the right to erect forts. It had, however, been contended by his colleague and others, that the Constitution gave *expressly* the right to erect forts, etc. This was a palpable mistake. The Constitution contained no such provision. The clause referred to by gentlemen was inserted for a totally different object; it was not to give the *power* to erect forts, that was taken for granted; but to give Congress "*exclusive legislation*" over them when erected. The object was to exclude State laws and State jurisdiction from our forts, and for very sound and obvious reasons. This was the object, and the only object of this clause so much relied on. So far from granting the power to erect forts, it evidently went upon the assumption that this power existed as a matter of course resulting from the general power over all the means necessary for carrying into effect the great objects and ends of Government.

Having thus established, and, as he thought, conclusively, the right to construct roads and canals for *mail* and *military* purposes, he came next to say a few words on the subject of those which appertained to the express power of "regulating commerce with foreign nations and *among the several States.*" This power carried with it, as a necessary incident, the right to construct *commercial* roads and canals. From this grant Congress derived precisely the same power to make roads and canals that it did sea-walls, light-houses, buoys, beacons, etc., along the seaboard. If the power existed over the one it existed over the other in every point of view; the cases were precisely parallel: it was impossible to draw a distinction between them. This power was essential to every Government—there was no Government under the sun without it. All writers on national law and political economy considered the right to construct roads and canals as belonging to the commercial power of all Governments.

There were great arteries of communication between distant divisions of this extensive empire, passing through many States, or bordering upon them, which the States never could and never would make. These works were emphatically national, and ought to be accomplished by national means.

He instanced the road now under consideration—it passed through Maryland, Pennsylvania, and Virginia, yet neither of these States would have given a dollar to make it. It passed mostly through mountainous and uninhabited regions. He adverted to the Potomac, Ohio, and Mississippi rivers. Important as these were to all the States, yet they were the internal concerns of none—they were mere boundaries to which the States would give nothing, while they had so many objects exclusively internal requiring all their means. For these reasons he was utterly opposed to the project of dividing the surplus revenue of the General Government among the several States; this would be to surrender the national means which the people had confided to this Government for national purposes to mere local and sectional objects, while those truly national would remain forever unprovided for. He did not claim for this Government the power to make roads and canals for all purposes. The powers of this Government and of the States were distinct and well defined. To the national Government belonged, under the Constitution, the power of making national roads and canals for national purposes. To the States belonged the power of providing for State and local objects. The roads and canals projected and executed by States and private companies were often highly important in a national point of view; and to such, in his opinion, this Government ought always to afford aid in a proportion corresponding with the interest the nation had in their accomplishment. When individuals were willing to go before and vest millions of their private funds in works strictly and truly national, connecting the remote sections of the Union together (of which we had two distinguished examples, one in this district and the other in a neighboring city, Baltimore), could this Government, charged with the care and guardianship of all the great interests of the nation, look on with cold indifference? Was it not our duty to lend a helping hand to encourage, to cheer, and sustain them in their noble and patriotic efforts?

To all the considerations of interest and patriotism which could influence States or individuals, to undertake works of this sort, this Government had superadded other high and important obligations. States and individuals were not bound, as was this Government, to provide the *means* of defending the nation; of transporting its mails; of regulating its commerce; of suppressing insurrections, repelling invasions; in short, of preserving the Union and advancing all its vast and various interests. And what, he asked, would more effectually promote all these great objects than the construction of internal improvements, connecting the widely separated parts of our common country more closely together? Notwithstanding all this, we have been gravely told by gentlemen, in the course of this debate, that this Government had nothing to do with internal improvements; that they belonged *exclusively* to the States!! Such arguments scarcely merited a serious reply. The reverse of the position would certainly be much more plausible.

Mr. Stewart said, he would now proceed to answer, as briefly as possible, some leading arguments urged by gentlemen in opposition to the bill under consideration. His colleague [Mr. Buchanan] had said that this bill proposed a greater stretch of power than the *sedition law*. This was an argument "*ad captandum vulgus*." He would not do his colleague the injustice to suppose that he was so ignorant of the Constitution of his country as seriously to address such an argument to the understanding of this House. The bill under consideration was necessary to carry into effect the express power of transporting the mail. What power of this Government was the sedition law intended to carry into effect? None. It was therefore not only clearly unconstitutional on this ground, but it went directly to abridge the freedom of the *press*, and, of course, was a plain and palpable violation of that provision in the Constitution which declares that "Congress shall make no law *abridging the freedom* of speech or *of the press*." Now, if his colleague could show any provision in the Constitution in the slightest degree impugning the right of Congress to pass this bill, then he might have some excuse for offering such an argument, otherwise he had none. The gentleman had, in a very labored effort, endeavored to prove that this Government had no kind of jurisdiction or control whatever over this road. Yet his own amendment recognized the existence of the very power which he denies. By his amendment he proposes what? That this Government shall cede the road to the States, with the power to erect gates and collect as much toll as was necessary to keep it in repair. But his whole argument went to prove that Congress did not possess the very power which his amendment assumed and proposed to transfer to the States. The gentleman's amendment and his speech were therefore at open war with each other, and would perhaps both perish in the conflict. Certainly both could not survive—one or the other must fall.

The gentleman, proceeding in his argument, had assumed premises which nobody would admit, and then, with an air of great triumph, he drew conclusions which even his own premises would not support. He takes for granted that this Government, with all its mail, military, and commercial powers, has no more right to make a road to carry these powers into effect, though a State, than any individual possessing none of these powers, would have. Thus having assumed what was utterly inadmissible, he triumphantly inquires whether an individual, having obtained leave to make a road through another's land, could put up gates and exact tolls? The gentleman says surely not. But he said surely yes, unless expressly prohibited by the contract. Suppose, by permission, I build a mill, said Mr. S., upon that gentleman's estate, and construct a bridge and turnpike road to get to it, have I not as much right to demand toll at the bridge as at the mill? Most undoubtedly; so that the gentleman's premises and his conclusion were alike fallacious and unsound. This position had been taken by both the gentlemen from Virginia [Mr. Barbour and Mr. Archer], to whom he would make the same reply. A most extraordinary argument had been advanced against military roads: the public enemy may get possession of them in war!! Was it possible that an American statesman could, at this time of day, urge such an argument? It might be addressed to a set of timid savages, secure in the midst of the wilderness. The enemy get possession of our roads, and therefore not make them! Such cowardly arguments would deprive us of every possible means of defence. The enemy, it might be said with equal propriety, may get our ships, our forts, our cannon, our soldiers, and therefore we ought not to provide them. What would the brave freemen of this country say to the men who would deny them roads to travel on, lest the enemy might take them from us in war? They would reply, with Spartan magnanimity, "let them come and take them."

It has been urged, with great zeal and earnestness, by the gentleman from Virginia [Mr. Barbour] that if this Government had the power to construct roads and canals on the principles contended for, that then we might take possession of the New York canal, and all the roads and canals in the country. Mr. S. disclaimed any such right; this would not be the use but the abuse of power. Congress was confined, by the Constitution, to the use of such means as were *necessary and proper*, and it would be neither proper nor necessary to take possession of the New York canal; it could be used for all the purposes of this Government, without committing such an outrage. Mr. S. said he held it, in all cases, to be the indispensable duty of every gentlemen who brought forward any measure of internal improvement, to demonstrate to the satisfaction of a majority of Congress, that it was national in its character; that it necessarily and properly belonged to the execution of some one of the express powers of this Government. Indeed, if he failed to do this, it was impossible that it could be adopted. Hence there was no danger of the dreadful consequences which gentlemen seemed to anticipate; these dangers were imaginary. The cases supposed could never happen, and if they did, it would be an abuse of power; and what power was there belonging to this Government that might not be abused? Congress had power enough to ruin the nation, and power that could not be controverted. Congress may impose taxes without any limitation; they may raise an army of a hundred thousand men; they may crush the people under these burdens; but it did not follow that because these powers might be abused that therefore they did not exist. On this principle there could be no power, for all power was liable to be abused by those to whom it was delegated. The great safeguard which the people had against the abuse of power was the *ballot-box*. This remedy they held in their own hands—it was the great palladium of their liberties; and it was the only remedy for the abuse of the great express powers of Government. But in relation to all the incidental or implied powers employed in the selecting of means there was a double check, the *ballot-box* and the *Supreme Court*. Congress may declare war against all the world, lay taxes, raise armies to any extent, and the Supreme Court could not interpose; but if they employ *means* to carry these measures into effect, which are not "necessary and proper" to obtain the end proposed by them, then the Supreme Court have said that they would feel themselves bound to pronounce such laws unconstitutional. Hence he contended that the power of internal improvement being an incidental power, was not only highly beneficial in its tendency, but also perfectly innocent and harmless. It was not the frightful Briareus described in such glowing colors by his colleague.

A great deal had been said on the subject of jurisdiction; that, if it existed at all, it must be *exclusive;* that it could not attach to soil, and much metaphysical refinement of this sort, which had little to do with the subject. On this point, the only sound and practical rule was, that this Government had a right to assume such jurisdiction over their roads as was necessary for their preservation and repair by such means as should be deemed most expedient, leaving every thing beyond that to the States. Thus far the constitution declared the legislation of Congress to be "the supreme law of the land, any thing in the constitution and laws of any State to the contrary notwithstanding." This, left to the laws of the States, the right to punish all offences and other acts committed upon the road, in the same manner as though they had occurred in any other part of their territory. Such had been the uniform practice of the government in executing all its powers up to the present time, and no complaint had ever been made or inconvenience experienced.

It has been universally conceded on all hands in this debate, that the consent of the States could not confer any jurisdiction or power on this Government beyond what it had derived from the constitution. This was too clear a proposition to admit of doubt. Yet the names of Jefferson, Madison, Monroe, and Gallatin, were introduced, and relied on. Did gentlemen forget that Mr. Gallatin was the very first man that ever suggested the plan for making the Cumberland road, and that it had been sanctioned and actually constructed under the administrations of Jefferson, Madison, and Monroe? Their opinions were thus reduced to practice, which was the best evidence in the world—"by their fruits shall ye know them."

Mr. S. said his colleague [Mr. Buchanan] had divided the powers of Government into two classes, *external* and *internal*. The first, he says, belong to the General Government, and the second, with a few exceptions, to the States. It was matter of astonishment that any one who had ever read the Constitution, should seriously advance such a proposition. He begged his colleague to look at the 8th section of the first article of the Constitution; which contained the enumeration of the powers of Congress, and he would find that so far as this Government was concerned, the reverse of his proposition was the fact; that of the eighteen substantive grants of power, there were but two external; all the rest operated internally upon and among the States, and were to all intents and purposes internal and not external powers: thus, by assuming false premises, almost any conclusion might be established. On such arguments as these (if arguments they would be called,) the Chief Justice of the United States bestowed a merited rebuke when he said that "ingenuity by assuming premises, may explain away the Constitution, and leave it a magnificent structure to look at; but totally unfit for use."

The radical vice of most of the arguments urged against this power, was found in this, that they treated this Government as an alien and a foreigner in its own country. The common parent and protector of all the states is habitually regarded with an eye of jealousy and distrust, instead of generous confidence. This course was calculated to create hostility; to beget hatred and heart burnings, where nothing should exist but affection and confidence. Such doctrines were anti-republican and dangerous; they tended to the destruction of the Union.

But we are told that internal improvements will destroy the States and produce disunion. Destroy the States by giving them money, by making roads and canals for their use at the national expense! Produce disunion by binding and uniting together distant parts of our common country, by promoting harmony of interest and feeling; creating mutual dependence of the agricultural, planting, and manufacturing districts, on each other for markets and supplies, by virtually removing the mountains that divide them; destroying time and space, and constituting us, in fact, as well as in theory, a united people. Yet all this, we are told, is to destroy the Union! Such logic was too refined for the comprehension of common sense. No, sir; destroy this power, and you cut one of the strongest cords; you break one of the firmest links in the chain of our Union; you rob this Government of one of its most popular and beneficent powers; you leave it nothing but its odious powers of taxation; of imposing burdens without benefits; of taking, without the power of giving.

He could not better express his ideas on this subject, than by adopting the language of the immortal Washington, who asserted the existence of this power in the General Government even before the formation of the present Constitution, when its powers, as all must admit, were much more circumscribed and limited than they now are. In 1784, when urging the opening of roads to the west, he says: "I wish every door to that country may be set wide open, and the commercial intercourse with it rendered as free and easy as possible. This, in my opinion, is the best, if not the only cement that can bind them to us for any length of time, and we shall be deficient in foresight and wisdom if we neglect the means of effecting it. Our interest is so much in unison with this policy, that nothing short of that ill-timed and misapplied parsimony and contracted way of thinking which intermingles so much in our public councils, can counteract it." Such was the language of the father of his country on this subject, more than forty-five years ago. If opposition to internal improvements was then justly denounced as "ill-timed and misapplied parsimony," as contracted and illiberal, what would be said of it now?

Mr. S. said he had trespassed already, he feared, too long

on the time and patience of the committee. He would notice but one or two topics more, and would detain them no longer. The opinion and the hope had been repeatedly expressed on this floor, that the system of internal improvement would be soon arrested. Sir, said Mr. S., that opinion is as unfounded as the hope is vain; the impulse is given; the spirit of improvement is abroad upon the earth; it has gone forth; it is the voice of the people, and will of the nation; its benefits and blessings are every where seen and felt, and its advantages demanded by the people. There were other active and powerful causes at this moment generating, and would soon be in full operation, causes which would give the system a resistless and overwhelming impulse; an impulse to which resistance would be as vain as human efforts to arrest the majestic march of the Mississippi, or to prevent the genial showers of heaven from descending to cheer and refresh a thirsty land. This required no spirit of prophecy to foresee. The causes to which he referred were plain and obvious. He pointed to the *rapid extinction of the national debt,* which would, in a few years, leave a surplus revenue of ten or twelve millions annually for these objects. He adverted to the progress of improvements throughout the country, furnishing to all conclusive evidence of their utility and importance; brushing away the cobweb arguments and metaphysical notions about "state rights." He also pointed to the effect of the *new census* about to be taken; the effect it would have in bringing a vast accession of strength to the cause of internal improvement. Nearly, if not all the new and growing States of the Union, were decidedly in its favor, while the States declining in the scale of political power were alone opposed to it. And to this opposition might perhaps be traced one of the principal causes of that decline. These States neglected to improve the bounties of Providence, and by denying the power of this Government over the subject, they excluded themselves from all participation in its expenditures. This was an evil which the people alone could correct. The remedy was in their own hands, and it was their own fault if they did not apply it. They would apply it, and he hoped yet to see even Virginia among the foremost states in the Union in favor of this policy, which she now denounced as unconstitutional.

Why were the population, the power, and prosperity of the South on the decline? All their productions found a ready and abundant market abroad. In the last ten years, their exports of cotton and tobacco alone amounted to more than all the other exports of the United States put together. Within that period, their exports of cotton and tobacco amounted to $320,000,000, while all the other exports of the nation amounted to less than $220,000,000. How was the decline of the South to be accounted for, but by referring it to the total neglect of those advantages of internal improvement, internal commerce, and internal supplies, which they had within their reach? They looked too much abroad, and not enough at home. They relied too much upon foreign supplies, and neglected too much their own internal resources. This he would not say was the sole cause, but he would express the decided opinion, that it was among the most powerful and efficient causes which had led to the unhappy results in that portion of our common country to which he had adverted.

We have been told that there is a great party in this country wedded to what they call "state-rights." This party was, on all occasions, found united in resisting this government in the exercise of what he considered its indispensable and most beneficial powers. They were always preaching up the dangers of this Government; endeavoring to alarm the people with the idea of consolidation; holding up before them frightful pictures and imaginary evils. They talked much of the public liberties, of usurpations, and oppressions. On some occasions they went so far as to call on the people to resist. It was time the people should examine these doctrines, and see what was their tendency, and on what foundation they rested. In his opinion, their tendency was first to weaken, and next to destroy this Government. It was gradually to undermine what could not be directly overthrown. It was to wean off the affections, and destroy the confidence of the people in their government; and, when these were gone, all was lost—this Government could live alone in the affections and confidence of the people. This was the vital spark which animated the system; it was the corner-stone that sustained the whole fabric. Destroy this, and the whole edifice, this temple of liberty, with all it contained, would be instantly a pile of indiscriminate ruins. He was far from imputing to any a disposition to destroy this Government; but were it possible for such a design to exist, how would it operate? Not by open violence. This would be premature and unavailing; but it would be by rendering the Government odious among the people, withdrawing from it their confidence, creating dissatisfaction, producing distrust, and finally, when its foundations were thus sapped, its strength and power destroyed; when the mine was dug, and the train laid, then to apply the match,

"Cry havoc, and let slip the dogs of war."

This was the only way in which treason could ever operate successfully, so long as this Government enjoyed the confidence of the people; so long as it retained their affections, so long as they remained virtuous and faithful to the constitution and themselves, all was safe. Without these, he repeated, all was lost.

Let us inquire, for a moment, whether there is, in fact, any kind of foundation for the apprehension and alarm lest this Government would swallow up the States and assume what the gentleman from Virginia [Mr. Archer] was pleased to call "*autocratical and Russian powers.*" What is this Government? How is it composed, and to whom is it responsible? The answer to these plain questions would not only show that all these apprehensions were vain, but that the real danger lay in the opposite direction; that there was much more danger of this Government being destroyed by the States, than there was of the States being destroyed by it. This was a Government of the people, formed by the people, and responsible to them. Those who administered it were elected by the States and the people of the States, and were responsible to them, and to them only. From whom do we derive our authority to sit here and legislate? From the people of the States. If we fail to guard and protect their rights, they will hold us responsible; but if, on the other hand, we fail in our duty to this Government; if we fail to guard and protect its rights, where is the responsibility? who is there to call us to account? Not the people of this national district of ten miles square. No, sir. Congress is responsible to the people of the States. Where then was the danger of the rights of the people and the rights of the States being destroyed by their own representatives? Such apprehensions were idle and unfounded. Were the States in any danger from the Senate? Whence did they derive their offices, and to whom were they responsible? They were elected by, and responsible to the legislatures of the several States; and had "state-rights" anything to fear from them? Certainly not. But had this Government nothing to fear? Were its rights and its powers in no danger? Sir, look at the bills and propositions on your table, and answer the question. It was high time there should be a party to defend the rights of this Government from undue encroachments.

A proposition is now under debate in the other House, to take the whole surplus revenue at the end of every session, and divide it among the States. What would be the effect of this measure? Would it not arrest every national work, paralyze all the efforts, and prostrate all the powers of this Government? Sir, adopt this proposition, and you make it the interest of the representatives of every State to swell the surplus and increase the dividend which they are to carry home to their constituents. And how is this object to be accomplished? By withholding appropriations from the army, the navy, forts, fortifications, and internal improvements; in short, from everything that would reduce the common fund to be distributed. If a fort or other public work is required in a particular district, all will unite against it, as it would favor one district at the expense of all the rest, and thus lead to an unequal distribution. What, then, is to become of this Government, when it is thus robbed by the States of the means of carrying into effect its great and essential powers? There were other propositions of similar import; among them was one to take the public lands, and divide them too among the States, or surrender them to the States in which they were located, in direct violation of their solemn pledge for the payment of the public debt. For these reasons he contended that, if there was danger of "usurpation," it was that this Government, and not the States, would be robbed of its legitimate powers. It was impossible for this Government to destroy the States; it was dependent upon the States for all the means of executing its indispensable powers; but how easy was it for the States to destroy this Government? It could be done in a moment. Let them refuse to elect senators and representatives, and the Government is at an end; it is destroyed at a blow. This Government cannot infringe upon the rights of the States without their own consent, expressed through their representatives in Congress. But suppose the States instruct their willing and obedient servants here to rob this Government of its power, its money, and its means, and transfer them to the States. Suppose we obey; to whom are we responsible? To those on whom we are dependent for favor? The people of the States, and their legislators who direct the act, and divide the spoil. He hoped such an event was remote; but if this happy Government was doomed to perish (which God forbid), it would perish not by having too much power, but too little; it would fail in consequence of its weakness, not of its strength.

But why, sir, this jealousy, this never-dying hostility to this Government? Why these attempts to fritter away, and destroy its most essential powers? Why these unceasing endeavors to bind it in manacles and chains, to paralyze its energies, and prostrate all its powers? Is it not this Government that guards the rights and protects the liberties of the people? Is it not this that secures them tranquillity in peace, and defence in war? Whether at home or abroad, it throws around every citizen the mantle of its protection, and by conferring on him the proud title of "*an American citizen*," secures him an honorable passport throughout the world. He considered this Union as the sacred repository of the happiness and best hopes of this people—as the last asylum of persecuted liberty on earth. Destroy it, and you destroy the influence of our bright example. You extinguish the light of our glorious revolution, which now blazes up to Heaven, illumining the path, and guiding the footsteps of those who are on their march to freedom.

This Government, therefore, instead of being regarded with what his colleague [Mr. Buchanan] was pleased to call "wholesome jealousy and distrust," should be regarded with wholesome confidence and affection; it should be dear and precious to the heart of every patriot, to the friends of freedom throughout the world. For himself, he never did, and he never would, belong to this jealous "party," no matter what its name, or what its professions; no matter by whom it might be led, or by whom it might be followed; no matter what seductive allurements of power and of patronage it might hold out to enlist the mercenary or the ambitious under its banners; so long as he considered its doctrines dangerous to the Union, prosperity, and liberty of the country, as destructive to the best interests of those whom he had the honor to represent, he would, regardless of consequences, resist it with an uncompromising opposition, he would resist every attempt to rob this Government of any of its great and essential powers; its power of protecting its own internal industry, and improving its own internal condition. Regarding these as the most important powers that this Government possessed, so they would be the last he would consent to surrender. The first he regarded as essential to our national independence, the last to our national defence. Without them, "the value of the Union" might well be made the subject of calculation. He belonged, Mr. S. said, to that party (and, thank God, there was such a party in this country), whose business it was not to destroy the confidence of the people in this Government by constant clamor about "state-rights," consolidation, usurpation, and oppression, but firmly to maintain the just rights and powers of this Government; to guard and protect it against all its enemies, whether foreign and domestic, open or insidious; to resist every attempt to trample upon the constitution and laws, or to render them odious among the people. This he considered "the great Republican party." This was the party to which he always had, and always would belong; and it was the party to which his colleague [Mr. Buchanan] always had been, and always would be opposed.

INTERNAL IMPROVEMENT.

DELIVERED IN THE HOUSE OF REPRESENTATIVES, U. S., JANUARY 28, 1824.

BUT the gentleman from Virginia [Mr. Archer], who has just addressed you, admits the power to make *military* roads and canals. This, Mr. S. said, he considered a surrender of the whole question. The gentleman says it properly belongs to the power "to raise armies and provide for the common defence," and thus admits the right of Congress to select the means to accomplish the ends of government; and if a majority of Congress think roads and canals necessary and proper for the transportation of the mail, and the regulation of commerce, they have, undoubtedly, upon the same principle, and by virtue of the same power, a right to make them. But even suppose you confine its exercise to *military* roads and canals; by this you can accomplish all the great objects contemplated by the friends of this bill. If the honorable gentleman will compare *Mr. Gallatin's* report, which embraces the whole subject for *mail, military,* and *commercial* purposes, with the report of Mr. Calhoun, now at the head of the War Department, on the subject of "Military Roads and Canals," he will find their systems, in all material respects, to be the same. Mr. Calhoun, in fact, says, at the close of his enumeration: "Many of the roads and canals which have been suggested are, no doubt, of the first importance to the commerce, the manufactures, the agriculture, and political prosperity of the country, but are not, for that reason, less useful or necessary for military purposes. It is, in fact, one of the great advantages of our country, enjoying so many others, that, whether we regard its internal improvement in relation to military, civil, or political purposes, very nearly the *same system, in all its parts,* is required. The road or canal can scarcely be designated, which is not highly useful for military operations, and which is not equally required for the industry or political prosperity of the community;" and had the roads and canals pointed out, he adds, "been completed before the late war, their saving, in that single contest, in men, money, and reputation, would have more than indemnified the country for the expense of their construction." He then recommends the very plan proposed by this bill for procuring the necessary plans and estimates, as preliminary to their execution; so that, by passing this bill, you do no more than has been required by the Secretary of War for *military* purposes alone; and the gentleman from Virginia [Mr. Archer], who has admitted the power to make military roads and canals, may, with perfect consistency, support this bill with a view to strengthen the military defences of the country. And, having the power to make roads and canals for the defence of the country, will it be seriously contended that the State through which they pass may defeat them, though indispensably necessary for the safety and best interests of the country? To give the power to defend the country, without the means of its execution, would be ridiculous and absurd; it would be a degree of folly which could not be imputed to the wise framers of our excellent Constitution; besides, these powers were perfectly innocent and harmless. What possible injury could result? If, in their exercise, Congress should transcend the limits of a sound discretion; if they should resort to means not "necessary and proper," to attain the end—the Supreme Court, possessing a power of supervision and control, will correct it. But, sir, if the liberties of this country—if the States have any thing to fear from the General Government, it is not from their *incidental* or resulting powers; it is from their great and *express* powers; the power to "raise armies," and to "lay taxes." Here their power is not only unlimited, but it is without check, without control.

But he not only thought the General Government possessed the power over the subject of roads and canals, but he considered the question settled; if any question could ever be settled by frequent and solemn decisions in Congress, this was. He found in the statute book a whole system of laws under the head of "roads and canals;" and were all these laws unconstitutional? Laws for the construction of the *Cumberland road* had received the sanction of every Executive, and of almost every Congress, since the administration of Mr. Jefferson, who had signed the first law on the subject. But the strongest and most unequivocal expression in favor of the power was to be found in the proceedings had in the last Congress, on the bill providing for the erection of toll-gates on the Cumberland road. This bill certainly carried the constitutional power of Congress over the subject, to its utmost limit. It assumed complete sovereignty and jurisdiction within the territory of the States, establishing tolls, and inflicting pains and penalties upon those who might disregard or violate its provisions; yet this bill, thus exerting the constitutional power of Congress to its utmost extent, passed in committee of the whole (though it encountered the powerful opposition of the honorable gentleman from Virginia, who had just spoken [Mr. Barbour], and several others), by a vote of more than *two to one*, and after an amendment was adopted, appropriating a sum of money to repair the road previous to the erection of the gates, the bill passed, by ayes and noes, by a large majority; and even *Virginia* and *North Carolina*, so remarkable for their constitutional scruples, stood divided on the passage of the bill, the former 8 to 12, the latter 5 to 5. And, in the *Senate*, where the constitutional powers of this Government were certainly well understood, where you find many of the most able, experienced, and enlightened constitutional lawyers in this or any other nation, this bill passed with all its powers, and all its provisions, gates, penalties, money, and all, by a vote of 29 to 7, and even some of the seven who voted against it, he understood, were influenced, not by any doubt of the power, but by a doubt of the expediency of degrading this great, free, national road to the level of common toll roads, for the sake of the trifling sum required to keep it in repair. By this strong and almost unanimous decision, the question, in Congress at least, ought to be considered as settled.

He came next to consider the second question—Is this measure expedient? And this, to his mind, was the most important branch of the subject. On this ground, the bill, he said, had met with very little opposition. Gentlemen who had denied the constitutional power of Congress over the subject, had generally admitted the expediency of the measure. Some objections, however, had been made to it on this ground, which first claimed his attention. The honorable gentleman from Virginia [Mr. Archer], has said that the national debt, of nearly $100,000,000, should be first paid. Mr. S. said, that he was quite sure that he felt as much anxiety as that honorable gentleman to discharge the national debt, and he would go as far to retrench the expenditure of the Government, to accomplish it. But the national debt, he said, had been overrated. The honorable gentleman would find, after deducting the 3 per cent. stocks, the subscription to the National Bank, and the amount of 7 per cents. which would be discharged by the balance now in the Treasury, the amount, to be redeemed, of the national debt, instead of $100,000,000, was, in fact, little more than $61,-000,000, which, by the regular application of the ordinary sinking fund, would be entirely extinguished in less than eight years. What, then, was to be done with the sinking fund of $10,000,000 per annum? Was it to be wasted in idle extravagance? Besides, Mr. S. said, many of the present sources of expenditure would soon be dried up. The annual appropriations for the erection of forts, and the gradual increase of the navy would soon be rendered unnecessary by the accomplishment of those objects. Our enormous pension list must soon be reduced by the hand of time, and the annual expenditure upon this Capitol, this splendid monument of national extravagance, which had cost as much as would have completed a canal from here to Cumberland, must cease. These results would produce an annual saving of nearly $3,000,000 per annum, which might be well applied to internal improvements; or, if gentlemen would consent to give to this object the increase of revenue, which would arise from the adoption of the *new tariff*, it would be sufficient for two or three of the first years of its operation.

Another objection made was, that this measure would lean to an *unequal* distribution of the public funds. This, Mr. S. said, must depend upon the plan hereafter adopted. For his own part, he was free to say that he would prefer a plan to distribute the fund set apart for this purpose, among the States according to their representation in this House; reserving to Congress the right to designate the objects upon which it should be expended within, or adjoining the several States; and, by referring to Mr. Gallatin's report, it would be seen that there was scarcely a State in the Union which was not intersected or bounded by some great national object of internal improvement. This fund, yielding an annual and certain aid to the States, would give a general impulse to improvements throughout the Union; it would stimulate and strengthen the efforts of the States, and induce them, in many cases, to commence great undertakings of this kind, which would never be attempted without it.

Thus, the distribution would be salutary; it would be just, equitable, and beneficial to every portion of the Union. But, Mr. S. said, he would ask the honorable gentleman from Virginia whether the expenditures of the General Government were, in other respects, *equal* among the States? Look at the immense expenditures on the seaboard, in the erection of forts and other public works of defence, in building and supporting a navy for the protection of *foreign* commerce, and for defending it against foreign aggression; the late war was emphatically a war in defence of "free-trade and sailors' rights," in support of which, the interior of the West had expended their full portion of blood and treasure. Of the $560,000,000 expended since the formation of the Government, how much had gone to the benefit of the interior, in promoting *internal* commerce among the States? Scarcely $2,000,000 for constructing the Cumberland Road, and this trifling sum the State of Ohio was required to refund. Was this an *equal*, was this, he asked, a fair distribution of the public funds? Must all be devoted to *foreign* commerce, and nothing to *internal* commerce among the States? Sir, said he, the interior is now laboring under a complication of difficulties, which rendered their situation truly distressing. The manufacturing establishments, which heretofore furnished a market for the farmer (for want of adequate protection), had sunk under the weight of foreign competition; without canals, the products of agriculture would not bear transportation to the Atlantic markets; thus, the farmer, without a market, was left without a motive to industry. Here Mr. S. mentioned a variety of facts, showing that the West paid annually a *tax* of near $3,000,000 for the transportation of goods, and a heavier duty was paid on glass and other articles carried from the West to Baltimore, than was paid by the foreign article in the same port; nineteen-twentieths of this expense would be saved by a single canal connecting the Eastern and Western waters. He then took an extensive view of the canals and internal improvements of England, where twenty-two canals crossed their mountains, uniting the Eastern and Western waters of that Kingdom. He also adverted to the policy of France, Holland, and several other European nations, and contrasted their policy in this respect with our own. While no nation, he said, possessed the same advantages, the same facilities, or the same inducements as this for internal improvements, yet none had done so little. *As a nation*, he said, we had done almost nothing; we were far behind the Holy Alliance, and had scarcely kept up with the *Ottoman Porte* in attending to the internal concerns of our own country, by developing its resources, and facilitating internal trade by internal improvements. If we were asked by our constituents why we lavished millions every year, for the benefit and protection of *foreign* commerce, and did nothing to promote *internal* commerce among the States, were we prepared to give them a satisfactory answer?

But, as nothing but what was *foreign* appeared to satisfy some gentlemen; as they appeared to have an aversion to everything that was *domestic*, that was *internal*, that was *American*, whether in reference to commerce or manufactures, still they might, he said, be gratified—they might have *foreign* commerce *at home*, at least if *distance* made commerce foreign. For instance, he said, our Atlantic merchants might be as profitably employed to themselves, and much more so to the country, in importing lead from Missouri, instead of bringing it from Europe. While the voyage would be equally *foreign* as to distance, it would be infinitely more secure and advantageous. In a single year (1816) we had imported from abroad more than 20,000,000 of pounds of lead. Every year it cost the nation more than half a million of dollars, while our own country furnished this article in inexhaustible quantities. In the West we had whole districts of country literally composed of *lead*, sufficient to supply the universe; yet, for want of the necessary facilities for transportation, such as this bill was intended to afford, these immense sources of national wealth, of national independence, remained, and must continue to remain, dormant and useless. This was a single instance selected to illustrate the policy of this measure, while the argument would apply with equal force to an almost infinite variety of other sources of wealth in the interior, as iron, glass, etc., the raw material of which remained buried in the earth, useless and unproductive, and which only required the plastic and vivifying touch of governmental patronage and protection to spring at once into useful and prosperous activity.

Mr. S. here introduced another argument in favor of this measure, drawn from its evident tendency to enhance the value of the public lands, of which the Government still had for sale more than 400,000,000 of acres, and with respect to which Congress had expressly, by the Constitution, power to make "*all needful rules and regulations*," and certainly there could be no "*regulation*" better calculated to increase their value, to facilitate their sale, and to induce their settlement, than a good system of roads and canals, opening a cheap, free, and easy communication with them. In support of this argument, Mr. S. read several extracts from Mr. Gallatin's report, made in 1808, which states, among other things, that "the opening of an inland navigation *from tide-water to the great lakes* would immediately give to the great body of lands bordering on those lakes as great value as if they were situate at the distance of one hundred miles by land from the sea-coast; and if the proceeds of the first 10,000,000 of acres which may be sold were applied to such improvements, the United States would be amply repaid in the sale of the other 90,000,000." Mr. S. also referred to some calculations made on the subject, in a letter addressed to Mr. Gallatin by Mr. Robert Fulton, to whose genius the world was so much indebted, in which he demonstrated that the public lands, 600 miles from the seaboard, would, by the use of canals, enjoy all the advantages of those within fifty miles of it by land. "Every mile of canal," he stated, "through the public lands, would accommodate 25,600 acres;" "and the land sold," says Mr. Fulton, "in 1806, averaged about two dollars per acre—with a canal it would produce six dollars. Thus, he says, only twenty miles of canal each year, running through national lands, would raise the value of 512,000 acres four dollars per acre, giving $2,048,000—a sum sufficient to make 136 miles of canal." Hence, it was evidently the interest and duty of the Government speedily to adopt a system of policy which, while it greatly increased its revenue and resources, would, at the same time, open a market to the West, facilitate trade and intercourse, unite the great geographical sections of the Union, and thus promote the permanent prosperity of the nation.

Sir, possessing as we do the only free government upon earth, blessed by Divine Providence with every variety of climate and of soil, unconnected with Europe, and strangers to the storms which disturb her repose, enjoying tranquillity at home, and at peace with all the world, it is the policy of this Government to turn its attention to its own internal improvement, to bring into activity its own immense resources, which, as yet, were but partially developed; to minister to the wants, and relieve the distresses of our own people, by seeking out and adopting appropriate remedies, by building up proud and permanent and glorious monuments of internal improvement, which will remain to the latest posterity as so many memorials of the wisdom and munificence of their ancestors. Unique in our situation, occupying a proud pre-eminence among the nations of the earth, sir, we owe a *great example* to the world, not by conquering and destroying nations, but by cultivating the arts of peace, by making our people as prosperous and as happy as they are free. His heart beat high with joy and gladness when he contemplated the delightful prospect which, he flattered himself, was rapidly rising into view, when this nation would cease to be dependent upon European skill and industry for the supply of its wants; when we should enjoy the utmost degree of prosperity; when New England, now sufficiently populous, instead of Old England, should become the great and principal seat of our manufacturing establishments—the South cultivating and supplying the *raw material*, while the West, offering to the hand of agriculture a rich and productive soil, will always afford the breadstuffs in abundance. Thus, the great sections of our Republic will become customers instead of rivals, mutually dependent upon each other both for a market and supply. Then, with the proposed system of internal improvement, by which the provisions of the West would find a rapid, cheap, and easy conveyance to the East, in exchange for return cargoes of manufactured articles, and the cottons of the South enjoying similar facilities of exchange with the North, our independence would become perfect, and our Union indissoluble.

In a country so extensive as this, spreading itself over an almost unlimited extent of territory, divided into great geographical sections by high and almost impassable mountains, and presenting an exposed *military* frontier of seven or eight thousand miles, a well regulated system of internal improvements, whether regarded in relation to its *military strength*, its *political stability*, or *commercial prosperity*, was of the utmost importance. With it we would be the *strongest*, without it the *weakest* nation on earth, possessing the same population and resources. Sir, this nation must depend for its security and its liberty not upon *standing armies*, but upon the virtue and patriotism of the people—on the militia, the citizen-soldiers of the Republic. Standing armies in time of peace he deprecated as inauspicious to freedom; he regarded them as a most destructive bane and intolerable burden. The strength of this nation therefore, in all emergencies, would be in proportion to the facility with which the *physical force* of the country could be promptly and rapidly concentrated at any point where its presence might be required, whether "to suppress insurrections" at home, or "to repel invasions" from abroad. Suppose your seaboard to be threatened by the combined fleets of Europe, without the possibility of knowing at what point you were to be attacked, what would be a standing army of even 100,000 men, distributed along a maritime frontier of three or four thousand miles, without facilities for prompt and rapid concentration? They would be weak and inefficient. How much more powerful and effectual would be a system of inland navigation, extending from the North to the South, connecting in one common chain the whole of your Atlantic cities, and thence, like the radii of a circle, penetrating the interior to its centre, enabling the whole physical strength of the country to be rapidly delivered at any given point, where they could move, with all the munitions of war, "*pari passu*" with the enemy, always fresh and unbroken by the fatigue of long and forced marches. These advantages are not imaginary. They have been already in some degree realized on the New York Canal, where we now transport troops and munitions of war more than three times the distance in the same period, and at less than one-third the former expense without fatigue to the soldier, or the destruction of property attendant upon land transportation. As a means of national defence therefore, roads and canals were incomparably the best. In peace, liberty had nothing to fear from roads and canals—from standing armies it had. In peace, forts were useless; nay, worse. They were a burden of expense. Roads and canals, whether in peace or in war, afforded every facility for commercial intercourse, and, if made by subscribing stock, would be, instead of a public burden, a constant source of revenue to the Government, presenting such facilities that, by stamping on the earth, an army will spring into existence and rush to the point of danger or alarm.

But, independent of their *military* and *commercial* advantages, roads and canals, considered in a *political* point of view, would form one of the most powerful bonds of union among the States. They virtually removed mountains, conquered time and space, brought distant parts of the country more nearly together, and united them by the strong ties of friendship, of interest, of intercourse. And here he begged leave again to quote the language of Washington, the Father of his Country, whose solemn advice could never be too often repeated. In speaking of the Western country, forty years ago, he says: "For my own part, I wish sincerely every door to that country may be set wide open, and the commercial intercourse with it rendered as free and easy as possible. This, in my opinion, is the *best,* if not the *only cement,* that can bind these people to us for any length of time; and we shall be deficient in foresight and wisdom if we neglect the means of effecting it. Our interest," he says, "is so much in unison with this measure that nothing short of that ill-timed and misapplied parsimony and contracted way of thinking, which intermingles so much in our public councils, can counteract it."

If the policy which opposed this measure forty years ago was justly considered *unwise, ill-timed, contracted,* and *illiberal,* what would be said of it now? Since then a new world, as if by magic, had sprung up in the West; the wilderness had yielded to the hand of industry; ships had taken the place of the Indian's canoe; and splendid cities and towns and cultivated fields had risen on the ruins of savage huts. If it then required roads and canals as the "*best and only cement,*" to hold together the East and the West, how much more are they required now? Then the Western people were surrounded by powerful and hostile savage tribes; they were not only dependent on the Atlantic States for protection and for supplies, but were bound to them by all the ties of a common kindred and of filial affection, bearing to the Eastern States the relation of the first colonies to the mother country. But how is it now? The population of the West is the growth of its own soil; their wealth and resources are increasing every day; they are becoming of themselves a great and powerful people, and, as they increased in weight, it would be the part of a wise policy to increase the number and strength of the ties which unite them to the East. Though it is true, sir, that the *West* cling to their brethren of the East with a fond affection and an ardent attachment; though they cheerfully perform an annual *pilgrimage* over yonder rough and rugged mountains, to worship *here* with "a more than Eastern idolatry" at this temple of liberty, this altar of our Union; yet, sir, remember that the time may come (which God forbid) when an unwise and unjust policy may weaken those attachments, however strong, and stifle those affections, however pure. Though all is sunshine now, still a cloud may yet appear to darken and to mar our political horizon. How long was it since the threat of resistance, the thunder of rebellion was heard on this floor from another quarter? Though he did not for his own part apprehend any danger at present, yet it was, he repeated, the part of a wise policy to strengthen by every possible means the ties which bind this Union together; for upon it depended the peace and the happiness and the best hopes of this people. Destroy this, and you extinguish the last lamp of liberty; you prostrate the last citadel of freedom. Thus, freedom left without a friend, and liberty without a sanctuary, the fell principles of "the Holy Alliance" would spread, unresisted, their gloomy dominion over the universe.

Sir, I feel that I have trespassed too long on the patience of the committee, and I will only add, that the power to pass this bill is as clear to my mind, as its exercise is expedient. It is almost the only power you possess of conferring benefits and blessings upon the States; of expending the people's money for the people's benefit; and its exercise, more than any other, would tend to promote and to perpetuate the union, harmony, and prosperity of this nation; and, as he considered this the most salutary power that the General Government possessed, so it would be the last that he would consent to surrender. It was a power which every well-regulated Government *must* possess—the power of *self-improvement.*

Sir, defeat this bill, and you give the *death-blow* to the best hopes and best interests of this nation. Pass it, and one other (he meant the *tariff*), and the 18th Congress will have nobly done its duty. It will be hailed by future generations as having laid the foundation of a system of policy which would soon raise this nation to the high and brilliant destiny that awaits it. Let the fate, however, of this measure be what it might, he would, at least, have the satisfaction of recording his name in its favor.

INTERNAL IMPROVEMENT.

Delivered in the House of Representatives, U. S., February 29th, 1828.

In opposition to the amendment offered by Mr. Drayton, of S. C., limiting the surveys, under the internal improvement act of 1824.

Mr. Stewart said he regarded the motion now made to restrict the appropriation proposed in the bill, to carry into effect the act of 1824, as a blow aimed at the foundation of the whole system of internal improvement.

The act of 1824, authorizing the organization of a corps of engineers to make surveys and estimates of such roads and canals as the President should deem of national importance, for mail, military, or commercial purposes, was considered by every body at the time as constituting the basis and foundation of a general system of internal improvement. This measure, after full and ample discussion, was adopted by a large majority in Congress. It was then foreseen, that the period of the final extinction of the national debt was fast approaching, when there would be ten millions of dollars, now applied to that debt, annually remaining in the treasury. To be in readiness for this event, it was thought wise to provide in time for its judicious and economical expenditure, by having all the advantages of our country, for works of internal improvement, fully explored by scientific engineers, and the results spread before Congress, so as to enable them to determine as to the relative importance of the various works, proposed; as also, to enable the Government to progress with the execution of such of them, in the meantine, as the means of the treasury would justify. Immediately after the act of 1824, the President organized this corps. Appropriations have been annually made, and the engineers have been diligently employed in carrying into effect the objects of that law—and now, when these engineers have just acquired the practical skill and experience necessary to qualify them for the performance of the great task set before them, when the work is in vigorous and successful prosecution, all of a sudden it is to be arrested, the corps disbanded, and the whole system virtually destroyed. And why is this course to be adopted? Mr. S. said, he had listened attentively to the arguments urged by gentlemen in its favor, which it appeared to him might all be classed under three heads. The first and leading ground of objection was, that it furnished the administration with the means of advancing its own *popularity*. Second, that *enough* had been done; and third, a want of *constitutional* power. Mr. S. said, he regretted to see the first political battery opened, and kept up with so much fury. Gentlemen seem disposed to sacrifice this important system, for the purpose of putting down the present administration. Such was the obvious and manifest result of their arguments. Mr. S. was sorry to see the debate assume this character. It resolved the whole subject into a mere *party question*. The true merits of the subject were lost sight of amid the fire and smoke of party excitement. This was too much the case at present, with everything brought before the House. Instead of attending to the business for which we are sent here, we employ our time in useless, nay, worse than useless discussions of the Presidential question—a question which it is for the people, and not for Congress to decide—a question which he hoped the people themselves would determine, and that it might never again devolve upon this House.

Mr. S. said, he felt it due to himself, however, to say that, never, since he had the honor of a seat upon that floor, had he introduced any subject having the remotest connection with the Presidential question, nor had he ever participated in the discussion of such topics, when introduced by others. He came here neither to attack nor defend the administration; he did not consider this the proper place for such discussions—the stump was a more appropriate theatre for such displays. But, sir, when I see attacks made upon the present administration, for the purpose of destroying a system of policy which I regard as essential to the prosperity of the country, I feel myself called on by an imperious sense of public duty to vindicate the system, and the men who are faithfully and honestly endeavoring to carry it into effect, and the more especially against charges which I believe to be without any just foundation. We are told, by the gentleman from Virginia [Mr. Rives], who has just resumed his seat, that this power has been abused by those entrusted with its execution, that much of the money has been expended on local, and not on national objects. Mr. S. said he had turned much of his attention to the subject, and he defied the gentleman to point out a single work surveyed, that was not of national importance, either for mail, military, or commercial purposes. It was easy to deal out general denunciations, but the gentleman had failed to make a single specification, though he held the whole list of surveys in his hand. Why not point out some particular instance in which this power had been abused? It is not the number of miles, or the extent of the cost, that makes a work national—a work of one mile in extent was often as national as one of a thousand miles. In the contemplated chain of inland navigation, from Boston to the South, extending more than a thousand miles, the land cuts, to connect bays and rivers, were often inconsiderable in extent, yet they constituted a part of the great line itself, and were as national as any part, or the whole put together. The repair of a bridge, or removal of an obstruction in any of your great mail roads, would be an object of national importance in reference to the mail; yet this the gentleman would regard as local. The gentleman has also endeavored to alarm the House by the exhibition of a long list of surveys, consisting of sixty-nine in number; but he has failed to inform us of the fact, that many of these surveys constitute but the several links of one great chain of interior communication. Many great national objects, Mr. S. contended, remained yet to be examined—our country had not yet been fully explored. The object was to present all our national advantages for internal improvement in a single view, to enable us to select the most important, to open the great arteries of communication first, and afterwards to supply the less important veins and tributaries. Until this was accomplished, the system would be incomplete—to stop now would be to leave the work half finished.

The gentleman from Virginia contends that these surveys are not worth the money they have cost: true—if the gentleman's plan prevails, they will be worth nothing. These maps were not made to be put up at auction to the highest bidder; they were procured to enlighten and guide us in the paths of future legislation—to show us what will be practicable, and what profitable—to enable us to avoid those improvident and wasteful expenditures, which must result from a want of accurate information. As to the auction value of public works, he would ask the gentleman what would the forts and fortifications, erected on the seaboard, at the expense of millions, bring at auction? The whole would not bring as much as the stock subscribed in 1824, in a single canal. What would this splendid edifice bring? What would the Cumberland Road bring? Nothing! Yet, does it follow that they are worth nothing to the nation? The value of public works is not to be estimated in dollars and cents, but by the benefits and blessings they confer on the country. These surveys, as a mere matter of topography, he contended, were worth to the country more than they cost, even if no improvements ever resulted from them. The gentleman has, with an air of confidence and triumph, charged the executive with the abuse of this power, because the act of 1824 requires the President to have such roads and canals surveyed as he shall deem of national importance; yet the President, he says, has not acted on his own opinion, but on information derived from members of Congress and others. And how, he would ask that honorable gentleman, is the President to form "his opinion" of the importance of proposed roads and canals, but from the information derived from others? Would the gentleman have the President to visit, personally, and inspect the route of every road and canal, before deciding on the propriety of a survey? Surely not! This would be requiring the President to perform the duties of Chief Engineer. The law, it is true, required the President to act upon his own opinion, but that opinion was to be formed from the best evidence he could obtain. When these duties were performed by a Virginia President, it was all right. We heard not a whisper of objection. But party feeling now seems to have so perverted the judgment of some gentlemen, that they appear to think the executive can do nothing right; while others, perhaps, think he can do nothing wrong. For his own part, Mr. S. said, he belonged to neither of these parties; he was ready to pronounce censure, or bestow praise, according to the dictates of impartial justice. He had but one rule of political action, and that was to support "*measures, and not men.*" By this maxim he had been, and should continue to be governed. He would support the *men* who supported the *measures* which he believed best calculated to promote the welfare and prosperity of the country; and he would oppose those opposed to those measures, without regard to names or parties. The measure now under consideration, was one which had great influence with him—he would support its friends, and oppose its enemies, now, henceforth, and forever, without regard to the men who might succeed or fail in the struggles going on for political power.

More surveys have already been made, gentlemen say, than can be executed. One work (the Chesapeake and Ohio Canal) it is said, will exhaust the surplus revenue for many years. Gentlemen, surely, had not referred to the facts in this case, or to the bill reported. What is asked in this case? Only one million of dollars, and that to be paid in five equal annual instalments—not so much as has been expended on a single fortification on the seaboard; and this was not asked as a gratuitous appropriation, but as a subscription to stock, which, while it would accomplish a great national work, alike important in peace and in war, would yield an annual revenue of more than six per centum on the investment; and would, therefore, in a mere pecuniary point of view, be highly advantageous to the Government. While we see the several States nobly advancing in the great work of internal improvement, and even incurring debts to a large amount, shall this Government, with stronger and more urgent inducements, fold its arms, and look on in listless indifference? States constructed internal improvements for commercial purposes merely; but the National Government have superadded to these other powerful inducements: the defence of the country in time of war—the transportation of the mail—and the uniting and binding together, by these powerful ties, the distant parts of this vast empire, were considerations which ought to weigh much with the General Government, in adopting this policy. But these were considerations which could have no influence at all with the individual States. Still they were outstripping the General Government in the grand and noble march of improvement.

Another gentleman [Mr. Hamilton] objects that the engineers are withdrawn, by these surveys, from their appropriate duties in the camp and garrisons. This was a service into which the officers (Mr. S. understood) were anxious to get; it was certainly a service in which they were more profitably employed, both for themselves and their country. The young officers thus escaped from the scences of vice, dissipation, and idleness, which too much prevailed in camps and garrisons, in time of peace. They were strengthened and invigorated, mentally and bodily, by a life of activity and exposure in the field. It was, therefore, better for the officers themselves to be thus employed, than to be confined to an idle and dissolute life in camps and garrisons, independent of the great advantages the country would, in future, derive from their valuable labors. But we are told that the organization of this corps has increased to a dangerous extent the already too great patronage of the executive. This Mr. S. denied. How, he asked, does the transfer of a corps of engineers from one species of service to another, increase the executive patronage? If these appointments were made *de novo* by the President, then there would be some color for the objection; but these men are officers, and are entitled to their pay, whether they are employed in the garrisons or in making surveys. It, therefore, he contended, led to no increase of the executive patronage.

It is also objected by gentlemen that the objects ought to be designated by Congress, and not left to the executive discretion. An attempt had been made to insert this provision in the act of 1824, at the time of its passage, but very few votes were given its favor. The utter impossibility of this kind of legislation was seen and acknowledged on all hands. Attempt to designate the surveys in this House to be made next season—every member will have some important national work in his district, and some, two or three, perhaps; if you provide for one, you must provide for all, or nothing can be done. Such a course of legislation would be alike idle and impracticable.

But another objection is urged by the honorable gentleman from New York [Mr. Oakley]. He contends that the money should be divided by Congress among the several States, to be expended as they might think proper. Does not the gentleman see, at once, that this would be to defeat the execution of every great national object, and to divert the national funds from their only legitimate purpose—the carrying into effect the great objects and powers of this Government, its defence in war, and its commerce in peace? Besides, it would be an evident violation of the Constitution, which requires the revenue to be applied to the payment of the debts, and to providing for the common defence and general welfare of the Union; by applying it to mere local and State purposes—to making county and township roads—while the great national works would remain forever unexecuted and unprovided for. Such a disposition of the national funds, he contended, therefore, would be alike impolitic and unconstitutional.

Mr. S. said he had noted other arguments urged by gentlemen against this measure, but feeling anxious to close this discussion, with a view to take up the tariff, he would not now detain the House with the notice he had intended to give them. On the question of constitutional power, which had been drawn so largely into this discussion, Mr. S. begged leave to say a few words in explanation of his own views, which were somewhat different from those expressed by the gentleman on the same side with himself. To his mind there was no power exercised by Congress more clearly granted, than the right to provide for the construction of roads and canals. There was no bill upon the files of the House, which Congress had, in his judgment, a clearer right to pass, than the bill under consideration. He did not claim this right, however, from the power to "provide for the common defence and general welfare," nor did he claim the right to make all roads and canals for all purposes; he claimed the right merely to construct such roads and canals as were "necessary and proper to carry into effect some one of the powers *expressly* granted to Congress by the Constitution," and, when it was shown that a particular road or canal was necessary and proper, as a means of carrying into effect any one of the express powers, he did not see how it was possible for gentlemen to deny our right to act upon it, unless they were prepared to pronounce all the laws in our statute books unconstitutional; for our legal code consisted of little else than legislative provision for carrying into effect the powers conferred upon Congress by the Constitution.

The Constitution, in the space of twenty lines, granted all the powers conferred on Congress. Having thus indicated, in the fewest possible words, the general powers, it concludes the grant with this comprehensive provision: "And Congress shall have the right to pass all laws necessary and proper for carrying into effect the foregoing powers," thus leaving to the wisdom and discretion of Congress the selection of the means "necessary and proper" for starting the machinery and keeping in successful motion the wheels of Government. To have attempted to point out in the Constitution the various means which might, from time to time, become necessary in carrying forward this vast Government, was impossible—it would have been to provide a code, and not a Constitution.

Among the powers expressly granted, we find the power—

"To raise armies and navies, and provide for the common defence;

"To regulate commerce with foreign nations, and among the several States; and

"To establish post-offices and post-roads."

He now put it to the candor and good sense of gentlemen to say if a particular road was "necessary and proper," as a means of defending the country in time of war, had not Congress clearly and expressly the right to construct it? They had expressly the right to provide all the means necessary and proper for the national defence—and, if a road was admitted to be necessary and proper for this purpose, there was an end of the question. What right have Congress to build forts and armories—to purchase cannon, etc.? The Constitution says nothing about such things as armories and cannon; yet our right to provide them is not disputed—and why? Because they are necessary and proper for our defence in time of war. If a road be necessary to transport your cannon to the points of attack, have you not precisely the same right to provide the one as the other? It is impossible to draw a distinction. No one at all conversant with the delays and disasters experienced during the late war, especially on the northwestern frontier, would deny the utility of good roads as a means of national defence.

By virtue of the power to regulate commerce with foreign nations, we build light-houses and sea-walls, clear out harbors, and erect buoys and beacons. The power to do these things has never been disputed—and why? Because they are necessary to facilitate the passage of ships and other vessels to and from our ports, along our bays and rivers. Now, if this may constitutionally be done, "to regulate commerce with foreign nations," how is it possible for gentlemen to deny our right to do the same thing in effect, by improving our interior navigation by canals, under the power "*to regulate commerce among the several States?*" If the right exists in the one case, it undoubtedly exists in the other. Ingenuity itself could not point out a difference. It was certainly as constitutional to build a *canal-wall* to facilitate commerce as to build a *sea-wall* for the same purpose.

As to the other power mentioned—the power "to establish post-offices and post-roads"—he would detain the House with but a very few words. By virtue of the first clause of this grant, "to establish post-offices," Congress has not merely established offices, but has passed whole volumes of laws and regulations, organizing a department, with all its various and complex machinery. It has enacted laws providing the severest punishments for offences committed against the mail, even to taking away the lives of the citizens of the States, and requiring the State courts to take cognizance of some of these offences; yet we hear no complaints about State rights or a want of constitutional power. Whence do you derive the power to do all this? The Constitution is silent on the subject. All it says is, that Congress may "establish post-offices." If, then, you may lawfully go into the States and hang up the citizens because you have a right "to establish post-offices," may you not, with much more propriety, and much more advantage to the States, expend your money among their citizens, in constructing post-roads under the same grant of power? Roads are not merely necessary, but *indispensably* necessary for the transportation of the mail, and Congress has certainly the right to construct them whenever it is necessary to carry this power into effect. Gentlemen say that we can use the State roads; but suppose the States should decline to make roads, especially across the mountains, where the mail must pass between the seat of Government and the western world, who will have the hardihood to say that Congress has not the power to open a road for this purpose, if necessary? The framers of the Constitution have required Congress to provide for the transportation of the mail, and have expressly given the right to do whatever is necessary and proper to carry this power into effect. A road is necessary; yet we are told that Congress has no power to construct it. We must wait till the States shall think proper to do it for us—wait till the States furnish the means of executing our powers. Such a construction must prostrate the general Government! As well might gentlemen require us to wait till the States should erect forts and fortifications, and provide the means of defence in time of war. No, sir; whenever a power is conferred on this Government by the Constitution, it is paramount and independent of all other powers; it carries with it as an inseparable incident all the means necessary for its full and complete execution, and the selection of these means is left by the express terms of the Constitution to the wisdom and sound discretion of Congress. It was impossible that it should be otherwise. The means of executing the powers of this Government, like every thing else, must change and vary with the advance of improvement and the progress of the arts. These were briefly his views of the constitutional power of Congress over the subject of roads and canals. Each power carried with it its own appropriate means of execution. The military power carried with it the power to provide military roads and canals; the commercial power carried commercial roads and canals; and the mail power carried with it the power to construct mail roads wherever necessary.

Mr. S. said, he would notice one other objection briefly, and he would detain the House no longer. We are told, said he, that this appropriation of $30,000 is a very extravagant and wasteful expenditure; that we are largely in debt; and that we ought to do nothing towards internal improvement till the national debt is paid off. Now, sir, there is no one appropriation in the whole range of public expenditure more important, or that looks forward to more beneficial results. As to the public debt, it was now paid off faster than the public interest or the creditors required. We had no right to pay the debt before it became payable; and eight and a half millions a year would as soon extinguish the debt as $80,000,000. He would, therefore, reduce the annual sinking fund to eight and a half millions. The balance, one and half millions, with the usual surplus, making about $2,000,000 a year, he would now apply annually to internal improvements. By this means we should acquire skill and experience by the time the debt was finally extinguished, some seven or eight years hence, when there would be an annual surplus of $10,000,000 a year. If we do nothing but hasten the payment of the debt, according to the views of some gentlemen, until the whole is paid off, what will be the effect? At the end of that time we will commence the work of internal improvement with a surplus of $10,000,000 a year, without skill, without experience, without practical engineers, without those improved plans of construction always the result of experience, and what would be the result? Would it not lead to wasteful and extravagant expenditures? Would not the great demand for labor, by the expenditure of $10,000,000 a year, and the increased quantity of money thus suddenly thrown into the market, so enhance the price of every thing as to require double the sum required at this time to do the same work? He, therefore, contended that it was the part of wisdom and sound policy to commence now with a judicious and economical expenditure of two or three millions a year, and throw forward a few years, if necessary, the final payment of the debt. This would lead to the most happy results, not only in reference to the advantages he had just referred to, but it would also return a portion of the money now paid into the treasury by the people to its ordinary channels of circulation; it would supply currency; stimulate industry; afford markets to the farmer; employment to laborers; and produce in other parts of our country the beneficial—the magical—effects which have resulted from the New York Canal.

These were some of his views, very imperfectly presented, of the policy which ought to be pursued. He thanked the House for their attention, and hoped the motion would not prevail, which he regarded as an attempt, virtually, to repeal the act of 1824, which constituted the basis of a system of policy from which, he firmly believed, this country had more to hope than from any other act of legislation ince the foundation of the Government.

REMARKS IN OPPOSITION TO THE MOTION OF JAMES K. POLK TO DEFEAT THE CUMBERLAND ROAD.

DELIVERED IN THE HOUSE OF REPRESENTATIVES, U. S., JUNE 16TH, 1834.

MR. STEWART expressed his surprise that this motion should come from the chairman of the Committee of Ways and Means [Mr. Polk], who, he understood, would interpose no obstacle to the passage of this bill, though from constitutional doubts he would be constrained to vote against it. But as that gentleman had, notwithstanding, thought proper to move the reduction of the sum from $652,000 to $300,000, he would not object to it, provided the gentleman would modify so as to strike out the provision in the bill which made this appropriation final, and thus make it conform to the bill reported by the Committee of Ways and Means, of which he was chairman; but if it was the object of the gentleman to reduce the sum more than one-half, and still retain the restriction which made the appropriation final, he would be obliged to resist it; and he now wished to know distinctly from the honorable chairman whether he would so modify his motion or not. [Mr. Polk signified his unwillingness so to modify, and said that his purpose was to reduce the sum and make it final, as he thought it sufficient, and the estimate extravagant.] Mr. Stewart said he would be glad to know upon what ground the gentleman undertook thus to condemn the estimates of the department of war as extravagant. The Secretary of War, the chief engineer, and the officers of the engineer corps, who made this estimate, had no interest in making it extravagant; besides, it was made after two years' operations on the road, when the precise cost of labor and materials was accurately ascertained. This estimate was printed and placed, more than two months ago, on the gentleman's table, giving in detail the exact quantity of work required to be done; every perch of stone, every drain, culvert, side wall, and bridge—every thing required to complete the road from one end to the other, with the precise cost of each item. Now, let the honorable chairman take up this estimate—no doubt he had examined it—let him point out a single item that is unnecessary, or too high; a single thing that is extravagant; let him put his finger on it, sir, and I will consent to strike it out; this he has not attempted. Why, then, shall the gentleman, without knowledge or examination, rise in his place, and, with his eyes shut, pronounce at random this minute and detailed estimate, made after two years' experience, by practical, disinterested, and scientific engineers, absurd and extravagant? Why ask this House to adopt his mere dictum in opposition to the enlightened opinions of the War Department, communicated to this House by the President himself; to do so would be equivalent to a vote of censure, which he hoped the House was not prepared to give. It is an easy matter, sir, for gentlemen to talk here about extravagance and prodigality; it is easy to say, as has been said, that this road has cost $50,000 a mile, and that the people upon it have made fortunes by getting contracts at extravagant rates; this is mere declamation. Look at the records in the department, and you will find that the most difficult portion of this road, made during the late war, in the midst of mountains, overcoming difficulties considered insurmountable, at a time when the price of labor and provisions was at the highest, passing sixty miles over mountains, cost less than $10,000 per mile; the next portion, from Uniontown to Washington, cost only $6,400 per mile, including bridges. A cheaper road, under similar circumstances, he contended, had never been constructed; and, so far from making fortunes, the fact was notorious, that there were more honest and industrious men ruined on this road by taking contracts too low, than there were who had made fortunes by getting them too high.

But how, it is asked, is the repair of this road now so expensive? By attending to a very brief statement of the facts, this would be readily understood. This road was originally constructed by laying down a substratum or pavement of loose stone one foot in thickness, and superadding six inches of fine stone to give it a smooth surface; and thus it was left without any system for its preservation, exposed to the uncontrolled action of the travel and the elements for more than fifteen years, during all of which time only three appropriations were made for its repair, amounting together to $178,000. The road was therefore in a most ruinous condition, the whole of the six inches of fine stone gone, and much of the rough pavement cut through and destroyed. In this condition the States of Pennsylvania, Maryland, and Virginia took it up, and passed the laws referred to in the bill providing for the erection of gates and the collection of tolls, whenever Congress should appropriate a sum sufficient to put the road in a "*complete state of repair.*" To these acts Congress has assented; and two appropriations, one in 1832 and the other in 1833, have been made, to carry these acts into effect, and thereby throw the burden of repairs from the national treasury on those who have the use and benefit of the road. The condition of the road was inspected personally by the Secretary of War, and also by General Gratiot, the chief engineer, who were satisfied, from its dilapidated and ruinous condition, that a complete and thorough repair, such as was expressly required by the State laws, could only be effected by taking up the road from its foundations, and reconstructing it on McAdam's plan, for which limestone (very scarce and expensive in the mountains) was the only suitable material; and it is mainly attributable to this fact that the expense of the repairs has been so great. In pursuance of this plan, more than two-thirds of the whole road has been taken up, and the first stratum of four and a half inches of fine broken limestone put down, and on much of it the second stratum, making nine inches of metal. It is, therefore, too late for the gentleman from Tennessee [Mr. Polk] to talk about a different plan; it is too late to rake up estimates made seven or eight years ago. The plan has been adopted by the executive department; it has been sanctioned by Congress, and has been two years in progress; and now, after the whole road (except about forty miles) has been taken up, and is partly completed on the plan adopted, the gentleman talks about a new system; it is too late, sir. Surely the gentleman would not himself consent to put broken sandstone on the fine limestone already put down. To do so, would, indeed, be a wanton waste of public money; it would not last six months; it would all be ground into sand before the next meeting of Congress, when a further appropriation would be required to place the road in a condition to receive gates; the State laws requiring, as a condition precedent, the "complete and thorough repair of the road," preliminary to the erection of gates.

The question, therefore, as to the *plan* and the *amount*

required, he regarded as definitively settled by the concurrent action of the department and of Congress: and the only question remaining to be decided was, whether the *whole* or a *part* only of the sum required, should now be appropriated. This was a question about which he felt very little solicitude, and should be perfectly satisfied with any decision the House might think proper to make. He would, however, suggest a few considerations which seemed to him to favor the appropriation of the whole sum.

In the first place, the department, having the certainty of funds, could regulate their operations accordingly; the whole road would at once be put under contract, and the work continued throughout the year, without the injurious delays which occur here in the passage of appropriation bills, by which the work has now been suspended for nearly eight months; and a considerable portion of the work done last summer had, during the winter and spring, been entirely destroyed by the combined action of the frost, rain, and travel, and must be again repaired at additional expense.

Again, Congress, by making a final appropriation, would be relieved from all further trouble with this most troublesome subject; and those interested in the road would find it to their interest to hasten the erection of gates, and promote an economical and profitable expenditure of the money, it being the last appropriation. But while Congress appropriate partially from time to time, they have no such interest. Hence he thought every consideration of economy and sound policy favored the appropriation of the entire sum at once. The gates would be sooner up, it would cost less, and be in every way better than to continue to encounter the delays and embarrassments which attended partial appropriations.

The objection urged against appropriating the whole sum by the chairman of the Committee of Ways and Means, on the ground that it would lock up this large sum in the treasury till the road was finished, was altogether unfounded. Surely that gentleman knows that the money would be drawn from the treasury only as wanted, and that till required, it would remain blended with the other funds, and applicable to the other wants of the Government. But the gentleman has also endeavored to alarm the House with the idea of a *deficiency* of revenue; and, standing as he did, in the attitude of chancellor of the exchequer, his opinions were entitled on that account to some weight. But here the gentleman again comes in direct collision with the

Secretary of the Treasury, who says, in his annual report, communicated early in the session, that after satisfying all the estimates for the service of the year, and discharging the last dollar of the public debt, there would still remain, exclusive of unavailable funds in the treasury on the 31st of December next, $2,981,796.05, nearly three millions of dollars; and a few days since, in answer to a call from the Senate, the secretary says, the revenue has so far overrun this estimate, and that the actual surplus, at the end of the year, after satisfying all demands, will exceed *four millions of dollars;* and yet, in the face of this statement, the chairman of the Committee of Ways and Means is found opposing his own bills, and withholding from the Government the sums required for the public service, lest there should be a deficit in the treasury. He was at a loss to conceive why this large surplus was to be retained; what benefit was it to the people to have their money idle when it could be put into profitable circulation? To retain it could profit no one except the stockholders of the deposit banks; but would the people be satisfied to see four millions of their money in the hands of rich bankers and stock-jobbers to speculate on, without paying one cent for the use of it? Yet such would be the effect of the gentleman's course. It was to give this money to the deposit banks, instead of giving it to the people, by expending it for their benefit on this great road, on which the mails and travel from this city and the seaboard to nine western States were in daily motion.

Much had been said about the enormous cost of this road; it was always selected as the theme for economical speeches. Why were gentlemen silent when other appropriations, much more useless and extravagant, were considered? If gentlemen would look to the facts, they would find that this road, from its commencement, twenty-eight years ago, had cost less, repairs and all, than the House in which we are now sitting; less than a single fortification now erecting a few miles below this city, still unfinished, and to which annual appropriations are granted without objection? Compare these objects in point of utility, and how do they stand? The road, even in time of war, for the transportation of troops, was more important than those forts; and, in time of peace, the road is invaluable; while the forts are not only useless, but a constant burden on the treasury. Why did not the honorable chairman think of economy and the condition of the treasury when the fortification and other appropriation bills were under consideration? Why are the interior and the West to be forever excluded from all participation in the benefits of public expenditure? It was a fact worthy of special notice, and he called the attention of the House to it, that in the whole volume of annual estimates of appropriations for the public service, amounting to upwards of twenty-three millions of dollars, there were but two objects embraced in all the interior and Western States; the one was the Cumberland road, the other the Ohio and Mississippi rivers; not another object could be found. He stated it as a fact, and he challenged contradiction; and it was a fact, to which he wished to call the attention of the American people, that the whole annual expenditures of this Government, in all the interior portion of the Union, did not amount annually, to half the sum expended on a single fortification! Yes, sir—draw a line one mile from the flow of the tides, one mile from the external boundary of the whole Union, and he affirmed that the whole expenditures within this circle, on public works of every description, did not amount annually, to one million of dollars; not one million out of twenty-four; not one-third part of the cost of this splendid edifice went to all the interior and West. The whole revenue (of which they paid their full proportion) was disbursed on the seaboard and the lakes, in the erection of forts and fortifications, harbors, light-houses, buoys and beacons, sea-walls, breakwaters, custom-houses, navies, dock-yards, and a thousand such objects; while the whole interior and West are put off with a reluctant appropriation of a few thousand dollars for the Cumberland Road, and the Ohio and Mississippi. Are we to be doomed forever to be mere tax payers, "hewers of wood and drawers of water" for the seaboard? Is our money, like our rivers, to flow in perpetual streams to the ocean, no portion of it returning? He hoped not; he hoped a sense of justice and liberality would prevail; if not, a spirit of retaliation might be engendered, productive of the most injurious effects.

We have just passed, almost without objection, the harbor bill, granting to the Atlantic and the lakes,............... $652,000
The fortification bill, granting,...................... 287,000
The annual light-house bill, for oil and salaries,..... 251,000
For new light-houses, etc.,........................ 395,000

$1,585,000

Besides some three or four millions more, for the support of the navy, and its appendages, dock-yards, etc. Thus, while we are granting, annually, some six or eight millions to be expended on the seaboard, without objection, is it reasonable or just for gentlemen from that quarter to refuse this pittance to preserve a great public road, necessary to enable us to come here, and mingle our voices with theirs in favor of these liberal, not to say lavish expenditures on the seaboard, every one of which could be defeated by the votes of the friends of this road? Under these circumstances, he submitted whether opposition from the seaboard to this appropriation could be justified or defended.

He regretted to find some of his own colleagues opposed to this appropriation, but trusted their opposition would be withdrawn when they reflected that many of the honest citizens of Pennsylvania, who had taken contracts on this road, and to whom large sums were due, would be ruined by the failure of this bill; and the more especially when they reflected that this money went not from Pennsylvania, but from the nation, to relieve a portion of the people of that State, who, while they sustain their full share of the burden, had no share in the benefits of an expenditure of more than twenty millions of dollars for improvements in that State. He expressed his astonishment that Western gentlemen, who travelled on this road, should be opposed to it; the destruction of this road would be a non-intercourse between this city and the West; or, if gentlemen ventured upon it at all, it would be at the hazard of their limbs and lives. If this portion of the road is to become impassable, why continue it further west? Why continue to appropriate money to extend the road through Ohio, Indiana, and Illinois? This road was made under a compact with the new States. It was made in consideration that they should exempt the public lands from taxation; they had complied; they had paid the consideration, and fulfilled the compact. But these States had no power to legislate for the preservation of this road; it was not within their jurisdiction; and it would be a violation of good faith and the spirit of the compact for this Government now to suffer this road, made for the benefit of the new States, and for an adequate consideration, to go to destruction.

Gentlemen had seized on this as a suitable occasion to raise the constitutional question and denounce the general policy of internal improvement as unwise, as leading to extravagant and unequal expenditures, and to unjust and oppressive taxation.

The constitutional power of Congress over the general subject, he said, was not involved in this question. This was not a proposition to construct an original work, but merely to preserve a work already constructed, and that, too, under a compact with the States. As to extravagant expenditures for internal improvements, about which so much had been said, he utterly denied it. Where or when had such expenditures occurred? Let gentlemen point out a case of useless or wasteful expenditure. This had not—it could not be done. Congress had legislated for internal improvements for forty years, and the whole expenditure for roads and canals throughout the Union did not amount to more than half as much as had been expended by the single State of Pennsylvania! It did not average half a million a year. Yet, to hear gentlemen declaim upon this subject, a stranger would suppose that this was almost the only source of public expenditure threatening the subversion of the Government. Who ever thought of incurring a debt or borrowing money to promote internal improvements? No one; the idea was never suggested. Its most ardent friends never claimed more than the mere surplus, after satisfying all the other wants of Government; and what injury or danger could result from this? None. He declared it to be his opinion that if the tariff of 1824 had not been sacrificed to the spirit of party the surplus revenue would now amount to at least twelve millions a year. It had averaged this sum for the last eight years. In 1832 more than eighteen millions had been applied to the public debt; and, had this tariff been continued, instead of fears of a deficiency in the treasury, we would now have at least twelve millions to distribute among the States for internal improvement. In ten years this would amount to one hundred and twenty millions. And what would be the effect of such an expenditure? Would not this soon become one of the most beautiful and prosperous countries under heaven—united and bound together by indissoluble bonds; new sources of national wealth everywhere opened; new activity and life imparted to every department of industry; agriculture, manufactures, and commerce all prosperous; in short, making our country what it ought to be and what it would be—the wonder and admiration of the world? And all this accomplished, too, without imposing one cent of internal taxation. This immense revenue would be paid by foreigners, levied on foreign goods, and paid by the foreigner, or his agent, for the privilege of importing and selling them here. And, whether the duties were on or off, all experience proved that the price to the American consumer was the same. When we reduce the duty the foreigner adds it to the price; he puts the duty into his own pocket instead of our treasury. He appealed to experience for the truth of this position. Last year we repealed the duty on some hundred articles, amounting, in many cases, to fifty or sixty per cent.—the duty on tea, coffee, spices of all kinds, fine linens, silks, etc. They now come in free of duty; and are they any cheaper? Not a cent. On the contrary, some of them have risen in price. Thus our treasury and our people lose $15,000,000, heretofore paid annually by foreigners into our treasury; lost, too, without advantage to any portion of the American people; but, on the contrary, with positive injury, by destroying domestic industry, and facilitating the introduction of millions of foreign goods which ought to be manufactured at home. He declared it to be his honest and firm conviction that the late repeal of the tariff, to appease nullification, would, if not soon corrected, destroy our manufactures, agriculture, revenue, and internal improvements, without benefiting in the slightest degree any individual in the United States. It would throw back this nation more than half a century in its late rapid and onward march to a condition of unrivalled prosperity and power.

He would pursue this subject no further, but return to the immediate question before the House; and, in conclusion, would state, in a few words, what he conceived to be the true and only question presented by the motion of the gentleman from Tennessee [Mr. Polk]. It was simply whether the House would concur with the Senate in granting the whole sum at once to complete the repairs, or whether they would appropriate a part now and the balance hereafter. Let the gentleman restrict it as he pleased, it would come to this in the end: the whole sum would be granted. The States have agreed to erect gates; but when? Not till the road was put in "complete repair." To this Congress has assented. A plan has been adopted and partly completed; it cannot be changed; $652,130 is required *to complete it.* The commissioners appointed by the States are not authorized by law to erect the gates till the repairs are *completed.* The sum now proposed by the amendment is obviously insufficient for this purpose; and, consequently, the gates cannot be legally erected. Hence, the question at the next session will be presented whether the road shall fall back on the treasury, to be kept free, as heretofore; or whether the compact with the States to "complete the repairs" shall be fulfilled, the gates erected, and this Government forever relieved from this perplexing subject. This was the true state of the question. He repeated he felt no great solicitude as to the decision whether the whole or a part should be now appropriated; he thought, however, the object would be sooner and better accomplished, and at less expense, by appropriating the whole sum to complete the work. If so, he would pledge himself never again to ask for another cent; and all the gentlemen immediately interested were, he believed, prepared to concur in this pledge. But if only a part of the sum required by the department to complete the work and erect the gates was now granted, no such pledge could or would be given.

[NOTE.—On taking the vote, Mr. Polk's motion was rejected; but the next day, in the absence of many friends of the road, it was reconsidered, and adopted by a small majority; but finally passed.]

EXTRACT FROM REPORT OF 112 PAGES, MADE BY COMMITTEE APPOINTED ON THE SIXTH OF DECEMBER, 1826, BY THE CHESAPEAKE AND OHIO CANAL CONVENTION, HELD IN THE CAPITOL, WASHINGTON CITY.

FOUNDED ON THE REPORT OF THE UNITED STATES BOARD OF INTERNAL IMPROVEMENT TO THE DEPARTMENT OF WAR.

MR. STEWART, from the said committee, made the following Report:

That the committee have given to the subject their unremitted attention since the time of their appointment, but find it impossible, in the short period allowed them, to make their report as full and as perfect as could have been desired.

They have examined, however, with great care and attention, the able and scientific report lately made by the Board of Internal Improvement, which, it is but just to say, reflects great credit on their industry and talents. The great error, however, into which the Board appear to have been betrayed by a want of accurate local information, is found to consist in the extravagance of the PRICES *of labor and materials*, established as the basis of their estimate, which estimate must of course rise or fall in a ratio corresponding with the increase or diminution of this standard.

The committee, therefore, with a view as well to test the accuracy of the estimate of the Board as to furnish one of their own, have found it necessary, in the first place, to establish an analysis and table of *prices*, corresponding to, and contrasted with, that of the Board. This being the most important, so the committee also found it to be the most difficult and delicate part of their task. They are happy, however, in being able to state that they have succeeded, with perfect *unanimity* among themselves, in adopting the following table of *prices*, which, they trust, will meet the approbation of the Convention.

In establishing these prices, the committee had recourse to the following sources of information:

1st. To the prices *actually paid* for labor and materials on canals now in progress both east and west of the mountains;
2d. To numerous reports of committees appointed along the immediate line of the canal, to collect facts and information on the subject;
3d. To the personal knowledge and observation of the members of the Convention, engineers, and others, from whom much valuable information was derived;
4th. The actual cost of similar works, executed in the immediate vicinity of the Chesapeake and Ohio Canal route, where all the circumstances, the labor, materials, and local facilities are the same:
5th. Offers made by responsible men to give security and execute the work. All these tests, the committee are happy to find, concur in establishing the *prices* they have adopted, and in proving, conclusively, that the work can be performed for about one-third part of the estimated cost.

And, finally, from the analysis detailed by the Board, of the prices on which their own estimate is grounded, the committee have inferred the source of the error of that estimate, and sought to harmonize the results of these facts, and of common experience, with the reasoning of the Board.

[NOTE.—Then follows the report of appendix of 112 pages.]

EXTRACTS FROM A REPORT OF 122 PAGES ON THE CHESAPEAKE AND OHIO CANAL,

MADE ON THE 22D OF MAY, 1826, BY MR. STEWART, AS CHAIRMAN OF THE COMMITTEE ON INTERNAL IMPROVEMENT, HOUSE OF REPRESENTATIVES, U. S.

MR. STEWART, from the Committee on Roads and Canals, to which the subject had been referred, made the following report:

The Committee on Roads and Canals, to whom was referred the joint memorial of the Central Committee and the Commissioners appointed by Virginia, Maryland, and the United States, to open books for the subscription of stock in the Chesapeake and Ohio Canal, with sundry petitions from the citizens of Pennsylvania and Maryland on the same subject, respectfully report:

That they have given the important subject referred to them all the consideration which the short time allowed at so late a period of the session would permit.

In presenting the subject to the consideration of the House, the committee propose, in the first place, to take a brief view of the early history of this measure, its origin and progress up to the present time; then to state some of the most important facts and results disclosed by the recent surveys, together with an estimate of the probable expense of the work, and the ways and means for its accomplishment, and finally present some of the benefits and advantages which it is believed will compensate the nation for the cost of its construction.

The committee have obtained possession of a variety of letters, reports, maps, and papers, connected with this subject, in the handwriting of General Washington, extracts from which are annexed to this report. From these papers it appears that the importance of improving the navigation of the Potomac river, which affords the nearest and most practicable connection with the Western waters, attracted the attention of the Colonial Government of Virginia whilst yet a province of Great Britain. Among the manuscripts referred to, the committee find a report, in the handwriting of General Washington, dated in 1754, stating all the difficulties and obstructions to be overcome in rendering the Potomac navigable, and he actually succeeded, says his biographer [Colonel John Marshall], in getting an act passed by the Colonial Government, "*to open the Potomac so as to make it navigable from tide water to Wills' Creek*, and the business was in a train which promised success when the Revolutionary War diverted the attention of its patrons, and of all *America from internal improvements* to the great objects of liberty and independence. As that war approached its termination, subjects which, for a time, had yielded their pretensions to consideration, reclaimed that place to which their real magnitude entitled them; and the internal navigation again attracted the attention of the wise and thinking part of society. Accustomed to contemplate America as his country, and to consider with solicitude the interests of the whole, Washington now took a more enlarged view of the advantages to be derived from opening both the eastern and the western waters, and for this, as well as for other purposes, after peace had been proclaimed, he traversed the western parts of New England and New York." And in a letter to the Marquis of Chastelleux, he says: "I have lately made a tour through the lakes George and Champlain, as far as Crown Point; then returning to Schenectady, I proceeded up the Mohawk river to Fort Schuyler; crossed over the Wood creek which empties into the Oneida lake, and affords the water communication with Ontario. I then traversed the country to the head of the eastern branch of the Susquehanna, and viewed the Lake Otswego, and the portage between that lake and the Mohawk river, at Conajoharie. Prompted by these actual observations, I could not help taking a more contemplative and extensive view of the vast inland navigation of these United States, and could not but be struck with the immense diffusion and importance of it; and with the goodness of that Providence which has dealt his favors to us with so profuse a hand. Would to God we may have wisdom enough to improve them! I shall not rest contented until I have explored the western country, and traversed those lines (or great part of them) which have given bounds to a new empire."

In the fall of the same year [1784], it appears that General Washington, being so deeply impressed with the importance of uniting the eastern and western waters, and devoting all his time and attention to it, actually explored the route of the Chesapeake and Ohio Canal as far as Pittsburg. When he returned he made out a detailed and accurate report of the distances, the advantages and disadvantages of the several routes, examined by him, and on comparing them he expressed, unequivocally, his opinion that the Potomac and Ohio afforded the nearest and most practicable route for the accomplishment of his favorite plan of approximating the eastern and western waters;* and what is a most remarkable fact, he at that early day predicted the accomplishment of the New York Canal, and that the trade of the West would soon be sufficient to supply with business not only the Potomac and Ohio, and New York canals, but also one through the Susquehanna to Lake Erie, which he thought would also be found practicable.

But a circumstance still more remarkable, and one which shows in a most striking point of view the character of this great and extraordinary man is, that among his manuscript papers endorsed in his own handwriting, the committee have found a map exhibiting the whole route of the *Chesapeake and Ohio Canal* indicating the *practicable point of connection*, which appears to be precisely the same recommended by the United States Board of Engineers in their report made to Congress at the last session! This map also exhibits the route of a road or portage to connect the Eastern and Western waters, commencing at Cumberland and terminating at the Youghiogany, precisely at the point where the present Cumberland road strikes that river, and without any material deviation in the intermediate space. Having made these surveys and reports, General Washington succeeded in getting a company incorporated by the concurrent acts of Virginia and Maryland to improve this navigation, of which company he consented, at the pressing solicitation of Mr.

---

* *Extract from the manuscript calculation of General Washington* [1784].

Distance from Detroit to the several Atlantic seaports:

From Detroit, by the route through Fort Pitt and Fort Cumberland,

To Alexandria (or Washington City)	607 miles.
" Richmond	840
" Philadelphia	745
" Albany	943
" New York	1103

At present, from the head of steamboat navigation, on the Ohio, at Pittsburg, the comparative distances by the New York and Chesapeake and Ohio Canals, stand thus:—

To New York, by French Creek and Lake Erie	784 miles.
From Pittsburg to Washington, by the Chesapeake and Ohio Canal,	346 "
Difference	438 in

favor of the Chesapeake and Ohio Canal.

And General Washington's views are confirmed by Mr. Gallatin, who, in his report on internal improvements, says, "the Potomac furnishes the shortest communication from tide water to the nearest western river."

Jefferson, Mr. Madison, and other distinguished individuals who cooperated with him, to accept the presidency. In his letters to the governors of Virginia and Maryland, to the members of Congress, and others, he labored incessantly to impress upon them the immense importance of opening a cheap and easy communication with the Western country by means of internal improvements. "He suggested the appointment of commissioners of integrity and abilities, exempt from the suspicion of prejudice, whose duty it should be, after an accurate examination of the Potomac, to search out the nearest and best portage between it and the streams capable of improvement which run into the Ohio. Those streams were to be accurately surveyed, the impediments to their navigation ascertained, and their relative advantages examined. The navigable waters west of the Ohio, towards the great lakes, were also to be traced to their sources, and those which empty into the lakes to be followed to their mouths. . . . . These things being done, and an accurate map of the whole presented to the public, he was persuaded that reason would dictate what was right and proper. . . . . For the execution of this latter part of his plan *he had also much reliance on* CONGRESS; and in addition to the general advantages to be drawn from the measure, he labored, in his letters to the members of that body, to establish the opinion that the surveys he recommended would add to the revenue by enhancing the value of the lands offered for sale. Nature," he said, "had made such an ample display of her bounties in those regions that the more the country was explored the more it would rise in estimation." The assent and cooperation of Maryland being indispensable to the improvement of the Potomac, he was equally earnest in his endeavors to impress a conviction of its superior advantages on influential indivi uals of that State. In doing so, he detailed *the measures which would unquestionably be adopted by* NEW YORK AND PENNSYLVANIA FOR ACQUIRING THE MONOPOLY OF THE WESTERN COMMERCE, *and the difficulty which would be found in diverting it from the channel it had once taken.* "I am not," he added, "for *discouraging the exertions of any State to draw the commerce of the Western country to its seaports. The more communications we open to it the closer we bind that rising world* (for indeed it may be so called) *to our interests, and the greater strength shall we acquire by it. Those to whom nature affords the best communication will,* IF THEY ARE WISE, *enjoy the greatest share of the trade. All I would be understood to mean, therefore, is,* THAT THE GIFTS OF PROVIDENCE MAY NOT BE NEGLECTED.

"*But the light in which this subject would be viewed with most interest, and which gave to it most importance, was its political influence on the Union. Nor need I press the necessity of applying the cement of interest to bind all parts of the Union together by indissoluble bonds; especially of binding that part of it which lies immediately west of us to the Middle States.*"

Thus it clearly appears that General Washington in 1784 entertained no doubts of the power of the National Government, to engage in a general system of internal improvement, even before the adoption of the present Constitution, when its powers, all admit, were much more limited than they are at present, and for the extension and enlargement of which the present Constitution was formed and adopted by the States.

Delighting to dwell on these patriotic, clear-sighted, and prophetic views of the Father of his Country on the subject of internal improvement, and believing that this gratification will be common to all, especially at a time when the subject is attracting so much of the public attention, the committee will venture to present some additional views and arguments urged by Washington in favor of the *Chesapeake and Ohio Canal.*

In a letter addressed to a *member of Congress,* when speaking of the importance of this subject and the dangers of a separation of the Eastern and Western States, unless measures were adopted to prevent it by facilitating intercourse between them, which he pronounced to be "the best, if not the only cement to bind them together." He adds, "this is a matter which, though it does not come before *Congress* WHOLLY, is in my opinion of great political importance, and ought to be attended to in time." And, in speaking of the danger of severation, he says, "It may be asked how are we to prevent this? Happily for us the way is plain. Our immediate interests, as well as remote political advantages, point to it; whilst a combination of circumstances render the present time more favorable than any other to accomplish it. Extend the inland navigation of the Eastern waters; communicate them as near as possible with those which run westward; open these to the Ohio; open also such as extend from the Ohio towards Lake Erie; and we shall not only draw the produce of the Western settlers, but the peltry and fur trade of the lakes, also to our ports; thus adding an immense increase to our exports, and binding those people to us by a chain which never can be broken."

His letter to the governor was communicated to the assembly of Virginia, and the internal improvements it recommended were zealously advocated by the wisest and most influential members of that body; while the subject remained undecided, General Washington, accompanied by the Marquis La Fayette, who had crossed the Atlantic, and had devoted part of his time to the delights of an enthusiastic friendship, paid a visit to the capital of the State. Never was reception more cordial, or more demonstrative of respect and affection, than was given to these beloved personages. But amidst the display of addresses and of entertainments which were produced by the occasion, the great business of promoting the internal improvements then in contemplation, was not forgotten; and the ardor of the moment was seized to conquer those objections to the plan, which yet lingered in the bosoms of those who could perceive in it no future advantages to compensate for the present expense.

An exact conformity between the acts of Virginia and Maryland, being indispensable to the improvement of the Potomac, the friends of the measure deemed it advisable to avail themselves of the same influence with the latter State, which had been successfully employed with the former; and a resolution was passed, soon after the return of General Washington to Mount Vernon, requesting him* to attend the legislature of Maryland, in order to agree on a bill which might receive the sanction of both States. This agreement being happily completed, the bills were enacted under which works, capable of being rendered the most extensively beneficial of anything yet attempted in the United States, have been nearly accomplished.

These acts were succeeded by one, which conveys the liberal wishes of the legislature, with a delicacy scarcely less honorable to its framers, than to him who was its object. The treasurer had been instructed to subscribe in behalf of the State, for a specified number of shares in each company. Just at the close of the session, when no refusal of their offer could be communicated to them, a bill was suddenly brought in, which received the unanimous

---

* General Gates was associated with him in the mission.

assent of both Houses, authorizing the treasurer to subscribe for the benefit of General Washington, the same number of shares* in each company as were to be taken for the State. To the enacting clause of this bill was prefixed a preamble,† in which its greatest value consisted. With simple elegance, it manifested to the world, that in seizing this occasion to make a donation, which would in some degree testify their sense of the merits of their most favored and illustrious citizen, the donors would themselves be the obliged. However delightful might be the sensations produced by this delicate and flattering testimony of the affection of his fellow-citizens, it was not without its embarrassments. From his early resolution to receive no pecuniary compensation for his services, he could not be persuaded to depart; and yet this mark of the gratitude and attachment of his country could not easily be rejected, without furnishing occasion for sentiments he was unwilling to excite. To the friend who conveyed to him the first intelligence of this bill, his difficulties were thus expressed:

"It is not easy for me to decide, by which my mind was most affected, upon the receipt of your letter of the sixth instant, surprise or gratitude. Both were greater than I had words to express.

"The attention and good wishes which the assembly has evinced, by their act for vesting in me one hundred and fifty shares in the navigation of the rivers Potomac and James, is more than mere compliment. There is an unequivocal and substantial meaning annexed. But, believe me, sir, no circumstance has happened since I left the walks of public life which has so much embarrassed me. On the one hand, I consider this act, as I have already observed, as a noble and unequivocal proof of the good opinion, the affection and disposition of my country to serve me, and I should be hurt, if, by declining the acceptance of it, my refusal should be construed into disrespect, or the smallest slight upon the generous intention of the legislature; or

---

* One hundred and fifty shares.

† "It is in these words: 'Whereas, it is the desire of the Representatives of this Commonwealth to embrace every suitable occasion of testifying their sense of the unexampled merits of George Washington, Esquire, towards his country; and it is their wish, in particular, that those great works for its improvement, which, both as springing from the liberty which he has been so instrumental in establishing, and as encouraged by his patronage, will be durable monuments of his glory, may be made monuments also of the gratitude of his country: *Be it enacted, etc.*'"

that an ostentatious display of disinterestedness, or public virtue, was the source of refusal.

"On the other hand, it is really my wish to have my mind, and my actions, which are the result of reflection, as free and independent as the air, that I may be more at liberty (in things which my opportunities and experience have brought me to the knowledge of,) to express my sentiments and if necessary, to suggest what may occur to me, under the fullest conviction that although my judgment may be arraigned, there will be no suspicion that sinister motives had the smallest influence in the suggestion. Not content then with the bare consciousness of my having in all this navigation business, acted upon the clearest conviction of the political importance of the measure, I would wish that every individual who may hear that it was a favorite plan of mine, may know, also, that I had no other motive for promoting it, than the advantage of which I conceived it would be productive to the Union at large, and to this State in particular, by cementing the Eastern and Western Territory together, at the same time that it will give vigor and increase to our commerce, and be a convenience to our citizens."

On the 22nd of December, in the same year, 1784, General Washington presided at Annapolis, at a convention of delegates, consisting of the most distinguished patriots of the Revolution, from Virginia and Maryland, at which it was resolved, among other things, "That it is the opinion of this conference that the removing the obstructions in the Potomac river, and making it navigable, will increase the commerce of Virginia and Maryland, *and greatly promote the interest of the United States*, by forming a free and easy communication and connection with the people settled on the Western waters, already considerable in numbers and rapidly increasing. It will afford them proof of our disposition to connect ourselves with them by the strongest bands of friendship and mutual interest."

In another letter, addressed to a member of Congress on this subject in 1784, General Washington uses this emphatic language; "For my own part I wish sincerely every door to that country (the West) may be set wide open, and the commercial intercourse with it rendered as free and easy as possible. This, in my opinion, is the *best*, if not the *only cement*, that can bind these people to us for any length of time; and we shall be deficient in foresight and wisdom if we neglect the means of effecting it. Our interest," he says, "is so much in unison with this measure, that nothing short of that ill-timed and misapplied parsimony and contracted way of thinking, which intermingles so much in our public councils, can counteract it."

If the policy which opposed this measure, more than forty years ago, was justly pronounced by Washington *unwise, ill-timed, contracted,* and *illiberal,* what would he say of it now? Since then, a new world, as if by magic, has sprung up in the West; the wilderness has yielded to the hand of industry; ships have taken the place of the Indian canoe; and splendid cities and towns, and cultivated fields, have risen and spread themselves over the ruins of savage huts. Then the means of the country were limited; the nation was in debt, and exhausted by the revolutionary conflict which had just terminated. If *then* the policy that opposed this measure was justly considered "contracted and illiberal" what must be said of it *now,* when the means and resources of the country are ample, and when the inducements to this measure, both in a commercial and political point of view, have so greatly increased with the increasing growth, population, and resources of the Western States, and as they increase in *weight,* so it is the part of a wise policy to increase the number and the strength of the ties which bind them to the East.

But to return to the narrative. It appears from an examination of the proceedings of the Potomac Company, incorporated by the concurrent acts of Virginia and Maryland, in 1784, that they went on to expend in the prosecution of the improvement of the natural bed of the river, until they expended $311,555, the amount of their subscribed stock, twenty years tolls, and the further sum of $174,000, borrowed by the Company of the State of Maryland, banks, and individuals, without having accomplished the object, which is now admitted, on all hands, can be obtained, only by an independent and continuous canal, placed above the influence of tides or freshets. For the accomplishment of such a canal, the States of Virginia and Maryland, by concurrent acts of legislation, have recently incorporated a company: in these acts, the Congress of the United States, on the 3rd of March, 1825, and the State of Pennsylvania, on the 7th of February, 1826, passed acts of concurrence; all of which have received the approbation of the original Potomac Company, and nine commissioners have been accordingly appointed, three by the President of the United States, and three by each of the States of Virginia and Maryland, to open books for the subscription of stock for the completion of the first section, as far as the great coal mines near Cumberland; and these commissioners are now waiting the final report and estimates of the Board of Internal Improvement, to enable them to enter on the discharge of the duties of their appointment.

LETTERS.

Letter to Mr. Stewart from Gen. Jno. Mason, successor of Gen. Washington as President of the Potomac Improvement Company.

GEORGETOWN, 11*th May*, 1826.

DEAR SIR:—I have received your esteemed note of the 6th instant. I need not say that I shall always be ready to contribute everything within my reach or power to one of the most sublime schemes conceived in any country, that of the Ohio and Chesapeake Canal; but, I pray you, sir, to be assured that it will, at all times, give me great pleasure to comply with any request of yours.

I have a large bundle of papers, collected by General Washington, committed to me by himself a year or two before his death, in relation to the object of which we are now in pursuit; some of them, unfortunately, I entrusted to gentlemen, who have not returned them. In looking over the collection, I perceive none that I suppose would be useful to our present purpose, but the *nine* papers I now send you; they all bear the stamp of authenticity from his own hand, either being of his autography or bearing an endorsement from his pen. They embrace a period, as you will perceive, from 1754 to 1785, and will evince throughout, with what interest and accuracy he looked to the object.

The communications of the winter 1784–5, have relation to a conference held at that time in Annapolis, between the States of Virginia and Maryland, regarding the opening of the Potomac river, and certain roads from its head waters to those of the Ohio; to which General Washington, General Gates, and Colonel Blackburn, were deputed on the part of Virginia, but the latter gentleman did not attend on account of indisposition.

I commit to you, my dear sir, on this occasion the same trust that was placed in me by the great author and compiler of these papers —make such use of their contents as to you may seem best for the cause in which they were prepared. Could he look down on us from the mansions above, he could but approve of the exertions now making to carry into execution the vast designs originated by his foresight and anxiety for the development of the resources of our country.

I annex a list of the papers sent, be pleased to return them to me when you have done with them, as they are precious relics. Should they be wanted at a future session, they will always be ready in my hands.

I am, with great regard and respect, dear sir, yours,

J. MASON.

ANDREW STEWART, Esq.

Summary of the reports of Mr. Johnson.

Sketches of the country between the waters of the Potomac, and those of the Youghiogany and Monongahela.

From Captain Hanway, to General Washington, as to the communication between the waters of the Potomac and those of the West.

Dr. Craik to General Washington, on the communication between Wills' creek and the Youghiogany.

The first in General Washington's hand writing—the others bearing his endorsements.

Letter from General Washington, of 20th July, 1770, known to have been to the late Governor Johnson, of Maryland.

Letter from same to Joseph Jones, and James Madison, of 28th November, 1784.

Letter from same to same, of 3d December, 1784.

Letter from same to James Madison, of 28th December, 1784.

Report of General Washington and General Gates to the General Assembly of the Commonwealth of Virginia, dated 28th December, 1784, respecting conference with the State of Maryland at Annapolis.

These last five in General Washington's handwriting.

Summary of the Reports of Mr. Johnson, Mr. Semple, and G. Washington, respecting the navigation of Potomac river—by General Washington.

From the mouth of Patterson's creek to the beginning of Shenandoah Falls, there is no other obstacles than shallow water; thence, for six miles, rocky, swift, and uneven water, in which distance there are four falls; the first, tolerably clear of rocks, but shallow, may be much amended by a passage on the Maryland side. Two miles from this, and half a mile below the mouth of the Shenandoah, is the spout; a considerable rapid of swift and uneven water, which is confined to a narrow passage; a passage to avoid this, by removing some rocks on the Maryland side, may be had. One of the other two falls is also swift and ugly, not much unlike the spout, but a passage between.

Eight miles lower down is another fall, but easy and passable. Two miles further are a cluster of small islands, with rocks and rapid water—from hence to the Seneca Falls fine smooth water. Seneca Falls not very difficult. Observations of G. W.—1754.

Mr. Semple.

From the Widow Brewster's (two miles above the Great Falls), there is good water for five miles to the Seneca Falls. Here continued rocks and rifts for near a mile, easily passed between an island and the main by raising short dams. From the Seneca Falls pretty good water to Payne's Falls. At most seasons this is a narrow rift of rocks extending across the river, which may be passed, though a natural channel inland. From hence to the spout, two miles, this is difficult and dangerous, made so by almost the whole water of the river being forced through a narrow, rocky passage, which subjects vessels to the danger of filling; to be avoided by a channel inland, a mile higher above Harper's Ferry, an obstacle more difficult and expensive, requiring a channel to be dug and walled along the river at least half a mile, with rocks therein. Head or beginning of Shenandoah Falls next obstacle; here there is already a natural channel between the main and an island. Hence to Fort Cumberland no other obstruction than shallow water in places.

MR. JOHNSON.

From a little below Fort Frederick to Caton's Gut little or no obstruction. House's Fall, another rift, between that and Antietam, and what is called Sheppard's Falls, a little below Shepherdstown, being the only obstructions, and which might easily be removed at very small expense. From Caton's Gut to Payne's Falls (about five miles).

VIRGINIA, *July 20th*, 1770.

SIR: I was honored with your favor of the 18th of June, about the last of that month, and read it with all the attention I was capable of. From that time till now I have not been able to inquire into the sentiments of any of the gentlemen of this side in respect to the scheme of opening the inland navigation of Potomac, by private subscription, in the manner you have proposed; and therefore any opinion which I may now offer on this head will be considered, I hope, as the result of my own private thinking, not of the public.

That no person concerned in this event wishes to see an undertaking of the sort go forward with more sincerity and ardor than I do, I can truly assure you, and will, at all times, give any assistance in my power to promote the design; but I leave you to judge from the trial, which before this you have undoubtedly made, how few there are (not immediately benefited by it) that will contribute anything worth while to the work, and how many small sums are requisite to raise a large one.

Upon your plan of raising money, it appears to me that there will be found but two kinds of people who will subscribe much towards it: those who are actuated by motives of public spirit, and those again who, from their proximity to the navigation, will reap the salutary effects of it, clearing the river. The number of the latter you must be a competent judge of; those of the former is more difficult to ascertain; for which reason I own to you that I am not without my doubts of your scheme falling through, however sanguine your first hopes may be from the rapidity of subscribers, for it is to be supposed that your subscription papers will probably be opened among those whose interests *must* naturally incline them to wish well to the undertaking, and consequently will aid it; but when you come to shift the scene a little, and apply to those who are unconnected with the river and the advantage of its navigation, how slowly will you advance!

This, sir, is my sentiment generally upon your plan of obtaining subscriptions for extending the navigation of Potomac; whereas I conceive, that if the subscribers were vested by the two legislatures with a kind of property in the navigation under certain restrictions and limitations, and to be reimbursed their first advances with a high interest thereon, by a certain easy toll on all craft proportionate to their respective burthens, in the manner that I am told works of this sort are effected in the inland parts of England—or upon the plan of turnpike-roads; you would add thereby a third set of men to the two I have mentioned, and gain considerable strength by it. I mean the moneyed gentry, who, tempted by lucrative views, would advance largely on account of the high interest. This I am inclined to think is the only method by which this desirable work will ever be accomplished in the manner it ought to be; for, as to its becoming an object of public expense, I never expect to see it. Our interests (in Virginia, at least) are too much divided; our views too confined, if out finances were better, to suffer that, which appears to redound to the advantage of a part of the community only to become a tax upon the whole—though in the instance before us, there is the strongest speculative proof in the world to me of the immense advantages which Virginia and Maryland might derive (and at a very small comparative expense), by making Potomac the channel of commerce between Great Britain and that immense territory; a tract of country which is unfolding to our view the advantages of which are too great and too obvious, I should think, to become the subject of serious debate, but which, through ill-timed parsimony and supineness, may be wrested from us and conducted through other channels, such as the Susquehanna (which I have seen recommended by some writer), the lakes, etc. How difficult it will be to divert it afterwards time only can show. Thus far, sir, I have taken the liberty of communicating my sentiments on the different modes of establishing a fund; but if from the efforts you have already made on the north side of Potomac it should be found that my views are rather imaginary than real (as I heartily wish they may prove), I have no doubts but the same spirit may be stirred up on the south side, if gentlemen of influence in the counties of Hampshire, Frederick, Loudon, and Fairfax will heartily engage in it, and receive all occasional sums, *received* from those who may wish to see a work of this sort undertaken, although they expect no benefit to themselves from it.

As to the manner in which you propose to execute the work, in order to avoid the inconvenience which you seem to apprehend from locks, I profess myself to be a very incompetent judge of it. It is a general received opinion I know, that, by reducing one fall, you too frequently create many; but how far this inconvenience is to be avoided by the method you speak of, those who have examined the rifts—the depth of water above, etc., must be infinitely the best qualified to determine. But I am inclined to think, that, if you were to exhibit your scheme to the public upon a *more extensive plan, than the one now printed, it would meet with a more general approbation; for so long as it is considered as a partial scheme, so long will it be partially attended to—whereas, if it was recommended to the public notice upon a* MORE ENLARGED PLAN, AND AS A MEANS OF BECOMING THE CHANNEL OF CONVEYANCE OF THE EXTENSIVE AND VALUABLE TRADE OF A RISING EMPIRE; and the operations to begin at the lower Landings, (above the Great Falls,) and to extend upwards as high as Fort Cumberland; or as far as the expenditure of the money would carry them; from whence the portage to the waters of Ohio must commence; I think many would be invited to contribute their mite, that otherwise will not. It may be said the expense of doing this will be considerably augmented. I readily grant it, but believe that the subscribers will increase in proportion; at any rate I think that there will be at least an equal sum raised by this means, and that the end of your plan will be as effectually answered by it.

G. WASHINGTON.

To Governor JOHNSON, of Maryland.

MOUNT VERNON, 3*d December*, 1784.

GENTLEMEN:—I returned yesterday from Annapolis, having conducted the Marquis La Fayette that far on his way to New York, and left him proceeding on the road to Baltimore, on Wednesday last.

This trip afforded me opportunities of conversing with some of the leading characters in the different branches of the Legislature of Maryland, on the subject of inland navigation, and the benefits which might arise from a commercial intercourse with the Western Territory. I was happy to find them so forcibly struck with the importance of these objects; and that there appeared the most favorable disposition to give encouragement to them.

Like us, they have two interests prevailing in their assembly—or rather in the present instance like ourselves have two ways by which the *same* interest is to be effected. The ill-grounded jealousies arising therefrom serves in some degree to embarrass this measure of public utility. The Baltimore interest has already obtained an act to encourage, and to empower a corporate company to remove the obstructions in that part of the Susquehanna, which lie within the territory of Maryland. And this, I perceive, is all that can be obtained in behalf of Potomac, from that quarter.

As no public money, therefore, is likely to be obtained from that State, and as little chance perhaps of getting it from this—should not the wisdom of both assemblies be exerted without delay to hit upon such a happy medium as will not on the one hand vest too much power and profit in a private company;—and on the other to hold out sufficient inducements to engage men to hazard their fortunes in an arduous undertaking? If the act does not effect this the object of it is defeated; and the business of course is suspended; which, in my opinion, would be injurious; as the present moment is important, favorable, and critical; and the spirit for enterprise greater now than it may ever be hereafter.

It is to be apprehended the money-lenders among the class of private gentlemen are but few; resort, therefore, must be had to mercantile funds, from whence nothing can be extracted if there is not a prospect of great gain, present or future—but to you, gentlemen, these observations are unnecessary, as you are better acquainted with public funds, and the circumstances of individuals than I am; and I am sure are not to learn that the motives which predominate most in human affairs is self-love and self-interest.

The bill I sent you is exceptionable in some parts, and gives discontent in others—so I am informed—for it came to my hands at a moment when I could not read, much less consider it. Would it not be highly expedient, therefore, as the session of both assemblies must soon draw to a close, for each to depute one or more members to meet at some intermediate place, and agree, (first knowing the sentiments of the respective assemblies,) upon an adequate bill to be adopted by both States? This would prevent dissimilar proceedings, as unproductive as no bill—save time—and bring matters at once to a point. A measure of this kind is consonant, I know, with the ideas of some of the leading members of the Maryland Assembly, who requested me to suggest it to my friends in our assembly, and inform them of the result.

From what I can learn, there was in the meeting held at Alexan-

24

dria too great a leaning to local advantages on one part, and too much compliance on the other part, to obtain general approbation of the bill which proceeded from it. I shall not pronounce on either side, but imperfections, if they really exist, at the meetings proposed, may be rectified; and a liberal plan adopted which shall have no eye to the interested views of a few individuals to the prejudice of the majority; who, rather than damp the spirit which was up, resolved, it is said, to submit to *any* plan, rather than impede the undertaking.

At such a meeting as has been suggested, of delegates from the two assemblies of Virginia and Maryland, might it not prove a politic step for them to agree upon a representation to be made by their respective assemblies *to the State of* PENNSYLVANIA, *of the political advantages which would flow from a close connection with the Western Territory; and to request their concurrence to make the communication through their State* AS EASY AND AS DIFFUSIVE AS POSSIBLE? —*pointing to the consequences which in the course of things must follow, if we do not open doors for their produce and trade. That State has many Delegates in the Assembly who would relish such a proposition highly.* It would on our parts appear attentive and respectful; and if rejected on theirs, place them (at least in the eyes of those people) in the wrong—and excite their reiterated applications, which most assuredly would effect it.

Another thing, in my opinion, should also be the object of this meeting, and that is to agree upon a sum, to be advanced by the States of *Virginia and Maryland*, for the purpose of opening a road between the eastern and western waters. The company (if one should be formed), and the bill have nothing to do with this—and the western settlers are not in circumstances to effect it themselves.

With very great esteem and regard,
I am, gentlemen,
Your most humble servant,
G. WASHINGTON.

JOSEPH JONES and JAMES MADISON, Esqs.

Extract of a Letter from James Craig to General Washington, dated Mount Vernon, October 2, 1784.

I have thought it might be more satisfactory to leave you the different accounts I received respecting the communication between the waters of the Youghiogany and the North Branch of the Potomac, that you might, from a view of the whole, collect an opinion for yourself. It appears to me, that the land carriage from the Fork of Youghiogany to Cumberland, which, from a variety of accounts, will not be more than thirty miles, is to be preferred to sixty miles of difficult navigation up the Little Crossing, and twenty miles land carriage afterwards, which is the distance from the Little Crossing on the Turkey-foot road to Cumberland. If the communication is to be carried on by the Little Crossing, the Turkey-foot road is to be preferred to Braddock's old road, as it is infinitely better, and above two miles shorter. Indeed I found the whole Turkey-foot road across the mountains much better and nearer than Braddock's road; that if there were good entertainment, no one could hesitate in the choice.

I have received of Lund Washington twelve pounds seven shillings and sixpence, being the expenses down. The general account of expenses must be deferred until I have the pleasure of seeing you.

OLD TOWN, *January* 26, 1785.

SIR:—In a short time after you left my office, I examined the falls of Cheat river, agreeable to your request; and find that it will be impossible to effect a navigation up it, through the Laurel hills. I have made the strictest inquiry where the most advantageous and nearest communication by land can be had, from the North Branch to the Western waters, and find it will be to the falls of the Tyger Valley Fork of the Monongahela river; it will not exceed forty miles from Logstones Ford on the North Branch to the said falls; and I have reason to believe, and am confident from my own knowledge of the greatest part of the way, and the information I have had of the other part, that a good road may be made. The falls of the Tyger Valley Fork is about nine miles from its junction with the West Fork, and upwards of thirty miles above the mouth of Cheat river, and near the centre of the most settled as well as most fertile part of the counties of Monongahela and Harrison, thence a navigation may easily be had up the West Fork; and consequently by a short land carriage down the Little Kenhawa.

I am, sir,
Your most obedient and very humble servant,
SAMUEL HANWAY.

His Excellency GENERAL WASHINGTON.

To the Honorable the Assembly of the Commonwealth of Virginia.

Pursuant to the resolves of the Honorable the Senate and House of Delegates, and conformably to the direction of the executive authority of the State, we repaired to the city of Annapolis, and held a conference with the gentlemen appointed by the legislature of Maryland: the result of which is contained in the enclosure No. 1.

In consequence of the opinion given by the conference the legislature of Maryland have passed the Act inclosed, No. 2, and the Resolves, No. 3.

It may be necessary for us to explain the reason for the provision in the act "that if subscriptions should be taken in, or a meeting of subscribers directed by the legislature of Virginia, at times different from those in the act, then there should be a meeting at the time appointed by Virginia; and subscriptions made at times by them appointed, should be received." It was thought by the conferees to be most proper to appoint certain times in the act; but as it was doubtful whether the act would get to Virginia in time to be adopted at the present session of the assembly, it was adjudged necessary to make a provision to accommodate the scheme to an act to be passed by Virginia, on the next session of their assembly without the necessity of having recourse again to the legislature of Maryland; but it is the opinion of the conferees, that an act upon similar principles to that passed by Maryland ought, if possible, to be passed by the assembly of Virginia at this session. This would give a speedy beginning to the work, and an opportunity of embracing the present favorable state of things for accomplishing the views of the two States.

The act appears to us, from every consideration we can give it, to be founded on just and proper principles, and to be calculated to answer in every respect the purposes for which it is designed: we conceive it a duty therefore to declare, that it meets our entire approbation.

The reasons why this act has not the signature of the Chief Magistrate are, because he is not present, and because it wants not this formality to give it validity.

We should do injustice to our feelings, were we not to add, that we have been happy in meeting gentlemen of liberality and candor, impressed with the importance of accelerating the purposes of the Legislature of Virgiria, of opening a free and easy intercourse with the Western Territory, and for the extension of inland navigation; and that there has been a perfect accordance of sentiment in the Legislature of the State.

Respectfully submitted by

G. WASHINGTON, and
HORATIO GATES.

ANNAPOLIS, *December 28th*, 1784.

MOUNT VERNON, 28*th November*, 1784.

GENTLEMEN:—After the several conversations we have had on the subject of inland navigation, and the benefits which would probably be derived from a commercial intercourse with the Western Territory, I shall make no apology for giving you the trouble of the enclosed. It is a matter of regret, however, that I cannot accompany them with some explanations and observations. It was intended they should have met me at Richmond, they missed me on the road—travelled to Baltimore—returned—and were put into my hands at the moment I was setting out for Annapolis, to which place I mean to accompany the Marquis La Fayette, who expects to embark about the middle of next month at New York for France. I could not think of withholding these papers until my return, as I shall probably accompany the above gentleman from Annapolis to Baltimore; therefore, in the order I receive, I send them to you; your own judgment in this business will be the best guide, but, in one word, it should seem to me that, if the public cannot take it up with efficient funds, and without those delays which might be involved by a limping conduct, it had better be placed in the hands of a corporate company. What encouragement, and what powers to give this company, deserve all the consideration which I persuade myself, you, gentlemen, will bestow. The Maryland Assembly is now sitting. If I should return in time I will have the power of writing to you again on the subject; in the meanwhile, if your leisure will admit, I should be glad to know your sentiments on, and what will probably be the issue of, this business.

I am, etc.,

G. WASHINGTON.

TO JOSEPH JONES AND JAMES MADISON, Esqrs.

ANNAPOLIS, 28*th December*, 1784.

DEAR SIR:—I have been favored with your letter of the 11th. The proceedings of the conference and act and resolutions of this Assembly consequently thereupon, herewith transmitted to the Assembly, are so full of explanations of the motives that governed in this business, that it is scarcely necessary for me to say anything in addition to them, except that State seems highly impressed with the importance of the objects which we have had under consideration, and are very desirous of seeing them accomplished.

We have reduced most of the tolls from what they were in the first bill, and have added something to a few others. Upon the whole, we have made them as low, as we conceived, from the best information before us, and such estimates as we had means to calculate upon, as they can be fixed without hazarding the plan altogether. We made the value of the commodity the governing principle in the establishment of the tolls; but having an eye to some bulky articles of produce, to the encouragement of the growth and manufacture of some others, as well as to prevent a tedious enumeration of the different species of all, we departed from the general rule in many instances.

The rates of tollage, as now fixed, may still appear high to some of the Southern gentlemen, when they compare them with those of the James' river, but as there is no comparison in the expense and risk of the two different undertakings, so neither ought there to be in the tolls. I am fully persuaded that the gentlemen who were appointed, and have had this matter under consideration, were actuated by no other motives than to hit (if they could do so) upon such a happy medium as would not give jealousy to the public on one hand, nor discouragement to adventurers on the other. To secure success and to give vigor to the undertaking, it was judged advisable for each State to contribute (upon the terms of private subscribers) to the expense of it, especially as it might have a happy influence on the minds of the Western settlers.* Though there is no obligation upon the State to adopt this, if it is inconvenient or repugnant to that opinion, yet I should be highly pleased to hear that they had done so, as also the resolution respecting the roads of communication, both of which look, in some degree, to different objects, are both very important. That by the Youghiogany (through Pennsylvania) is particularly so for the fur and peltry of the lakes, because it is the most direct route by which they can be transported, whilst it is also exceedingly convenient to the people inhabiting the Ohio, or Alleghany, above Fort Pitt, the lower parts of the Monongahela, and all the Youghiogany.

Matters might, perhaps, have been better digested if more time had been allowed, but the fear of not getting the report to Richmond before the Assembly should have risen, occasioned more hurry than accuracy, or even real dispatch. But to alter the act now further than to accommodate it to circumstances where it is essential, unless there be discovered something obviously wrong, it will not do. The bill passed this Assembly with only nine dissenting voices, and got through both Houses in a day, so earnest were they to get it to you in time.

* It is to be observed that only part of this money can be called for immediately, even if the subscription fills, and afterwards, no faster than the work advances.

It is now near twelve at night, and I am writing with an aching head, having been constantly employed on this business since the 22d, without any assistance from my colleagues, General Gates being sick and Colonel Blackburn not attending: but for this I would say more.

I am, etc.,

G. WASHINGTON.

JAMES MADISON, Esq.

CHESAPEAKE AND OHIO CANAL.

THE 4th of July, 1825, was celebrated on Clay Island, in the Yohogany River, by the brigade of engineers, under the charge of James Shriver, Esq., to survey the route of the Chesapeake and Ohio Canal, and the neighboring citizens of Smithfield, etc. It was a large party, and the affair was conducted in a very handsome style. The toasts also were good, and highly appropriate. One of them was:

Our Guest from Fayette, the HON. A. STEWART. The zealous and able advocate of internal improvement. The first to propose in Congress the design of connecting the East and the West by the Chesapeake and Ohio Canal. He merits and has our warmest thanks.

This toast was received by the company with much warmth of feeling; and, accordingly, Mr. Stewart rose to make suitable acknowledgments, and delivered the following address:

Mr. President and Gentlemen: I would do violence to my own feelings, as well as injustice to you, were I not to express my grateful—my sincere acknowledgments for the flattering compliment you have paid me, and for the still more flattering manner in which it has been received by this numerous and respectable assembly. A compliment, I assure you, as unexpected as it is unmerited by me. That I have been *zealous* in my endeavors, however humble, to promote the great cause of internal improvements, I will not pretend to deny. Regarding it, as I did, a cause in which not only my immediate constituents had a deep and vital interest, but as one in which the good and glory of my country was concerned, I could not but be zealous.

But, gentlemen, when your partiality carries you so far as to give me credit for *ability* as well as *zeal* in the discharge of my public duties, candor, on my part, requires me to say that you give me credit for more than I have any just right to claim.

You have also been so kind as to attribute to me the honor of having first proposed, in Congress, "the design of uniting the Eastern and Western waters by the Chesapeake and Ohio Canal." Though I was the first to bring this subject before Congress, yet, I assure you, the honor was at that time by no means enviable, though I asked but $10,000 to make the necessary surveys; yet so general was the impression that the project was utterly impracticable, that when the vote was taken I found myself in a very lean minority; to increase my mortification, on my return home, I found the same unfavorable sentiments entertained by many of those whom I had the honor to represent. Stimulated rather than discouraged by opposition, I determined to have the necessary surveys made upon my own responsibility. This determination I made known to Mr. James Shriver, who I found occupied in selecting materials on the subject, who, at once, with a promptitude and patriotic zeal that did him the greatest honor, undertook the task, and in a short time, with a party of public spirited young men, who joined us in the expedition, we repaired to the summit level, where Mr. Shriver remained for a considerable part of the season, in the midst of hills and mountains which no human foot before had, perhaps, ever trod, until he collected the materials for the work, which he has since published. And this work, it is but justice to say, gave the first great impulse to this movement. It was the result of these surveys, which Mr. Shriver exhibited in person at the Canal Convention at Washington City, that removed all doubt as to the practicability of this work. During the next session of Congress, $30,000 were appropriated, and a board, composed of the most able and accomplished engineers in this or perhaps any other country, assisted by several brigades of topographical engineers, many of whom I have the pleasure to see present on this occasion, gave the whole route a thorough examination, and their report demonstrated not only that it was practicable but that it could be accomplished, at an expense small compared with the magnitude and utility of the work. During the last session, a bill was passed appropriating $40,000 to continue the surveys, to which, in the House of Representatives, there was not a word of opposition. Also, another act was passed, with the *unanimous* assent of *sixteen States*, and but thirty-four negative votes, confirmatory of the laws of Virginia and Maryland, incorporating companies to prosecute the work to the Pennsylvania line, under which nine commissioners have recently been appointed to carry this object into effect. This, gentlemen, is a brief outline of the origin and progress of the work thus far. As to the future, it is not for me to speak.

But, gentlemen, if we look to the unexampled rapidity

with which this work has gained upon the public confidence—if we look to these strong and unequivocal expressions of national feeling in its favor, to which I have adverted—if we look to the general and diffusive nature of its benefits—its connection with the seat of the national Government, uniting, by a canal of less than 320 miles, streams whose waters wash the shores of a majority of all the States in the Union; opening a direct communication through the very heart of the Republic, connecting the Atlantic seaboard with the boundless Valley of the Mississippi,—in short, if we advert to the peaceful and prosperous situation of our country; the abundance and excellence of labor, and especially the flourishing condition of our national finances, affording an annual surplus of more than *thirteen millions* beyond the ordinary expenditures of the Government, applicable to the national debt and internal improvements, under favor, also, of an administration pledged in its outset to the great cause of internal improvements, I think it may be safely affirmed, that, with such prospects before us, we have every thing to hope, and nothing to fear.

But it has been suggested that Pennsylvania, under the influence of a contracted, illiberal and suicidal policy, will refuse her consent to this measure, and thus embarrass, if not defeat, the accomplishment of this grand national design. The suggestion is a slander. Pennsylvania, the second State of our confederacy, can never prove so faithless to herself and to the nation. What State in the Union has so deep, so vital an interest in the success of this measure as Pennsylvania? This canal, commencing in Washington City and terminating at the lakes, will pass for more than 250 miles through Pennsylvania, thus making her territory the great theatre of one of the most splendid works ever erected by the art or ingenuity of man. Not only conferring wealth upon her people, by the immediate expenditure of millions of money among them, but securing to her benefits and blessings which will descend to her latest posterity; making her the grand thoroughfare for all the rich, unbounding and fertilizing commerce moving through this connection between the Atlantic and Western States: and is it to be supposed that Pennsylvania is weak or wicked enough to reject such a boon, freely offered to her acceptance by the rest of the Union? Such a suspicion cannot be indulged. Where is the traitor politician who would thus sacrifice the best interests of the State at the shrine of a mean, illiberal and perverse policy? For should the general Government be thus expelled from our territory to a more southern connection, what must be the consequence? With a national canal passing round us on the south, and the New York Canal on the north, Pennsylvania would be left without a market and without commerce, to wither and decline.

But it is said that Pennsylvania intends uniting the eastern and western waters by the Juniata and Conemaugh. If the State is examined from the one extreme to the other, I venture to affirm, no point of connection will be found throughout her territory so eligible as that chosen by the United States.

By referring to the reports and recent surveys, it will be found that, by connecting the Susquehanna and Potomac, through the Canadoguinit and Conogocheague creeks, which can be easily accomplished, the distance from Philadelpia to Pittsburgh will be less than by the route of the Juniata and Conemaugh. And by a glance at the map, it will also appear that from Harrisburg, the point of divergence, the route by the Potomac and Yohogany will pass through counties in Pennsylvania with a population, according to the census of 1820, of 157,043 (exclusive of Allegheny and Westmoreland), sending sixteen representatives to the State legislature; while the counties on the route, from the same point by the Juniata and Conemaugh, have but 70,797 of a population, and only seven representatives; yet the latter is called the Pennsylvania route!

A still more important consideration in favor of this route, is, that it has been ascertained to be perfectly practicable, at a comparatively moderate expense, furnishing *three times* the quantity of water required at the summit, with a tunnel of only one and three-fourths miles; while, with respect to the Juniata route, not only the United States engineers express strong doubts whether "nature has furnished the possibility of a canal by that route," but the only gentleman of the Pennsylvania board of any experience pronounces this route, in his report, to be "utterly impracticable," without a tunnel of seven miles, at a depth of nearly 900 feet under ground.

But there is a fourth consideration, which, with Pennsylvania, ought to be conclusive. This connection through the State will be made at the expense of the Union, while the other (were it practicable), must be accomplished at the exclusive expense of Pennsylvania, leading to a system of heavy and oppressive taxation, or creating a debt which will rest like an incubus upon the commonwealth, for, perhaps, a century to come. If, then, this route be the *nearest* even from Philadelphia to Pittsburg; if it will accommodate more than *double the population* in Pennsylvania; if it is decidedly the *most practicable*, and if it is to be accomplished *without any expense* to Pennsylvania, making her territory the great highway for the immense commerce between the Atlantic and Western States, through a canal, in every point of view, more magnificent and important than that of New York; can Pennsylvania, with such facts before her, doubt as to the course she ought to pursue? Ought she not to be the first and foremost advocate of this measure? But if this great national design, this great bond of union between the East and West, did not touch the territory of Pennsylvania, if she had but a common interest in its success, would it comport with the character of the great and patriotic State of Pennsylvania, yielding to an illiberal and contracted policy, to oppose the execution of a work which must not only confer the most lasting benefits on our country, but stand an eternal monument to the honor and glory of the Republic?

Let other nations boast of their palaces, their pyramids and splendid piles, erected at the people's expense, to pamper the pride or perpetuate the power of some pageant monarch, or proud usurper. Yet be it our pride to expend the people's money for the people's benefit, in building up proud and permanent, and glorious monuments of internal improvement, alike useful in peace and in war; uniting the distant parts of this extended, and extending Republic, to which our children's children may look, in after times, and bless and praise the wisdom and munificence of their ancestors.

And when was there a period in our history more auspicious to the commencement of the great work of internal improvement than the present? At peace with all the world; unconnected with Europe, and strangers to the storms which disturb her repose; unique in our situation, abundant in resources, the freest government on earth, and a country embracing in its wide domain every variety of climate and of soil, intersected everywhere by vast mountains, lakes and rivers, extending their arms from the east to the west, and from the west to the east, as if to clasp each other, and imploring, as it were, the aid of industry and art to unite them in the sacred bonds of a perpetual union, making them the fruitful sources of wealth—of intercourse—of harmony and love, to the boundless millions that repose upon their border, awakening, by their plastic touch, to new activity and life, every branch of industry, agriculture, manufactures and commerce; opening every where new and abundant sources of wealth, which must, otherwise, forever remain dormant and unknown.

If internal improvements have decorated and adorned, and enriched other countries, why shall they not ours? What country under heaven presents such advantages or such inducements? If the traveller in Europe be every where delighted on his journey by magnificent roads and splendid canals, shall he come here to be disappointed? Shall this proud Republic lag behind the monarchies of Europe in improving its own condition: in conferring benefits and blessings on its people? Or should the time come (which God forbid) when this happy Government, sharing the fate of former Republics, shall fall beneath the power of some successful Cæsar, shall it be permitted to the proud usurper, looking abroad over the desolated land, to ask in triumph the fallen friends of liberty, Where are the benefits left by your boasted Republic? Where the foot-steps of its power, or the monuments of its glory? Where the remains of any of the boasted blessings which it has conferred upon the people?—none—none. Nothing left by which the Republic is to be remembered or regretted—nothing to recall to recollection the happy days gone by—nothing to rekindle the sacred love of liberty in the bosoms of her votaries—nothing to call forth the tear of regret for its fall. No, gentlemen, this must not, cannot be. Let us advance in the goodly work in which we are engaged; let us fill the land with these evidences of republican wisdom, and republican magnificence. These will be found our best security in times of danger—they will be found the most effectual means of counteracting the sad vicissitude to which I have adverted.

But I perceive I am getting into a boundless field. I have already trespassed too long on your attention; permit me to repeat my obligations, my grateful acknowledgments for this manifestation of your confidence and kindness; and believe me, gentlemen (for I speak in the sincerity of my heart), when I say that if I could even for a moment indulge the pleasing dream that my humble and unimportant name should ever be associated with any thing connected with the good and glory of my country, I would not desire for it a more exalted niche in the temple of fame than that in which your kindness has this day been pleased to place it. *

---

* Mr. S. here pointed to his name, which appeared suspended, with a number of others, from the boughs of the trees over the temple of liberty.

BREAKING GROUND OF THE CHESAPEAKE AND OHIO CANAL, 1828.

FRIDAY last, the 4th of July, the anniversary of the Declaration of the Independence of the United States, was a proud day for the District of Columbia—for the States interested in an open navigation from the Chesapeake to the lakes, and to the waters of the Mississippi—for the friends of internal improvements every where.

On that day, which, by concurrent votes of the president and directors of the Chesapeake and Ohio Canal Company, and the corporations of Washington, Georgetown and Alexandria, had been fixed upon for breaking ground upon the line of the canal, this interesting ceremony took place, in the order prescribed by the committee of arrangement, as heretofore published, which was most successfully carried into effect by General Thornton and Colonel Stull, marshals of the day, and the aids whom they appointed.

At an early hour, the members of the several corporations, and those who were invited to accompany them and the president and directors of the canal company on this interesting excursion, began to assemble at Tilley's hotel, and cordial greetings were exchanged between them. At half past 7 o'clock the President of the United States arrived, escorted by Captain Turner's and Captain Tyler's troops of cavalry, under the command of Major Stewart, who politely tendered their services, on this occasion, which were found highly useful throughout the day.

Amongst the gentlemen composing the company, thus assembled at the invitation of the committee of arrangement, were (besides the President of the United States) the secretaries of the treasury, war, and navy departments, Mr. Rush, General Porter, and Mr. Southard; the Postmaster General, Mr. McLean; Senators of the United States, Mr. J. S. Johnston and Mr. Bouligny, and Mr. Washington, Representative in Congress; Mr. Vaughan, the minister of Great Britain to the United States; Baron Krudener, the minister of Russia, and Baron Maltitz, secretary of legation from the same power; the Chevalier Huygens, minister from the Netherlands; Baron Stackelberg, chargé d'affaires from the king of Sweden; Mr. Lisboa, secretary of legation from the emperor of Brazil; Mr. Hersant, vice-consul general of France,—comprising all the representatives of foreign powers at this moment in the city and able to attend. Among the other invited guests was the commander of the army, General Macomb, and General Stuart and Colonel Brooke, surviving officers of the revolutionary army.

The invitations were necessarily circumscribed within the limits of the accommodation which the boats procured by the committee of arrangements were calculated to afford. It was a subject of unmixed regret to the committee that the same accommodation could not be extended to all, which they were able to provide for a few only. Besides those invited, a great number of the most respectable citizens of the district and adjoining States, either accompanied the procession by water, or kept pace with it by land.

About eight o'clock the procession was formed on Bridge street, and moved on, to the excellent music of the full band of the marine corps, to High street wharf, where they embarked in perfect order: as previously arranged, and the boats immediately set forward, amidst the cheers of the crowds which lined the wharves.

The President of the United States, to whom General Mercer had presented the spade, stepped forward, and, with an animation of manner and countenance, which showed that his whole heart was in the thing, thus addressed the assembly of his fellow citizens:

"Friends and fellow citizens: It is nearly a full century since Berkeley, Bishop of Cloyne, turning towards this fair land which we now inhabit, the eyes of a prophet, closed a few lines of poetical inspiration with this memorable prediction:

'Time's noblest empire is the last;'

A prediction which, to those of us whose lot has been cast by divine Providence in these regions, contains not only a precious promise, but a solemn injunction of duty, since upon our energies, and upon those of our posterity its fulfilment will depend. For, with reference to what principle could it be, that Berkeley proclaimed this, the last, to be the noblest empire of time? It was, as he himself declares, on the transplantation of *learning and the arts* to America. Of learning and the arts. The four first acts—the empires of the old world, and of former ages—the Assyrian, the Persian, the Grecian, the Roman empires—were empires of conquest; dominions of man over man. The empire which his great mind, piercing into the darkness of futurity, foretold in America, was the empire of learning and the arts—the dominion of man over himself, and over physical nature—acquired by the inspirations of genius, and the toils of industry; not watered with the tears of the widow and the orphan; not cemented in the blood of human victims; founded not in discord, but in harmony—of which the only spoils are the imperfection of nature, and the victory achieved is the improvement of the condition of all. Well may this be termed nobler than the empire of conquest, in which man subdues only his fellow-men.

"To the accomplishment of this prophecy the first necessary step was the acquisition of the right of self-government by the people of the British North American colonies, achieved by the Declaration of Independence, and its acknowledgment by the British nation. The second was the union of all these colonies under one general confederated government—a task more arduous than that of the preceding separation, but at last effected by the present constitution of the United States.

"The third step, more arduous still than either or both the others, was that which we, fellow citizens, may now congratulate ourselves, our country, and the world of man, that it is taken. It is the adaptation of the powers, physical, moral, and intellectual, of this whole union, to the improvement of its own condition: of its moral and political condition, by wise and liberal institutions—by the cultivation of the understanding and the heart—by academies, schools, and learned institutes—by the pursuit and patronage of learning and the arts: of its physical condition, by associated labor to improve the bounties, and to supply the deficiencies of nature; to stem the torrent in its course; to level the mountain with the plain; to disarm and fetter the raging surge of the ocean. Undertakings, of which the language I now hold is no exaggerated description, have become happily familiar, not only to the conceptions, but to the enterprise, of our countrymen. That, for the commencement of which we are here assembled, is eminent among the number. The project contemplates a conquest over physical nature, such as has never yet been achieved by man. The wonders of the ancient world, the pyramids of Egypt, the Colossus of Rhodes, the temple of Ephesus, the mausoleum of Artemisia, the wall of China, sink into insignificance before it—insignificance in the mass and momentum of human labor, required for the execution—insignificance in the comparison of the purposes to be accomplished by the work when executed. It is, therefore, a pleasing contemplation to those sanguine and patriotic spirits who have so long looked with hope to the completion of this undertaking, that it unites the moral power and resources—first, of numerous individuals—secondly, of the corporate cities of Washington, Georgetown, and Alexandria—thirdly, of the great and powerful States of Pennsylvania, Virginia, and Maryland—and, lastly, by the subscription authorised at the recent session of Congress, of the whole Union.

"Friends and fellow-laborers, we are informed by the holy oracles of truth, that, at the creation of man, male and female, the Lord of the universe, their Maker, blessed them, and said unto them, be fruitful and multiply, and replenish the earth, *and subdue it.* To subdue the earth was, therefore, one of the first duties assigned to man at his creation; and now, in his fallen condition, it remains among the most excellent of his occupations. To subdue the earth is preeminently the purpose of the undertaking, to the accomplishment of which the first stroke of the spade is now to be struck. That it is to be struck by this hand, I invite you to witness—[Here the stroke of the spade]*—and in performing this act, I call upon you to join me in fervent supplication to Him from whom that primitive injunction came, that he would follow with his blessing this joint effort of our great community, to perform his will in the subjugation of the earth for the improvement of the condition of man. That he would make it one of his chosen instruments for the preservation, prosperity, and perpetuity of our union. That he would have in his holy keeping all the workmen by whose

* Attending this action was an incident which procured a greater sensation than any other that occurred during the day. The spade which the President held struck a root, which prevented its penetrating the earth. Not deterred by trifling obstacles from doing what he had deliberately resolved to perform, Mr. Adams tried it again, with no better success. Thus foiled, he threw down the spade, hastily stripped off and laid aside his coat, and went seriously *to work.* The multitude around, and on the hills and trees, who could not *hear*, because of their distance from the open space, but could *see* and understand, observing this action, raised a loud and unanimous cheering, which continued for sometime after Mr. Adams had mastered the difficulty; when a Jackson man in the crowd exclaimed in a loud voice, "*A Hickory root,*" which gave rise to a tremendous shout by the Jackson men, this celebration occurring just before the election between Adams and Jackson in 1828.

labors it is to be completed. That their lives and their health may be precious in his sight; and that they may live to see the work of their hands contribute to the comforts and enjoyments of millions of their countrymen.

"Friends and brethren, permit me further to say, that I deem the duty, now performed at the request of the president and directors of the Chesapeake and Ohio Canal Company, and the corporations of the District of Columbia, one of the most fortunate incidents of my life. Though not among the functions of my official station, I esteem it as a privilege conferred upon me by my fellow-citizens of the district. Called, in the performance of my service heretofore as one of the representatives of my native commonwealth; in the senate, and now as a member of the executive department of the government, my abode has been among the inhabitants of the district longer than at any other spot upon earth. In availing myself of this occasion to return to them my thanks for the numberless acts of kindness that I have experienced at their hands, may I be allowed to assign it as a motive operating upon the heart, and superadded to my official obligations, for taking a deep interest in their welfare and prosperity. Among the prospects of futurity which we may indulge the rational hope of seeing realized by this junction of distant waters, that of the auspicious influence which it will exercise over the fortunes of every portion of this district, is one upon which my mind dwells with unqualified pleasure. It is my earnest prayer that they may not be disappointed.

"It was observed that the first step towards the accomplishment of the glorious destinies of our country was the Declaration of Independence. That the second was the union of these States under our federative government. The third is irrevocably fixed by the act upon the commencement of which we are now engaged. What time more suitable for this operation could have been selected than the anniversary of our great national festival? What place more appropriate from whence to proceed, than that which bears the name of the citizen warrior who led our armies in that eventful contest to the field, and who first presided as the chief magistrate of our union? You know that, of this very undertaking, he was one of the first projectors; and if, in the world of spirits, the affections of our mortal existence still retain their sway, may we not, without presumption, imagine that he looks down with complacency and delight upon the scene before and around us?

"But, while indulging a sentiment of joyous exultation, at the benefits to be derived from this labor of our friends and neighbors, let us not forget that the spirit of internal improvement is catholic and liberal. We hope and believe that its practical advantages will be extended to every individual in our union. In praying for the blessing of heaven upon our task, we ask it with equal zeal and sincerity upon every other similar work in this confederation; and particularly upon that which, on this same day, and perhaps at this very hour, is commencing from a neighboring city. It is one of the happiest characteristics in the principle of internal improvement, that the success of one great enterprise, instead of counteracting, gives assistance to the execution of another. May they increase and multiply, till, in the sublime language of inspiration, every valley shall be exalted, and every mountain and hill shall be made low; the crooked straight; the rough places plain. Thus shall the prediction of the Bishop of Cloyne be converted from prophecy into history, and, in the virtues and fortunes of our posterity, the last shall prove the noblest empire of time."

As the President concluded, a national salute was fired by a detachment of United States artillery posted upon the ground. As soon as the cheering which followed the close of the President's speech had subsided, the chairman of the committee of arrangements delivered the following brief address:

"In the name of the committee of arrangements of the corporations of the district, I tender to the president and directors of the canal company, and to this crowd of gratified spectators, our congratulations on the happy commencement of this great work.

"To the president of the company, we and the country are indebted for his early, persevering, and successful efforts in the great cause, the triumph of which we have this day assembled to honor; and we cordially respond to those emotions which the occasion is so well calculated to inspire in his breast.

"To the President of the United States we are under obligations for the kindness and cheerfulness with which he accepted our invitation to practically begin the labor, which is to unite, by closer ties of amity and interest, the inhabitants of the borders of the Atlantic, of the margins of the lakes, and of the rapidly peopling forests and prairies of the interior. In the name of our corporations, we return our acknowledgments to him for the countenance and aid which this undertaking has constantly received from him.

"To the director from the State of Pennsylvania, who may be considered, in his present relation to us, the representative not merely of his own State but of the whole West, we offer our cordial felicitation on the prospect of the early completion of the work which has just now been symbolically begun, and of which he too has been the zealous and efficient advocate.

"To the almost unanimous support of the senators and representatives of the Western States, united to that afforded by valuable friends from other States, we of the Atlantic shore, greatly owe the aid which Congress has liberally granted to this undertaking. It is our earnest hope, that, in the advantages to be derived from the opening of this great channel of commerce—from the construction of this great central chain of union—the States of the West will find their most sanguine calculations surpassed by the reality, and that, in the result, the whole sisterhood of States will be made sensible of the benign influence of liberal legislation."

When the chairman had concluded:—

Mr. Stewart (the director above referred to), after returning his thanks to the committee from the three corporations of the district, for the flattering terms in which they had noticed him in the address delivered by their chairman, begged to avail himself of this occasion, to tender also his grateful acknowledgments to the stockholders now present, for the distinguished and unexpected honor they had conferred on him, by calling him from a distant residence, to a seat at the board of directors. He had, however, to regret that, owing to his very limited experience, he could bring to the board little more than his hearty good will; and an ardent desire to do every thing in his power to give energy to the prosecution of this great work to a speedy and successful termination; a work pre-eminently national in all its aspects, commenced, as had been well remarked by the president of the company, under the most cheering auspices, by the hands of the chief magistrate of the greatest republic on earth, and in the presence of the official representatives of several of the most refined and powerful nations of Europe.

"Designated by you, gentlemen (said Mr. S.) as the representative of the Western States, on this occasion I may venture to tender you their thanks for the just tribute you have paid to the liberal and magnanimous spirit by which they have been governed. I need not say that the people of the West take a deep and lively interest in the success of this great enterprise. They have spoken their sentiments by much higher authority, by their immediate representatives in Congress: for, in eight of the nine Western States there was but one vote against the liberal appropriation granted at the last session to this object, and to which we are so greatly indebted for the gratification we all experience on this glorious and joyful occasion.

"Looking, as we do, in the West, with intense interest to the accomplishment of the great object, it would be unjust, on this occasion, to withhold the expression of our obligations to our brethren in the East, for their liberal support; for, in eight of the Eastern States, likewise, there were but eight votes in the House against this appropriation. Our obligations, however, are confined to no section; they belong to the whole union. Justly regarding this as an object eminently national, the representatives from all portions of our country, influenced by a liberal and enlightened policy, extended to it a generous support. This liberality, however, was not confined to this object alone, but was extended largely and freely to others—to Tennessee, to Ohio, to Pennsylvania.

"You have very justly, gentlemen, described this as 'a great central chain of union between the Atlantic and Western States.' I am happy, however, in the conviction that there are other and stronger ties which bind us together—ties of a higher and nobler origin—ties 'not made with hands,' but found in the hearts, in the affectionate attachment, in the patriotic devotion of the people to the government and union of the States. These are the bonds of union, after all, to which we must look, and on which we must rely; these are the bonds which we are called on by every patriotic feeling to cherish, to strengthen, and increase. Every attempt, no matter from what quarter it may come, to dissolve these bonds, to weaken these ties, which bind the people to the union, to the constitution, and laws of their country, should, as it must, meet the indignant reprobation of every true patriot. For, should this union be destroyed, what becomes of this fair land, with all its cheering prospects? Where will persecuted liberty longer look for an asylum? Where will the patriot turn his eyes for safety? What becomes of *our bright example* to the friends of freedom throughout the world? Gone! extinguished forever.

"But I will dismiss this reflection as inappropriate to the occasion, as an event beyond the reach of anticipation, to which we should never look but to avoid it.

"I present you, gentlemen, and all present, the congratulations of the West on this occasion; and permit me to express the hope that we will be able to complete the work, now so happily begun, as far as Cumberland in three years from this day; and, by a union and co-operation with our friends at Baltimore, when the two works become united on the Potomac river, with a common object and a common interest, may we not indulge the hope that the day is not distant when we shall again assemble, at the summit level, to celebrate an event still more glorious than this—the mingling of the waters of the Chesapeake and Ohio; when we may truly exclaim, without the aid of Berkeley's spirit of prophecy,

'Art's noblest, triumph, is the last.'"

These addresses being concluded, the spade was taken, and sods of earth dug in succession by the president of the canal company, the mayors of Washington, Georgetown and Alexandria, the Secretaries of the Treasury, War, and Navy, the Postmaster-General, the Commander of the army, the Revolutionary officers present, the directors of the canal company, and then by a great number of other persons.

After a few moments of repose, the procession again formed, and returned to the boats, and by the way of the canal back to the tide-water, where they re-embarked on board the steam boats.

A cold collation was then partaken of on board the boats, with a relish sharpened by exercise, and by the gratification, free from the least particle of alloy, which the whole excursion and the incidents of the day had afforded to all.

At the table on the deck of the *Surprize*, the President of the United States, being called upon for a toast, gave the following:

"*The Chesapeake and Ohio Canal*—Perseverance!"

The president of the canal company, on being called upon for a sentiment, gave the following:

"*The Constitution of the United States*—The offspring of mutual concession, may it be preserved by mutual forbearance!"

The Secretary of the Treasury, being also called on for a toast, gave the following, which only spoke the universal feeling:

"*The Chesapeake and Ohio Canal*—May its completion

be as productive of public benefits, as its commencement has been of social pleasure."

By this time the steam boats had arrived opposite to Georgetown; and, after lying in the stream a few minutes, proceeded down the river, and swept up to Davidson's wharf, in the city, where most of the passengers were landed, at about half past two o'clock; and the company dispersed to their respective homes, with the kindest feelings in themselves and to one another.

Thus ended the most delightful commemoration of this eventful day that we have ever witnessed, and thus auspiciously was begun the work upon the Chesapeake and Ohio Canal.—*Niles' Register, Vol.* 34, *p.* 325, 1828.

CONNELLSVILLE RAILROAD.

EARLY HISTORY OF THE ROUTE—ITS SURVEY BY GENERAL WASHINGTON—HE PREDICTS PENNSYLVANIAN OPPOSITION—PRESENT AND FUTURE OF THE ROAD.

At a late celebration [1871] at the town of Confluence, Pa., on the Pittsburg, Connellsville, and Baltimore Railroad, the venerable Hon. Andrew Stewart was called upon for a speech. Remarkable interest was excited by the address of the aged orator and life-long friend of the new route.

Mr. Stewart opened with a high and merited compliment to the town of Confluence, which, from its many local advantages, must soon become an important mountain city. With three converging rivers at this point, and where, no doubt, three railroads would soon unite—one from the South, and another from the North, and a third, the great road whose completion we now celebrate, up the middle toe of the Turkey foot. These rivers and roads would bring to this highly favored point the rich agricultural, mineral, and lumber supplies furnished by the mountains and valleys traversed by the rivers and roads to which he had referred.

Mr. S. then went on at length to state many new and very interesting facts, showing the great superiority of this road over all other roads crossing the Alleghany Mountains, as to distance, grades, safety, cheapness, etc.

NATURE'S GRADES.

The distance from Pittsburg to Washington was a fraction less than 300 miles, and although it passed over nine mountains, which cross its pathway at right angles, yet, strange to say, it has but a single summit, from which, descending east and west, two graduated inclined planes, one following the Youghiogany, at an average grade of thirteen feet per mile, 120 miles to Pittsburg, never losing sight of the river or crossing it once, and, of course, following the river could have no ascending grades. The eastern plane, in like manner, descending from the same summit, by the waters of the

Potomac, 180 miles, at an average grade of twelve feet per mile to Washington City. These were important facts, showing the superiority of this line, which had never been stated.

Nature had done much more for this route. She seems to have made it on purpose for this road. In removing these nine mountains, six west and three east of the summit, nature had done more work to make a pathway for this road than could have been done by all the men and money, mattocks and shovels, in the whole world in a hundred centuries; but this is not all that nature has done for this her favorite route. She has deposited at its single summit the richest mines of coal and ore ever discovered, where an eastern train having ascended from tide water, with a full load to this summit, may take double the quantity from a switch, which will follow on this descending grade of thirteen feet per mile, without being felt by the engine or seen by the engineer until it reaches Pittsburg; and in like manner a western train may double its load with iron or coal at this summit, and carry it to the tides of the ocean, aided by gravity, without any increase of power or expense.

EFFECT ON MONOPOLY.

But there were other facts, he said, showing the great superiority of this work, especially over its great rival and enemy, the Pennsylvania road, a matter in which the people are deeply interested. This fact was, that, since the opening of this road, the Pennsylvania road had to reduce her charges about one-third—28 on travel, and 40 per cent. on freight, making a clear gain to the people using this road of more than half a million a month, or $6,000,000 a year. If such are the effects of the competition of this road in a few weeks, what will it be when it is finally finished and fully equipped?

The Pennsylvania road having no longer the power to take away our charter, the Supreme Court having pronounced this outrageous legislation unconstitutional and void; they are now endeavoring to cut off our western connections by obtaining control of all the roads going westward from Pittsburg. In this they will be equally unsuccessful. Western connections for this road will soon be opened, and, in the meantime, let the Pennsylvania road and her subordinates bring the trade and travel to Pittsburg, where, being free to choose, they will take this road, being the shortest, safest, and cheapest line, and, when it is full, those it cannot accommodate will take the Pennsylvania or some other route.

GENERAL WASHINGTON ON NATIONAL HIGHWAYS.

Mr. Stewart then went on to state a great variety of new and highly interesting facts in reference to the origin and early history of this route, which facts, he said, he had found in a large box containing a bushel or more of the original reports, letters, etc., in the handwriting and manuscripts of General Washington, which had been handed over by him shortly before his death to General John Mason, of Georgetown, his successor as president of the company having charge of the work by which he (Washington) intended to connect the East and West, by route of the Potomac and Youghiogany rivers. Throughout these letters and reports, addressed to the Legislatures of Virginia and Maryland, members of Congress and others, he contended that roads across the mountains were the only means of keeping the East and West united; without them, for many reasons, he said, separation was inevitable.

Mr. Stewart had himself condensed the substance of these papers in the supplement to a report on the subject made by him to the nineteenth Congress, of which he was a member, in 1826. It would then be seen that Washington, the first year after the close of the revolutionary war, in 1784, not only re-examined this route, but also, with a view to institute a comparison with other routes, actually explored the route of the New York Canal to the lakes; also the line of the Pennsylvania improvements, by the Juniata and Conemaugh, from Philadelphia to Pittsburg, and likewise the route of the James river and Kanawha in Virginia, giving the comparative advantages and distances of each, and predicting their accomplishment; but he pronounced this the shortest and in every way the best route, and with remarkable sagacity and foresight he predicted that the hostility of the Pennsylvania Legislature might embarrass and delay the passage of this work through this State, but said the people of the western part of the State, so deeply interested, would resist this unjust and illiberal policy, and "reiterate" their just claims until they would finally succeed—which prophecy has just been fulfilled.

GENERAL WASHINGTON'S FIRST SURVEY.

General Washington's first report of his examination of this route was made to the Colonial Legislature of Virginia in 1754, when he was only twenty-two years of age. In the same year, with the aid of some Virginia volunteers, he actually cut out this route from Cumberland to "Washington's Meadows," five or six miles south of the Connellsville road, at the Ohio Pyle Falls, when he was met and driven back by 1100 French and Indians, after a three days' battle, which ended by an honorable capitulation, on the 4th of July, 117 years ago. Washington took out a warrant for this tract of land, embracing "Fort Necessity," his first battle-field, and owned it to the day of his death. The next year, in company with General Braddock, he aided in opening this road from "Fort Necessity" to "Braddock's Fields," near Pittsburg. General B. died of his wounds, and was buried near "Fort Necessity," in the middle of Braddock's road (to conceal the place of his interment from the enemy), where, in 1802, when a boy, Mr. S. saw his bones disinterred in the presence of Thomas Fawcett, an old mountain hunter, who pointed out the spot where Braddock was buried, who then and always said he shot Braddock, for driving his brother Joseph from behind a tree, and in order to save the army, which was accomplished by Washington taking command.

HIS LATER SURVEY.

As soon as Washington resigned his commission as commander-in-chief, he mounted his war-horse, armed with compass and chain, and dashed into the mountains, amid savage beasts of prey, and Indians still more savage, and made the maps and surveys to which he had referred, crossing the river about a mile above "Turkey Foot," where we now stand. He then descended the river in a canoe to the "Ohio Pyle Falls," with an Indian guide, who, on beholding the falls, exclaimed, "Ohio Pyle!" which, in English, means "Beautiful Falls." Here they left their canoe, and proceeded west by land. Shortly after this, Washington was again called from this his favorite work, by his election to the Presidency of the United States, but immediately on surrendering this office, at the end of eight years, he resumed the presidency of the company in charge of this work, and prosecuted it unceasingly until he took a cold, resulting in quinsy, which ended his glorious life. This work he commenced at twenty-two, and he followed it up to the day of his death.

MR. STEWART TAKES UP THE WORK.

Beginning where Washington quit, Mr. S. said, in 1821, more than half a century ago, he asked Congress for an appropriation of $30,000 to survey this route, but failed to satisfy them of its practicability. To remove this difficulty, he got James Shriver, an able civil engineer, with some other young gentlemen to go with him to the summit level, and make the surveys necessary to show the practicability of this work, which he had printed, and placed a copy on every member's table, when, at the next session, he succeeded in obtaining the appropriation of $30,000. Mr. Calhoun, then Secretary of War, immediately organized a corps of topographical engineers to make the surveys, commencing on the top of the mountain, where, Mr. S. said, he afterwards met Mr. Calhoun, and slept in a tent with him for several weeks. He evinced the greatest interest in the work, and advocated the construction of the summit section first, for the purpose of showing its practicability, and securing its completion east and west. After the completion of the surveys, liberal subscriptions of stock were made by Congress, the District cities, Virginia, Maryland, and individuals, and on the 4th of July, 1828, the first shovelful of earth was removed by the hands of John Q. Adams, then President of the United States, in the presence of the foreign ministers, heads of departments, members of Congress, and a vast concourse of people. This work was thus commenced as a canal at Washington City, and prosecuted to completion as far as Cumberland, at a cost of $11,000,000; here the canal was superseded by the construction of a railroad, and opened as such from Cumberland to Pittsburg, thus consummating this great and favorite object of the "Father of his Country," connecting the East and West by the waters of the Potomac and Youghiogany.

ENEMIES, AND FINAL TRIUMPH OVER THEM.

Mr. S. then went on, at some length, to speak of the numerous delays and embarrassments experienced by the company from the jealousy and hostility of the Pennsylvania Railroad, and also from the attempt of the president and part of the stockholders to abandon the work and surrender the charter, in which, after a protracted struggle, they were fortunately defeated. If lost then, it would have been lost forever.

Mr. S. said he had detained the meeting too long, but he could not conclude without a word in reference to the gentlemen to whom we are most indebted for the completion of this work. To John W. Garrett, he said, we are most indebted, more than to any other man, living or dead; next to Mr. Garrett, to Mr. Hughart, the president, and Mr. Latrobe, chief engineer, and their able corps of assistants. Others, it is true, have done some of the wind work. Some of us have helped to kindle the fire and blow the bellows, but Mr. Garrett raised the money, he put the iron on the anvil, while Messrs. Hughart, Latrobe, and assistants have wielded the ponderous sledges and directed the powerful blows that worked out this glorious result. He, therefore, in conclusion, asked three times three united cheers for Garrett, Hughart, Latrobe, and their assistants, which were given with a heartiness and sincerity that showed the vast audience was in entire sympathy with him.

PITTSBURG AND CONNELLSVILLE BRANCH ROADS.

In this connection, the following items of intelligence, from the *Cumberland (Md.) News*, of the 15th of August, show how rapidly as well as effectually, the Connellsville Railroad is building up the country along its route:

"The branch railroad from Mineral Point, on the Con nellsville Railroad, to the town of Somerset, in Somerset county, ten miles in length, has been graded and ballasted, and the work of laying the rails was begun yesterday, and will be completed by September 2d, if no unforseen event occurs to interfere.

"The branch road from Garrett Station to Berline, in Somerset county, distance eight miles, has been let, and is to be completed within ninety days.

"A large part of the grading on the branch from Meyer's Mills, near Dale City, to Salisbury, has been completed, and the work is progressing quite vigorously."—*Baltimore Sun, Aug.* 19, 1871.

LETTERS

RECOMMENDING THE PUBLICATION OF

MR. STEWART'S SPEECHES IN 1851.

[*From Daniel Webster.*]

MARSHFIELD, *August 15th*, 1851.

DEAR SIR:—I am glad to hear you contemplate publishing Mr. Stewart's speeches on the tariff. I have heard or read most if not all of them. They are able, plain, practical, original, and exhaustive, adapted to the comprehension of the plainest people. Their publication cannot fail to do a great deal of good, and will I doubt not be received with public favor, and be extensively circulated and read. When published I will be pleased to purchase a number of copies.

Yours respectfully,
D. WEBSTER.

[*From Governor Hunt of New York.*]

ALBANY, *August 25th*, 1851.

DEAR SIR:—I will render you any aid in my power in publishing the speeches of the Hon. Andrew Stewart in favor of the protective policy. Having heard most of his speeches in Congress I was enabled to form a correct estimate of their merits. He was eminently successful in simplifying the tariff question, and making the practical operations of the system perfectly plain to the most common understandings.

Yours respectfully,
WASHINGTON HUNT.

[*From Hon. Reverdy Johnson.*]

SARATOGA SPRINGS, *August 16th*, 1851.

SIR:—Yours of the 2nd finds me here. The publication of Mr. Stewart's speeches during his most useful and distinguished career in Congress, which you are about to publish, will be a valuable aquisition to the political knowledge of the country. To a mind remarkably practicable and discriminating he has united untiring industry, guided by a pure and enlightened patriotism. His labors have been signally promotive of the great and true interests of the nation, and I shall be surprised if the work is not received with general favor throughout the country.

With regard, your obedient servant,
REVERDY JOHNSON.

[With many others of like tenor.]

[*From Speaker Winthrop.*]

WASHINGTON, *March 2nd*, 1847.

GENTLEMEN :—I have the honor to acknowledge your letter of the 26th ult., inviting me to be present at a Public Dinner to be given to the Hon. Andrew Stewart. I am deeply sensible of the fitness of the compliment to the distinguished Representative from the Eighteenth District of Pennsylvania. The labor of the whole country owes him a debt of gratitude. No man in the Union has asserted the claims of all branches of American industry, to the fostering care of the Government, more ardently or more ably. New England appreciates his services no less than Pennsylvania, and I earnestly hope that some son of New England may be with you, to express her sentiments on the occasion. For myself, I regret sincerely that indispensable engagements will deprive me of the pleasure of availing myself of your very kind invitation.

I am, very respectfully,
your obliged friend and obedient servant,
ROBT. C. WINTHROP.

Hon. E. Joy Morris, and others, Committee, etc.

[The above from speaker Winthrop, with many others of like import from eminent members of the Senate, House, etc., was received and published, with the speeches and proceedings at the dinner given complimentary to Mr. Stewart, in the Assembly buildings, Philadelphia, on the 6th of March, 1847.]

INDEX.

THE END.

CATALOGUE

OF

PRACTICAL AND SCIENTIFIC BOOKS,

PUBLISHED BY

HENRY CAREY BAIRD,

INDUSTRIAL PUBLISHER,

No. 406 WALNUT STREET,

PHILADELPHIA.

☞ Any of the Books comprised in this Catalogue will be sent by mail, free of postage, at the publication price.

☞ MY NEW AND ENLARGED CATALOGUE, 95 pages 8vo., with full descriptions of Books, will be sent, free of postage, to any one who will favor me with his address.

ARMENGAUD, AMOUROUX, AND JOHNSON.—THE PRACTICAL DRAUGHTSMAN'S BOOK OF INDUSTRIAL DESIGN, AND MACHINIST'S AND ENGINEER'S DRAWING COMPANION: Forming a complete course of Mechanical Engineering and Architectural Drawing. From the French of M. Armengaud the elder, Prof. of Design in the Conservatoire of Arts and Industry, Paris, and MM. Armengaud the younger and Amouroux, Civil Engineers. Rewritten and arranged, with additional matter and plates, selections from and examples of the most useful and generally employed mechanism of the day. By WILLIAM JOHNSON, Assoc. Inst. C. E., Editor of "The Practical Mechanic's Journal." Illustrated by 50 folio steel plates and 50 wood-cuts. A new edition, 4to. . $10 00

ARLOT.—A COMPLETE GUIDE FOR COACH PAINTERS. Translated from the French of M. ARLOT, Coach Painter; late Master Painter for eleven years with M. Ehrler, Coach Manufacturer, Paris. With important American additions . . $1 25

ARROWSMITH.—PAPER-HANGER'S COMPANION: A Treatise in which the Practical Operations of the Trade are Systematically laid down: with Copious Directions Preparatory to Papering; Preventives against the Effect of Damp on Walls; the Various Cements and Pastes adapted to the Several Purposes of the Trade; Observations and Directions for the Panelling and Ornamenting of Rooms, &c. By JAMES ARROWSMITH. 12mo., cloth $1 25

BAIRD.—THE AMERICAN COTTON SPINNER, AND MANAGER'S AND CARDER'S GUIDE:

A Practical Treatise on Cotton Spinning; giving the Dimensions and Speed of Machinery, Draught and Twist Calculations, etc.; with notices of recent Improvements: together with Rules and Examples for making changes in the sizes and numbers of Roving and Yarn. Compiled from the papers of the late ROBERT H. BAIRD. 12mo. $1 50

BAKER.—LONG-SPAN RAILWAY BRIDGES:

Comprising Investigations of the Comparative Theoretical and Practical Advantages of the various Adopted or Proposed Type Systems of Construction; with numerous Formulæ and Tables. By B. Baker. 12mo. $2 00

BAKEWELL.—A MANUAL OF ELECTRICITY—PRACTICAL AND THEORETICAL:

By F. C. BAKEWELL, Inventor of the Copying Telegraph. Second Edition. Revised and enlarged. Illustrated by numerous engravings. 12mo. Cloth . . . .

BEANS.—A TREATISE ON RAILROAD CURVES AND THE LOCATION OF RAILROADS:

By E. W. BEANS, C. E. 12mo. . . . $2 00

BLENKARN.—PRACTICAL SPECIFICATIONS OF WORKS EXECUTED IN ARCHITECTURE, CIVIL AND MECHANICAL ENGINEERING, AND IN ROAD MAKING AND SEWERING:

To which are added a series of practically useful Agreements and Reports. By JOHN BLENKARN. Illustrated by fifteen large folding plates. 8vo. $9 00

BLINN.—A PRACTICAL WORKSHOP COMPANION FOR TIN, SHEET-IRON, AND COPPER-PLATE WORKERS:

Containing Rules for Describing various kinds of Patterns used by Tin, Sheet-iron, and Copper-plate Workers; Practical Geometry; Mensuration of Surfaces and Solids; Tables of the Weight of Metals, Lead Pipe, etc.; Tables of Areas and Circumferences of Circles; Japans, Varnishes, Lackers, Cements, Compositions, etc. etc. By LEROY J. BLINN, Master Mechanic. With over One Hundred Illustrations. 12mo. $2 50

BOOTH.—MARBLE WORKER'S MANUAL:

Containing Practical Information respecting Marbles in general, their Cutting, Working, and Polishing; Veneering of Marble; Mosaics; Composition and Use of Artificial Marble, Stuccos, Cements, Receipts, Secrets, etc. etc. Translated from the French by M. L. BOOTH. With an Appendix concerning American Marbles. 12mo., cloth . . $1 50

BOOTH AND MORFIT.—THE ENCYCLOPEDIA OF CHEMISTRY, PRACTICAL AND THEORETICAL:

Embracing its application to the Arts, Metallurgy, Mineralogy, Geology, Medicine, and Pharmacy. By JAMES C. BOOTH, Melter and Refiner in the United States Mint, Professor of Applied Chemistry in the Franklin Institute, etc., assisted by CAMPBELL MORFIT, author of "Chemical Manipulations," etc. Seventh edition. Complete in one volume, royal 8vo., 978 pages, with numerous wood-cuts and other illustrations. $5 00

BOWDITCH.—ANALYSIS, TECHNICAL VALUATION, PURIFICATION, AND USE OF COAL GAS:

By Rev. W. R. BOWDITCH. Illustrated with wood engravings. 8vo. $6 50

BOX.—PRACTICAL HYDRAULICS:

A Series of Rules and Tables for the use of Engineers, etc. By THOMAS BOX. 12mo. $2 50

BUCKMASTER.—THE ELEMENTS OF MECHANICAL PHYSICS:

By J. C. BUCKMASTER, late Student in the Government School of Mines; Certified Teacher of Science by the Department of Science and Art; Examiner in Chemistry and Physics in the Royal College of Preceptors; and late Lecturer in Chemistry and Physics of the Royal Polytechnic Institute. Illustrated with numerous engravings. In one vol. 12mo. . $1 50

BULLOCK.—THE AMERICAN COTTAGE BUILDER:

A Series of Designs, Plans, and Specifications, from $200 to to $20,000 for Homes for the People; together with Warming, Ventilation, Drainage, Painting, and Landscape Gardening. By JOHN BULLOCK, Architect, Civil Engineer, Mechanician, and Editor of "The Rudiments of Architecture and Building," etc. Illustrated by 75 engravings. In one vol. 8vo. $3 50

BULLOCK.—THE RUDIMENTS OF ARCHITECTURE AND BUILDING:

For the use of Architects, Builders, Draughtsmen, Machinists, Engineers, and Mechanics. Edited by JOHN BULLOCK, author of "The American Cottage Builder." Illustrated by 250 engravings. In one volume 8vo. $3 50

BURGH.—PRACTICAL ILLUSTRATIONS OF LAND AND MARINE ENGINES:

Showing in detail the Modern Improvements of High and Low Pressure, Surface Condensation, and Super-heating, together with Land and Marine Boilers. By N. P. BURGH, Engineer. Illustrated by twenty plates, double elephant folio, with text. $21 00

BURGH.—PRACTICAL RULES FOR THE PROPORTIONS OF MODERN ENGINES AND BOILERS FOR LAND AND MARINE PURPOSES.

By N. P. BURGH, Engineer. 12mo. $2 00

BURGH.—THE SLIDE-VALVE PRACTICALLY CONSIDERED:

By N. P. BURGH, author of "A Treatise on Sugar Machinery," "Practical Illustrations of Land and Marine Engines," "A Pocket-Book of Practical Rules for Designing Land and Marine Engines, Boilers," etc. etc. etc. Completely illustrated. 12mo. $2 00

BYRN.—THE COMPLETE PRACTICAL BREWER:

Or, Plain, Accurate, and Thorough Instructions in the Art of Brewing Beer, Ale, Porter, including the Process of making Bavarian Beer, all the Small Beers, such as Root-beer, Ginger-pop, Sarsaparilla-beer, Mead, Spruce beer, etc. etc. Adapted to the use of Public Brewers and Private Families. By M. LA FAYETTE BYRN, M. D. With illustrations. 12mo. $1 25

BYRN.—THE COMPLETE PRACTICAL DISTILLER:

Comprising the most perfect and exact Theoretical and Practical Description of the Art of Distillation and Rectification; including all of the most recent improvements in distilling apparatus; instructions for preparing spirits from the numerous vegetables, fruits, etc.; directions for the distillation and preparation of all kinds of brandies and other spirits, spirituous and other compounds, etc. etc.; all of which is so simplified that it is adapted not only to the use of extensive distillers, but for every farmer, or others who may wish to engage in the art of distilling By M. LA FAYETTE BYRN, M. D. With numerous engravings. In one volume, 12mo. $1 50

BYRNE.—POCKET BOOK FOR RAILROAD AND CIVIL ENGINEERS:

Containing New, Exact, and Concise Methods for Laying out Railroad Curves, Switches, Frog Angles and Crossings; the Staking out of work; Levelling; the Calculation of Cuttings; Embankments; Earth-work, etc. By OLIVER BYRNE. Illustrated, 18mo., full bound $1 75

BYRNE.—THE HANDBOOK FOR THE ARTISAN, MECHANIC, AND ENGINEER:

By OLIVER BYRNE. Illustrated by 185 Wood Engravings. 8vo. $5 00

BYRNE.—THE ESSENTIAL ELEMENTS OF PRACTICAL MECHANICS:

For Engineering Students, based on the Principle of Work. By OLIVER BYRNE. Illustrated by Numerous Wood Engravings, 12mo. $3 63

BYRNE.—THE PRACTICAL METAL-WORKER'S ASSISTANT:

Comprising Metallurgic Chemistry; the Arts of Working all Metals and Alloys; Forging of Iron and Steel; Hardening and Tempering; Melting and Mixing; Casting and Founding; Works in Sheet Metal; the Processes Dependent on the Ductility of the Metals; Soldering; and the most Improved Processes and Tools employed by Metal-Workers. With the Application of the Art of Electro-Metallurgy to Manufacturing Processes; collected from Original Sources, and from the Works of Holtzapffel, Bergeron, Leupold, Plumier, Napier, and others. By OLIVER BYRNE. A New, Revised, and improved Edition, with Additions by John Scoffern, M. B , William Clay, Wm. Fairbairn, F. R. S., and James Napier. With Five Hundred and Ninety-two Engravings; Illustrating every Branch of the Subject. In one volume, 8vo. 652 pages . $7 00

BYRNE.—THE PRACTICAL MODEL CALCULATOR:

For the Engineer, Mechanic, Manufacturer of Engine Work, Naval Architect, Miner, and Millwright. By OLIVER BYRNE. 1 volume, 8vo., nearly 600 pages $4 50

BEMROSE.—MANUAL OF WOOD CARVING: With Practical Illustrations for Learners of the Art, and Original and Selected designs. By WILLIAM BEMROSE, Jr. With an Introduction by LLEWELLYN JEWITT, F. S. A., etc. With 128 Illustrations. 4to., cloth $3 00

BAIRD.—PROTECTION OF HOME LABOR AND HOME PRODUCTIONS NECESSARY TO THE PROSPERITY OF THE AMERICAN FARMER:
By HENRY CAREY BAIRD. 8vo., paper 10

BAIRD.—THE RIGHTS OF AMERICAN PRODUCERS, AND THE WRONGS OF BRITISH FREE TRADE REVENUE REFORM.
By HENRY CAREY BAIRD. (1870) 5

BAIRD.—SOME OF THE FALLACIES OF BRITISH-FREE-TRADE REVENUE-REFORM.
Two Letters to Prof. A. L. Perry, of Williams College, Mass. By HENRY CAREY BAIRD. (1871.) Paper 5

BAIRD.—STANDARD WAGES COMPUTING TABLES:
An Improvement in all former Methods of Computation, so arranged that wages for days, hours, or fractions of hours, at a specified rate per day or hour, may be ascertained at a glance. By T. SPANGLER BAIRD. Oblong folio $5 00

BAUERMAN.—TREATISE ON THE METALLURGY OF IRON.
Illustrated. 12mo. $2 50

BICKNELL'S VILLAGE BUILDER.
55 large plates. 4to. $10 00

BISHOP.—A HISTORY OF AMERICAN MANUFACTURES:
From 1608 to 1866; exhibiting the Origin and Growth of the Principal Mechanic Arts and Manufactures, from the Earliest Colonial Period to the Present Time; By J. LEANDER BISHOP, M. D., EDWARD YOUNG, and EDWIN T. FREEDLEY. Three vols. 8vo.,
$10 00

BOX.—A PRACTICAL TREATISE ON HEAT AS APPLIED TO THE USEFUL ARTS:
For the use of Engineers, Architects, etc. By THOMAS BOX, author of "Practical Hydraulics." Illustrated by 14 plates, containing 114 figures. 12mo. $4 25

CABINET MAKER'S ALBUM OF FURNITURE:
Comprising a Collection of Designs for the Newest and Most Elegant Styles of Furniture. Illustrated by Forty-eight Large and Beautifully Engraved Plates. In one volume, oblong
$5 00

CHAPMAN.—A TREATISE ON ROPE-MAKING:
As practised in private and public Rope-yards, with a Description of the Manufacture, Rules, Tables of Weights, etc., adapted to the Trade; Shipping, Mining, Railways, Builders, etc. By ROBERT CHAPMAN. 24mo. $1 50

CRAIK.—THE PRACTICAL AMERICAN MILLWRIGHT AND MILLER.

Comprising the Elementary Principles of Mechanics, Mechanism, and Motive Power, Hydraulics and Hydraulic Motors, Mill-dams, Saw Mills, Grist Mills, the Oat Meal Mill, the Barley Mill, Wool Carding, and Cloth Fulling and Dressing, Wind Mills, Steam Power, &c. By DAVID CRAIK, Millwright. Illustrated by numerous wood engravings, and five folding plates. 1 vol. 8vo. $5 00

CAMPIN.—A PRACTICAL TREATISE ON MECHANICAL ENGINEERING:

Comprising Metallurgy, Moulding, Casting, Forging, Tools, Workshop Machinery, Mechanical Manipulation, Manufacture of Steam-engines, etc. etc. With an Appendix on the Analysis of Iron and Iron Ores. By FRANCIS CAMPIN, C. E. To which are added, Observations on the Construction of Steam Boilers, and Remarks upon Furnaces used for Smoke Prevention; with a Chapter on Explosions. By R. Armstrong, C. E., and John Bourne. Rules for Calculating the Change Wheels for Screws on a Turning Lathe, and for a Wheel-cutting Machine. By J. LA NICCA. Management of Steel, including Forging, Hardening, Tempering, Annealing, Shrinking, and Expansion. And the Case-hardening of Iron. By G. EDE. 8vo. Illustrated with 29 plates and 100 wood engravings. $6 00

CAMPIN.—THE PRACTICE OF HAND-TURNING IN WOOD, IVORY, SHELL, ETC.:

With Instructions for Turning such works in Metal as may be required in the Practice of Turning Wood, Ivory, etc. Also an Appendix on Ornamental Turning. By FRANCIS CAMPIN, with Numerous Illustrations, 12mo., cloth . . $3 00

CAPRON DE DOLE.—DUSSAUCE.—BLUES AND CARMINES OF INDIGO.

A Practical Treatise on the Fabrication of every Commercial Product derived from Indigo. By FELICIEN CAPRON DE DOLE Translated, with important additions, by Professor H. DUSSAUCE. 12mo.

CAREY.—THE WORKS OF HENRY C. CAREY:

CONTRACTION OR EXPANSION? REPUDIATION OR RESUMPTION? Letters to Hon. Hugh McCulloch. 8vo. 38

FINANCIAL CRISES, their Causes and Effects. 8vo. paper 25

HARMONY OF INTERESTS; Agricultural, Manufacturing, and Commercial. 8vo., paper $1 00
Do. do. cloth $1 50

LETTERS TO THE PRESIDENT OF THE UNITED STATES. Paper $1 00

MANUAL OF SOCIAL SCIENCE. Condensed from Carey's "Principles of Social Science." By KATE McKEAN. 1 vol. 12mo. $2 25

MISCELLANEOUS WORKS: comprising "Harmony of Interests," "Money," "Letters to the President," "French and American Tariffs," "Financial Crises," "The Way to Outdo England without Fighting Her," "Resources of the Union," "The Public Debt," "Contraction or Expansion," "Review of the Decade 1857—'67," "Reconstruction," etc. etc. 1 vol. 8vo., cloth $4 50

MONEY: A LECTURE before the N. Y. Geographical and Statistical Society. 8vo., paper 25

PAST, PRESENT, AND FUTURE. 8vo. $2 50

PRINCIPLES OF SOCIAL SCIENCE. 3 volumes 8vo., cloth $10 00

REVIEW OF THE DECADE 1857—'67. 8vo., paper 50

RECONSTRUCTION: INDUSTRIAL, FINANCIAL, AND POLITICAL. Letters to the Hon. Henry Wilson, U. S. S. 8vo, paper 50

THE PUBLIC DEBT, LOCAL AND NATIONAL. How to provide for its discharge while lessening the burden of Taxation. Letter to David A. Wells, Esq., U. S. Revenue Commission. 8vo., paper 25

THE RESOURCES OF THE UNION. A Lecture read, Dec. 1865, before the American Geographical and Statistical Society, N. Y., and before the American Association for the Advancement of Social Science, Boston 50

THE SLAVE TRADE, DOMESTIC AND FOREIGN; Why it Exists, and How it may be Extinguished. 12mo., cloth $1 50

LETTERS ON INTERNATIONAL COPYRIGHT. (1867.) Paper 50

REVIEW OF THE FARMERS' QUESTION. (1870.) Paper 25

RESUMPTION! HOW IT MAY PROFITABLY BE BROUGHT AROUT. (1869.) 8vo., paper 50

REVIEW OF THE REPORT OF HON. D. A. WELLS, Special Commissioner of the Revenue. (1869.) 8vo., paper 50

SHALL WE HAVE PEACE? Peace Financial and Peace Political. Letters to the President Elect. (1868.) 8vo., paper 50

THE FINANCE MINISTER AND THE CURRENCY, AND THE PUBLIC DEBT. (1868.) 8vo., paper . . 50

THE WAY TO OUTDO ENGLAND WITHOUT FIGHTING HER. Letters to Hon. Schuyler Colfax. (1865.) 8vo., paper $1 00

WEALTH! OF WHAT DOES IT CONSIST? (1870.) Paper 25

CAMUS.—A TREATISE ON THE TEETH OF WHEELS:
Demonstrating the best forms which can be given to them for the purposes of Machinery, such as Mill-work and Clock-work. Translated from the French of M. CAMUS. By JOHN I. HAWKINS. Illustrated by 40 plates. 8vo. $3 00

COXE.—MINING LEGISLATION.
A paper read before the Am. Social Science Association. By ECKLEY B. COXE. Paper 20

COLBURN.—THE GAS-WORKS OF LONDON:
Comprising a sketch of the Gas-works of the city, Process of Manufacture, Quantity Produced, Cost, Profit, etc. By ZERAH COLBURN. 8vo., cloth 75

COLBURN.—THE LOCOMOTIVE ENGINE:
Including a Description of its Structure, Rules for Estimating its Capabilities, and Practical Observations on its Construction and Management. By ZERAH COLBURN. Illustrated. A new edition. 12mo. $1 25

COLBURN AND MAW.—THE WATER-WORKS OF LONDON:
Together with a Series of Articles on various other Waterworks. By ZERAH COLBURN and W. MAW. Reprinted from "Engineering." In one volume, 8vo. . . $4 00

DAGUERREOTYPIST AND PHOTOGRAPHER'S COMPANION:
12mo., cloth $1 25

DIRCKS.—PERPETUAL MOTION:

Or Search for Self-Motive Power during the 17th, 18th, and 19th centuries. Illustrated from various authentic sources in Papers, Essays, Letters, Paragraphs, and numerous Patent Specifications, with an Introductory Essay by HENRY DIRCKS, C. E. Illustrated by numerous engravings of machines. 12mo., cloth $3 50

DIXON.—THE PRACTICAL MILLWRIGHT'S AND ENGINEER'S GUIDE:

Or Tables for Finding the Diameter and Power of Cogwheels; Diameter, Weight, and Power of Shafts; Diameter and Strength of Bolts, etc. etc. By THOMAS DIXON. 12mo., cloth. $1 50

DUNCAN.—PRACTICAL SURVEYOR'S GUIDE:

Containing the necessary information to make any person, of common capacity, a finished land surveyor without the aid of a teacher. By ANDREW DUNCAN. Illustrated. 12mo., cloth. $1 25

DUSSAUCE.—A NEW AND COMPLETE TREATISE ON THE ARTS OF TANNING, CURRYING, AND LEATHER DRESSING:

Comprising all the Discoveries and Improvements made in France, Great Britain, and the United States. Edited from Notes and Documents of Messrs. Sallerou, Grouvelle, Duval, Dessables, Labarraque, Payen, René, De Fontenelle, Malapeyre, etc. etc. By Prof. H. DUSSAUCE, Chemist. Illustrated by 212 wood engravings. 8vo. $10 00

DUSSAUCE.—A GENERAL TREATISE ON THE MANUFACTURE OF SOAP, THEORETICAL AND PRACTICAL:

Comprising the Chemistry of the Art, a Description of all the Raw Materials and their Uses. Directions for the Establishment of a Soap Factory, with the necessary Apparatus, Instructions in the Manufacture of every variety of Soap, the Assay and Determination of the Value of Alkalies, Fatty Substances, Soaps, etc. etc. By PROFESSOR H. DUSSAUCE. With an Appendix, containing Extracts from the Reports of the International Jury on Soaps, as exhibited in the Paris Universal Exposition, 1867, numerous Tables, etc. etc. Illustrated by engravings. In one volume 8vo. of over 800 pages $10 00

DUSSAUCE.—PRACTICAL TREATISE ON THE FABRICATION OF MATCHES, GUN COTTON, AND FULMINATING POWDERS.

By Professor H. DUSSAUCE. 12mo. . . . $3 00

DUSSAUCE.—A PRACTICAL GUIDE FOR THE PERFUMER:
Being a New Treatise on Perfumery the most favorable to the Beauty without being injurious to the Health, comprising a Description of the substances used in Perfumery, the Formulæ of more than one thousand Preparations, such as Cosmetics, Perfumed Oils, Tooth Powders, Waters, Extracts, Tinctures, Infusions, Vinaigres, Essential Oils, Pastels, Creams, Soaps, and many new Hygienic Products not hitherto described. Edited from Notes and Documents of Messrs. Debay, Lunel, etc. With additions by Professor H. DUSSAUCE, Chemist. 12mo. $3 00

DUSSAUCE.—A GENERAL TREATISE ON THE MANUFACTURE OF VINEGAR, THEORETICAL AND PRACTICAL.
Comprising the various methods, by the slow and the quick processes, with Alcohol, Wine, Grain, Cider, and Molasses, as well as the Fabrication of Wood Vinegar, etc. By Prof. H. DUSSAUCE. 12mo. $5 00

DUPLAIS.—A COMPLETE TREATISE ON THE DISTILLATION AND MANUFACTURE OF ALCOHOLIC LIQUORS:
From the French of M. DUPLAIS. Translated and Edited by M. McKENNIE, M D. Illustrated by numerous large plates and wood engravings of the best apparatus calculated for producing the finest products. In one vol. royal 8vo. $10 00

☞ This is a treatise of the highest scientific merit and of the greatest practical value, surpassing in these respects, as well as in the variety of its contents, any similar volume in the English language.

DE GRAFF.—THE GEOMETRICAL STAIR-BUILDERS' GUIDE:
Being a Plain Practical System of Hand-Railing, embracing all its necessary Details, and Geometrically Illustrated by 22 Steel Engravings; together with the use of the most approved principles of Practical Geometry. By SIMON DE GRAFF, Architect. 4to. $5 00

DYER AND COLOR-MAKER'S COMPANION:
Containing upwards of two hundred Receipts for making Colors, on the most approved principles, for all the various styles and fabrics now in existence; with the Scouring Process, and plain Directions for Preparing, Washing-off, and Finishing the Goods. In one vol. 12mo. $1 25

EASTON.—A PRACTICAL TREATISE ON STREET OR HORSE-POWER RAILWAYS:

Their Location, Construction, and Management; with General Plans and Rules for their Organization and Operation; together with Examinations as to their Comparative Advantages over the Omnibus System, and Inquiries as to their Value for Investment; including Copies of Municipal Ordinances relating thereto. By ALEXANDER EASTON, C. E. Illustrated by 23 plates, 8vo., cloth $2 00

FORSYTH.—BOOK OF DESIGNS FOR HEAD-STONES, MURAL, AND OTHER MONUMENTS:

Containing 78 Elaborate and Exquisite Designs. By FORSYTH. 4to., cloth $5 00

*** This volume, for the beauty and variety of its designs, has never been surpassed by any publication of the kind, and should be in the hands of every marble-worker who does fine monumental work.

FAIRBAIRN.—THE PRINCIPLES OF MECHANISM AND MACHINERY OF TRANSMISSION:

Comprising the Principles of Mechanism, Wheels, and Pulleys, Strength and Proportions of Shafts, Couplings of Shafts, and Engaging and Disengaging Gear. By WILLIAM FAIRBAIRN, Esq., C. E., LL. D., F. R. S., F. G. S., Corresponding Member of the National Institute of France, and of the Royal Academy of Turin; Chevalier of the Legion of Honor, etc. etc. Beautifully illustrated by over 150 wood-cuts. In one volume 12mo. $2 50

FAIRBAIRN.—PRIME-MOVERS:

Comprising the Accumulation of Water-power; the Construction of Water-wheels and Turbines; the Properties of Steam; the Varieties of Steam-engines and Boilers and Wind-mills. By WILLIAM FAIRBAIRN, C. E., LL. D., F. R. S., F. G. S. Author of "Principles of Mechanism and the Machinery of Transmission." With Numerous Illustrations. In one volume. (In press.)

GILBART.—A PRACTICAL TREATISE ON BANKING:

By JAMES WILLIAM GILBART. To which is added: THE NATIONAL BANK ACT AS NOW IN FORCE. 8vo. . . . $4 50

GESNER.—A PRACTICAL TREATISE ON COAL, PETROLEUM, AND OTHER DISTILLED OILS.

By ABRAHAM GESNER, M. D., F. G. S. Second edition, revised and enlarged. By GEORGE WELTDEN GESNER, Consulting Chemist and Engineer. Illustrated. 8vo. . . . $3 50

GOTHIC ALBUM FOR CABINET MAKERS:

Comprising a Collection of Designs for Gothic Furniture. Illustrated by twenty-three large and beautifully engraved plates. Oblong $3 00

GRANT.—BEET-ROOT SUGAR AND CULTIVATION OF THE BEET:

By E. B. Grant. 12mo. $1 25

GREGORY.—MATHEMATICS FOR PRACTICAL MEN:

Adapted to the Pursuits of Surveyors, Architects, Mechanics, and Civil Engineers. By Olinthus Gregory. 8vo., plates, cloth $3 00

GRISWOLD.—RAILROAD ENGINEER'S POCKET COMPANION.

Comprising Rules for Calculating Deflection Distances and Angles, Tangential Distances and Angles, and all Necessary Tables for Engineers; also the art of Levelling f om Preliminary Survey to the Construction of Railroads, intended Expressly for the Young Engineer, together with Numerous Valuable Rules and Examples. By W. Griswold. 12mo., tucks. $1 75

GUETTIER.—METALLIC ALLOYS:

Being a Practical Guide to their Chemical and Physical Properties, their Preparation, Composition, and Uses. Translated from the French of A. Guettier, Engineer and Director of Founderies, author of "La Fouderie en France," etc. etc. By A. A. Fesquet, Chemist and Engineer. In one volume, 12mo. $3 00

HATS AND FELTING:

A Practical Treatise on their Manufacture. By a Practical Hatter. Illustrated by Drawings of Machinery, &c., 8vo. $1 25

HAY.—THE INTERIOR DECORATOR:

The Laws of Harmonious Coloring adapted to Interior Decorations: with a Practical Treatise on House-Painting. By D. R. Hay, House-Painter and Decorator. Illustrated by a Diagram of the Primary, Secondary, and Tertiary Colors. 12mo. $2 25

HUGHES.—AMERICAN MILLER AND MILLWRIGHT'S ASSISTANT:

By Wm. Carter Hughes. A new edition. In one volume, 12mo. $1 50

HUNT.—THE PRACTICE OF PHOTOGRAPHY.

By ROBERT HUNT, Vice-President of the Photographic Society, London. With numerous illustrations. 12mo., cloth . 75

HURST.—A HAND-BOOK FOR ARCHITECTURAL SURVEYORS:

Comprising Formulæ useful in Designing Builders' work, Table of Weights, of the materials used in Building, Memoranda connected with Builders' work, Mensuration, the Practice of Builders' Measurement, Contracts of Labor, Valuation of Property, Summary of the Practice in Dilapidation, etc. etc. By J. F. HURST, C. E. 2d edition, pocket-book form, full bound $2 50

JERVIS.—RAILWAY PROPERTY:

A Treatise on the Construction and Management of Railways; designed to afford useful knowledge, in the popular style, to the holders of this class of property; as well as Railway Managers, Officers, and Agents. By JOHN B. JERVIS, late Chief Engineer of the Hudson River Railroad, Croton Aqueduct, &c. One vol. 12mo., cloth $2 00

JOHNSON.—A REPORT TO THE NAVY DEPARTMENT OF THE UNITED STATES ON AMERICAN COALS:

Applicable to Steam Navigation and to other purposes. By WALTER R. JOHNSON. With numerous illustrations. 607 pp. 8vo., ... $10 00

JOHNSTON.—INSTRUCTIONS FOR THE ANALYSIS OF SOILS, LIMESTONES, AND MANURES

By J. W. F. JOHNSTON. 12mo. 35

KEENE.—A HAND-BOOK OF PRACTICAL GAUGING,

For the Use of Beginners, to which is added a Chapter on Distillation, describing the process in operation at the Custom House for ascertaining the strength of wines. By JAMES B. KEENE, of H. M. Customs. 8vo. . . . $1 25

KENTISH.—A TREATISE ON A BOX OF INSTRUMENTS,

And the Slide Rule; with the Theory of Trigonometry and Logarithms, including Practical Geometry, Surveying, Measuring of Timber, Cask and Malt Gauging, Heights, and Distances. By THOMAS KENTISH. In one volume. 12mo. . . $1 25

KOBELL.—ERNI.—MINERALOGY SIMPLIFIED:

A short method of Determining and Classifying Minerals, by means of simple Chemical Experiments in the Wet Way. Translated from the last German Edition of F. VON KOBELL, with an Introduction to Blowpipe Analysis and other additions. By HENRI ERNI, M. D., Chief Chemist, Department of Agriculture, author of "Coal Oil and Petroleum." In one volume. 12mo. $2 50

LANDRIN.—A TREATISE ON STEEL:

Comprising its Theory, Metallurgy, Properties, Practical Working, and Use. By M. H. C. LANDRIN, Jr., Civil Engineer. Translated from the French, with Notes, by A. A. FESQUET, Chemist and Engineer. With an Appendix on the Bessemer and the Martin Processes for Manufacturing Steel, from the Report of ABRAM S. HEWITT, United States Commissioner to the Universal Exposition, Paris, 1867. 12mo. . . $3 00

LARKIN.—THE PRACTICAL BRASS AND IRON FOUNDER'S GUIDE.

A Concise Treatise on Brass Founding, Moulding, the Metals and their Alloys, etc.; to which are added Recent Improvements in the Manufacture of Iron, Steel by the Bessemer Process, etc. etc. By JAMES LARKIN, late Conductor of the Brass Foundry Department in Reany, Neafie & Co.'s Penn Works, Philadelphia. Fifth edition, revised, with extensive Additions. In one volume. 12mo. $2 25

LEAVITT.—FACTS ABOUT PEAT AS AN ARTICLE OF FUEL:
With Remarks upon its Origin and Composition, the Localities in which it is found, the Methods of Preparation and Manufacture, and the various Uses to which it is applicable; together with many other matters of Practical and Scientific Interest. To which is added a chapter on the Utilization of Coal Dust with Peat for the Production of an Excellent Fuel at Moderate Cost, especially adapted for Steam Service. By H. T. LEAVITT. Third edition. 12mo. $1 75

LEROUX.—A PRACTICAL TREATISE ON THE MANUFACTURE OF WORSTEDS AND CARDED YARNS:
Translated from the French of CHARLES LEROUX, Mechanical Engineer, and Superintendent of a Spinning Mill. By Dr. H. PAINE, and A. A. FESQUET. Illustrated by 12 large plates. In one volume 8vo. $5 00

LESLIE (MISS).—COMPLETE COOKERY:
Directions for Cookery in its Various Branches. By MISS LESLIE. 60th edition. Thoroughly revised, with the addition of New Receipts. In 1 vol. 12mo., cloth . . $1 50

LESLIE (MISS). LADIES' HOUSE BOOK:
a Manual of Domestic Economy. 20th revised edition. 12mo., cloth $1 25

LESLIE (MISS).—TWO HUNDRED RECEIPTS IN FRENCH COOKERY.
12mo. 50

LIEBER.—ASSAYER'S GUIDE:
Or, Practical Directions to Assayers, Miners, and Smelters, for the Tests and Assays, by Heat and by Wet Processes, for the Ores of all the principal Metals, of Gold and Silver Coins and Alloys, and of Coal, etc. By OSCAR M. LIEBER. 12mo., cloth $1 25

LOVE.—THE ART OF DYEING, CLEANING, SCOURING, AND FINISHING:
On the most approved English and French methods; being Practical Instructions in Dyeing Silks, Woollens, and Cottons, Feathers, Chips, Straw, etc.; Scouring and Cleaning Bed and Window Curtains, Carpets, Rugs, etc.; French and English Cleaning, etc. By THOMAS LOVE. Second American Edition, to which are added General Instructions for the Use of Aniline Colors. 8vo. 5 00

MAIN AND BROWN.—QUESTIONS ON SUBJECTS CONNECTED WITH THE MARINE STEAM-ENGINE:
And Examination Papers; with Hints for their Solution. By THOMAS J. MAIN, Professor of Mathematics, Royal Naval College, and THOMAS BROWN, Chief Engineer, R. N. 12mo., cloth $1 50

MAIN AND BROWN.—THE INDICATOR AND DYNAMOMETER:
With their Practical Applications to the Steam-Engine. By THOMAS J. MAIN, M. A. F. R., Ass't Prof. Royal Naval College, Portsmouth, and THOMAS BROWN, Assoc. Inst. C. E., Chief Engineer, R. N., attached to the R. N. College. Illustrated. From the Fourth London Edition. 8vo. $1 50

MAIN AND BROWN.—THE MARINE STEAM-ENGINE.
By THOMAS J. MAIN, F. R. Ass't S. Mathematical Professor at Royal Naval College, and THOMAS BROWN, Assoc. Inst. C. E. Chief Engineer, R. N. Attached to the Royal Naval College. Authors of "Questions Connected with the Marine Steam-Engine," and the "Indicator and Dynamometer." With numerous Illustrations. In one volume 8vo. $5 00

MARTIN.—SCREW-CUTTING TABLES, FOR THE USE OF MECHANICAL ENGINEERS:
Showing the Proper Arrangement of Wheels for Cutting the Threads of Screws of any required Pitch; with a Table for Making the Universal Gas-Pipe Thread and Taps. By W. A. MARTIN, Engineer. 8vo. 50

MILES—A PLAIN TREATISE ON HORSE-SHOEING.
With Illustrations. By WILLIAM MILES, author of "The Horse's Foot"

MOLESWORTH.—POCKET-BOOK OF USEFUL FORMULÆ AND MEMORANDA FOR CIVIL AND MECHANICAL ENGINEERS.
By GUILFORD L. MOLESWORTH, Member of the Institution of Civil Engineers, Chief Resident Engineer of the Ceylon Railway. Second American from the Tenth London Edition. In one volume, full bound in pocket-book form $2 00

MOORE.—THE INVENTOR'S GUIDE:
Patent Office and Patent Laws: or, a Guide to Inventors, and a Book of Reference for Judges, Lawyers, Magistrates, and others. By J G. MOORE. 12mo., cloth $1 25

NAPIER.—A MANUAL OF ELECTRO-METALLURGY:
Including the Application of the Art to Manufacturing Processes. By JAMES NAPIER. Fourth American, from the Fourth London edition, revised and enlarged. Illustrated by engravings. In one volume, 8vo. $2 00

NAPIER.—A SYSTEM OF CHEMISTRY APPLIED TO DYEING:
By JAMES NAPIER, F. C. S. A New and Thoroughly Revised Edition, completely brought up to the present state of the Science, including the Chemistry of Coal Tar Colors. By A. A. FESQUET, Chemist and Engineer. With an Appendix on Dyeing and Calico Printing, as shown at the Paris Universal Exposition of 1867, from the Reports of the International Jury, etc. Illustrated. In one volume 8vo., 400 pages $5 00

NEWBERY.—GLEANINGS FROM ORNAMENTAL ART OF EVERY STYLE;
Drawn from Examples in the British, South Kensington, Indian, Crystal Palace, and other Museums, the Exhibitions of 1851 and 1862, and the best English and Foreign works. In a series of one hundred exquisitely drawn Plates, containing many hundred examples. By ROBERT NEWBERY. 4to. $15 00

NICHOLSON.—A MANUAL OF THE ART OF BOOK-BINDING:
Containing full instructions in the different Branches of Forwarding, Gilding, and Finishing. Also, the Art of Marbling Book-edges and Paper. By JAMES B. NICHOLSON. Illustrated. 12mo. cloth $2 25

NORRIS.—A HAND-BOOK FOR LOCOMOTIVE ENGINEERS AND MACHINISTS:
Comprising the Proportions and Calculations for Constructing Locomotives; Manner of Setting Valves; Tables of Squares, Cubes, Areas, etc. etc. By SEPTIMUS NORRIS, Civil and Mechanical Engineer. New edition. Illustrated, 12mo., cloth $2 00

NYSTROM.—ON TECHNOLOGICAL EDUCATION AND THE CONSTRUCTION OF SHIPS AND SCREW PROPELLERS:
For Naval and Marine Engineers. By JOHN W. NYSTROM, late Acting Chief Engineer U. S. N. Second edition, revised with additional matter. Illustrated by seven engravings. 12mo. $2 50

O'NEILL.—A DICTIONARY OF DYEING AND CALICO PRINTING:
Containing a brief account of all the Substances and Processes in use in the Art of Dyeing and Printing Textile Fabrics: with Practical Receipts and Scientific Information. By CHARLES O'NEILL, Analytical Chemist; Fellow of the Chemical Society of London; Member of the Literary and Philosophical Society of Manchester; Author of "Chemistry of Calico Printing and Dyeing." To which is added An Essay on Coal Tar Colors and their Application to

Dyeing and Calico Printing. By A. A. FESQUET, Chemist and Engineer. With an Appendix on Dyeing and Calico Printing, as shown at the Exposition of 1867, from the Reports of the International Jury, etc. In one volume 8vo., 491 pages . . $6 00

OSBORN.—THE METALLURGY OF IRON AND STEEL:

Theoretical and Practical: In all its Branches; With Special Reference to American Materials and Processes. By H. S. OSBORN, LL. D., Professor of Mining and Metallurgy in Lafayette College, Easton, Pa. Illustrated by 230 Engravings on Wood, and 6 Folding Plates. 8vo., 972 pages $10 00

OSBORN.—AMERICAN MINES AND MINING:

Theoretically and Practically Considered. By Prof. H. S. OSBORN, Illustrated by numerous engravings. 8vo. (*In preparation.*)

PAINTER, GILDER, AND VARNISHER'S COMPANION:

Containing Rules and Regulations in everything relating to the Arts of Painting, Gilding, Varnishing, and Glass Staining, with numerous useful and valuable Receipts; Tests for the Detection of Adulterations in Oils and Colors, and a statement of the Diseases and Accidents to which Painters, Gilders, and Varnishers are particularly liable, with the simplest methods of Prevention and Remedy. With Directions for Graining, Marbling, Sign Writing, and Gilding on Glass. To which are added COMPLETE INSTRUCTIONS FOR COACH PAINTING AND VARNISHING. 12mo., cloth, $1 50

PALLETT.—THE MILLER'S, MILLWRIGHT'S, AND ENGINEER'S GUIDE.

By HENRY PALLETT. Illustrated. In one vol. 12mo. . $3 00

PERKINS.—GAS AND VENTILATION.

Practical Treatise on Gas and Ventilation. With Special Relation to Illuminating, Heating, and Cooking by Gas. Including Scientific Helps to Engineer-students and others. With illustrated Diagrams. By E. E. PERKINS. 12mo., cloth . . . $1 25

PERKINS AND STOWE.—A NEW GUIDE TO THE SHEET-IRON AND BOILER PLATE ROLLER:

Containing a Series of Tables showing the Weight of Slabs and Piles to Produce Boiler Plates, and of the Weight of Piles and the Sizes of Bars to Produce Sheet-iron; the Thickness of the Bar Gauge in Decimals; the Weight per foot, and the Thickness on the Bar or Wire Gauge of the fractional parts of an inch; the Weight per sheet, and the Thickness on the Wire Gauge of Sheet-iron of various dimensions to weigh 112 lbs. per bundle; and the conversion of Short Weight into Long Weight, and Long Weight into Short. Estimated and collected by G. H. PERKINS and J. G. STOWE $2 50

PHILLIPS AND DARLINGTON.—RECORDS OF MINING AND METALLURGY:

Or, Facts and Memoranda for the use of the Mine Agent and Smelter. By J. ARTHUR PHILLIPS, Mining Engineer, Graduate of the Imperial School of Mines, France, etc., and JOHN DARLINGTON. Illustrated by numerous engravings. In one vol. 12mo. . $2 00

PRADAL, MALEPEYRE, AND DUSSAUCE.—A COMPLETE TREATISE ON PERFUMERY:

Containing notices of the Raw Material used in the Art, and the Best Formulæ. According to the most approved Methods followed in France, England, and the United States. By M. P. PRADAL, Perfumer-Chemist, and M. F. MALEPEYRE. Translated from the French, with extensive additions, by Prof. H. DUSSAUCE. 8vo. $10

PROTEAUX.—PRACTICAL GUIDE FOR THE MANUFACTURE OF PAPER AND BOARDS.

By A. PROTEAUX, Civil Engineer, and Graduate of the School of Arts and Manufactures, Director of Thiers's Paper Mill, 'Puy-de-Dômé. With additions, by L. S. LE NORMAND. Translated from the French, with Notes, by HORATIO PAINE, A. B., M. D. To which is added a Chapter on the Manufacture of Paper from Wood in the United States, by HENRY T. BROWN, of the "American Artisan." Illustrated by six plates, containing Drawings of Raw Materials, Machinery, Plans of Paper-Mills, etc. etc. 8vo. $5 00

REGNAULT.—ELEMENTS OF CHEMISTRY.

By M. V. REGNAULT. Translated from the French by T. FORREST BENTON, M. B., and edited, with notes, by JAMES C. BOOTH, Melter and Refiner U. S. Mint, and WM. L. FABER, Metallurgist and Mining Engineer. Illustrated by nearly 700 wood engravings. Comprising nearly 1500 pages. In two vols. 8vo., cloth $10 00

REID.—A PRACTICAL TREATISE ON THE MANUFACTURE OF PORTLAND CEMENT:

By HENRY REID, C. E. To which is added a Translation of M. A. Lipowitz's Work, describing a new method adopted in Germany of Manufacturing that Cement. By W. F. REID. Illustrated by plates and wood engravings. 8vo. $7 00

RIFFAULT, VERGNAUD, AND TOUSSAINT.—A PRACTICAL TREATISE ON THE MANUFACTURE OF COLORS FOR PAINTING:

Containing the best Formulæ and the Processes the Newest and in most General Use. By MM. RIFFAULT, VERGNAUD, and TOUSSAINT. Revised and Edited by M. F. MALEPEYRE and Dr. EMIL WINCKLER. Illustrated by Engravings. In one vol. 8vo. (*In preparation.*)

RIFFAULT, VERGNAUD, AND TOUSSAINT.—A PRACTICAL TREATISE ON THE MANUFACTURE OF VARNISHES:

By MM. RIFFAULT, VERGNAUD, and TOUSSAINT. Revised and Edited by M. F. MALEPEYRE and Dr. EMIL WINCKLER. Illustrated. In one vol. 8vo. (*In preparation.*)

SHUNK.—A PRACTICAL TREATISE ON RAILWAY CURVES AND LOCATION, FOR YOUNG ENGINEERS.

By WM. F. SHUNK, Civil Engineer. 12mo., tucks . . $2 00

SMEATON.—BUILDER'S POCKET COMPANION:

Containing the Elements of Building, Surveying, and Architecture; with Practical Rules and Instructions connected with the subject. By A. C. SMEATON, Civil Engineer, etc. In one volume, 12mo. $1 50

SMITH.—THE DYER'S INSTRUCTOR:

Comprising Practical Instructions in the Art of Dyeing Silk, Cotton, Wool, and Worsted, and Woollen Goods: containing nearly 800 Receipts. To which is added a Treatise on the Art of Padding; and the Printing of Silk Warps, Skeins, and Handkerchiefs, and the various Mordants and Colors for the different styles of such work. By DAVID SMITH, Pattern Dyer, 12mo., cloth $3 00

SMITH.—THE PRACTICAL DYER'S GUIDE:

Comprising Practical Instructions in the Dyeing of Shot Cobourgs, Silk Striped Orleans, Colored Orleans from Black Warps, ditto from White Warps, Colored Cobourgs from White Warps, Merinos, Yarns, Woollen Cloths, etc. Containing nearly 300 Receipts, to most of which a Dyed Pattern is annexed. Also, a Treatise on the Art of Padding. By DAVID SMITH. In one vol. 8vo. $25 00

SHAW.—CIVIL ARCHITECTURE:

Being a Complete Theoretical and Practical System of Building, containing the Fundamental Principles of the Art. By EDWARD SHAW, Architect. To which is added a Treatise on Gothic Architecture, &c. By THOMAS W. SILLOWAY and GEORGE M. HARDING, Architects. The whole illustrated by 102 quarto plates finely engraved on copper. Eleventh Edition. 4to. Cloth. $10 00

SLOAN.—AMERICAN HOUSES:

A variety of Original Designs for Rural Buildings. Illustrated by 26 colored Engravings, with Descriptive References. By SAMUEL SLOAN, Architect, author of the "Model Architect," etc. etc. 8vo. $2 50

SCHINZ.—RESEARCHES ON THE ACTION OF THE BLAST-FURNACE.

By CHAS. SCHINZ. Seven plates. 12mo. $4 25

SMITH.—PARKS AND PLEASURE GROUNDS:

Or, Practical Notes on Country Residences, Villas, Public Parks, and Gardens. By CHARLES H. J. SMITH, Landscape Gardener and Garden Architect, etc. etc. 12mo. $2 25

STOKES.—CABINET-MAKER'S AND UPHOLSTERER'S COMPANION:

Comprising the Rudiments and Principles of Cabinet-making and Upholstery, with Familiar Instructions, Illustrated by Examples for attaining a Proficiency in the Art of Drawing, as applicable to Cabinet-work; The Processes of Veneering, Inlaying, and Buhl-work; the Art of Dyeing and Staining Wood, Bone, Tortoise Shell, etc. Directions for Lackering, Japanning, and Varnishing; to make French Polish; to prepare the Best Glues, Cements, and Compositions, and a number of Receipts, particularly for workmen generally. By J. STOKES. In one vol. 12mo. With illustrations $1 25

STRENGTH AND OTHER PROPERTIES OF METALS.

Reports of Experiments on the Strength and other Properties of Metals for Cannon. With a Description of the Machines for Testing Metals, and of the Classification of Cannon in service. By Officers of the Ordnance Department U. S. Army. By authority of the Secretary of War. Illustrated by 25 large steel plates. In 1 vol. quarto $10 00

SULLIVAN.—PROTECTION TO NATIVE INDUSTRY.

By Sir EDWARD SULLIVAN, Baronet. (1870.) 8vo. . $1 50

TABLES SHOWING THE WEIGHT OF ROUND, SQUARE, AND FLAT BAR IRON, STEEL, ETC.

By Measurement. Cloth 63

TAYLOR.—STATISTICS OF COAL:

Including Mineral Bituminous Substances employed in Arts and Manufactures; with their Geographical, Geological, and Commercial Distribution and amount of Production and Consumption on the American Continent. With Incidental Statistics of the Iron Manufacture. By R. C. TAYLOR. Second edition, revised by S. S. HALDEMAN. Illustrated by five Maps and many wood engravings. 8vo., cloth $6 00

TEMPLETON.—THE PRACTICAL EXAMINATOR ON STEAM AND THE STEAM-ENGINE:

With Instructive References relative thereto, for the Use of Engineers, Students, and others. By WM. TEMPLETON, Engineer 12mo. $1 25

THOMAS.—THE MODERN PRACTICE OF PHOTOGRAPHY.

By R. W. THOMAS, F. C. S. 8vo., cloth 75

THOMSON.—FREIGHT CHARGES CALCULATOR.

By ANDREW THOMSON, Freight Agent $1 25

TURNING: SPECIMENS OF FANCY TURNING EXECUTED ON THE HAND OR FOOT LATHE:

With Geometric, Oval, and Eccentric Chucks, and Elliptical Cutting Frame. By an Amateur. Illustrated by 30 exquisite Photographs. 4to. $3 00

TURNER'S (THE) COMPANION:

Containing Instructions in Concentric, Elliptic, and Eccentric Turning; also various Plates of Chucks, Tools, and Instruments; and Directions for using the Eccentric Cutter, Drill, Vertical Cutter, and Circular Rest; with Patterns and Instructions for working them. A new edition in 1 vol. 12mo. $1 50

URBIN—BRULL.—A PRACTICAL GUIDE FOR PUDDLING IRON AND STEEL.

By ED. URBIN, Engineer of Arts and Manufactures. A Prize Essay read before the Association of Engineers, Graduate of the School of Mines, of Liege, Belgium, at the Meeting of 1865–6. To which is added a COMPARISON OF THE RESISTING PROPERTIES OF IRON AND STEEL. By A. BRULL. Translated from the French by A. A. FESQUET, Chemist and Engineer. In one volume, 8vo. $1 00

VOGDES.—THE ARCHITECT'S AND BUILDER'S POCKET COMPANION AND PRICE BOOK.

By F. W. VOGDES, Architect. Illustrated. Full bound in pocket-book form. $2 00

In book form, 18mo., muslin 1 50

WARN.—THE SHEET METAL WORKER'S INSTRUCTOR, FOR ZINC, SHEET-IRON, COPPER AND TIN PLATE WORKERS, &c.

By REUBEN HENRY WARN, Practical Tin Plate Worker. Illustrated by 32 plates and 37 wood engravings. 8vo. . . $3 00

WATSON.—A MANUAL OF THE HAND-LATHE.

By EGBERT P. WATSON, Late of the "Scientific American," Author of "Modern Practice of American Machinists and Engineers," In one volume, 12mo. $1 50

WATSON.—THE MODERN PRACTICE OF AMERICAN MACHINISTS AND ENGINEERS:

Including the Construction, Application, and Use of Drills, Lathe Tools, Cutters for Boring Cylinders, and Hollow Work Generally, with the most Economical Speed of the same, the Results verified by Actual Practice at the Lathe, the Vice, and on the Floor. Together with Workshop management, Economy of Manufacture, the Steam-Engine, Boilers, Gears, Belting, etc. etc. By EGBERT P. WATSON, late of the "Scientific American." Illustrated by eighty-six engravings. 12mo. $2 50

WATSON.—THE THEORY AND PRACTICE OF THE ART OF WEAVING BY HAND AND POWER:

With Calculations and Tables for the use of those connected with the Trade. By JOHN WATSON, Manufacturer and Practical Machine Maker. Illustrated by large drawings of the best Power-Looms. 8vo. $10 00

WEATHERLY.—TREATISE ON THE ART OF BOILING SUGAR, CRYSTALLIZING, LOZENGE-MAKING, COMFITS, GUM GOODS,

And other processes for Confectionery, &c. In which are explained, in an easy and familiar manner, the various Methods of Manufacturing every description of Raw and Refined Sugar Goods, as sold by Confectioners and others . . . $2 00

WILL.—TABLES FOR QUALITATIVE CHEMICAL ANALYSIS.

By Prof. HEINRICH WILL, of Giessen, Germany. Seventh edition. Translated by CHARLES F. HIMES, Ph. D., Professor of Natural Science, Dickinson College, Carlisle, Pa. . . $1 25

WILLIAMS.—ON HEAT AND STEAM:

Embracing New Views of Vaporization, Condensation, and Expansion. By CHARLES WYE WILLIAMS, A. I. C. E. Illustrated. 8vo. $3 50

WORSSAM.—ON MECHANICAL SAWS:

From the Transactions of the Society of Engineers, 1867. By S. W. WORSSAM, Jr. Illustrated by 18 large folding plates. 8vo. $5 00

WÖHLER.—A HAND-BOOK OF MINERAL ANALYSIS.

By F. WÖHLER. Edited by H. B. NASON, Professor of Chemistry, Rensselaer Institute, Troy, N. Y. With numerous Illustrations. 12mo. $3 00

www.ingramcontent.com/pod-product-compliance
Lightning Source LLC
LaVergne TN
LVHW021145110826
845150LV00005B/1128